European Union Committee

19th Report of Session 2007–08

The Future of EU Regional Policy

Report with Evidence

Ordered to be printed 8 July 2008 and published 16 July 2008

Published by the Authority of the House of Lords

London : The Stationery Office Limited

£20.00

HL Paper 141

The European Union Committee

The European Union Committee is appointed by the House of Lords "to consider European Union documents and other matters relating to the European Union". The Committee has seven Sub-Committees which are:

Economic and Financial Affairs, and International Trade (Sub-Committee A)
Internal Market (Sub-Committee B)
Foreign Affairs, Defence and Development Policy (Sub-Committee C)
Environment and Agriculture (Sub-Committee D)
Law and Institutions (Sub-Committee E)
Home Affairs (Sub-Committee F)
Social and Consumer Affairs (Sub-Committee G)

Our Membership

The Members of the European Union Committee are:

Lord Blackwell
Baroness Cohen of Pimlico
Lord Dykes
Lord Freeman
Lord Grenfell (Chairman)
Lord Harrison
Baroness Howarth of Breckland
Lord Jopling
Lord Kerr of Kinlochard
Lord Maclennan of Rogart
Lord Mance
Lord Plumb
Lord Powell of Bayswater
Lord Roper
Lord Sewel
Baroness Symons of Vernham Dean
Lord Tomlinson
Lord Wade of Chorlton
Lord Wright of Richmond

The Members of the Sub-Committee which carried out this inquiry (Economic and Financial Affairs, and International Trade, Sub-Committee A) are:

Baroness Cohen of Pimlico (Chairman)
Lord Giddens (until February 2008)
Lord Haskins
Lord Kerr of Kinlochard
Lord Maclennan of Rogart
Lord Moser
Lord Renton of Mount Harry
Lord Steinberg
Lord Trimble
Lord Watson of Richmond
Lord Woolmer of Leeds

Information about the Committee

The reports and evidence of the Committee are published by and available from The Stationery Office. For information freely available on the web, our homepage is:
http://www.parliament.uk/parliamentary_committees/lords_eu_select_committee.cfm
There you will find many of our publications, along with press notices, details of membership and forthcoming meetings, and other information about the ongoing work of the Committee and its Sub-Committees, each of which has its own homepage.

General Information

General information about the House of Lords and its Committees, including guidance to witnesses, details of current inquiries and forthcoming meetings is on the internet at
http://www.parliament.uk/about_lords/about_lords.cfm

Contacts for the European Union Committee

Contact details for individual Sub-Committees are given on the website.
General correspondence should be addressed to the Clerk of the European Union Committee, Committee Office, House of Lords, London, SW1A 0PW
The telephone number for general enquiries is 020 7219 5791.
The Committee's email address is euclords@parliament.uk

CONTENTS

Oral Evidence

Written evidence

NOTE: References in the text of the report are as follows:
(Q) refers to a question in oral evidence
(p) refers to a page of written evidence

FOREWORD—What this report is about

The present policies to tackle regional disparities in Europe are rooted in the creation of the Social Fund in 1958. In the intervening time expenditure on the policies has grown to the extent that 36% of the EU budget in 2008—0.38% of EU GNI—will be spent in this area. Although money is transferred through Member State exchequers, entitlement is on the whole dependent on the wealth of the regions: poorer regions in a richer Member State may be eligible for assistance.

The European Social Fund is still in place, and has been joined by the European Regional Development Fund and the Cohesion Fund: the triumvirate of Funds is colloquially known as the Structural Funds. The majority of this funding targets the poorest third of European regions, but approximately one fifth is distributed across the remaining regions with the aim of improving their competitiveness.

With work now beginning to examine the priorities for the European budget in the period after 2014, we have chosen to examine the distribution, management and impact of the Funds. We continue to support the underlying principle of intervention in the market to counter the uneven distribution of the benefits and costs of the single market, but wish to ensure that this support is delivered in an efficient and effective manner.

We find that the Funds are effective and, in general, fit for purpose. The evidence we received suggests that the size of the funding distributed to the poorest regions under the Convergence Objective is approximately correct. We also heard that the absorption cap in the poorest countries operates at an appropriate level to match the ability of regions to use the funds.

We consider in detail the distribution of funds to richer regions and wealthier Member States under the Competitiveness Objective. We find that objections about the cost of management of the funds are overstated. While we recognise that many Member States would lose funding as a result, we suggest that the future of the Competitiveness Objective should be reviewed during the forthcoming review of the EU budget. The funding and scope of the Convergence Objective, which supports the poorest regions, is appropriate and it should remain.

The Future of EU Regional Policy

CHAPTER 1: INTRODUCTION AND BACKGROUND

1. Economic cohesion has been a policy consideration for the European Community for half a century. In this period it has become increasingly important and it is likely that it will remain a priority: if the Lisbon Treaty is ratified, Article 3 of the Treaty on European Union will state that the Union "shall work for the sustainable development of Europe based on balanced economic growth and ... promote economic, social and territorial cohesion, and solidarity among Member States."[1] The Treaty also recognises that it is important that all Member States and regions share in this increasing prosperity and, more specifically, that there is a convergence in living standards across the various regions. The EU seeks to achieve this through its Regional Policy for which the European Structural and Cohesion Funds provide the financing.[2]

2. Article 158 of the Treaty establishing the European Community as currently in force states that the Community will aim to reduce "disparities between the levels of development of the various regions and the backwardness of the least favoured regions or islands, including rural areas." The Lisbon Treaty will amend this text, and, if adopted, Article 174 of the Treaty on the Functioning of the European Union will state:

   "the Union shall aim at reducing disparities between the levels of development of the various regions and the backwardness of the least favoured regions.

   Among the regions concerned, particular attention shall be paid to rural areas, areas affected by industrial transition, and regions which suffer from severe and permanent natural or demographic handicaps such as the northernmost regions with very low population density and island, cross-border and mountain regions."

3. While the rationale for a regional policy is grounded in the Treaty, its current embodiment, summarised later in this Chapter, is being considered—along with all of the Union's policies—as part of the 2008/9 Review of the EU Budget agreed at the December 2005 European Council. It is with the Budget Review in mind that we consider the Structural and Cohesion Funds, and European regional policy in general—the first time that we have focused on this significant European policy for several years.[3]

---

1 A similar expression was in Article 2 of the Treaty establishing the European Community.

2 'Cohesion policy' is often used synonymously with regional policy (defining the term region broadly to include both individual Member States and their regions) and is distinct from the 'Cohesion Fund' which is one of the financial instruments used in furtherance of Cohesion Policy. To avoid confusion, the term regional policy, rather than cohesion policy, is used in this Report.

3 The Funds were discussed in Chapter 4 of European Union Committee, 6th Report (2004–05): *Future Financing of the European Union* (HL 62). The last report to focus solely on the Funds was European Communities Committee, 30th Report (1997–98): *The Reform of the Structural Funds and the Cohesion Fund* (HL 138).

4. This report is one of several produced by this Committee in preparation for the 2008/9 Budget Review: last year we considered the income side of the budget,[4] and this year we have already looked at the Common Agricultural Policy.[5] Taken together, these reports will cover both the income to the budget and nearly all of its expenditure. When the Commission publishes proposals for budget reform we will consider them in detail, as part of our scrutiny remit.

5. This report is also made in the light of the Commission's Fourth Report on Economic and Social Cohesion[6] which noted some of the challenges with which regional policy may be confronted in the coming years. In his oral evidence to us, Mr Ahner, Director General, DG Regional Policy, suggested that the principal alternative to the current allocation of funds would be to leave regional development to market forces (Q 261). We do not support this alternative prospect, and in this report set out some proposals for change.

6. Regional policy is by its nature difficult to evaluate: it is very difficult to determine what path the economy might have taken without intervention. However, **we start this report from the stance of agreement with the European Union's Treaty-based aims to increase growth and to reduce disparities between regions, and we support the use of economic and knowledge transfer from rich to poor regions as a means to undertake this. EU economic growth is not a zero-sum game: the stronger and more competitive the EU economy as a whole, the better for all Member States. But the benefits and costs of the single market are not distributed evenly and we support intervention in the market to counter both unemployment and under-utilisation of resources in poorer regions, and costs arising from issues such as congestion and over-population in richer regions.**

The Development of European Regional Policy

7. Although Article 158 of the Treaty establishing the European Community mentions social cohesion, the degree of success of regional policy is largely judged on the reduction of regional differences in Gross Domestic Product (GDP) per head.

---

[4] European Union Committee, 12th Report (2006–07): *Funding the European Union* (HL 64).

[5] European Union Committee, 7th Report (2007–08): *The Future of the Common Agricultural Policy* (HL 54).

[6] COM(2007) 273. European Commission, *Growing Regions, Growing Europe. Fourth Report on Economic and Social Cohesion.* May 2007. The Commission is obliged by Article 159 of the Treaty establishing the European Community to produce a report every three years on the progress made towards achieving economic and social cohesion.

BOX 1

Different Measures of Regional Prosperity

A standard indicator of regional prosperity is GDP per head.[7] GDP measures the level of output and GDP per head has the advantage that it is easily understood and widely used in international comparisons of standards of living (when measured using Purchasing Power Parity). GDP per head has, however, a number of disadvantages as a measure of regional disparities:

- The figure is distorted by cross regional commuting. The Commission state that "this has not had a significant impact on the allocation of structural funding".[8] Open Europe cited the case of Lüneburg, a prosperous residential area of Hamburg, which because of commuting has a low GDP per head and hence attracted considerable Objective 1 (now Convergence) funding (p 21).
- GDP excludes a number of important items of income, especially pensions and unemployment benefits. A prosperous region with a large number of pensioners could have a relatively low value of GDP per head.
- A regional life-style where there is a high preference for leisure can lead to a low value of the GDP per head, although the region is relatively prosperous.

For the Cohesion Fund criteria, the Commission uses Gross National Income (GNI) which is GDP less net taxes on production and imports, less compensation of employees and property income paid to other countries plus similar items receivable from abroad. This is a preferable measure of prosperity. It is possible that a country or region with a high level of GDP per head could have a relatively low GNI per head if much of its income goes abroad. This might occur because of high levels of inward investment. GDP per capita would overstate the prosperity of the region or country compared with GNI per capita. The classic example of this is Ireland.

8. Policies to tackle regional disparity have been in place for fifty years. The European Social Fund, European Agricultural Guidance and Guarantee Fund (EAGGF) and the European Regional Development Fund (ERDF) were created in 1958, 1962 and 1975 respectively. Of these, the ERDF was the first explicit regional fund, and was based on the then existing premise that regional policy should be still a national rather than Community concern. Initially there was nothing to stop the Member States substituting the ERDF funds for their own regional expenditure, effectively turning the ERDF payments into a rebate.

9. In 1986, the Single European Act allowed for a regional policy designed to counter any negative repercussions of the single market. An agreement at the February 1988 European Council doubled the funding allocated to the structural funds and increased the emphasis on the poorer regions as part of a significant review of the EC budget. The reforms, made in preparation for the single market, gave the Commission a much greater role in the delivery, implementation and regulation of the Policy. The Funds could no longer be used by the Member States as they saw fit, as how and where they were spent now required Commission approval. The principles incorporated in these reforms still remain at the heart of regional policy.

---

[7] This is very closely related to Gross Value Added per head: GVA plus taxes on products less subsidies on products equals GDP. The two measures are so similar that we treat them as equivalent.

[8] COM(2007) 273. European Commission *Growing Regions, Growing Europe. Fourth report on Economic and Social Cohesion*, May 2007, (p.11 "The Impact of Commuting on GDP per Head".)

10. A concern to assist the poorer Member States cope with the challenge of the single market (and in particular the need for adequate investment in infrastructure) without breaching the convergence criteria[9] required for the EMU led to the creation of the Cohesion Fund in 1994. Rather than supporting poorer regions, this focussed on support for the poorer Member States (defined as those countries with a Gross National Income per head below 90% of the EU average).

11. In the late 1990s, some Member States raised concerns about the relatively lacklustre performance of the European Union as a whole in terms of productivity growth and the levels of unemployment. This led to the Lisbon Strategy[10], published in 2000 and relaunched in 2005. It now has two major targets at the European level—increasing the share of public and private investment in R&D to 3% of GDP; and securing an employment rate of 70%, both by 2010. The implications of the strategy for EU regional policy is that it should focus on three priorities: improving the attractiveness of regions and cities in the Member States; encouraging innovation, entrepreneurship and growth in the knowledge economy; and creating more and better jobs. It has two major targets at the European level—increasing the share of public and private investment in R&D to 3% of GDP; and securing an employment rate of 70%, both by 2010.

12. As a consequence, the aim of the Structural and Cohesion Funds became not only the reduction of income inequalities, but also the sustained increase in the growth rates of poorer regions. The Commission stated that "cohesion policy has been recognized as a key instrument at the Community level contributing to the implementation of the growth and jobs strategy—not just because it represents one third of the Community budget, but also because strategies designed at local and regional levels must also form an integral part of the effort to promote growth and jobs. The role of SMEs (small and medium-sized enterprises), the need to meet local skill demands, the importance of clusters, the need for local innovation centres is such that in many cases strategies also have to be built from below, at the regional and local levels."[11]

Measuring Disparities

13. The importance of regional policy has grown with the progressive enlargement of the EU. The States that have acceded in the past five years had lower GDP per head than the Union they were joining and their accession has by itself had the statistical effect of considerably widening disparities between Member States and between regions. The extent of these current differences is visible in Table 1. The poorest regions are to be found in Romania and Bulgaria, where all nine regions have a GDP per head that is below one-third of the EU average. The Nord-Est in Romania has the lowest GDP per head in the EU with an index of 24. At the other end of the spectrum, the richest regions are Inner London, UK (303); Luxembourg (264); Bruxelles-Cap./Brussels Hfdst, Belgium (241); and Hamburg, Germany (202). The GDP per head of some regions, especially the large cities and Luxembourg, is overstated due to

---

9 These were a budget deficit of less than 3% of GDP, public debt below 60% of GDP, an inflation rate within 1.5 percentage points of the three EU countries with the lowest rate, long-term interest rates within 2 percentage points of the three lowest interest rates in the EU, and an exchange rate that was within the normal fluctuation margin of the European exchange-rate mechanism.

10 European Union Committee, 28th Report (2005–2006): *A European Strategy for Jobs and Growth* (HL 137).

11 COM(2006) 281. European Commission *The Growth and Jobs Strategy and the Reform of European cohesion policy. Fourth Progress Report on Cohesion*, p. 8.

commuting patterns: commuters to the region where they work contribute to that region's GDP but are not classed as inhabitants.

TABLE 1

Regional GDP per Head in the European Union, 2005[12]

Country	Year of Accession	GDP per head (PPS, EU27 = 100) National	Richest Region	Poorest Region
Bulgaria	2007	35.3	52.2	26.9
Romania	2007	35.4	74.8	24.2
Latvia	2004	49.9	n.a.	n.a.
Poland	2004	51.3	81.2	35.0
Lithuania	2004	53.2	n.a	n.a.
Slovakia	2004	60.6	147.9	43.1
Estonia	2004	62.9	n.a.	n.a.
Hungary	2004	64.3	104.9	40.9
Portugal	1986	75.4	106.3	59.8
Czech Republic	2004	76.6	160.3	59.8
Malta	2004	77.4	n.a.	n.a.
Slovenia	2004	86.9	104.7	71.6
Cyprus	2004	92.6	n.a.	n.a.
Greece	1981	96.4	131.1	59.1
Spain	1986	103.0	133.9	69.7
Italy	1958	104.8	136.7	66.9
France	1958	111.9	172.6	50.5
Finland	1995	115.1	139.5	85.3
Germany	1958	115.2	202.1	74.2
United Kingdom	1973	119.3	302.7	77.4
Belgium	1958	121.1	240.5	79.5
Sweden	1995	123.8	172.2	105.4
Denmark	1973	126.7	161.0	94.9
Austria	1995	128.8	142.7	88.7
Netherlands	1958	131.1	164.0	96.3
Ireland	1973	143.7	158.1	104.3
Luxembourg	1958	264.3	n.a.	n.a.

12 Source: Eurostat News Release, 12 February 2008, Regional GDP per Inhabitant in the EU27. PPS is purchasing power standard, which corrects for differences in national prices not taken into account by exchange rates. "Region" refers to NUTS2 regions (see Box 2). n.a. denotes not applicable. Estonia, Cyprus, Latvia, Lithuania, Luxembourg and Malta are all treated as single regions. Germany on its accession was West Germany.

BOX 2

The NUTS Regional Classification

NUTS—Nomenclature of Territorial Units for Statistics—are the standard regions used in the EU regulations and by the Commission. Most of the regions are based on administrative criteria rather than functional or analytical criteria such as economic and social characteristics. A Member State is divided into NUTS1 regions which in turn are subdivided into NUTS2 regions and NUTS3 regions. If the country is small, such as Luxembourg, it can appear simultaneously as a NUTS1, NUTS2 and NUTS3 region.

The population of the NUTS regions at the same level can differ considerably. At the NUTS1 level, the range is from Nordrhein-Westfalen in Germany with a population of 18 million to Åland in Finland which only has 26,000 inhabitants. At the NUTS2 level, the Île de France has a population of 11 million while 14 regions have fewer than 300,000 inhabitants. At the NUTS3 level the range is from over 3 million (e.g. Madrid and Barcelona) to under 50,000.

There is also considerable variation in the area and population density of the NUTS2 regions. The largest region in terms of area is Pohjois-Soumi in Finland which is 133,580 sq. km. At the other extreme is a region in Spain that is only 13 sq. km. The NUTS2 region with the greatest population density is, perhaps not surprisingly, Inner London with 9,073 inhabitants per sq. km and in stark contrast is French Guiana with only 2 people per square km. (In the United Kingdom, the Highlands and Islands are the most sparsely populated with a density of 9 people per square km.)

The United Kingdom has 12 NUTS1 regions, 37 NUTS2 regions and 133 NUTS3 regions (all listed in Appendix 4). The current regional policy is calculated using the NUTS classifications adopted in 2003: there are 268 NUTS2 regions in the EU. The map on page 15 shows the NUTS2 regional boundaries. The NUTS classification and the regional boundaries are amended from time to time by Eurostat[13].

Our Inquiry

14. The membership of Sub-Committee A that undertook this inquiry is set out in Appendix 1. We are grateful to those who submitted written and oral evidence, who are listed in Appendix 2; all the evidence is printed with this report. Appendix 4 sets out the countries that comprise the EU10, EU15, EU25 and EU27; Appendix 5 lists the United Kingdom statistical regions. There is a glossary in Appendix 6.

15. We also thank the Sub-Committee's specialist adviser Dr John McCombie, Department of Land Economy, University of Cambridge. We make this report for debate in the context of the EU Budget as a whole.

[13] A slightly revised version of the NUTS classification came into force on 1 January 2008, under which the number of NUTS2 regions is now 271. It is likely that decisions on eligibility taken on the basis of the previous classification will remain for the whole budget period, and as a consequence we refer to the 268 regions in this report.

CHAPTER 2: THE EUROPEAN UNION STRUCTURAL AND COHESION FUNDS

The Current Funds

16. Three Funds are used for regional policy:

- The *European Regional Development Fund* (ERDF) finances direct aid for investment in companies (particularly small and medium-sized enterprises), infrastructure, financial instruments (such as capital risk funds and local development funds) and technical assistance[14] measures. It is allocated on a regional basis.
- The *European Social Fund* (ESF) finances projects in the labour market that improve skills (human capital) and access to employment opportunities and social integration. It is again allocated on a regional basis.
- The *Cohesion Fund* finances developments in transport networks which have been identified as priority projects by the EU; projects related to the environment; and energy and transport projects with clear environmental benefits. It is allocated at the Member State level, with finance from the Fund conditional on compliance with the Stability and Growth Pact requirement of not running an excessive public deficit.

17. The Funds are allocated to meet three objectives:

- The *Convergence Objective* is "aimed at the speeding up the convergence of the least-developed Member States and regions".[15] It is the main instrument of regional policy and accounts for 81.5% of spending. It covers the areas of "improvement of the quality of investment in physical and human capital, the development of innovation and of the knowledge society, adaptability to economic and social changes, and of the protection and improvement of the environment and administrative efficiency".[16] It is focussed on the poorer regions, defined at NUTS2 level. (See Box 2 for a discussion of the NUTS regions.) Different eligibility requirements apply under this Objective based on which Fund the spending is being sourced from. These are summarised in Table 3.
- The *Regional Competitiveness and Employment Objective* is designed to act "outside the least developed regions ... at strengthening regions' competitiveness and attractiveness as well as employment by anticipating economic and social changes, including those linked to the opening of trade"[17]. The Objective accounts for 16% of regional funding and is funded by the ERDF and ESF. Every region not covered by the Convergence Objective is eligible and it is up to the Member States to decide which of their regions should receive funding. This Objective

14 Technical assistance provides funding for those activities that enhance the quality and efficiency of the implementation of ERDF projects.

15 Council Regulation (EC) No. 1083/2006 of 11 July 2006 laying down general provisions on the European Regional Development Fund, the European Social Fund and the Cohesion Fund and repealing Regulation (EC) No. 1260/1999, Article 3(a).

16 Ibid, Article 3, 2(a).

17 Ibid, Article 3, (6).

recognises that even the richest Member States have areas that are struggling. As these areas may be further disadvantaged by the integration of EU markets and, more generally, by globalisation, they may need regional aid.

- The *European Territorial Cooperation Objective* has the aim of "strengthening cross-border co-operation through joint local and regional initiatives."[18] Unlike the other Objectives, it operates at the NUTS3 level (although in practice a NUTS2 region can be designated, if all its NUTS3 regions are chosen). This means that it operates in regions that are also eligible for the first two Objectives and, with its narrow remit and relatively small budget, it is a complement to them.

18. Regions that formerly qualified for Objective 1 status[19] under the 2000–2006 financial framework, but are now no longer eligible for convergence funding, receive transitional competitiveness funding as "phasing in" regions. The accession of the 10 new Member States had the statistical effect of lowering the EU GDP per head by about 12.5%. This made some regions and countries that would have been eligible for support under the old calculation, ineligible. These areas have been given tapering transitional support up until 2013, known as "phasing out" regions when under the convergence objective.

19. Table 2 summarises the interaction between the Funds and Objectives. The map shows the eligibility of regions during the current Financial Perspective.

---

[18] Ibid, Article 3, 2(c).

[19] In the 2000–2006 period, Objective 1 regions were those that had a GDP per head less than 75% of the EU average.

MAP

Structural Funds 2007–13: Convergence and Regional Competitiveness Objectives

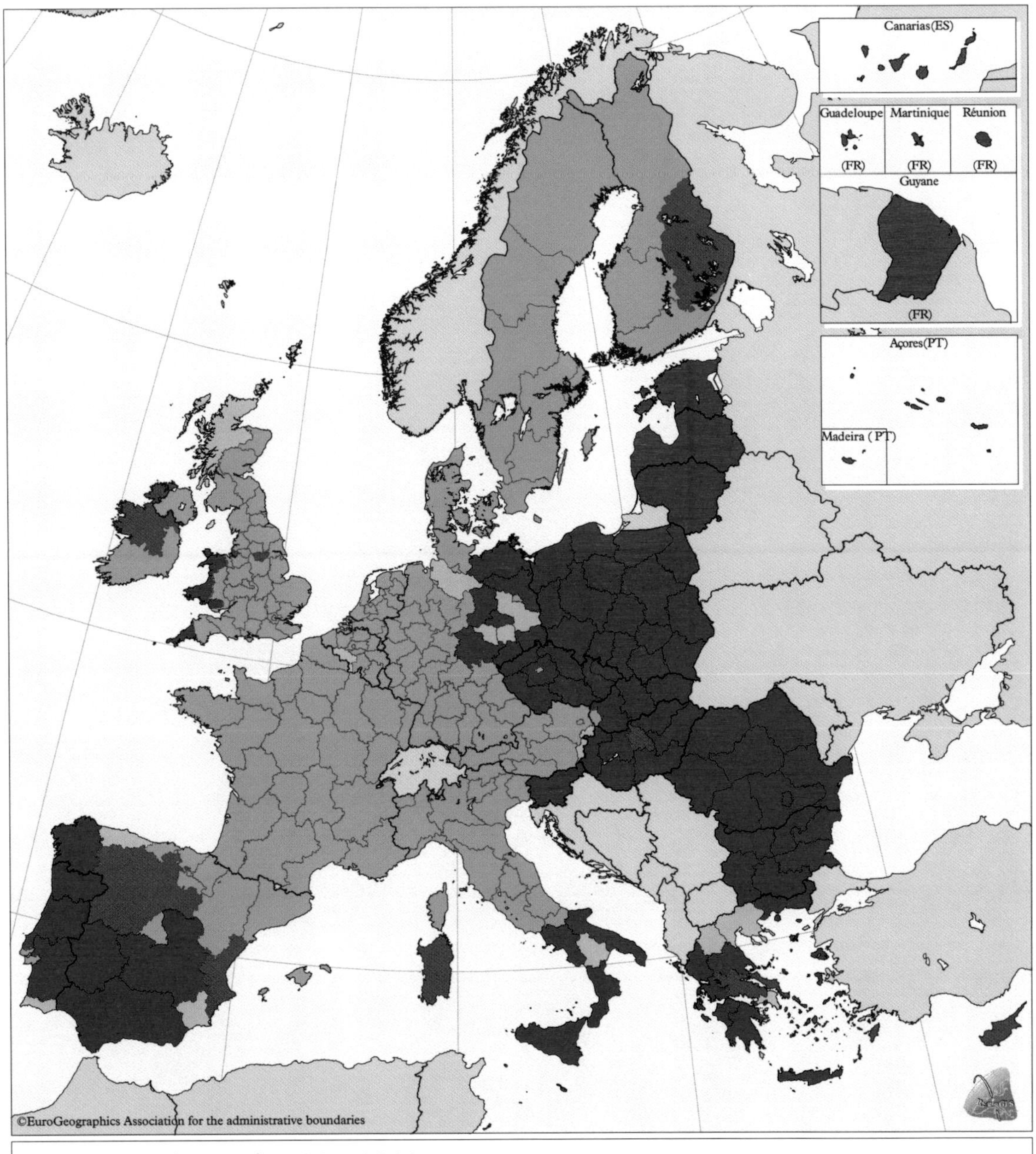

Structural Funds 2007-2013:
Convergence and Regional Competitiveness Objectives

- Convergence Regions
- Phasing-out Regions
- Phasing-in Regions
- Competitiveness and Employment Regions

0 1,000km

Source: European Commission

Position as of October 2006.

Regional boundaries in Bulgaria and Romania are indicative only.

TABLE 2

Regional Policy Architecture (2007–13)[20]

Objective	Financial Instruments	Eligibility	Financial Allocation (Million €, 2004 prices)	Regions/countries receiving allocation
Convergence	ERDF ESF	NUTS2 regions whose GDP per head is less than 75% of the EU average (shaded red on the map)	177,083 (57.5%)	84 regions (31.7% of EU27 population)
		Tapering transitional support up to 2013 for regions that would have been eligible if the threshold had remained 75% of the EU15 GDP per head average and not the EU25 (“**phasing out**”)[21] (shaded pink on the map)	12,521 (4.1%)	16 regions (3.4% of EU27 population)
	Cohesion Fund	Member States whose GNI per head is less than 90% of the Community average for the period 2001–03	58,308 (18.9%)	All new Member States, Portugal and Greece
		Tapering transitional support for Member States that would have remained eligible for the Cohesion Fund if the threshold had remained 90% of the EU15 GNI per head average and not the EU25[21]	3,250 (1.0%)	Spain
			Subtotal: 251,162 (81.5%)	

[20] Sources: European Commission: Cohesion Policy, 2007–13 Commentaries and Official Texts Luxemburg, Office for the Official Publications of the European Communities. Commission Communication *The Growth and Jobs Strategy and the Reform of European Cohesion Policy. Fourth Progress Report on Cohesion* (Table 3).

[21] The accession of the 10 new Member States to the European Union had the statistical effect of lowering the EU GDP per head by about 12.5%. This support will not be renewed after 2013.

Regional Competitiveness and Employment	ERDF ESF	All NUTS2 regions not covered by the Convergence Objective or by transitional support (shaded light grey on the map)	38,742 (12.6%)	All regions not covered elsewhere (61% of the EU27 population)
		Transitional support for NUTS 2 regions which were covered by Objective 1 in the 2000–06 framework (which corresponds to the present Convergence Objective) but whose GDP per head now exceeds 75% of the EU15 GDP per head average ("**phasing in**")[22] (shaded dark grey on the map)	10,385 (3.4%) Subtotal: 49,127 (15.9%)	13 regions (3.9% of the EU27 population)
European Territorial Cooperation	ERDF	(i) Cross-border co-operation. NUTS3 regions that have maritime, national or EU borders (ii) Trans-national co-operation. All European NUTS3 regions are eligible but the Commission has identified 13 co-operation zones (iii) Inter-regional co-operation and setting up networks and exchanges of experience. All European NUTS3 regions are eligible	Subtotal: 7,750 (2.5%)	
			Total: 308,041 (100%)	

22 This also includes Cyprus which, due an overestimate of its GDP per head, did not have Objective 1 status.

Intervention Principles

20. The implementation of the Structural and Cohesion Funds is controlled by a number of intervention principles, some of which date from the 1988 reforms with others added since. The principle of *concentration* is where, because of limited financial resources, the Commission seeks to target the funds both spatially and sectorally. This forms the rationale for having the three Objectives discussed above and the accompanying eligibility conditions, although in previous programmes there were more Objectives. A major innovation of the 1988 reforms was the *programming* principle which represents a move away from funding project-by-project to funding on a multi-annual basis. The 1988 reforms also introduced the principle of decisions being made in a *partnership* between the Commission and the Member State, their regional organisations and other public bodies and non-governmental organisations. The principle of *proportionality* was introduced into the latest financial framework with the aim that the total spend on administration, control and monitoring should not be disproportionate to the total expenditure on a particular project. Why this is required is discussed in Chapter 4.

21. *Subsidiarity* is a fundamental EU principle, enshrined in the Treaties, that requires the decentralization of powers to the lowest level of government that is compatible with efficient policy delivery. For the Structural and Cohesion Funds to respect the subsidiarity principle, their provision must achieve something that the Member States by themselves could not achieve, i.e. they must "add value". In the case of the poorer Member States where the Funds represent a net contribution to their resources, the principle is straightforwardly met: the Funds represent a net contribution to the resources of the Member States. However, many witnesses argued that when richer Member States who are net contributors to the EU budget are merely receiving back funds that they have already contributed, this principle is breached. We return to this issue in Chapter 3.

22. A condition of the Structural and Cohesion Funds is that expenditure should also leverage in additional spending by the Member States on their own regional policy or from the private sector. Under the principle of *co-financing*, the maximum contribution that the EU will make to a particular project varies between 50% and 85%, with the EU making a greater contribution to the projects of the new Member States than the other richer Member States.

23. Furthermore, the Structural and Cohesion Funds are designed not merely to replace national public expenditure: there must be *additionality*. The objective is to ensure that the Member State does not reduce their own related public expenditure in the 2007–13 period when compared with the previous Financial Perspective. Member State expenditure is only verified by the Commission with respect to the Convergence Objective.[23] As the Funds comprise only 0.38 of the EU's GNI and are small compared with the public expenditure in many Member States they are best seen as seed corn, leveraging in further funding, both from the Member States because of the co-financing regulations, but also from the private sector.

24. For those Member States in the European Union prior to 1 May 2004, 60% of expenditure under the Convergence Objective and 75% of expenditure under the Regional Competitiveness and Employment Objective must

---

[23] For the methodology employed see the European Commission, Directorate-General Regional Policy, "Commission Methodological Paper Giving Guidelines on the Calculation of Public or Equivalent Structural Spending for the Purposes of Additionality", Working Document No.3, December 2006.

explicitly meet the aims of the *Lisbon Strategy*.[24] The spending categories eligible under the Lisbon Strategy are:

- Research and technological development, innovation and entrepreneurship
- Information society
- Transport
- Energy
- Environment protection and risk prevention
- Increasing the adaptability of workers and firms, enterprises and entrepreneurs
- Improving access to employment and sustainability
- Improving the social inclusion of less-favoured persons
- Improving human capital.[25]

The Current 2007–2013 Financial Framework

25. Regional policy's share of the budget has also increased over time: as Table 3 shows, by 1988 the share was 17% and since then it has slowly risen and is budgeted to be 38% by 2013. This growth has been at the expense of payments to agriculture, for which the share of the budget has gradually decreased over time. For the 2007–2013 Financial Framework, the total funding available is €308 billion at 2004 prices[26] which constitutes approximately 0.38% of the EU's GNI. However, the proportion of the budget allocated to regional policy has not risen significantly in recent years despite the increased disparity in wealth in the enlarged EU.

TABLE 3[27]

Policies' shares of the EU budget

Year	Percentage of European Budget[a]		Size of EU Budget[a] as % of EU GNP or GNI
	Regional Policy	Common Agricultural Policy	
1975	6.2	70.9	0.53
1980	11.0	68.6	0.80
1985	12.8	68.4	0.92
1988	17.2	60.7	1.12
1993	32.3	53.5	1.20
2000	34.8	44.5	1.07
2007	36.7	47.1	1.04
2013	38.1	43.0	0.93

24 As set out in the *Integrated Guidelines for Growth and Jobs* (2005–2008)—Council Decision 2005/600/EC of 12 July 2005.

25 Article 9(3) and Annex IV of Council Regulation (EC) No. 1083/2006 of 11 July 2006 laying down general provisions on the European Regional Development Fund, the European Social Fund and the Cohesion Fund and repealing Regulation (EC) No. 1260/1999 include a list of the priorities underlying each of the above categories.

26 2004 prices are often used by the Commission as the reference point for the 2007–13 Financial Perspective. The Commission and the Government equated this amount to €347 billion at current prices (p 58).

27 Sources: European Commission, *The Community Budget: Facts in Figures, 2000*; European Navigator at www.ena.lu and Commission documents. Notes: [a] Total appropriations for payments. 1998, 1993, 2000 and 2007 are the first years of the Financial Frameworks, Sources: European Navigator at www.ena.lu, European Commission, EU Budget 2006—Financial Report.

26. Table 4 shows the allocation of the Structural and Cohesion Funds between the Member States for the financial framework 2007–2013. It includes the allocation for the Convergence Objective and also for the total funding a country receives from all of the Funds. The biggest beneficiary is Poland with €60 billion (19.4% of the total), followed by Spain (€32 billion, 10.2%) and then Italy (€26 billion, 8.3%).

TABLE 4[28]

Indicative Financial Allocations: 2007–2013

Country	*National*	*Convergence Objective*		*Total EU Regional Funds*			
	GDP per head, €, 2005	Million €	€ per head in recipient regions	Million €	€ per head in recipient country	Share of GDP %	Share of total regional funds %
Bulgaria	7,913	5,888	753	6,047	768	3.15	2.0
Romania	7,933	16,912	778	17,316	795	3.00	5.6
Latvia	11,180	4,010	1,725	4,090	1,749	3.52	1.3
Poland	11,482	59,048	1,546	59,698	1,562	3.43	19.4
Lithuania	11,914	5,999	1,737	6,096	1,757	3.42	2.0
Slovak Republic	13,563	9,663	1,796	10,264	1,904	3.30	3.3
Estonia	14,093	3,011	2,221	3,058	2,247	3.31	1.0
Hungary	14,393	20,243	1,998	22,451	2,210	3.22	7.3
Portugal	16,891	18,316	1,750	19,147	1,847	1.82	6.2
Czech Republic	17,156	22,979	2,252	23,698	2,323	3.25	7.7
Malta	17,330	747	1,878	761	1,922	2.35	0.2
Slovenia	19,462	3,646	1,827	3,739	1,874	1.70	1.2
Cyprus	20,753	193	265	580	812	0.56	0.2
Greece	21,589	17,447	1,585	18,217	1,658	1.34	5.9
Spain	23,069	23,411	1,566	31,536	778	0.49	10.2
Italy	23,474	19,255	1,112	25,647	449	0.25	8.3
Germany	25,797	14,323	933	23,449	284	0.14	7.6
France	25,077	2,838	1,623	12,736	208	0.10	4.1
Finland	25,774	0	0	1,533	295	0.13	0.5
United Kingdom	26,715	2,594	949	9,468	160	0.07	3.1

28 € in 2004 purchasing power parities except GDP per head which is 2005. *Sources:* OECD (2007), *Economic Surveys: European Union*, Table 7.4, p.144. European Commission (2006) *The Growth and Jobs Strategy and Reform of EU Cohesion Policy*. The difference between the Total and the Convergence Objective is made up of spending under the Competitiveness and Territorial Cooperation Objectives.

Belgium	27,135	579	452	2,020	195	0.09	0.7
Sweden	27,721	0	0	1,682	188	0.08	0.5
Denmark	28,375	0	0	545	101	0.04	0.2
Austria	28,852	159	568	1,301	161	0.07	0.4
Netherlands	29,374	0	0	1,697	105	0.05	0.6
Ireland	32,197	0	0	815	207	0.06	0.3
Luxembourg	59,202	0	0	58	130	0.02	0.0
Not allocated				392			0.1
EU27 All Member States				308,041			100.0
EU12 New Member States				158,190			51.4
EU15 Pre 2004 Member States				149,851			48.6

27. Although GDP/GNI per head is used to determine the eligibility of the region/Member State for funding, the actual moneys received are determined by a formula that involves other criteria. These are the Member State's relative prosperity, the number of people unemployed (Convergence Objective only) and in addition, for the Regional Competitiveness and Employment Objective, the number of jobs needed to reach an employment rate of 70%, the number of workers employed with a low education level, and population density.

28. As a result of the application of this formula and, in some cases, the absorption cap (discussed in paragraph 35), there is no clear relationship in the Convergence Objective regions between the value of Funds received per head and national GDP per head. This is shown in Table 4. Regions in some of the wealthier Member States receive more funding per inhabitant than eligible regions in the poorer countries. The United Kingdom will receive, over the 2007–13 Financial Framework, a total of approximately €9.5 billion (at 2004 prices) of which €2.6 billion is for the Convergence Objective. The two regions eligible for this are Cornwall & the Isles of Scilly and West Wales & the Valleys (covering 2.5 million people). The Highlands and Islands are eligible for phasing out assistance. €6.2 billion is allocated to Regional Competitiveness and Employment Funding and Merseyside and South Yorkshire are eligible for phasing in funding (see paragraph 18). The phasing in and phasing out regions together cover a further 3 million people. €0.6 billion is available under the Territorial Co-operation Objective. The EU funding only covers 75% and 50% of the eligible expenditure under the Convergence and Regional Competitiveness and Employment Objectives respectively. This means that relatively large additional funds will also be

available from the required United Kingdom public and private "match funding".

Implementation

29. Implementation of regional policy involves a dialogue between the Commission and the Member States and their regional organisations, and encompasses what is termed "multi-level governance". Broadly, the Commission sets out the strategy to be observed and the Member States put forward proposals for the individual projects and programmes for agreement by the Commission.

30. The European Council sets, and Council and the European Parliament then fine tune, the amounts in the Financial Perspective to be allocated to the Structural and Cohesion Funds. The Commission, in consultation with the Member States, draws up the *Community Strategic Guidelines on Cohesion* which set out the broad guidelines for the use of the Funds. The guidelines are used to produce the aims for each Objective and are now aligned with the Lisbon Strategy priorities. For the 2007–13 period, the *Guidelines* identified three main priorities, as noted in paragraph 11:

- improving the attractiveness of Member States, regions and cities by improving accessibility, ensuring adequate quality and level of services, and preserving their environmental potential;
- encouraging innovation, entrepreneurship and the growth of the knowledge economy by research and innovation capacities, including new information and communication technologies; and
- creating more and better jobs by attracting more people into employment or entrepreneurial activity, improving adaptability of workers and enterprises and increasing investment in human capital.

31. Each Member State is required to produce a *National Strategic Reference Framework* (NSRF) which sets out the country's economic strengths and weaknesses and how it intends to implement the EU regional policy priorities, taking account of local conditions. The Member State will have received an indicative allocation of funding. After negotiations between the Member State and the Commission, the NSRF is validated by the Commission. The funding for the Convergence Objective is ring fenced for the eligible regions, except for the Cohesions Fund. As long as it acts within the NSRF, the Member State can propose exactly how and where the funds all allocated under the Regional Competitiveness and Employment Objective are to be allocated. *Operational programmes* then spell out in detail the projects to be implemented, taking into account the NSRF. There are, in total, 455 operational programmes in the EU for the 2007–13 exercise. Following approval, the Commission authorizes expenditure and subsequently, together with the relevant Member State, monitors and evaluates the projects.

32. In the United Kingdom, the Government has allocated ERDF Regional Competitiveness funding between the United Kingdom's Competitiveness regions[29] by reference to population, GDP and levels of innovation, enterprise and skills. For the ESF Regional Competitiveness Funds, the

[29] All regions other than Cornwall, West Wales & the Valleys, and the Highlands & Islands.

criteria are numbers of jobless people, numbers of working-age people with no qualifications, and numbers of working-age people with low qualifications.[30]

Allocation between the Member States

33. The accession of the new Member States in 2004 and 2007 has had a major impact on the distribution of the funds. Because of the enlargement and the overall EU budget constraint, the original EU15 will receive 36% less support in this Financial Perspective compared with the last.[31] The United Kingdom's Structural Funds allocation fell by nearly a half. Nevertheless, the richer Member States (i.e. the original EU15 less Greece and Portugal) are set to receive a substantial share of the Structural and Cohesion Funds over the period 2007–2013. They received 36% of the budget commitments with the remaining 64% allocated to the poorer Member States. With the ending of transitional relief for some of the richer Member Sates and their regions, the share of the poorer Member States will rise to 67% in 2013 (p 58).

34. The Commission gives each Member State indicative annual sums for each of the seven years of the financial framework. The fact that the funding is guaranteed for seven years is seen as one of the advantages of multi-annual programming.

35. The amount allocated to each Member State depends on the population of regions or Member States falling within the various objective categories and the various allocation formulae which differ between the objectives.[32] However, the size of the funds for which the new Member States would be eligible under the allocation formulae is so large that there are doubts as to whether they have the capacity to use them efficiently. Consequently, an absorption cap based on a sliding scale, related to the Member States' GNI per head, has been introduced; while this applies in theory to all Member States, in practice the constraint is only triggered for some of the new Member States. For example, the cap for countries whose average GNI per head in 2002/3 was less than 40% of the EU average limits the total contribution of the Funds to about 3.8% of GNI. This can result in a reduction of around a half of the funds available for a number of the new Member States,[33] although the amounts allocated can still amount to around 20% of total public and private investment in these countries.

36. As the Funds are territorially concentrated, they can also form a not insignificant proportion of a region's investment, even within the richer Member States. This is notwithstanding the fact that the funds received by several of the richer Member States amount to less than 0.1 % of GDP each.

Alternatives to grants

37. Both the Government and Graham Meadows, former Director General, Regional Policy, European Commission suggested that especially for the

---

30 National Strategic Reference Framework for EU Structural Funds Programmes, 2007–2013, HC Deb 23 October 2006 cols 72WS–74WS.

31 Bachtler, J., Wishlade, F. and Méndez, C. (2007) *New Budget, New Regulations, New Strategies: The 2006 Reform of EU Cohesion Policy* (Figures 9 and 10, p.37), European Policy Research Paper no.63, European Policies Research Centre, University of Strathclyde.

32 Annex II of Council Regulation (EC) No.1083/2006 of 11 July 2006.

33 See Table 14, p.27 of Bachtler, J., Wishlade, F., and Méndez, C. op. cit.

richer regions, more use could be made of loans as opposed to grants, and in particular of recyclable loans (Q 245, pp 57, 79). We heard from Mr Meadows (Q 245) that as late as 1989, Marshall Aid funds were still being recycled in Germany. The advantage of recyclable loans, as opposed to grants from the Funds, is that the money is returned to the region at the end of the programming period when they are repaid. They can thus be used repeatedly time and again over a long period. The Government suggested this could be facilitated through more extensive use of the EIB[34] (p 57). **We would welcome increased use of loans and invite the Government, in their response, to outline what steps they are taking to encourage their use.**

34 The European Investment Bank was established in 1958 and raises considerable sums of money on the capital markets for lending to the Member States. Priority is given to projects for developing less-developed regions. In 2006, €27.5 billion, or two-thirds of total EIB lending, went to regional development in the EU27. The Commission is already in partnership with the EIB in JASPERS (Joint Assistance to Support Projects in European Regions), JEREMIE (Joint European Resources for Micro-to-Medium Enterprises) and JESSICA (Joint European Support for Sustainable Investment in City Areas). JEREMIE is an initiative with the European Investment Fund, of which the major shareholders are the EIB and the Commission. (See also Communities and Local Government, *Financing Investment in Sustainable Cities and Communities in Europe—the Role of the European Investment Bank,* 2007.)

CHAPTER 3: PROPOSALS FOR CHANGE

Measuring the Policy's impact

38. As Table 2 explains, the distribution of the Structural and Cohesion Funds is based upon disparities in GDP per head, and it is judged on its success at reducing those disparities (Q 127). There are alternative approaches that could be used. One is to measure relative prosperity in terms of income directly accruing to the inhabitants of a region or in terms of their actual consumption. Two common measures are primary income (per head), which is defined as income before taxes and transfer payments, and disposable income (per head) which is income after taxes and benefits. Primary and disposable income overcome the commuting problem (see Box 1), and disposable income takes into account government transfers. A further measure is actual individual consumption (AIC) per head. AIC comprises household final consumption expenditure (goods and services purchased by households directly) as well as the consumption of individual services, notably health and education services provided by government and non-profit organisations.

39. The use of other indicators to pick up economic changes at a local level (such as reductions in disparities in health, unemployment, degree of social exclusion) that the funds might have brought about would be desirable. These are sometimes masked by the broader economic measures used by the Commission. However, GDP per head is used primarily because it is the indicator for which there are the most reliable and consistent data across the regions.

40. Professor Bachtler, University of Strathclyde, informed us that determining the effectiveness of regional policy, especially in quantitative terms, is quite a difficult proposition (Q 103). A major problem in studies of the effectiveness of the Funds is how to measure what might have otherwise occurred (p 18): the fact that disparities may be widening, or not closing very rapidly, is not in itself an indication that EU regional policy is ineffective since the position might have been worse in the absence of the policy.

41. On the one hand, the opening up of markets, exposure to greater competition, and the diffusion of best-practice production techniques can all increase the rate of economic growth in the lagging regions. An important proviso is that the regions have the necessary flexibility and social institutions to take advantage of these opportunities. Thus the rapid growth of many of the poorer regions, or Member States, could be largely due to greater integration with European and world markets and have very little to do with the Structural and Cohesion Funds. On the other hand, agglomeration and other economies of scale mean that increased integration could be to the detriment of the lagging (often peripheral) regions.[35] In these circumstances, there is a trade off between equity and efficiency. The view of Mr Ahner, Director General, DG Regional Policy is that economic growth should be

[35] There is now considerable theoretical and empirical literature on this issue. Introductions to the various approaches may be found in Armstrong, H., and Taylor, J., *Regional Economics and Policy,* Blackwell, 2000; Barro, R.J., and Sala-i-Martin, X., *Economic Growth,* MIT (2nd ed,) 2003; and Brakman, S., Garretsen, H and van Marrewijk, C., *An Introduction to Geographical Economics, Trade Location and Growth,* Cambridge University Press, 2001.

spread evenly throughout the EU (Q 250). In his view, the concentration of growth in just a few areas brings with it problems of such as increased congestion and pollution and loss from the growth potential of the lagging regions (Q 250).

42. There are other reasons why it is difficult accurately to assess the effectiveness of the Funds. For example, many of the funded projects such as those improving the skills of the labour force or increasing the infrastructure may have a long lead time before they have any marked impact on the growth of GDP per head. The experience of national regional policies, including that of the United Kingdom, shows just how difficult it is to achieve a rapid convergence in regional prosperity. Many of the earlier studies on the effectiveness of the Funds use figures that are now somewhat dated. The Funds may have a much greater effect on the new Member States, given that their regions have levels of GDP per head that are lower than the lagging regions in the richer Member States (see Table 1). Consequently, they may have more scope for catching up, aided by the Funds.

43. Despite these problems, the effectiveness of the Funds has been extensively analysed. The Commission itself undertakes regular assessments of the impact of the Funds including detailed evaluations at the project level. These have used a bottom-up technique and attempt to assess the degree of employment creation at the local level, using data generated by the programme and from surveys. The Commission has also used a more aggregative approach through macro-economic simulation models. Other studies have used statistical techniques which attempt to estimate the effect of the Funds, controlling for the effect of other factors such as the impact of the single market. Some of the evidence is more anecdotal: Mr Meadows (Q 226) claimed that that the revival in fortunes of Cornwall could be traced to when it was given Objective 1 status.

44. One approach to assessing the impact of the EU's regional policy is to compare the performance of the Member States and regions that have received funds either with those that are not eligible or with the EU average. The period since the accession of new Member States is too short for any evaluation to be meaningful, but it is possible to consider the performance of the original Cohesion countries: Greece, Spain, Ireland and Portugal. During the period 1995–2005, Ireland grew at four percentage points above the EU15 average, and the country now has the second highest GDP per head in the EU. Spain and Greece have also exceeded the EU15 average growth rate by 0.7 and 1.5 percentage points respectively. The only disappointment has been Portugal, which recorded a growth rate above the EU average until 1999, but which since has grown at a rate well below the EU average. In 2005 it had a level of GDP per head below that of the Czech Republic and Slovenia[36]. At a regional level, there were 50 lagging regions for the EU15 (i.e. regions with a per head income below 75% of the EU average) in 1995 and by 2004 12 of these with a combined population of 10 million had moved above 75% of EU average GNI per head. Against this must be set the fact that five regions (with a population of 6 million) had slipped below 75%.[37] The Commission also points out that in spite of the convergence of

---

36 COM(2007) 273. European Commission, *Growing Regions, Growing Europe. Fourth Report on Economic and Social Cohesion*. May 2007 (p 5).

37 Ibid. (p 7).

low income countries, regional disparities within countries still remain large[38] (see Table 1).

45. Open Europe stated that convergence was very slow, with 43 of 44 regions originally granted Objective One status in 1989 still eligible for such funding in 2003 (p 19). The Government pointed out that the position had greatly improved in recent years: Mr McFadden MP, Minister of State for Employment Relations and Postal Affairs, provided detailed data indicating that by the 2007–13 programme only 30 of the 44 regions remained eligible for funding under the convergence objective and 9 of these were under the transitional arrangements (p 71). However, as noted in paragraph 44, some regions had become eligible for funding for the first time. Dr Robert Leonardi, London School of Economics, also provided evidence highlighting high growth rates in Member States whose regions were receiving funding (Q 122).

46. An alternative method of assessing the effectiveness of the use of the Funds could include the levels of private inward investment, which would reflect the market's confidence in the new Member State. Open Europe described an absence of evidence to date to support any "added value" delivered by the Funds (p 18). The Commission told us that they were currently studying the impact of the Funds on inward investment and we look forward to seeing the result of their research (Q 288).

47. **We agree with those witnesses who argue that the Funds have helped to reduce disparities in Europe. We welcome work to measure the impact of European regional policy on levels of private inward investment.**

Spending priorities

48. Professor Bachtler argued that some of the spending under the Funds in the past may not have been the most appropriate means of investment, with an excessive emphasis on infrastructure at the expense of education and human capital (Q 103). Dr Bradley and Professor Untiedt, Economic Modelling and Development Systems, agreed (p 122). They compared favourably the Irish Structural and Cohesion Funds, which were used in a programme of expenditure first weighted towards education and only subsequently infrastructure, with the Portuguese use of the Funds. The emphasis of the latter was primarily on infrastructure, notwithstanding the low level of education in Portugal. But we also heard from witnesses that a basic level of transport infrastructure is a necessary prerequisite for the attraction of new firms and inward investment (Q 286, p 109).

49. As discussed in Chapter 1, under the 2007–13 Financial Perspective regional policy is linked explicitly to the Lisbon Agenda. The Structural and Cohesion Funds are seen by the Commission as a key instrument in the implementation of the re-launched growth and jobs strategy. EU15 Member States are required to earmark 60% of the expenditure under the Convergence Objective and 75% under the Regional Competitiveness and Employment Objective for Lisbon objectives. In the United Kingdom, this amounts to € 964 million per year (2008 prices). As Mr Boijmans, Deputy Head of Unit, Poland, at DG Regio, pointed out, even in the case of Poland

---

38 Ibid.

where there is an acute need for improvements in infrastructure, the country has also "committed itself to the objectives of the Lisbon Strategy to create wealth and jobs and to have a more forward looking strategy than purely building roads and sewerage plants. It has allocated almost 64 per cent of its budget to Lisbon-relevant areas of expenditure which is quite high taking into account the size of Poland, the size of the budget and the situation the budget is in" (Q 286).

50. In the fourth report on Economic and Social Cohesion[39], the Commission identifies new challenges that may have an uneven impact and widen social and economic disparities. The Government explained that, in their view, the National Integrated Guidelines for Jobs and Growth and the National Reform Programmes set out the challenges the EU faces and "there is no need for a separate set of challenges to be identified for cohesion policy" (p 57). The Minister wrote that "Cohesion Policy should remain focussed on achieving sustainable growth and jobs. If the scope of Cohesion Policy were widened [to include issues such as climate and demographic change] then this could result in a shift in resources away from addressing disparities in economic development" (p 59).

51. **We believe that allowing the regions to draw up regional spending plans, emphasising local infrastructure or education priorities, reflects the fact that one policy does not fit all.**

52. **While the reduction in discrepancies in citizens' prosperity should be the policy's primary focus, we welcome integration with the Lisbon Strategy. Given the importance of innovation and human capital in the knowledge economy, if lagging regions and Member States are to accelerate their growth, improvements in these areas will be important. We are encouraged to learn that new Member States are also taking account of the strategy in their regional plans. However, the major impetus for the implementation of the Lisbon Agenda must come at the Member State level—the contribution to the Agenda under the Competitiveness Objective is marginal when compared with national public expenditure but can attract project finance from other sources. The problem of increasing the competitiveness of the European Union is of course greater than can be addressed solely by regional policy.**

53. **On broader issues such as climate change, we agree with the Government that the Structural and Cohesion Funds should not be used other than for reducing regional disparities.**

Absorption Cap and co-financing

54. The 2008 EC budget allocates €47.3 billion[40] to the Funds: this represents 36.1% of the total EC Budget and 0.38% of EU GNI. For comparison, BERR's total budget in the United Kingdom equates to approximately 0.2% of UK GNI.

55. As explained in paragraph 35, nearly all the new Member States find that their receipts from the Structural and Cohesion Funds are capped. This has reduced the amount that some of the new Member States would otherwise have

---

39 COM(2007) 273.

40 At 2008 prices: SEC (2008) 514.

received by about half. Mr Ahner stated that at present the least developed regions in the EU are not able to absorb more than is already allocated to them (QQ 273, 275). Ms Lorens, Head of Delegation for the Regional Representation for Lubelskie in Poland, told us that in the period 2004–06 her region could use only 80% of its allocation of funds, but that they expected a higher utilisation rate in the current budgetary period. Lack of management expertise was the principal limit to using even more (QQ 26, 300–303). This example illustrates the argument of several witnesses, including the Government, that increasing the share of funds that the new Member States receive of itself is not a sufficient prerequisite for increasing their economic performance (pp 57, 109, 122, 125, QQ 104, 206, 271).

56. Evidence has shown[41] that fraud and mismanagement occur predominantly at the national rather than the EU level. The Polish regions highlighted the difficulties that they have faced: in Wielkopolska the Funds are administered by 80 understandably inexperienced officials which increases the likelihood of low absorption and mismanagement of projects funded by the EU budget (QQ 316–317). The Polish witnesses also highlighted the regular departure of public sector administrators in Poland to higher paid positions in the private sector (Q 318).

57. Steps are being taken to alleviate some problems: the Commission uses its experience to provide advice on audit and project management[42], while richer Member States provide training and advice in areas where they have particular expertise: for example, the Office of National Statistics has advised Eastern European countries on the collection of statistics.[43] However, Commissioner Hübner explained that increasing administrative capacity would not by itself lead to a removal of the absorption cap as the Commission also examined the impact of the Funds on the region's macro-economic situation; for example, the Commission examined whether the region's labour market could support additional spending (Q 376).

58. **We support assistance with, and expenditure on, raising administrative capacity which will lead to long-term benefits.**

59. Witnesses told us that co-financing should continue, even for the poorest Member States (p 78). The need to provide national funds for a project provides an added incentive (in addition to the formal monitoring procedures) to ensure that the money is well spent. **We agree that co-financing should continue.**

Relationship with other policies

60. Understandably, witnesses representing regions would be happy were the regional policy budget to increase (Q 303, p 109). Other witnesses expressed concerns: as well as the issue of absorption capacity (discussed above), witnesses argued that there were several other measures that the Commission

---

41 European Union Committee, Fiftieth Report (2005–06) Financial Management and Fraud in the European Union: Perceptions, Facts and Proposals (HL 270).

42 Under our scrutiny remit, the Committee has examined: the Court of Auditors' Report on the 2006 Budget (OJ C 273, 15 November 2007, p 1), and Member States' responses (7210/08); the Commission's action plan to strengthen its supervision of the distribution of funds (7323/08); and the Commission's response to the Court of Auditors' Report on the management of major projects financed by the Funds (7487/08).

43 European Union Committee, Twelfth Report (2006–07) *Funding the European Union* (HL 64).

could use to support growth. Dr Bradley and Professor Untiedt noted that as the budget is a political decision, the share of the budget allocated to regional support "might be reduced compared to the Lisbon Strategy forms of interventions (for example non-spatial bounded support for R&D)" (p 125).

61. Mr Boyfield stated that the policy "is bribing citizens of the EU with their own money" (p 43) and argued that the size of the Funds should be reduced. Open Europe suggested that the Structural and Cohesion Funds are treated as a "'political sweetener' rather than a development tool" (p 14).

62. We heard no calls for an increase in the size of the EU's total budget and **we consider that no pressure should be placed on the Own Resources or the budget ceiling**. Any additional money for the Structural and Cohesion Funds would therefore have to come at the expense of other policies. Global Vision described the possibility of CAP funding reducing to zero as "highly unlikely" (p 135); we agree. Instead, as argued in our recent report *The Future of the Common Agricultural Policy*,[44] we would prefer to see increased funding for the European Agricultural Fund for Rural Development (EAFRD) at the expense of agricultural price support.

63. As we concluded in that report, the types of admissible actions currently organised around the three axes of the EAFRD should be recast more broadly to include more non-agricultural measures. Funds might thus be used to improve communications, infrastructure, and amenities in rural areas so as to ensure that rural communities are not disadvantaged by their rurality. The ultimate aim would be to ensure that environmental and economic objectives are available to improve the economic viability of rural areas. A recast Pillar II[45] such as we envisage in the report could be used to tackle the relative deprivation of rural areas compared to urban areas even in relatively rich Member States, and to target pockets of deprivation in otherwise wealthy rural areas. In practice, this would mean that all Member States would continue to benefit from access to CAP funds.

64. **We hope that the 2008/09 Budget Review will result in a reduction of spending on agricultural price support and increased support for the EAFRD, and at the same time increased coordination between European regional policy and rural development policy.**

Concentration of funding

65. The issue of allocating part of the budget to prosperous regions, or to pockets of deprivation within the most developed Member States of the EU, is a contentious one and was raised by nearly all witnesses, many of whom opposed the practice. At present 100 regions[46] out of the 268 EU NUTS2 regions receive about 80% of the total budget dedicated to Structural Funds. The remaining 20% is available to all the other EU regions.

66. Global Vision argued that the principle of subsidiarity strongly suggested that the most developed Member States should take responsibility for their regional policy (p 134). Other witnesses disagreed, describing the

---

[44] European Union Committee, 7th Report (2007–08) (HL 54).

[45] The CAP is split into two pillars. Pillar I encompasses Direct Payments and Market Support and Pillar II is Rural Development.

[46] 84 Convergence Regions and 16 Phasing Out Regions.

pan-European character of the policy Objectives (Q 261, pp 76–77, 135–137). Economic challenges—such as loss of competitiveness, unemployment, and lack of investment in innovation—occur in less developed regions across the EU irrespective of whether they are in a rich or poor Member States. Mr Meadows cast doubt on whether Member States would be able or willing to administer common actions inter-governmentally in the absence of supranational co-ordination (Q 231). We were also told that that the requirements of EU regional policy—in terms of audit, financial management, control and monitoring—are forcing changes to domestic systems of policy and governance, helping to reform public management and institutional operation both in Member States that lacked experience and know-how before accession (Q 104) and in the EU15 (QQ 138, 217). Mr Ahner told us that he was not convinced that it was acceptable to divide countries into donors and recipients (Q 275).

67. Professor Tarschys, Stockholm University, dismissed the idea of the Structural and Cohesion Funds as a unifying policy: "if we understand cohesion to mean a sense of togetherness, then it seems likely that all EU policies make some modest contributions towards this goal, but it is not self-evident that the Structural Funds are more efficient in this respect than other policies. To find measures that give particular value for money in pursuing the sense of European community, one should probably look to such fields as education, culture, mass media, sports and youth mobility" (p 137). This, however, understates the Treaty-based aim of the Funds to reduce discrepancies in citizens' prosperity.

68. Mr Meadows argued that the seven-year implementation period that is applied to projects funded by the Structural Funds offers the advantage of continuity beyond regional or national electoral cycles and medium-term stability to design and deliver projects. He added that this might be lost if Member States administered their own policies (p 77); we are not wholly convinced. Mr Meadows also noted that the adoption of common themes and objectives at the EU level for projects that are executed in regions within different Member States across the EU offers the possibility to exchange information and knowledge. Regional actors as well as the Commission learn from best practice in other parts of the EU (p 77). EU funded projects also allow for synergies, especially for regions in the same geographical area that are separated by national borders but suffer from similar structural disadvantages due to their geographical location. In addition, the Commission's evidence suggests "about a quarter" of the money spent in the poorer regions is recycled via trade to the richer regions (Q 250).

69. Some witnesses referred to the cost of administration, the risk of fraud and the time-consuming bureaucracy in applying and distributing the grants as good reasons for returning control of policy to the national level in richer Member States (Q 37, pp 16–17, 43, 134). However, as we discuss in Chapter 4, the cost of administration, relative to the total size of the budget, is not significant. The European Court of Auditors has found that mismanagement of EU funds happens mostly at Member State level and that the weaknesses in the management structures that lead to fraud or misallocation of funds occur in richer Member States as much as they

do in poorer.[47] **The cost of administering Structural Funds in the richer countries is not by itself a compelling argument in favour of ending Structural Fund programmes in richer Member States.**

70. In their written evidence, the Government stated that "in line with the principle of subsidiarity, those Member States which have the institutional and financial strength to fully develop and pursue their own devolved and decentralised regional policies in support of these objectives should be encouraged and enabled to do so" (p 58). In oral evidence, Pat McFadden MP, Minister of State in the Department for Business, Enterprise and Regulatory Reform, supplemented that statement. He told us that the Government would like to see a greater share of Structural Funds spent on the Member States and regions that really need it (i.e. the poorer Member States) (Q 184). In evidence to another inquiry, Kitty Ussher MP, Economic Secretary to HM Treasury, stated that the Government believed wealthier Member States have ways of addressing fundamental economic disparities which are not available to poorer Member States. The Minister added that wealthier Member States should take a "broader principled view" and give up some of their receipts.[48]

71. This is a position that we have previously argued for: in 2005 we concluded that "EU regional expenditure should focus on those economic and social areas where it is best able to make a contribution to growth and solidarity in Europe. In the period from 2007 to 2013 the potential for adding most value will lie in the new Member States. However, even in the new Member States, EU cohesion spending should remain transitional, time-limited and geographically focused ... Support should be tapered and should not become a permanent policy instrument."[49] We also concluded that the richest thirteen Member States should not receive any regional funds.

72. During this inquiry we have carefully examined this conclusion and the potential financial consequences. We have also examined a more nuanced suggestion: that the funding currently allocated to the Competitiveness Objective of the rich Member States to be diverted to the Convergence Objective, thus expanding the latter's reach. This proposal would mean that poor regions in otherwise rich Member States would remain eligible for funding, and all countries would continue to qualify for the small amount of funding allocated to the European Territorial Cooperation Objective. Table 5 sets out the funding that the rich Member States would lose had this change occurred before the start of the current Financial Perspective and the amount saved instead used to increase the funding to the existing roster of Convergence Objective regions and Member States. It should be noted that this loss differs from the current value of the Regional Competitiveness and Employment funding (including phasing in funding). This is because an adjustment has been made for the additional funding the convergence regions of the rich Member States would now receive.

---

47 7210/08.

48 Q 4, European Union Committee, 18th Report (2007–08): *The 2009 EC Budget* (HL 140).

49 European Union Committee, 6th Report (2004–05): *Future Financing of the European Union* (HL 62).

TABLE 5

Net loss to Member States if Competitiveness Objective funds are transferred to Convergence Objective funding, 2007–2013[50]

Country	Value, € millions	Value as % of Member State's EU regional policy income
Belgium	1,281	59
Denmark	491	83
Germany	6,777	27
France	9, 429	68
Ireland	738	84
Italy	3, 031	11
Luxembourg	49	78
Netherlands	1,600	87
Austria	965	68
Finland	1,545	93
Sweden	1,566	86
United Kingdom	6, 336	62

73. Had all EU regional funding (except the European Territorial Cooperation Objective) in the rich Member States been channelled into the Cohesion Objective during the current Financial Perspective the cost to the United Kingdom would have been around € 905 million per year at 2008 prices.

74. The Commission highlighted the leverage effects of allocating funds to wealthier regions and argued that the objectives of geographically balanced and environmentally sustainable development supported the current approach to distribution (QQ 261–262, 264–268). Mr Dufeil, Head of Unit, Spain at DG Regio, gave the example of Baden-Wurttemberg where the Commission had used the leverage of its €20 million annual allocation to the region to achieve "an upper level of efficiency" by encouraging the region to support pilots and projects that might be applicable to other areas of the EU (QQ 264).

75. **The political reasons advanced are not by themselves compelling enough to agree with the concept of distributing EU funds within Member Sates which are net contributors to the EU budget. In principle, we agree with the Government: funding should be concentrated in the poorest regions and should reflect the principle of subsidiarity. The sums involved in the Competitiveness Objective are too small to have significant behavioural and financial leverage effects.**

76. **We recognise that some Member States, including the United Kingdom, would as a consequence lose much of their income from the Structural and Cohesion Funds. Such a significant change would arouse opposition even in the wealthier Member states but it is a change that should be explored in the context of a satisfactory outcome (involving substantial**

50 2008 prices. Values for the Competitiveness Objective include the phasing-in funding. Values are total for the Financial Perspective, not per annum.

CAP Reform) to the imminent strategic review of the EU Budget and of EU policies on Economic and Social Cohesion.

77. **The eligibility criterion for the convergence objective is otherwise suitable. We continue to expect that richer Member States should remain responsible for the majority of their own regional funding. In addition, as we have already outlined (paragraph 64), an expanded EAFRD could work alongside the Structural and Cohesion funds to tackle deprivation in rural areas in all Member States.**

78. Further fine tuning is needed for those regions which are just above the borderline for support and do not receive significant rural development funding. Dr Garcia-Duran and Dr Millet, University of Barcelona, described these as "medium rural medium income" regions and suggested that they receive support "either ... from the Structural Funds or from a reviewed and adapted Research and Development Policy" (p 133). Mr Meadows expressed concern about regions which did not have sustainable growth and which "leave eligibility and then bounce back into it, like planes which do not take off" (Q 234). **We support continuation of the principle of phasing in and phasing out payments for regions around the boundary rather than a simple line between full eligibility and none.**

Regions and the measurement of wealth

79. As discussed in Box 2, the size of an NUTS2 region varies across the European Union. It is possible for pockets of deprivation to exist within an otherwise wealthy region, but distributing European Funds at the NUTS3 level would not necessarily help: Hastings and Thanet were cited as examples of urban deprivation in an otherwise wealthy NUTS2 region (South East England), but both are also relatively poorer than their NUTS3 regions (East Sussex CC and Kent CC, respectively) (p 21). METREX also highlighted issues arising from the relationship between a city and its hinterland; they suggested that up to 80% of the larger City regions[51] "are weak or have unrealised potential" (p 3). We were relieved to hear from Mr Meadows that it is no longer possible to manipulate regional boundaries to make areas eligible for funds (QQ 235–236).

80. Similarly, witnesses also outlined problems with the current measures used to calculate the wealth of a region: Dr Bradley and Professor Untiedt noted that the "main problem introduced by using the NUTS2 classification is that areas where people have their home and work outside the region (or abroad) are favoured" (p 126).

81. **Some redesignation is needed in the definition of regions to ensure, as far as possible, that regions at each level of the NUTS hierarchy have broadly similar characteristics. When the quality of the statistics allows, we would support an improvement in the methodology used for calculating a region's prosperity in order better to reflect the impact of the funds. We do not support the creation of additional levels of bureaucracy, but we recognise the need for enhanced cooperation between urban areas and their rural peripheries to promote sustainable and balanced economic growth.**

---

[51] METREX's supplementary evidence noted that there are about 100 such areas within the EU 27, Norway and Switzerland. They contain between 60 and 70% of Europe's population.

CHAPTER 4: ADMINISTRATION

Administration costs

82. Open Europe (p 15) quoted figures from November 2003 that the annual cost to the UK Department of Work and Pensions of administering the Funds was £10 million, and suggested that six other departments also involved in the administration faced budgets of the same magnitude. A share in the annual £366 million budget of thc Regional Development Agencies (RDAs) was also attributed to the Funds (p 15). We examined Open Europe's suggestion[52] that the cost to the UK of administering the funds is £670 million per year, and dismissed it (QQ 66–72).

83. We asked the Government and the RDAs about the cost of administering the Structural Funds in the UK. The Minister estimated that, in 2008, the administration costs to central Government and the devolved administrations, above those co-financed by the Funds through Technical Assistance, would be £15.45 million (p 69). The RDAs stated their annual cost of administering the European Regional Development Fund is £11 million. The contribution of the RDAs towards their Regional Representational Offices is £1.5 million (2006–2007) (pp 126–129). This gives the United Kingdom a total administration cost of around £28 million per year, against the United Kingdom's current allocation of Structural Funds of approximately €1.5 billion (£1.2 billion) per annum.

84. The United Kingdom also contributes towards the Commission's expenditure on administering Regional Policy in its entirety across the EU. In 2008, this is estimated to be €83 million EU wide[53].

BOX 3

Regional Representation in Brussels

Mr Boyfield, consultant economist, was struck by the "profusion" of Regional Representational Offices in Brussels and questioned their "rent-seeking" behaviour (p 43). 264 of the NUTS2 regions have chosen to be represented in Brussels, either directly or through the Regional Representational Offices of their NUTS1 region. These Offices are not part of the EU's institutional framework. They perform representational and advocacy tasks, and promote their region vis-à-vis the EU institutions and other regions. They collect information on funding opportunities and advise their regional authorities as well as the private sector on how to gain access to these funds. The size of these representations varies. There are regions with just one member of staff based in Brussels (e.g. Lubelskie, Poland), and others that have 45 permanent members of staff (e.g. Valencia, Spain). The 12 UK NUTS1 regions (9 English RDAs, Wales, Scotland and Northern Ireland) are each represented in Brussels; the smaller NUTS2 regions do not maintain individual offices.

The degree of success of the Representational Offices also varies. Witnesses told us that they perform a series of useful functions: above all they are very effective in helping their regions take advantage of different funding sources (QQ 8, 292, 322–325, 343). It is clear, however, that decisions on programmes and fund distribution occur in the region and not in the Brussels

52 Should the EU run Regional Policy? Open Europe, December 2007.

53 This includes the ERDF, Cohesion Fund, Social Fund and the Instrument for Pre-Accession Assistance which is also administered by DG Regio. http://eur-lex.europa.eu/budget/data/D2008_VOL4/EN/nmc-titleN164FB/nmc-chapterN16534/index.html#N16534.

office. We are grateful to the Polish (Lubelskie and Wielkopolska) and Spanish (Valencia) Regional Representational Offices in Brussels for the valuable information they gave us, and to the East Midlands Regional Development Agency for coordinating responses from the English regions.

Administrative burden

85. Bureaucracy constitutes a hurdle for those wishing to apply for EU funding. Several witnesses raised this concern: Mr Meadows, former Director General of DG Regio, highlighted this issue as one which gave the policy a "bad reputation" (p 74). Items that we have considered under our scrutiny remit highlight the tension that exists between the need for audit and control of expenditure, and the burden of administration. In particular, following the European Court of Auditors report on the 2006 Budget[54], the Commission and Member States noted that there was some disagreement between the Court of Auditors, the Commission and Member States over the interpretation of the audit and management requirements. Action to provide more guidance and clarification is being taken[55].

86. The Commission emphasised that they have to strike a balance between calls from the European Parliament for more rigorous auditing and complaints by the regions which find the mechanisms in place far too rigorous, restricting and bureaucratic. Mr Ahner added that the Commission is looking for ways to address the problem of bureaucracy and invited both regions and recipients of funds to table "concrete suggestions" on how the administration of the funds can be made less bureaucratic (Q 284).

87. We were told that the EU regional policy is run in a very decentralised manner (pp 74, 76 QQ 25, 250). The local and the regional level are extensively involved, not just in administering and spending the funds allocated to them, but also through input into the decision making process at EU and Member State levels. Several witnesses emphasised that there is a dialogue between all levels regarding the design of operational programmes and projects to deliver the Funds' priorities (pp 123, QQ 9, 268). The Government noted that the partnership approach enhanced transparency, cooperation and coordination in the design and delivery of policy (p 58). Professor Bachtler argued that the Commission probably has less influence now than at any time since the expansion of the Structural Funds in 1988 (Q 108).

88. However, this decentralisation can increase the administrative burden. Some Member States add their own layers of bureaucracy to the Commission's (QQ 285, 314). Scotland Europa told us that the experience of applicants was that the layers of audit bodies involved in the programmes (local, regional, national, European) was increasing the burden upon them (Q 29). This does not mean that obtaining public funds is necessarily more cumbersome and bureaucratic than obtaining private sector investment: the Spanish region of Valencia told us that obtaining funding for their projects from the EU is less complicated than obtaining it from the banking sector in Spain (Q 360).

---

[54] (OJ C 273) The Court of Auditors have also highlighted (in Special Report 1/2008) the varying quality of information provided to the Commission by project promoters in Member States.

[55] 7210/08 and 7323/08.

89. **An underlying theme in the evidence we received was the tension between reducing administrative cost, and maintaining high quality financial management. The evidence we received did not demonstrate that the cost of administration, relative to the total size of the budget, is significant in the United Kingdom. Extrapolation to countries receiving larger contributions from the funds might suggest further efficiencies and we dismiss witnesses' claims that the regional policies are beset by a costly bureaucracy.**

90. **We welcome the trend towards the Commission taking a strategic view of policy and the regions drawing up the local spending plans. There does appear to be significant bureaucracy for applicants to the funds; while some clarification is needed, we are content that it is not excessive. We note that the Commission is aware of the balance it needs to strike between control and ease of distribution and that it is actively seeking ways to address the bureaucracy. We support their invitation for suggestions of how the administrative burden can be alleviated, at each of the EU, national and regional level.**

CHAPTER 5: SUMMARY OF CONCLUSIONS

91. We start this report from the stance of agreement with the European Union's Treaty-based aims to increase growth and to reduce disparities between regions, and we support the use of economic and knowledge transfer from rich to poor regions as a means to undertake this. EU economic growth is not a zero-sum game: the stronger and more competitive the EU economy as a whole, the better for all Member States. But the benefits and costs of the single market are not distributed evenly and we support intervention in the market to counter both unemployment and under-utilisation of resources in poorer regions, and costs arising from issues such as congestion and over-population in richer regions. (paragraph 6)

92. We would welcome increased use of loans and invite the Government, in their response, to outline what steps they are taking to encourage their use. (paragraph 37)

93. We agree with those witnesses who argue that the Funds have helped to reduce disparities in Europe. We welcome work to measure the impact of European regional policy on levels of private inward investment. (paragraph 47)

94. We believe that allowing the regions to draw up regional spending plans, emphasising local infrastructure or education priorities, reflects the fact that one policy does not fit all. (paragraph 51)

95. While the reduction in discrepancies in citizens' prosperity should be the policy's primary focus, we welcome integration with the Lisbon Strategy. Given the importance of innovation and human capital in the knowledge economy, if lagging regions and Member States are to accelerate their growth, improvements in these areas will be important. We are encouraged to learn that new Member States are also taking account of the strategy in their regional plans. However, the major impetus for the implementation of the Lisbon Agenda must come at the Member State level—the contribution to the Agenda under the Competitiveness Objective is marginal when compared with national public expenditure but can attract project finance from other sources. The problem of increasing the competitiveness of the European Union is of course greater than can be addressed solely by regional policy. (paragraph 52)

96. On broader issues such as climate change, we agree with the Government that the Structural and Cohesion Funds should not be used other than for reducing regional disparities. (paragraph 53)

97. We support assistance with, and expenditure on, raising administrative capacity which will lead to long-term benefits. (paragraph 58)

98. We agree that co-financing should continue. (paragraph 59)

99. We consider that no pressure should be placed on the Own Resources or the budget ceiling. (paragraph 62)

100. We hope that the 2008/09 Budget Review will result in a reduction of spending on agricultural price support and increased support for the EAFRD, and at the same time increased coordination between European regional policy and rural development policy. (paragraph 64)

101. The cost of administering Structural Funds in the richer countries is not by itself a compelling argument in favour of ending Structural Fund programmes in richer Member States. (paragraph 69)

102. The political reasons advanced are not by themselves compelling enough to agree with the concept of distributing EU funds within Member Sates which are net contributors to the EU budget. In principle, we agree with the Government: funding should be concentrated in the poorest regions and should reflect the principle of subsidiarity. The sums involved in the Competitiveness Objective are too small to have significant behavioural and financial leverage effects. (paragraph 75)

103. We recognise that some Member States, including the United Kingdom, would as a consequence lose much of their income from the Structural and Cohesion Funds. Such a significant change would arouse opposition even in the wealthier Member states but it is a change that should be explored in the context of a satisfactory outcome (involving substantial CAP Reform) to the imminent strategic review of the EU Budget and of EU policies on Economic and Social Cohesion. (paragraph 76)

104. The eligibility criterion for the convergence objective is suitable and the overall split in funding between the objectives is, on balance, appropriate. We continue to expect that richer Member States should remain responsible for the majority of their own regional funding. In addition, as we have already outlined, an expanded EAFRD could work alongside the Structural and Cohesion funds to tackle deprivation in rural areas in all Member States. (paragraph 77)

105. We support continuation of the principle of phasing in and phasing out payments for regions around the boundary rather than a simple line between full eligibility and none. (paragraph 78)

106. Some redesignation is needed in the definition of regions to ensure, as far as possible, that regions at each level of the NUTS hierarchy have broadly similar characteristics. When the quality of the statistics allows, we would support an improvement in the methodology used for calculating a region's prosperity in order better to reflect the impact of the funds. We do not support the creation of additional levels of bureaucracy, but we recognise the need for enhanced cooperation between urban areas and their rural peripheries to promote sustainable and balanced economic growth. (paragraph 81)

107. An underlying theme in the evidence we received was the tension between reducing administrative cost, and maintaining high quality financial management. The evidence we received did not demonstrate that the cost of administration, relative to the total size of the budget, is significant in the United Kingdom. Extrapolation to countries receiving larger contributions from the funds might suggest further efficiencies and we dismiss witnesses' claims that the regional policies are beset by a costly bureaucracy. (paragraph 89)

108. We welcome the trend towards the Commission taking a strategic view of policy and the regions drawing up the local spending plans. There does appear to be significant bureaucracy for applicants to the funds; while some clarification is needed, we are content that it is not excessive. We note that the Commission is aware of the balance it needs to strike between control and ease of distribution and that it is actively seeking ways to address the bureaucracy. We support their invitation for suggestions of how the administrative burden can be alleviated, at each of the EU, national and regional level. (paragraph 90)

APPENDIX 1: SUB-COMMITTEE A (ECONOMIC AND FINANCIAL AFFAIRS, AND INTERNATIONAL TRADE)

Sub-Committee A

The members of the Sub-Committee which conducted this inquiry were:

Baroness Cohen of Pimlico (Chairman)
Lord Giddens (until February 2008)
Lord Haskins
Lord Kerr of Kinlochard
Lord Maclennan of Rogart
Lord Moser
Lord Renton of Mount Harry
Lord Steinberg
Lord Trimble
Lord Watson of Richmond
Lord Woolmer of Leeds

Declaration of Interests

A full list of Members' interests can be found in the Register of Lords Interests:

http://www.publications.parliament.uk/pa/ld/ldreg.htm

APPENDIX 2: LIST OF WITNESSES

The following witnesses gave evidence. Those marked ** gave both oral and written evidence; those marked * gave oral evidence only.

**	Professor John Bachtler
**	Department for Business, Enterprise & Regulatory Reform
*	DG Regional Policy, European Commission
	emda on behalf of the English RDAs
	Dr Patricia Garcia-Duran & Dr Montserrat Millet
	Global Vision
*	Commissioner Hübner, European Commission
	Jorge Nunes Ferrer, Centre for European Policy Studies
**	Keith Boyfield Associates
*	Dr Robert Leonardi, London School of Economics
*	Lubelskie Regional Representation (Poland)
**	Graham Meadows
**	METREX
**	Open Europe
*	Scotland Europa
*	South West Regional Development Agency
	Professor Daniel Tarschys, Stockholm University
	Professor Dr Gerhard Untiedt & Dr John Bradley
*	Valencia Regional Representation (Spain)
*	Wielkopolska Regional Representation (Poland)

Additional written evidence was received from:

- Yorkshire Forward
- Business Europe

It has not been printed but is available for inspection at the Parliamentary Archives (020 7219 5316).

We would like to take the opportunity to thank all our witnesses for their submissions to our inquiry.

APPENDIX 3: CALL FOR EVIDENCE

Under the 2007–2013 Financial Perspective Structural Funds[56] constitute around 35% of the EU's budget. The enlarged EU, migration, and the commitments made under the Lisbon Agenda all impact upon the design of the EU's regional policy, and there is an underlying requirement for the Funds to be effective and sustainable. In the light of the forthcoming review of the EU Budget, the Sub-Committee, under the Chairmanship of Baroness Cohen of Pimlico, has decided to conduct an inquiry into the future of the European regional policies.

The inquiry will seek to answer the following questions:

- What should be the objectives of the EU's Structural Funds? How can the Funds become more effective in supporting public policies in Member States and regions? What mechanisms of delivery could make the policy more performance-based and more user-friendly?
- Do Structural Funds meet the principle of subsidiarity? Could the same cohesion objectives be met through repatriation of the distribution of these funds?
- What impact has enlargement had on Structural Funds, and are any changes necessary to meet the challenges of further enlargement?
- How will the EU's commitments on combating climate change manifest themselves in the distribution of Structural Funds for the post-2013 period? How will the response to other challenges facing the EU economy (e.g. migration, growth of the service sector) shape future policies?
- What criteria should guide decisions on the proportion of the EU budget to be allocated to Structural Funds?
- Are the current eligibility tests for regions to receive support under the EU's Structural Funds relevant, fair and appropriate? Should they remain in place after 2013? Is it appropriate that they are discussed simultaneously with wider agreements on allocating EU budget spending?
- What would be the effect of linking the availability of Structural Funds with compliance to Broad Economic Policy Guidelines?

The Sub-Committee would welcome written comments on these issues.

[56] In this document, the term "Structural Funds" is used to refer to the European Social Fund, the European Regional Development Fund, the European Agricultural Guidance & Guarantee Fund, as well as the Cohesion Fund.

APPENDIX 4: THE EU CLASSIFICATION

The EU15 refers to those Member States who formed the European Union prior to 2004, namely, Austria, Belgium, Denmark, Finland, Germany, Greece, Spain, France, Ireland, Italy, Luxembourg, The Netherlands, Portugal, Sweden and the United Kingdom.

The EU10 refers to the new Member States who joined the European Union in 2004, namely the Czech Republic, Estonia, Cyprus, Latvia, Lithuania, Hungary, Malta, Poland, Slovenia and Slovakia.

The EU25 refers to the EU15 and EU10 Member States.

The EU27 is the EU25 plus Bulgaria and Romania who joined in 2007.

APPENDIX 5: LIST OF UNITED KINGDOM NUTS REGIONS

NUTS1	NUTS2	NUTS3
NORTH EAST (ENGLAND)		
	Tees Valley and Durham	
		Hartlepool and Stockton-on-Tees
		South Teesside
		Darlington
		Durham CC
	Northumberland and Tyne and Wear	
		Northumberland
		Tyneside
		Sunderland
NORTH WEST (ENGLAND)		
	Cumbria	
		West Cumbria
		East Cumbria
	Cheshire	
		Halton and Warrington
		Cheshire CC
	Greater Manchester	
		Greater Manchester South
		Greater Manchester North
	Lancashire	
		Blackpool
		Lancashire CC
	Merseyside	
		East Merseyside
		Liverpool
		Sefton
		Wirral
YORKSHIRE AND THE HUMBER		
	East Yorkshire and Northern Lincolnshire	
		Kingston upon Hull, City of
		East Riding of Yorkshire
		North and North East Lincolnshire
	North Yorkshire	
		York

NUTS1	NUTS2	NUTS3
		North Yorkshire CC
	South Yorkshire	
		Barnsley, Doncaster and Rotherham
		Sheffield
	West Yorkshire	
		Bradford
		Leeds
		Calderdale, Kirklees and Wakefield
EAST MIDLANDS (ENGLAND)		
	Derbyshire and Nottinghamshire	
		Derby
		East Derbyshire
		South and West Derbyshire
		Nottingham
		North Nottinghamshire
		South Nottinghamshire
	Leicestershire, Rutland and Northamptonshire	
		Leicester
		Leicestershire CC and Rutland
		Northamptonshire
	Lincolnshire	
		Lincolnshire
WEST MIDLANDS (ENGLAND)		
	Herefordshire, Worcestershire and Warwickshire	
		Herefordshire, County of
		Worcestershire
		Warwickshire
	Shropshire and Staffordshire	
		Telford and Wrekin
		Shropshire CC
		Stoke-on-Trent
		Staffordshire CC
	West Midlands	
		Birmingham
		Solihull
		Coventry
		Dudley and Sandwell
		Walsall and Wolverhampton

NUTS1	NUTS2	NUTS3
EAST OF ENGLAND		
	East Anglia	
		Peterborough
		Cambridgeshire CC
		Norfolk
		Suffolk
	Bedfordshire and Hertfordshire	
		Luton
		Bedfordshire CC
		Hertfordshire
	Essex	
		Southend-on-Sea
		Thurrock
		Essex CC
LONDON		
	Inner London	
		Inner London—West
		Inner London—East
	Outer London	
		Outer London—East and North East
		Outer London—South
		Outer London—West and North West
(ENGLAND)		
	Berkshire, Buckinghamshire and Oxfordshire	
		Berkshire
		Milton Keynes
		Buckinghamshire CC
		Oxfordshire
	Surrey, East and West Sussex	
		Brighton and Hove
		East Sussex CC
		Surrey
		West Sussex
	Hampshire and Isle of Wight	
		Portsmouth
		Southampton
		Hampshire CC
		Isle of Wight
	Kent	
		Medway
		Kent CC

NUTS1	NUTS2	NUTS3
SOUTH WEST (ENGLAND)		
	Gloucestershire, Wiltshire and Bristol/Bath area	
		Bristol, City of
		Bath and North East Somerset, North Somerset and South Gloucestershire
		Gloucestershire
		Swindon
		Wiltshire CC
	Dorset and Somerset	
		Bournemouth and Poole
		Dorset CC
		Somerset
	Cornwall and Isles of Scilly	
		Cornwall and Isles of Scilly
	Devon	
		Plymouth
		Torbay
		Devon CC
WALES		
	West Wales and The Valleys	
		Isle of Anglesey
		Gwynedd
		Conwy and Denbighshire
		South West Wales
		Central Valleys
		Gwent Valleys
		Bridgend and Neath Port Talbot
		Swansea
	East Wales	
		Monmouthshire and Newport
		Cardiff and Vale of Glamorgan
		Flintshire and Wrexham
		Powys
SCOTLAND		
	Eastern Scotland	
		Angus and Dundee City
		Clackmannanshire and Fife
		East Lothian and Midlothian
		Scottish Borders
		Edinburgh, City of
		Falkirk
		Perth & Kinross and Stirling
		West Lothian

NUTS1	NUTS2	NUTS3
	South Western Scotland	
		East Dunbartonshire, West Dunbartonshire and Helensburgh & Lomond
		Dumfries & Galloway
		East Ayrshire and North Ayrshire mainland
		Glasgow City
		Inverclyde, East Renfrewshire and Renfrewshire
		North Lanarkshire
		South Ayrshire
		South Lanarkshire
	North Eastern Scotland	
		Aberdeen City and Aberdeenshire
	Highlands and Islands	
		Caithness & Sutherland and Ross & Cromarty
		Inverness & Nairn and Moray, Badenoch & Strathspey
		Lochaber, Skye & Lochalsh, Arran & Cumbrae and Argyll & Bute
		Eilean Siar (Western Isles)
		Orkney Islands
		Shetland Islands
NORTHERN IRELAND		
	Northern Ireland	
		Belfast
		Outer Belfast
		East of Northern Ireland
		North of Northern Ireland
		West and South of Northern Ireland

APPENDIX 6: GLOSSARY

CAP	Common Agricultural Policy
EAFRD	European Agricultural Fund for Rural Development
EAGGF	European Agricultural Guidance & Guarantee Fund
EMU	European Monetary Union
ERDF	European Regional Development Fund
ESF	European Social Fund
GDP	Gross Domestic Product
GNI	Gross National Income
GVA	Gross Value Added
NSRF	National Strategic Reference Framework
NUTS	Nomenclature of Territorial Units for Statistics
ONS	Office for National Statistics
RDA	Regional Development Agency
SMEs	Small & Medium-sized Enterprises

APPENDIX 7: REPORTS

Recent Reports from the Select Committee

Priorities of the European Union: evidence from the Minister for Europe and the Ambassador of Slovenia (11th report session 2007–2008, HL Paper 73)

The Treaty of Lisbon: an impact assessment (10th Report session 2007–08, HL Paper 62)

The Future of the Common Agricultural Policy (7th Report session 2007–08, HL Paper 54)

The Single Market: Wallflower or Dancing Partner? (5th Report session 2007–08, HL Paper 36)

The Commission's Annual Policy Strategy for 2008 (23rd Report session 2006–07, HL Paper 123)

Session 2007–2008 Reports prepared by Sub-Committee A

The 2009 EC Budget (18th Report session 2007–08, HL Paper 140)

The euro (13th Report session 2007–2008, HL Paper 90)

Solvency II (6th Report, HL Paper 42)

Current Developments in European Trade Policy (1st Report, HL Paper 8)

Other Relevant Reports prepared by Sub-Committee A

The 2008 EC Budget (33rd Report session 2006–07, HL Paper 160)

Financial Management and Fraud in the European Union: Responses to the Report (19th Report session 2006–07, HL Paper 98)

Funding the European Union (12th Report session 2006–07, HL Paper 64)

A European Strategy for Jobs and Growth (28th Report session 2005–06, HL Paper 137)

Minutes of Evidence

TAKEN BEFORE THE SELECT COMMITTEE ON THE EUROPEAN UNION (SUB-COMMITTEE A)

TUESDAY 8 JANUARY 2008

Present	Cohen of Pimlico, B (Chairman)	Trimble, L
	Maclennan of Rogart, L	Watson of Richmond, L
	Moser, L	Woolmer of Leeds
	Steinberg, L	

Memorandum by METREX—The Network of European Metropolitan Regions and Areas

Introduction to METREX

1. METREX is the Network of European Metropolitan Regions and Areas. The acronym stands for Metropolitan Exchange. The twin objectives of the Network are the exchange of knowledge and understanding on metropolitan spatial planning and development issues between practitioners (politicians, officials and their advisers) and the contribution of a metropolitan dimension to European affairs. In effect, METREX is a self-help network of those responsible for strategic decision-making at the metropolitan level.

2. METREX was founded in 1996, with the support of the then DGXVI (Regional Policy), at the Glasgow Metropolitan Regions Conference. It now has Members from 50 of the 100+ recognised metropolitan regions and areas of Europe. It has Members from most EU countries and a number of EU neighbours, for example, Russia and Turkey. It is, therefore, highly representative of European metropolitan opinion (see also www.eurometrex.org).

Context—The Metropolitan Dimension—Meeting the Challenges

3. By "metropolitan" METREX means the larger city-regions of Europe, generally with populations over 500k, which share many common strategic problems and opportunities. They number 100+ and comprise perhaps 60%+ of the European population of 490 million. They are the main drivers of the European economy.

4. There are many strategic issues that can only be addressed effectively at the metropolitan level. For example, promoting urban competitiveness and cohesion, balancing the need for urban renewal and regeneration with urban extension, integrating land use and transportation, assessing the environmental impact of major development options and mitigating the emission of greenhouse gases.

5. In many parts of Europe, most notably in Germany, there is recognition of the value of a metropolitan approach. Germany has restructured its local government to set up 11 Metropolregions focussed on the main cities and their areas of influence. It has done this because it recognises that to remain competitive German urban areas must have the competencies and capabilities to address their key strategic issues in a comprehensive and integrated way.

6. The European Spatial Planning Observation Network (ESPON), which is the primary research network on spatial planning issues supported by the European Union, has assessed and categorised European metropolitan areas (see www.espon.eu). It has concluded that although Europe has a number of metropolitan areas of global or European significance many have latent potentials or structural weaknesses that need to be addressed if the EU's Lisbon Strategy is to be realised.

7. The Structural Funds need to recognise the importance of the metropolitan dimension to the Lisbon and Gothenburg agendas for sustainable economic and environmental development. Social cohesion within Europe also has a metropolitan dimension.

8. Effective metropolitan governance, as Germany and other countries have concluded, is central to the realisation of many EU and National objectives and to meeting Europe's challenges in the future. The European Economic and Social Committee (EESC) has strongly advocated the recognition of a metropolitan

dimension to European Affairs in Opinions it has offered to the European Parliament (see www.eesc.europa.eu)

9. It is in this context that METREX offers its written evidence.

Subsidiarity

10. The Structural Funds should respond to the key issues that the EU and its constituent nation States can foresee in the medium to longer term, that is, beyond the next 10 years and towards the next 25+ years. Most of the agenda for the next five years is programmed and much of the agenda for 5–10 years is planned.

11. There are certain key strategic issues that only the EU can address effectively. These include, for example, external and internal connectivity and how the EU can function as an integrated social and economic entity and external and internal population movement and change, economic change, and environmental change and their consequences.

12. By addressing such key strategic issues the EU can set the context for national and metropolitan policy. The concept of subsidiarity relies on a clear common understanding of the issues that need to be addressed, and which can only be addressed effectively, at the various levels of government.

13. The EU does not have an integrated medium/longer term perspective that addresses and responds to the key social, economic and environmental issues that can be foreseen. It has the European Spatial Development Perspective (ESDP) of 1999 but this was limited in scope and is now dated.

14. The Structural Funds should be the means through which key medium/longer term European strategic issues are addressed in an integrated way. First the issues need to be identified and considered. There could then be a structured European dialogue on the most effective means of implementing a European perspective and the metropolitan contribution that could be made to this.

Objectives of the EU's Structural Funds

15. In this context the objective of the EU's Structural Funds should be to respond to the agreed key medium/ longer term European strategic issues identified in a European Perspective. It could be expected that connectivity, as exemplified in the current TEN programme, would remain an issue and that areas facing social, economic and environmental stress of European significance would continue to be supported. The current dilemma of the balance to be struck between funds for cohesion and funds for competitiveness would remain. In reality these two issues are closely interrelated.

16. However, if the EU was to actively promote a metropolitan dimension to European affairs, for the same good reasons that have led Germany to do so for its own competitiveness, then Europe would have a new and effective level of governance through which, and with which, to work. Metropolitan governance mechanisms can range from the voluntary to the statutory, with various combinations in between.

17. The metropolitan level of governance could reasonably be invited to assess its medium to longer-term problems and opportunities, on a SWOT basis, and to identify those that would be beyond its resources to respond to. It could make the case for EU support across a range of social, economic and environmental issues. The key requirement could be to demonstrate the added value of considering these in an integrated way, with EU support. For example, improved internal connectivity to respond to areas of social exclusion, improve access to economic opportunities and the mitigate greenhouse gas emissions.

Delivery Mechanisms, Allocation Criteria, Eligibility and Compliance

18. Metropolitan areas, with appropriate governance, represent an effective delivery mechanism for action to implement a European Perspective for the future, and the consequential Structural Fund priorities. They also represent areas over which integrated Metropolitan Strategies can be formulated to deal with their own key issues on a SWOT basis.

19. It might be expected that the Structural Funds would be allocated, on a proportionate basis, to those metropolitan areas that had clearly demonstrated in their Strategies how they would contribute to the realisation of a European Perspective and how they would address the priorities emerging from their own metropolitan SWOT analyses. In effect, to enable European metropolitan areas to become as strong as they possible can be collectively and individually.

20. The Scottish Regional Authorities, from before the Scottish Parliament was constituted, offer a good and proven example of how such as approach can work within the UK. More recently, the establishment of the "Metropolregions" within Germany confirms and endorses the practicality and effectiveness of such an approach.

Enlargement

21. The ESDP was concerned with the issue of better urban balance across the wider Europe and the need for the peripheral areas to balance the core (London/Paris/Rhine/Ruhr area). In the absence of an up to date European perspective METREX has produced a Framework to provide a context for action at the metropolitan level, through the PolyMETREXplus project under the EU's Interreg IIIC Programme (see www.eurometrex.org). The Framework concludes that better European urban balance can be achieved through the fostering and development of cluster and corridors of metropolitan areas cooperating for greater competitiveness.

22. Examples of such a "polycentric" approach include the Saxon Triangle (Dresden/Leipzeg/Chemnitz/Halle), Eurocity Basque (San Sebastian/Biarritz), Øresund (Copenhagen. Malmö) and the Po (Torino/Milano/Bologna/Veneto) and Ebro valleys (Zaragoza/Barcelona). There are similar opportunities in Silesia and the Baltic States.

Climate Change

23. METREX has promoted the EUC02 80/50 project under the EU's Interreg IVC programme. A partnership of 24 metropolitan areas, led by the Metropolregion Hamburg, aimes to use the GRIP model and process (see www.euco2.org and www.grip.co.uk) to assess individual metropolitan energy use and greenhouse gas sources and emissions, explore mitigation scenarios and adopt effective Mitigation Strategies to deliver an 80% reduction, over 1990 level, by 2050.

24. This is an example of the metropolitan dimension in action in partnership with the EU.

17 December 2007

Supplementary memorandum by METREX

What defects are there in the current management and distribution of the Funds?

Metropolitan dimension

By metropolitan we mean the larger European city regions, with populations of 500,000 or more, and their areas of influence. Areas of influence can be defined by journey to work areas, housing market areas and retail catchment areas.

There are about 100 such areas within the wider Europe of the EU 27 + 2 (Norway and Switzerland). They contain some 60–70% of Europe's population of 490 million and their social, economic and environmental well-being is central to both the Lisbon and Gothenburg agendas. They are the building blocks for a more competitive and sustainable Europe.

However, the work of ESPON (the European Spatial Planning Observation Network), in categorising European metropolitan areas, has revealed that only a very few, perhaps 20–30, are strong in global and European terms and that most are weak or have unrealised potential (Framework page 92).

All metropolitan areas can strive to become as strong, individually, as possible. However, they can also combine for collective strength in clusters or corridors and there are a number of examples of this approach. Such clusters can develop critical mass and enable specialisations to be developed. This is the Framework approach.

Structural Funds defects

Funds can be allocated either by pointing the way forward through objectives and criteria or leading the way forward though visions, frameworks or perspectives.

For example, the EU now has social, economic and territorial cohesion objectives. The ESDP (European Spatial Development Perspective 1999) is concerned about the better urban balance of Europe, with so much of the wealth generating capacity being concentrated in the core area. It would be possible to produce an EU vision of what better urban balance would like, as the Framework attempts to do.

The Structural Funds could then be allocated, positively, on the basis of those metropolitan regions and areas that can demonstrate how they can help to progress the realisation of the EU vision.

In addition, funds could be allocated on the basis of metropolitan SWOT analyses and an assessment of the resources needed to address the key strategic issues arising.

Does the creation of metropolregions add an additional level of bureaucracy?

Metropolitan governance

METREX experience is that there is a range of key strategic issues that can only be addressed effectively, and in an integrated way, at the metropolitan level. Informed metropolitan decision-making is required in the public interest. This can be through co-operation between existing levels of governance (the voluntary model) or through bodies or authorities with specific and targeted competencies (the statutory model). There are examples in Europe of these models and combinations of them.

Informed decision-making can be through in house resources (an additional level of bureaucracy), the pooling of existing resources (the voluntary model) or out sourcing.

7 January 2008

Examination of Witnesses

Witnesses: Mr Donald MacInnes, Scotland Europa, Mr Phil McVey, South West of England Regional Development Agency and Mr Roger Read, METREX, examined.

Q1 ***Chairman:*** Good morning and welcome to the Committee. Could I say that we do record everything that is said here but you will get a transcript of it so that you can make corrections of things which might have been better put, if that happens. I know you have had a list of the topics but I would like you all to start out by saying what it is that your organisation does because this is a new subject for us and not all of us are absolutely familiar with what these various groups do. We very much wanted to talk to people who were, as it were, at the sharp end, at the end where the money got to. The first question, which I am going to ask, really applies only to Mr MacInnes and Mr McVey, and Mr Read gets his chance in a few moments. Against the background would Mr MacInnes and Mr McVey start out by telling us, roughly speaking, about their organisations and what they do?

Mr MacInnes: I am Donald MacInnes, I am the Chief Executive of an organisation called Scotland Europa. We are a membership organisation. Approximately 60 members pay our fee to represent them in Brussels. In Scotland we also represent Scottish Enterprise and provide the EU funding service for Scottish Enterprise. They get around £30 million a year in EU funds for around 300 live projects we have just now.

Mr McVey: Good morning. My name is Phil McVey, I am Director of European Programmes in the South West of England Regional Development Agency. We are a non-departmental public body—there is one agency in each of England's regions, including London—responsible for leading sustainable economic development within the region. We receive funding each year from central government, in addition to which from this year we receive approximately £50 million each year of European funding, which we are administering on behalf of the UK government in the region working with partners.

Q2 ***Chairman:*** That is quite a familiar structure. If I may start by asking both of you, answering in turn or as you like, what are your guiding principles as you distribute funds received from the EU? To what extent are you allowed to use your own discretion in setting the parameters for distribution? Do you believe the devolution in the United Kingdom of decision-making to the devolved administrations and the RDAs has been successful?

Mr MacInnes: Our guiding principles are that we like to use the funds to support our economic strategy in Scotland. We have a clear economic strategy which was called Smart Successful Scotland, it has now been renewed in the autumn, and our aim is to support business innovation, research and development, workforce development and also regeneration of deprived areas. To what extent do we have discretion: yes, we do have a large degree of discretion within these parameters, especially in the new programme where we are taking a much more strategic approach to funding. Rather than having to apply on individual projects, we are free to apply on a strategic basis; to do that we apply to support our priority industries. We have six priority industries that we particularly want to support because by supporting them from a public point of view we think they make a disproportionate impact on the economy. Whether devolution and decision-making to devolved administrations has been advantageous, we have not noticed a big difference in that. When it comes specifically to Structural Funds we have not noticed a big difference on whether that has been advantageous. In a whole lot of other areas, of course, there are comments on that. The area we like to support more in terms of going forward is innovation and research and development, and particularly tying some of the issues we have to do with regeneration with the bigger issues across Europe in climate change and so on. We find it very difficult to square that circle, particularly using Structural Funds. I think it is easier to do that using the bigger funds like the Framework Programmes in research and development.

Mr McVey: Our guiding principles are along similar lines, in that we take as the starting point for how we use the funds in the region our regional economic strategy, which sets out on behalf of partners what we hope to achieve in the economy in the South West. Underpinning that is very much the environment as being an economic driver, so that we do not see issues such as climate change as a disadvantage, but we should see them as an opportunity within the economy. As well as that regional principle in terms of how we would use the funds within the region, we also keep very much to the top of our mind two other things: one, that these are European funds, so we work within the framework set up by the European Commission and all the Member States for the use of the funds. There is something called the National Strategic Reference Framework that sets out how the UK will distribute the funds and we work very closely with that. Then critically (and I would say this as someone who lives in the far South West of England) we align the funds with local economic strategies. I think about Cornwall and the Isles of Scilly which will receive a considerable injection of European funds over the next seven years. That area has its own economic strategy as we have. As well as taking account of the top-down national regional strategies, we have built the use of the funding around that local economic strategy as well so that, for example, in Cornwall and the Isles of Scilly partners are very keen to see the further development of the renewable energy sector in Cornwall and the Isles of Scilly. We have worked with them to ensure that the European programmes will help to deliver that aspiration. In terms of the second part of the question about the development of decision-making—and I should make it clear that this is the first time that Regional Development Agencies have actually been responsible for the funds, so it might be a little early to say what the outcome will be—even in the planning of the programmes in the South West of England with the RDA in the lead we have seen a much greater emphasis on ensuring that the activities in the European programmes, and the sort of outcomes we are going to achieve, are much more aligned with existing strategies in the region. At the outset of the programme we have got a set of things we want to achieve that are much more, as I say, closely aligned with overall aspirations.

Q3 ***Lord Steinberg:*** May I ask a question particularly of Mr MacInnes but maybe you can come in as well. You said there were six principal industries that you were supporting and working on. Could you tell us what those are, please? I am particularly interested to know whether tourism forms any part of that, and would ask Mr McVey the same thing.

Mr MacInnes: From a Scottish Enterprise point of view the six priority industries are: life sciences; energy; financial services; tourism; creative industries and there is another one as well.

Q4 ***Lord Steinberg:*** Obviously not an important one!

Mr MacInnes: I cannot remember the other one. These are basic industries.

Q5 ***Lord Steinberg:*** Are the monies allocated on a fairly even basis, or do some take a particular priority?

Mr MacInnes: No, not evenly. Some of these industries are much more advanced than others. For instance, the work we do in financial services is about workforce development skills, to have skills coming through for the big financial services industry that we have. In energy it is the combination of supporting the oil and gas in Aberdeen, for instance, plus also supporting new projects in renewables. In creative industries it is to support a young industry across Scotland, particularly in Dundee.

Q6 ***Lord Watson of Richmond:*** You particularly mentioned innovation several times. To what extent are you in the business of picking winners, and what is the process which led you down that path? Secondly, if you could just clear up something which has slightly puzzled me. I may have misunderstood

what you were saying, Mr MacInnes, but I thought you said that your organisation was a membership organisation? Presumably you have to be very careful about this so there is no relationship between a company becoming a member and paying a fee presumably and having any kind of access to these funds?
Mr MacInnes: No, there is no relationship. On innovation we believe that by supporting young companies which have a capacity to grow faster than others we can make a disproportionate impact on the economy.

Q7 ***Lord Watson of Richmond:*** I am sorry, my question is: how do you judge which have the greater potential to develop, because that is picking winners?
Mr MacInnes: We have two particular programmes that we work on. One is called the Proof of Concept Fund where we have achieved about £10 million of ERDF funding for that, and that is for people who are working on research at universities and have not yet got a commercial idea but by supporting them we think that the idea might become commercial and it would lead to a substantial company being set up. We work closely with the universities on that one so it is very specific. The other fund we have is what we call the Scottish Co- investment Fund, and again we want to attract people who want to grow businesses of scale. We do not make the choices ourselves; we allow either universities or companies to come to us. On the question of our members, it is not individual companies who are members of Scotland Europa, it is people like the universities, local authorities and so on.

Q8 ***Lord Maclennan of Rogart:*** I am sorry, I am still trying to get a little more clarity in my mind about how you operate. Are you in a negotiating position with the funders in the European Union about the objectives, or is this discussion about prioritisation in a sense entirely internal to Scotland?
Mr MacInnes: We have an office in Brussels where we work to promote our members' interests and that ranges from helping them to understand what legislative issues might be coming up, to helping them with funding for individual projects. The large part of what we do with Scottish Enterprise, which is one of our members, is on Structural Funds and helping them to obtain funding for their individual projects.

Q9 ***Lord Maclennan of Rogart:*** What proportion of the funds allocated to Scotland is administrated by your organisation?
Mr MacInnes: On business development funds it is round about 70 per cent.

Q10 ***Chairman:*** Mr McVey, would you like to comment inasmuch as these questions apply to your area?
Mr McVey: I would like to comment, if I might, on the question related to sectors. The South West of England in the recent economic strategy has priority sectors, and tourism is one of those priority sectors. In relation to how we might make use of the European Structural Funds within the region we are taking a slightly different approach, which is we recognise the value of certain sectors to the economy but the programmes themselves are much more about ensuring that we invest in companies that are going to deliver high quality, high value jobs in the future regardless of sector; and that is a slightly different approach to what might have been taken in the past through European Structural Fund Programmes. There is no allocation to a sector of funding, but what there is is a definite concentration of funding upon businesses that we believe might bring those better jobs in the future, and that is very important in the South West of England where the average wage rate is below the national average in many parts of the region. It does relate to the subsequent question about picking winners which is always a difficult issue. I do not know if anybody has got the answer to that one in particular. Similar to Scotland, we have a proof of concept programme whereby we can reward inventors, if you like, to ensure that those ideas get transferred to the market, get transferred to businesses as quickly as possible, and that is something Structural Funds are going to do as well. If I may in relation to the third point about the relationship with Brussels, certainly in terms of the Structural Fund, the South West RDA is responsible for 100 per cent of the main Structural Fund Programmes coming into the South West region. It has been a very open dialogue with Brussels about the prioritisation of the funding and how we might use it within the region. The sectoral issue is a particular one, where Brussels started from the standpoint of wanting to see clear sectoral prioritisation and money allocated to sectors on the basis of their importance in the region. We persuaded them that actually a different approach, a sectoral aligned approach, might be one that in the longer run would bring greater benefits because, as I say, we invest on the basis of outputs and impacts we are getting in terms of jobs and growth, rather than on a particular sector's historical performance.
Chairman: Thank you very much. The guns will turn on Mr Read shortly. Lord Trimble, I think your question probably applies more to this point than to Mr Read's operation, if you would like to ask it.

Q11 ***Lord Trimble:*** Just reflecting on the involvement of devolved administrations, I was quite surprised in our early days when a senior official in the Department of Finance told me that European Structural Funds were quite often more trouble than they were worth; that they led to a distortion of public expenditure priorities because the money was not additional to devolved administration, the money went to HMT; and consequently the Treasury put pressure on the administration to pursue public expenditure which would draw down money from Brussels rather than very often pursuing public expenditure priorities the administration would have pursued, were it not that. You referred to the dialogue with Brussels; do you have any sort of dialogue with the Treasury?

Mr McVey: Not directly, is the straight answer to that. As a Regional Development Agency we do not because we deal through the Department for Business Enterprise and Regulatory Reform and Communities and Local Government, so that is our route for dialogue. The issue as to whether Structural Funds distort public expenditure within the region is one that is discussed quite a lot. If I refer to Cornwall and the Isles of Scilly—where it has been put to us that, because there is a concentration of Structural Funds in Cornwall and the Isles of Scilly, other parts of the South West Region do not receive as much domestic funding as they might through the Regional Development Agency—in fact, all the evidence is that the Regional Development Agency would have, and indeed has spent the domestic money in Cornwall and the Isles of Scilly anyway because of the economic conditions in that part of the far South West. The distortion is not at the level that people might be arguing.

Mr MacInnes: The situation with us is very similar. In fact, maybe to put it in an historical context, our principal relationship was with the Scottish Office previously, then the Scottish Executive and the Scottish Government. We do not have a direct relationship with the Treasury as such.

Q12 ***Lord Trimble:*** Do you come under any pressure from the Scottish administration?

Mr MacInnes: No, we agree the programme with them and we have done that for the programme for 2007-2017.

Q13 ***Lord Trimble:*** If there was any Treasury influence it would be on the Scottish administration and then fed through indirectly to yourselves?

Mr MacInnes: Yes.

Q14 ***Lord Woolmer of Leeds:*** Mr Read, in this country the idea of city regions being very important drivers of development and so on is now well established—500,000-plus population and so on, as you say in your notes. You say in your written evidence that Structural Funds need to recognise the importance of the metropolitan dimension (city regions, I assume) to the various agendas for sustainable economic and environmental development. Does that imply that the Structural Funds do not currently do that? What is it that you are critical of; and what is it that needs to be put right in your view?

Mr Read: Would you like me to say something about METREX and myself?

Q15 ***Chairman:*** Yes, please. If you could introduce the organisation.

Mr Read: METREX is a network of city regions, city regions and their area of influence. We use the term "metropolitan" to describe that. As I have said, there are about 100, with a population over half a million. It was founded in 1996. It is a self-help network for practitioners. By "practitioners" we mean politicians, officials and their advisers; so everybody who is involved in strategic decision-making at that level to just exchange knowledge and information, and also to contribute what we term the "metropolitan dimension" to European affairs. So those are the two objectives. It is self-funding; it is a club. In our view there are two ways in which the funds might be approached. It is possible to point directions, as the EU has done with climate change, to say we have an objective of an 80 per cent reduction over 1990 by 2050. METREX has responded to that through the INTERREG programme with a submission where all our members will try and reduce their levels of emission; so it is a responsive approach. The other approach which is really the main thrust of our evidence to you is that in 1999 the European Spatial Development Perspective was produced. It took about ten years to produce and nothing has happened since 1999. We have now got the situation where the EU has social, economic and territorial cohesion as its objective. One of the issues is: what is "territorial cohesion"? There was a view on this which said that the overall balance in Europe leads to problems in terms of cohesion and competitiveness, so much being in the core and so little being round the periphery. The work of ESPON, which is the advisory research organisation to DG Regio, suggests that perhaps 20-30 of Europe's metropolitan regions are strong. The vast number of them have a range of interrelating problems of all kinds. If better balance is an objective, better territorial balance, in our view it can only be achieved by co-operation between a lot of the metropolitan areas around the periphery. What we would like to see in a word (and it is something we have tried to produce ourselves) is a framework for Europe; so that in allocating the funds it will be possible for Europe to say, "We have a vision, framework, perspective, whatever you like, of the medium to longer-term; we would invite you to contribute to its realisation"; so positive leadership rather than pointing the direction with objectives and criteria. "This is where we would like you to go; please go there; make proposals to us". This document has been produced under the INTERREG programme by METREX and METREX members really in order to provide it with a context, with a plan in effect. Our response really to the question is that we would like to see a clear view of the long-term future of Europe, a clear vision for that; and an invitation for metropolitan areas which we regard as the building blocks to realise that vision, to participate and contribute. That is what is happening at the moment in the absence of this. This has been produced because of the vacuum above. I know you have a concern about subsidiarity. Our view of subsidiarity is that every level of decision-making has an obligation to say, "These are the issues which we have to address, because they cannot be addressed effectively anywhere else"; and to then say how they are going to do that. At the moment there does not seem that direction from the European level of "This is where we want to go. This is how we intend to get there. We invite you to join us on the journey". I think in essence that is the position we have on the funds.

Q16 ***Lord Woolmer of Leeds:*** In England (and I do not know the situation in Scotland terribly well, Mr MacInnes, so you may later put me right) the idea of city region issues is embedded in the way in which a number of policies are developed. Certainly in the, North East, North West and Yorkshire, the northern regions, this is central to the work of the Regional Development Agencies. Is not all this adding another layer of bureaucracy if you start saying the metropolitan regions have got to have a separate route into Brussels and so on? In England at least is this not the job of the Regional Development Agencies; because at the end of the day policies have to be coherent and city regions have to fit into a wider policy and so on? I hear what you say, and people all talking is very interesting and very helpful, but in terms of the Structural Funds what is it you think needs to be put right that is not being put right at the moment? I am trying to get to something concrete as opposed to lots of discussion producing documents?
Mr Read: If one accepts that the city region level is a key level for strategic decision-making, there are all sorts of mechanisms we are aware of across Europe for doing that—just a voluntary coming together of existing organisations at one level, what you might term the "voluntary approach". Recognising that there are decisions that have to be taken at that level, let us take all the stakeholders together to try and take that on a voluntary basis; and there are mechanisms which are that model. There are other models which you might term the "statutory approach" where an authority is set up with competences and powers to address big issues if there is economic restructuring going on in a crisis situation. It is a pity that our President from Stuttgart is not here because, as you know, Germany has set up 11 metropolitan regions; and they have set them up because they are concerned about the competitiveness of Germany, and recognition that there are key decisions which have to be taken at that level. The Stuttgart Metropolitan area, which was the first one to be set up, is half of Baden-Wurttemberg, and it was set up by Baden-Wurttemberg. It was set up because they recognised there was a decision-making level there that had to be established. I think there are a number of models you can use for strategic decision-making at that level. It does not necessarily have to lead to a further level of bureaucracy. For example, in Scotland in the Glasgow area, where there are eight authorities, they are both the local planning authority and the strategic planning authority. They can only exercise their strategic powers collectively together so there is nothing extra. So they do both those things in different sorts of ways. I do not think it follows that there has to be a further level of bureaucracy. The key thing is that the area that is appropriate ought to be covered, and the decision-making mechanism is there. It is an informed decision-making because we want informed decision-making and it does require some sort of back-up.

Q17 ***Lord Maclennan of Rogart:*** You are not seeking, are you, for a nexus of metropolitan regions decision-making authority which has to be recognised in the decision-making process in Brussels?
Mr Read: No. In order to achieve the territorial cohesion if that is an objective, and it would appear to be, then our view is that that will be brought about effectively by metropolitan areas co-operating particularly around the periphery. If there is no mechanism at the metropolitan level then it is difficult to organise that co-operation. Examples like the Oresund arrangement or the Eurocity Basque of Biarritz and San Sebastian combining, those sorts of mechanisms are required for collective strength around the periphery in order to get some sort of balance with the core. It is difficult to achieve that collective strength around the periphery unless the mechanisms are there to co-operate with one another.

Q18 ***Lord Maclennan of Rogart:*** Is that organisation a matter for the member governments, the Member States, in our view, to make sure that these concerns are reflected in national policy and national agencies; or are you actually trying to change the practice of the European Commission in considering the

implementation of effective Structural Fund distribution?
Mr Read: I think Europe city regions make good partners with the EU and good mechanisms through which they can achieve their objectives.

Q19 ***Lord Maclennan of Rogart:*** Mr Read, I understand the point but I am trying to see if you are looking for a constitutional or institutional change. Are you actually saying that the mechanisms do not work to achieve your goals; or are you saying you would just like your roles to be rather better understood at national levels?
Mr Read: If the city region is regarded as a basic building block across Europe for decision-taking then I think METREX would advocate that mechanisms are set up to take decisions that are needed at that level, and the mechanisms can vary completely. In some cases they are set up by government nationally, as it has been with Germany, and in other cases it is completely a bottom-up arrangement where all of the authorities in the city region area decide to come together for their own good reasons to co-operate and be stronger. There is nothing dictatorial about this—it is simply saying that a decision-making mechanism at the city region level across Europe enables Europe to interact with that. There are lots of models for it; but crucially it enables those mechanisms to co-operate around the periphery. If they are not there then organising that co-operation is that much more difficult.

Q20 ***Chairman:*** Is this meant to be a place where people talk to each other; or are you advocating the funding actually coming in at the city regional level?
Mr Read: Our main point is not so much the funding coming in at the city region level. Our main point is that, in addition to have some objectives and some issues which Europe would like everybody to engage in, it would be good to have something by way of vision, framework or perspective at the European level to which others could then contribute. A level which would then contribute very effectively with that would be the city region level. A number of countries have decided to go down that road and set that up, and funding goes through them; but that is not, I do not think, the key issue. The key issue at the moment is the absence of a clear vision for the future of Europe at that level.
Chairman: The next question I was going to ask was about the future. We will pass that one by and I will ask Lord Watson to ask his question.

Q21 ***Lord Watson of Richmond:*** I would just like to follow up on one thing Mr Read has said, because I think we have got a slight feeling that maybe inadvertently you have opened Pandora's Box. The truth is, depending on how you interpret "territorial cohesion" (and this is one of those phrases, is it not: what does it mean; how does one set of territorial cohesions relate to another) you may be straying into a huge minefield which, at the end of the day, is about whether Structural Funding ought to try and produce greater economic equality, or at least equality of opportunity between regions. As you know, that is an entirely unresolved question within the European Union; very controversial and much more sensitive post-enlargement than it was pre-enlargement. We are right into the minefield of all minefields at this point. Therefore, I would like from you a clear definition of your understanding of "territorial cohesion"; and to link that, if I may, to the question on subsidiarity again, which is: by going down this sort of route, and indeed Structural Funds themselves, are they basically not trespassing on sovereign decisions by government, but actually creating a situation in which they insist that decision-making is taken at this level and not at perhaps a more political level?
Mr Read: Our vision of better balance is set out here. As I mentioned earlier, of the 100 metropolitan areas in Europe maybe 20 or 30 are strong (question: what defines "strong?"), but have a number of collective strengths; but the vast majority of them have a range of significant weaknesses; they have potential but significant weaknesses.

Q22 ***Lord Watson of Richmond:*** Is the implication of that, in your mind anyway, that the 20 should somehow help the 80?
Mr Read: Not at all, but those are just the circumstances. The question is: is everybody happy with that? Looking to the future, do they think that situation is likely to get worse? Is that imbalance likely to increase? What could one do about it? What would be beneficial to all to do something about it? The conclusion that came out from this is, looking at the connectivity of Europe, it is like a spider's web, it is very radial and there are not too many opportunities to go north, south, east, west or, indeed, around the periphery. There is the connectivity issue. Does the periphery need to be connected better to itself?

Q23 ***Lord Watson of Richmond:*** You are arguing, in a way, that as connectivity does not currently exist—this is not an issue relevant to subsidiarity? One is not taking away from Member States because they do not do it anyway?
Mr Read: Indeed. It is an issue of connectivity that has not been resolved as yet. Within that framework, north, south, east, west and peripheral connectivity being improved, that the weaker metropolitan areas should cluster together for collective strength, as they are progressively doing regardless of European policy. For example, in the Po Valley there is an

initiative of all the Italian cities there to develop their collective strength. There are similar initiatives around the periphery: the Saxon Triangle, Dresden, Leipzig and Chemnitz, coming together for collective strength.

Q24 ***Lord Watson of Richmond:*** And here?
Mr Read: Here, the Northern Way and the Midlands Way would be good comparable examples, exactly. It is that form of collective action around the periphery, enabled by better overall communications, which is how we see better overall balance evolving. In our view, it is evolving in that way on a bottom-up basis. It would be nice to have some recognition that that is the way it ought to go from the top as well as from the bottom.

Q25 ***Chairman:*** Can I also address Lord Watson's questions to Mr McVey and Mr MacInnes because we were looking for a view on subsidiarity from all of you?
Mr McVey: On the subsidiarity question, I have been working on Structural Funds since 1999 and what has amazed me in that time is that the governance structures for European programmes to me demonstrate the principles of subsidiarity more than almost anything I have worked with in the past; in that we have local, regional, national and European decision-making decisions being made at the most appropriate levels. If I think about someone at the sharp end and the way we have actually worked up the current European programmes, although they have been done, as I have said, within the context of European guidelines, what is actually going to happen with the money is something that is very much determined at a local level. To take a pragmatic view of perhaps not worrying too much about where the money is coming from or who owns it, what we are able to do with it at a regional local level is the most important factor.
Mr MacInnes: Our experience is similar to that. We find that the more we talk about subsidiarity the more local decision-making comes into play, the more then we have a responsibility for an audit trail for a whole new set of administration of these programmes. We do find some applicants reluctant to apply for funding simply because of the burden of administration which is probably, in part at least, caused by local decision-making, whether people want to be sure that they have a good audit trail for a project.

Q26 ***Lord Moser:*** At the foot of all this really is the overall scale of Structural Funds. I wonder whether you would like to comment, any of you, on the criteria that should determine the scale of the overall EU budget going to the Structural Funds; and whether at the present time, in your view, it is adequate to do the job you think the Structural Funds should do, or too much or too little? The overall scale?
Mr MacInnes: I suppose our experience from a customer point of view is that we have many more applications than we have money available. I imagine if you look at it from that point of view that there is not sufficient funding. There may well be other sources of funding for some of these applications; and some of them might not be appropriate for Structural Funds. In fact some of the other EU funding programmes may be more appropriate. Going into the future, I think that would be more and more the case, with more emphasis on business innovation and research and development, where these programmes are linked, for instance, with the big issues of climate change and so on. It may well be that Structural Funds will become less significant, and that the other programmes become more significant. We are finding already there is a strong appetite for applicants to go for framework programmes for research and development, for lifelong learning programmes and INTERREG programmes and so on.
Mr McVey: Yes, I am very much on the same lines. From a regional perspective you would expect us always to say there is not enough money for the region for these sorts of programmes. However, there is something about having a limited budget that gives focus to your activities. It makes you make decisions about what you are going to spend the money on. Certainly in terms of developing the current programme, that has been a really good discipline knowing that there is this limited amount of money that you want to achieve set objectives with. In terms of criteria for the future programmes, I guess we would argue for a radical shift here. There is still unfinished business in terms of the internal market and parts of the European Union that are lagging in terms of economic performance. We would still want to see criteria put in place, for example, for regions whose gross domestic product is below 75 per cent of the EU average, to ensure there was sufficient budget for them to improve their economic performance. Similarly we would want some criteria put in place that would ensure, for those regions that fall into a bit of a no-man's land between the criteria for the current convergence programmes and being at 100 per cent of the EU average for GDP, there was some money made available for them to address issues maybe to do with skills shortages or particular issues within their economy around maybe the take-up of innovation within businesses. For example, we would want to ensure there was still some Structural Funding available to enable that gap to be filled. There is an unresolved issue, not for debate today, in terms of the size of the overall budget, and the unresolved issue of the Common Agricultural Policy

in terms of more needing to be done from a regional perspective to ensure more of that money is diverted towards economic development activities.

Q27 ***Lord Moser:*** I am very ignorant about the process. Somebody in Brussels decides how much you are going to get for the South West. To what extent is that actually related to your express needs, to your shopping list so to speak; or is it just a figure and you have to do the best you can within it?
Mr McVey: The process is primarily at Member State level with Brussels in terms of determining an allocation for Member States based on various factors, including gross domestic product and others. At a regional level the UK Government agrees the criteria with the Commission, by which it will distribute money to the regions. That is based upon a mixture of need and opportunity. For example, in the South West because we have parts of the region, such as Cornwall and the Isles of Scilly, whose GDP historically has been much lower than the EU average, we do receive concentrations of funding to meet that need, as well as some funding related to opportunities around parts of the region where there is potential for businesses to be more competitive. There is a mixture of money based on the need and potential.

Q28 ***Chairman:*** Mr Read, do you have any comment on this bit of it?
Mr Read: No, other than just to reiterate again, if there was a longer-term vision that had been funded by the EU that would be the other way of looking at it, rather than trying to access the need from the bottom up to say, "This is where we are trying to get to. We think these are the resources required to get there. We invite you to make use of those resources and help us realise the goal".

Q29 ***Lord Watson of Richmond:*** This Committee spent a lot of time last year looking at the difficult issues of fraud within the European Union. I wanted therefore to ask you one question about audit trails, as you raised the audit trail question. We listened to a lot of people from the Commission in particular arguing that the possibility of fraud was really something which fundamentally focussed in the Member States rather than the institutions. Therefore I just wonder, in terms of the audit trail for monies that are granted under Structural Funding, where does the audit go; what is your reporting line on how the money has been spent?
Mr MacInnes: There are a number of audit bodies, from the European Court of Auditors to the DG Regio audits through to Member State audits and local audits for programmes, so there is a whole range of levels of audits, and the experience of applicants is that that audit burden is becoming very heavy indeed.

Q30 ***Lord Watson of Richmond:*** So they are likely to find themselves with audit reporting lines which are going to regional government in the UK, national government and Brussels?
Mr MacInnes: Yes.
Lord Watson of Richmond: Thank you.

Q31 ***Lord Woolmer of Leeds:*** I suppose a question for all of you: do you think that the current eligibility tests for regions to receive support under the Structural Funds are relevant, fair and appropriate?
Mr McVey: I recognise that I may have answered this question already in response to the previous question, but I think that the current tests have delivered for the South West region levels of funding that have enabled us to make significant differences to the economy in parts of the region, and that will continue with the new programmes. It is important—and I think I have already said this—that there are still tests in place that enable need to be recognised at a regional level and a sub-regional level as well. However, that is something for us as a region to determine. As I have already said, I would like to see in place tests that do recognise the gross domestic product of regions in relation to the EU average but also do something to capture the needs of those regions which, although on the face of it are relatively prosperous, have within them pockets of real need in terms of economic performance that lag behind the rest of the region and Europe.

Q32 ***Lord Woolmer of Leeds:*** But do those tests currently apply? Are you saying they do apply now and you want them to remain?
Mr McVey: The tests apply and I think, although enlargement and further enlargement brings further restrictions upon how the budget can be spread, there is a need to have tests in the future that would consider some of the issues that are here at the moment.
Mr MacInnes: From a Scotland point of view, I expect the two parts of Scotland that have done best out of the funds would be Highlands & Islands and Glasgow & West Central Scotland in terms of deindustrialisation and so on. I think the tests that would apply at that time over the last 20 years have been appropriate and have made a substantial difference in focusing funds on the areas that needed to be focused on. As we go forward it is more difficult to know what these tests ought to be, with more emphasis now on innovation, research and development. It is not clear that the funding should go, for instance, to the areas and to the applicants that it went to over the last programme period, so I

think whilst the tests are relevant they also have to change for the next programme.

Q33 ***Lord Woolmer of Leeds:*** So looking to post-2013, what changes do you fear might happen that you would not like to see and what changes would you like to happen?
Mr MacInnes: The changes we would like to happen: again, just more emphasis on workforce development, on innovation, on research and development, and also on making sure that areas of local regeneration that need to be regenerated locally are still done. I think that the big infrastructural projects that have been funded in the past will not happen in the future in the same way and there may be a concern that there are still some of these needing to be done but that they will not be addressed in the same comprehensive way that they were in the past.
Mr McVey: I think the fear would be that because of enlargement, because of restrictions on the budget, that there would be an emphasis just on need which would mean certain Member States on the face of it might not receive any Structural Funds in the future, or certainly some regions in the UK might not receive Structural Funds in the future. To echo what Donald was saying, there is the need for regeneration in certain parts of the UK so that somehow needs to be recognised in the criteria. I also support very strongly the point that Donald was making about the need for competitiveness-type activities to be supported and criteria to be in place to support those, so around innovation and research and development. That certainly is the way forward with much of the funding.

Q34 ***Chairman:*** I think I would like to do a sweep-up question which is how can the funds become more effective in supporting other policies to deal with climate change and managed migration, et cetera, in Member States and regions? I would like a quick answer from all three if I might.
Mr Read: I can say something about where we stand on climate change in terms of METREX members. There is a computer model produced by the Tyndall Centre in East Anglia called GRIP which enables metropolitan areas to look at their sources of energy and the emissions that are generated and the source of those emissions within the metropolitan areas. We have a proposition going forward under INTERREG at the moment where every metropolitan area does that. They do an inventory of their emissions and the sources and then look at various reduction scenarios and come up with an integrated strategy to do that, which involves all of the stakeholders—to use the jargon—all of those who have a contribution to make to reducing emissions, sitting round the table, which is one of the reasons why you need a decision-making mechanism at the metropolitan level in order to come up with an integrated greenhouse gas reduction strategy. After metropolitan areas have come up with that, relatively quickly and say the way forward for us is whatever it is—heating in the north, cooling in the south or whatever—then there would be an issue of how those strategies could be supported. I think the EU could say that metropolitan areas should produce mitigation strategies, assess the extent to which you can deal with those entirely from your own resources and the extent to which you need supplementary resources beyond that, either through the Structural Funds or nationally.
Mr MacInnes: I think there is a case to be made for the fact that Structural Funds ought not to address these wider issues. There are other mechanisms or other interventions which should be used for addressing climate change, immigration and so on. Structural Funds only apply in certain areas and these wider issues apply right across the EU, and other interventions should be used for these. I think particularly programmes like the Framework Programmes for research and development, where a lot of money is going into climate change research, should be used more extensively than structural funds for these wider policy issues that are around.
Mr McVey: I might have mentioned earlier that there was huge enthusiasm during the development of our current Structural Fund programmes for the programmes to not necessarily address the underlying issues of climate change and migration but for the funds to be used in a way that recognised that those are issues, they are there; how can we, through economic strategies and Structural Funds, gain some economic advantage as a consequence? Whether that is by ensuring that migrants have the right skills to contribute to the economy or, in terms of climate change, for example ensuring that the local economy builds renewable energy infrastructure, encourages businesses to be more energy efficient and so on, so practical actions at the local and regional level.
Chairman: Thank you very much. Have I swept aside any questions that colleagues were waiting to ask?

Q35 ***Lord Steinberg:*** I would just like to ask one. In relation to climate change, which is the "buzz" situation at the moment, do you not sometimes feel in the allocation of your funds that too much emphasis is being placed on this, whereas Britain's emissions are very tiny compared to the rest of the world and that the money could be used—I know this is not a popular thing to say—more sensibly in other areas within the development of your industries that you are interested in promoting?

Mr McVey: In terms of how the funds are being applied in the region, although the European Commission were very supportive of us using them to address climate change issues, in particular to work towards a low carbon economy, I should make it clear that was a regional partnership decision, and in Cornwall and the Isles of Scilly in particular a partnership decision there, to go in that direction, to recognise that climate change is an issue and to say, right, in terms of our economy what can we do with the Structural Funds to address aspects of that issue?

Mr MacInnes: I think climate change is too big an issue to be addressed through the Structural Funds.

Mr Read: The only comment I would make is that climate change and energy use are clearly inter-related and most metropolitan areas are concerned to secure their energy futures, and if that has to be on a renewable basis, on a local basis, then that just seems sensible in terms of the cost of carbon fuels in the future, so taking climate change action by securing renewable energy resources for the future helps your economy and helps climate change; it is not a competition there.

Chairman: Thank you all very much for coming. It is very good of you and we have learnt a lot from you. Thank you very much.

Further supplementary memorandum by METREX

Lord Woolmer asked me yesterday whether METREX was advocating an additional level of government for European metropolitan regions and areas. I may not have made the METREX position explicit.

Governance and Government

We do advocate a level of governance at the metropolitan level but not necessarily a level of government. The distinction is between governance as the capability for decision-making and government, which can add competencies (powers) and resources.

I can perhaps illustrate this through the situation in Scotland. Here the government consists of the Scottish Parliament and 32 local Councils. However, there are also five city regions or metropolitan areas across which strategic decision-making is required. Across the Glasgow metropolitan area the eight Councils concerned have set up a level of governance, through a joint committee, without adding to the levels of government.

Across Europe metropolitan areas are making appropriate administrative arrangements to manage change and these range from such informal governance to elected government, as in Germany. The choice often depends on the perception of the scale and intensity of change that has to be managed and the effectiveness of decision-making and implementation that is required.

In addition, many European metropolitan regions and areas are cooperating for collective strength and competitiveness and this is particularly important outside the prosperous core if the Lisbon agenda is to be realised. The European jargon is coopetition.

This is the approach advocated in the METREX Framework.

However, such coopetition is not possible without metropolitan governance of some kind through which it can be progressed. In this sense the Benchmark approach facilitates the realisation of the Framework.

ERDF Implications

METREX advocates the production of a European perspective or framework to clarify how the related objectives of social, economic and territorial cohesion can be achieved and the allocation of financial resources accordingly. European metropolitan regions and areas would then be key partners in the realisation of such an overview.

In reality cooperation at the metropolitan level and between metropolitan areas is happening across Europe, driven by the practical need for competitiveness. The allocation of ERDF resources should reflect this reality (for example, the Northern Way initiative in England) and support it as one way of progressing the realisation of the Lisbon Agenda.

9 January 2008

TUESDAY 15 JANUARY 2008

Present	Cohen of Pimlico (Chairman)	Steinberg, L
	Haskins, L	Trimble, L
	Kerr of Kinlochard, L	Watson of Richmond, L
	Moser, L	Woolmer of Leeds, L

Memorandum by Open Europe

1. *What should be the Objectives of the EU's Structural Funds? How can the Funds become more effective in supporting public policies in Member States and regions? What mechanisms of delivery could make the policy more performance-based and more user-friendly?*

1.1 For the Structural and Cohesion Funds (SCF) to become more effective in supporting public policy, at least five major reforms need to take place:

(i) Better targeting of funds both amongst and within regions to focus effort on the worst off areas.

(ii) Lower deadweight costs and less bureaucracy both for public and private actors.

(iii) Better project selection to focus on genuinely growth and employment enhancing programmes.

(iv) Better coordination with, and less constraints on, national policies.

(v) Stronger systems to reduce fraud and mismanagement.

1.2 We argue that these flaws predominantly stem from the very involvement of the EU in regional policy in the first place, and will be very hard to fix through micro-reforms. Rather, we suggest the complete repatriation of regional policy to the UK. We also suggest that all Member States should have the option to opt out of the SCF.

1.3 First, the poor targeting (both in terms of projects and areas) has its roots in the EU's budget negotiations themselves. Historically and today still, the evidence suggests that the SCF are treated more as "political sweetener" than a development tool. The influential Sapir report for the Commission rightly argued that,

> "National political constraints mean that each government worries more about being able to flag a negotiation success (ie obtaining a significant share of EU money to be spent in its own territory) than about being sure that money is spent on worthwhile projects, let alone those fostering convergence in the EU as a whole".[1]

1.4 Likewise, as often pointed out in academic literature, the classic EU horse-trading often makes the SCF function as a "side-payment", as with the so-called "Integrated Mediterranean Programme" from which Greece was promised some €2 billion, in return for its vote on the accession of Portugal and Spain.[2] The Cohesion Funds was likewise set up to "compensate" for the forthcoming monetary union. Hence, the SCF are not a needs-driven policy, but more based on contingencies in negotiations. This, in turn, paves way for arbitrary allocation processes. Should control of regional policy be brought back to the Member States which so choose, at the very least, the bargain-driven element of the SCF would be become less significant.

1.5 The poor targeting is also tied to EU-specific rules on the rate of spending. The European Court of Auditors (ECA), amongst others, has pointed to problems with the Commission's N + 2 rule. The rule means that the commitment by the member states to spend the allocated funds must lead to payments within two years of being entered into the budget or the money will be cancelled. The objective behind the rule is to prevent unused funds from storing up and ensuring that the spending is well planned. However, the ECA argues, it provides a tremendous incentive for the member states to spend where the money can be quickly absorbed, rather than where it can lead to long-term and sustainable gains.

1.6 An ECA report concluded that for the 2000–06 financial period, "budgetary allocations were determined less by a well established development strategy and the effectiveness of the Structural Funds than by maximising likely take-up of funding".[3] It found several instances where money had been reshuffled from projects that were deemed effective and deserving, to projects that simply could absorb the funds.

[1] Sapir et al "An Agenda for a Growing Europe; making the EU Economic System Deliver", July 2003.

[2] Allen, "Cohesion and the Structural Funds: Competing Pressures for Reform?" in Wallace, Wallace and Pollack *Policy-Making in the European Union*, 2005.

[3] *European Court of Auditors*, "Special Report No 1/2007, concerning the implementation of the mid-term processes on the Structural Funds 2000–06", 5 June 2007.

1.7 A better solution—which would make the delivery of the SCF substantially more result-based—would be to leave governments free to choose the investment project to be financed by EU transfers, but oblige them to declare beforehand the expected results of the project. Disbursement of the funds could then be made in lump sums, and would depend upon reaching these results—rather than ability to spend. This is essentially the solution the Sapir-report and others have suggested. However, from such a system there is a relatively small step to bringing back regional policy to the national level altogether.

1.8 Moreover, if the SCF truly are to add value to domestic policy, the heavy bureaucracy of the SCF must be downsized and the deadweight loss drastically reduced. The cumbersome bureaucracy involved in the SCF is universally acknowledged.[4]

1.9 On the EU level, substantial resources are spent on administration and overlapping committees. For example, the Committee of the Regions (CoR), costing some €140 million a year; some €70 million is spent under the label "Working in Europe: Social dialogue and mobility" and another €120 million on "Employment, social solidarity and gender equality". There is also the Assembly of the European Regions. Also the EU's Economic and Social Committee, costing some €120 million a year, has a specific unit for the SCF. It is far from clear what all these committees and groups actually achieve. All in addition to the admin costs involved in DG Regio.[5]

1.10 On the national level, there are no less than seven different Whitehall departments involved in the SCF—the DWP, BERR, Treasury, DEFRA, CLG, DFT and DCMS. For the DWP, the yearly administrative cost involved in the ESF is reported at £10 million.[6] For the other departments, such figures have not been possible to obtain but could well be of the same magnitude.

1.11 On top of this the regional tier adds substantial costs. An evaluation of the Peace 2 programme in Northern Ireland concluded that out of the £641.2 million that was allocated for the programme, £57.1 million—or 11%—was absorbed by administration.[7] A report from the Scottish Parliament put the annual figure for administering the SCF in Scotland at £30.9 million, equivalent to 10% of the funds allocated.[8]

1.12 The English GOs and RDAs (and at present regional assemblies) cost £366 million to administer. It has not been possible to distinguish between the administrative costs created by the SCF and other spending. Nor would it be possible to get rid of the regional tier while the EU's current spending framework stays in place. Regardless, it is clear that also at the regional level, the bureaucratic cost is high.

Region	*Admin cost, RDA*	*Overseas spending, RDA*	*Admin cost, Government Office for Region*	*Grants, Regional Assembly*	*Total*
North East	22,607	836	13,055	2,073	38,571
North West	38,144	577	17,400	3,045	59,166
Yorks & Humber	19,290	606	13,286	2,339	35,521
West Midlands	20,000	1,056	14,972	2,518	38,546
East Midlands	16,000	375	11,496	2,507	30,377
East	10,900	180	12,672	2,469	26,221
South West	19,290	672	14,766	2,470	37,198
South East	21,222	443	14,095	3,771	39,531
London	29,500		17,881	*65(admin)*	112,381
Total	166,063	4,745	129,624	21,436[9]	366,868

Sources: GLA, Greater London Authority Consolidated Budget 2006–07, February 2006, p 9; *Hansard,* 19 July 2007, Column 494W; *Hansard,* 22 May 2006, Column 1460W; *Hansard* 10 May 2006, Column 376WA onwards; Hansard, 11 January 2007, Column 738WA.

1.13 The combined SCF-related administrative costs of the EU, national and regional policies suggests that even while spending the same amount of money on regional/regeneration policies as at present, it would be possible to save hundreds of millions in administrative costs by sweeping away the costly bureaucracy necessitated by the EU's regional policies.

4 For the administrative burden of the SCF, see: "'London's Perspective'—Consultation on the future of EU Structural Funds post-2006", *London Partners*, House of Commons, May 2006, 2003; *Hansard*, 17 June 2004 : Column 275WH; DTI/ODPM, "Evaluation of the Added Value and Costs of the European Structural Funds in the UK", November 2003; Bachtler, John & Taylo, Sandra, *European Policies Research Centre*, "The Added Value of the Structural Funds: A Regional Perspective", June 2003.
5 Ibid.
6 *House of Commons Work and Pensions Committee*, "European Social Fund", Sixth Report of Session 2002–03 Volume I.
7 *PA*, 10 September 2007.
8 Scottish Parliament, European and External Relations Committee Official Report 6 June 2006.
9 Figure include £244,000 for the English Regions Network.

1.14 Beyond this, cutting out the EU-level would presumably lead to significant savings also for recipients, given that the EU's bureaucracy and regulations, almost universally, are perceived as more cumbersome than its national counterparts.[10]

1.15 Again, as widely acknowledged, the EU's regulations are today overdone and too inflexible to accommodate the specific needs of 27 countries and hundreds of regions—at different stages of their development. Something that is made worse by the lack of "opt-outs" for smaller-sized projects, or projects with special needs. The requirement to keep records for 12 years, regardless of project size, is a case in point. As has been noted elsewhere, it seems odd that a small café offering intermediate job opportunities for the mentally ill should be under the same accounting rules as a multi-million pound infrastructure project.[11]

1.16 The obvious risk is that the cost of both the extra bureaucracy and regulations are passed down to the stakeholders at the bottom of the chain, hitting smaller players that have a much harder time to absorb the costs, ie small or struggling firms and community or voluntary organisations. There are examples of small projects that drown in this paper work, such as a training organisation funded by the ESF with only 12 trainers that had to employ five support staff in order to fulfill all the administrative requirements of the SCF.[12] This runs completely contrary to the supposed aim of the SCF, in as far as the policy is meant to encourage local initiatives and subsidiarity.

1.17 The entire structure of administrative control and audit seems to be both disproportionate to the small amount of funds given and out of touch with economic reality. As a DTI/ODPM report pointed out, there is little evidence that the rigorous regulations have actually led to better and more efficient spending.[13] It would of course make sense to create a system of opt-outs for smaller actors, and regulate with more attention paid to specific, local needs—such as including social housing among the eligible funding activities.

1.18 However, notwithstanding some flexibility for the UK in 2007-2013 in terms of reporting requirements, British proposals to simplify and streamline the regulations seem often to conflict with the Commission's ideas and rules. For example, a type of fast-track procedure for projects of less than £50,000—which would make life a lot easier for smaller players—did not comply with the Commission's rules on open and competitive tendering. Similarly, the UK attempted to drop the requirement to keep records for 12 years, but was found to be in breach of EU-regulations.[14] Gordon Brown has acknowledged that, "There are many things that we want to do to encourage local skills and research and development, and local businesses, but we're not able to do because of the existing rules".[15]

1.19 All of this seems to support the conclusion that the best way for the SCF to support public policy in the UK is through the complete repatriation of the funds.

1.20 In addition, corruption and mismanagement remain at large, undermining sound public spending and policy. The ECA found that at least 4 billion euros of the money that the EU Commission handed out in 2006 "should not have been". Of the projects the ECA audited, only 31% "were found to be free from error". The ECA warned that there was a "high risk" that the project costs were "overstated" and that there were large numbers of claims for "ineligible expenditure." The report stated that there was generally "a lack of evidence to support the calculation of overheads or the staff costs involved".[16]

1.21 But the ECA usually only monitor some 90 projects, and the Commission only audits 5% of the projects given money. Its figures could well be underestimates. For example, Italy's tax and fraud investigator, Guardia di Finanza, noted in its latest annual report that €433 million worth of EU money was subject to outright fraud in Italy alone in 2006.[17]

1.22 As the ECA also has pointed out[18], the SCF are particularly prone to errors, due to the set-up. There are several reasons for this:

(i) The large number of programmes and projects which are implemented over several years.

(ii) The large number of eligibility conditions which are hard to follow and sometimes open to divergent interpretations.

(iii) The variety of entities and actors which for different reasons intervene in the management process.

---

[10] A report for the DTI and the ODPM found that 60–65% of SCF stakeholders thought that more or significantly more resources were required to implement and apply for SCF programmes, when compared to UK domestic programmes. Only 5% found the EU easier to deal with. (*DTI/ODPM 2003*).

[11] *Hansard*, 17 June 2004 : Column 275WH.

[12] Ibid.

[13] *DTI/ODPM*, "Evaluation of the Added Value and Costs of the European Structural Funds in the UK", November 2003.

[14] *Hansard*, 17 June 2004 : Column 275WH.

[15] *BBC*, 6 March 2003.

[16] *European Report*, 10 July 2007.

[17] *Spiegel Online*, 22 March 2007.

[18] *European Court of Auditors*, "Special Report No 1/2007, concerning the implementation of the mid-term processes on the Structural Funds 2000–06", 5 June 2007.

(iv) The large number of diverging countries and regions subject to the same centralised regulations.

1.23 These are all issues relating to the scale and complexity of the SCF. By bringing back regional policy to the national level, the number of instances where fraud and mismanagement could take place would radically decrease. And the spending would be easier to audit.

2. *Do Structural Funds meet the principle of subsidiarity? Could the same cohesion objectives be met through repatriation of these funds?*

2.1 The complex regulatory culture of the SCF can undermine both localised, small-scale projects (see above), as well as the ability of regional and local authorities to channel money to where the needs are and where the funds can do most good.

2.2 A well-known example is that the SCF cannot be used for schooling or social housing projects—paradoxically as this was initially seen as breaching precisely the subsidiary principle. Stephens (1999) has noted that "Arguably, the current asymmetry between allowing European funds to be used to attract physical capital, but excluding housing as a key aspect of enhancing human capital, is itself a breach of subsidiarity."[19]

2.3 An obvious example is Cornwall—the only region in the UK that will receive Objective One funding throughout the 2007–13 financial perspective. One of the main problems in Cornwall is of course the disproportionately high property prices, due to the number of houses sold as second homes to wealthy outsiders (estimates vary—some argue levels are as high as up to 50% in some districts). In some areas the average house price is 17 times the average annual income in the region—while average income, in turn, is 25% below the national average. As a consequence, Cornwall has seen what MP Matthew Taylor calls a "shocking" rise in the number of people seeking social housing.[20]

2.4 In this scenario it would be sensible to at least have the flexibility to direct structural funds money towards social housing—as that is clearly a need on the ground.

2.5 Conversely, while it is clear that EU management of the structural funds prevents the UK Government from doing things it wants to do, it is difficult to argue that the EU's involvement in running UK regional policies allows anything to happen which could not be achieved by the UK Government. It is clear that EU management of UK regional policy is a violation of the subsidiarity principle.

3. *What impact has the enlargement had on Structural Funds, and are any changes necessary to meet the challenges of further enlargement?*

3.1 One of the more apparent effects is that the SCF since enlargement have become bigger and therefore even harder to manage and audit.

3.2 As for the UK, the significance of the SCF has obviously decreased due to the "statistical effect". For the UK as a whole, the annual allocation of the structural funds will amount to about 0.1–0.15% of national GDP for the 2007–13 financial perspective. Across the regions, the share of GDP varies between approximately 0.2% (Northern Ireland) and 0.02% (South East).[21] This is of course not enough to have any significant macro-economic effect. Despite the further decreased significance of EU funds, the complex regulations and the bureaucratic structure will stay in place, and hence so will the limitations on how the UK can run its regional policy.

3.3 In an enlarged Union, it therefore makes even less sense for the EU-15—particularly countries such as the UK—to be enrolled in the SCF. Allowing for the option of opting out of the policy, could be a major step towards focussing the SCF on the MS and regions that actually are in most need—as well as sizing down the programme and thus making it more manageable. In addition, the targeting of the SCF must be radically improved (see above and below) if the SCF are going to have a real impact on growth and jobs in the EU-27 and beyond.

4. *What criteria should guide the decisions on the proportion of the EU budget to be allocated to Structural Funds?*

4.1 The key is to move away from bargain-driven deals and towards development-focussed strategies. As long as the richer MS are in the game, political domestic constraints will inevitably force them to strike deals, and the budget will continue to balloon, without the funds necessarily having their desired effect. Both for the purpose of fiscal discipline and better targeting of funds, the UK Government's proposal to have all MS with

[19] Quoted in "The EU budget: a historic missed opportunity, *Open Europe*, 20 December 2005.
[20] *Observer*, 19 November 2007.
[21] *DTI*, 2007; ONS, 2007.

a GDP above 90% of the EU average managing and paying for their own regional policy, should be one of the main criteria for deciding how much money to inject into the SCF. If this indeed is the main criteria, the EU's overall regional budget could be cut by as much as 48% (given that 48% of the funds were allocated to the EU-15 for the 2007–13 period).[22]

4.2 There must also be an honest discussion about the SCF's track record. As with the CAP, the failed aspects of the SCF cannot be allowed to simply stay in place. For example, the absence of evidence in support of the SCF's added value must be considered also in the budget negotiations.[23] Where MS consider the value added to be absent, funds should not be allocated.

4.3 In addition, focus must be put on impact. While it is widely agreed that the evidence is inconclusive as to the precise effectiveness of the SCF—and that the counterfactual is virtually impossible to determine—several indicators seem to suggest that the SCF are simply not delivering where they should. Most generally, convergence between regions is simply not happening.

4.4 A recent OECD report noted that regional disparities in Europe are not falling, or at best are declining very slowly. At the current rate of convergence, the report stated, it would take 170 years to halve divergence across the regions in the EU.[24] The report argued that this should put a big question mark next to the SCF.

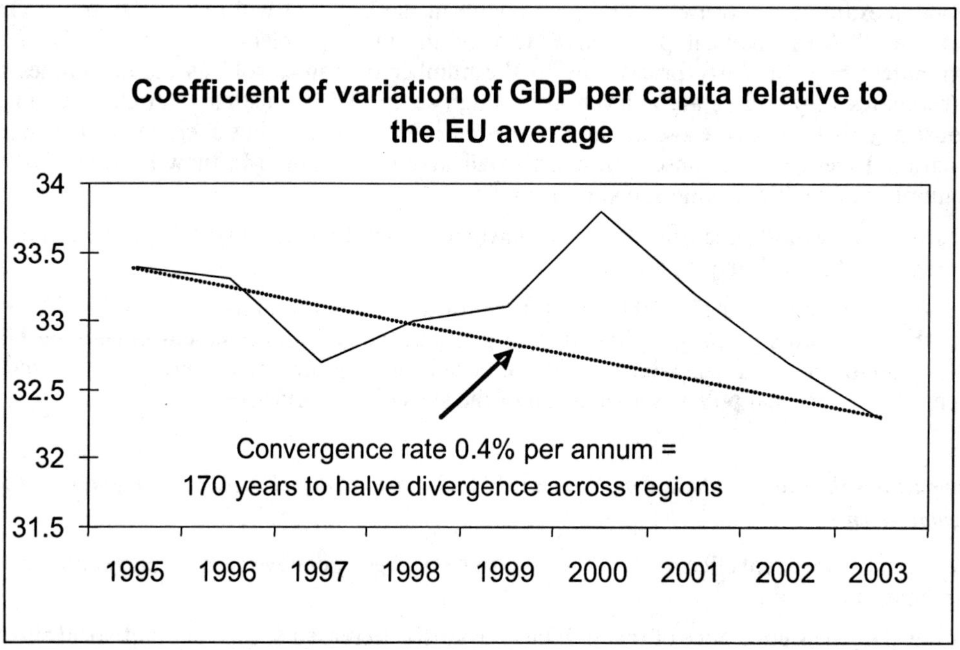

Source: OECD 2007.

[22] Inforegio 2006.

[23] For a discussion on the lack of value added, see: HM Treasury, "A Modern Regional Policy for the United Kingdom", March 2003; *CRG Research*, Cardiff University & Fitzpatrick Associates, "Mid-term Evaluation of the Objective 1 Programme for West Wales and the Valleys", September 2003; Jan Shury et al". A quantitative survey of companies supported by European Social Fund Objective 3", *Department for Work and Pensions*, Research Report No 361; Sapir et al "An Agenda for a Growing Europe; making the EU Economic System Deliver", July 2003.

[24] *OECD*, "Economic survey of the European Union 2007: Making the most of regional cohesion policy", 20 September 2007.

4.5 A paper by Gardiner *et al* concludes that both when looking at regional GDP per capita and regional productivity, regional convergence in the EU is at best a slow process of only 1–2% per annum. Meaningful convergence would take decades to achieve.[25]

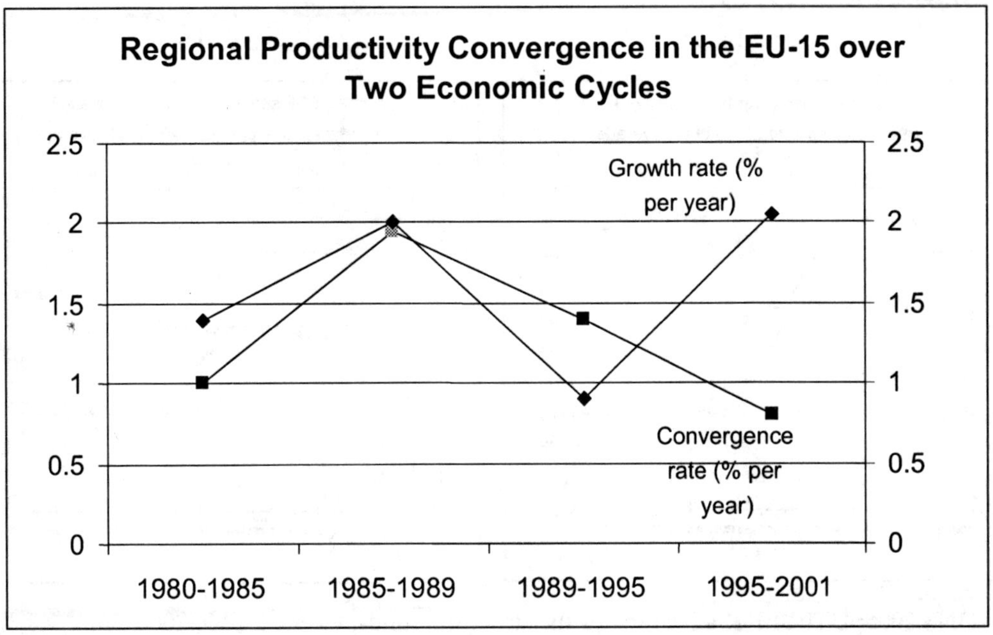

Source: Gardiner et al 2004.

4.6 And as the Sapir report has argued, the available empirical data on economic convergence in the EU gives a very different picture depending on whether one looks at the Member States, or its NUTS 1 regions across the Union.[26] Although convergence of GDP per capita has taken place between member states, inequality within each country accounted for roughly half of total EU regional inequality in the early 1980s, but this rose to about two thirds by the mid-1990s (while inequality between countries fell by about a third during that period).

4.7 Even the Commission's report admits the continuing divergence across the regions (in passing), stating that "in spite of progress, absolute disparities remain large. This is partly as a result of recent enlargement and partly as growth tends to concentrate—during the initial phases of development—in the most dynamic areas within countries".[27]

4.8 Elsewhere, the report also points out that in the period 2000–04, real GDP per head fell in 27 regions and in 24 regions it grew by less than 0.5% a year. In five regions, GDP per head slipped below 75% of the EU average.

4.9 The Commission seems to argue that such discrepancies reflect different stages of development and will naturally disappear in due course. However, first, as we saw, convergence is very slow—170 years to halve welfare gaps can hardly be an acceptable rate. Secondly, Objective One regions—those with an average GDP under 75% of the EU average—have remained remarkably stable. Of the 44 regions originally granted Objective One status in 1989, 43 were still eligible for such funding in 2003.

4.10 Meanwhile, households in the EU's poorer regions have increased their dependency on grants and social transfers for their disposable income.[28]

4.11 In the UK, when comparing EU funding with the GVA per indices there seems to be little evidence that the structural funds have had a net effect on wealth and job creation. If the structural funds were efficient, we would expect to detect some sort of boost in a regions' GVA as EU funding increases. This is not the case, however. Although not a hugely meaningful comparison, it still undermines the Commission's case, as the very idea behind the SCF is to raise GVA per head, as poorer regions are granted aid precisely on the basis of their low levels of GVA per capita relative to the EU average.

[25] Gardiner et al, "Competitiveness, Productivity and Economic Growth across the European Regions", *Regional Studies*, December 2004.
[26] Sapir et al, "An Agenda for a growing Europe: Making the EU Economic System Deliver", Report of an Independent High-Level Study Group established on the initiative of the President of the European Commission.
[27] *European Commission*, Fourth Report on Economic and Social Cohesion, 5 May, 2007.
[28] *Eurostat*, Private household income in the European Union regions, 2003, 25/2007.

4.12 Also more meaningful measures show that economic opportunities remain unevenly spread across the UK, and are unaffected by the SCF. The one-fifth of the UK's population that live in the poorest local areas still only accounts for about 13% of national income—with few signs of any significant upward mobility taking place in the last decade.[29]

North East[30]

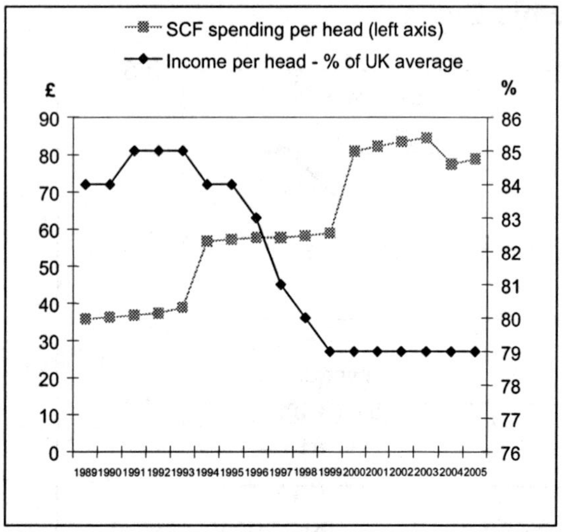

Wales

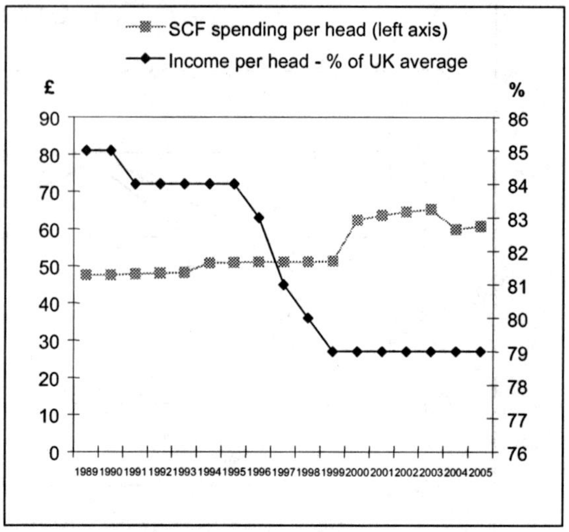

Sources: ONS 2005; DTI/BERR allocation of the structural funds, 89–93, 94–99, 2000–06.

4.13 Like in the case of value added, if there is no solid evidence that the SCF lead to convergence—evidence usually tend to tip the other way—nor any measurable impact of funds, what is the justification for continuing with the programme in its current size and shape—particularly with the deadweight losses in mind. These are all issues that have to inform the decision on how much money to allocate to the regional budget post-2013.

5. *Are the current eligibility tests for regions to receive support under the EU's Structural Funds relevant, fair and appropriate? Should they remain in place after 2013? Is it appropriate that they are discussed simultaneously with wider agreements on allocating EU budget spending?*

5.1 First, the EU's criterion for special status regions—75% of average EU GDP—is outdated. It may have made sense when the regions were either well above or well below the threshold. Since enlargement, however, the regions are now much more evenly scattered, with several areas being around the threshold. This opens up for regions with similar wealth levels, receiving very different amounts of funding.

5.2 Secondly, the Commission's preferred measure for wealth—the Gross Value Added (GVA) measure—is open to substantial criticism.[31] GVA measures the contribution to the economy of each individual producer, industry or sector. GDP is derived from GVA by adding taxes and subtracting subsidies on products.[32] Essentially, GVA measures output divided by population.[33]

5.3 However, as often noted, since GVA does not take commuting into account, it tends to produce an upwards bias for regions that have large levels of inward commuting, and vice versa. Thus, for example allocation of Objective One (now Convergence) spending can be distorted by the fact that some NUTS 2 regions, for example, are urban areas or cities (ie Hamburg, Bremen or even Inner and Outer London), whereas others are coastal or rural areas. The urban areas naturally have higher GVA per head, due to concentration of financial and business services, more value-added activities and so forth. Areas with a large share of inwards commuters will have artificially high GVA per head. The reverse is then true for areas where

[29] *Financial Times*, 15 December 2007.

[30] The tables compare GVA per head indices to the allocated SCF per head for the North East and Wales regions between 1989 and 2005. For the North East, SCF doubled during the period while GVA per head dropped 6% compared to the UK average. In Wales, funding increased by close to 16%, while GVA fell by 7%. The trend recurs in Yorkshire, where funding almost doubled during the time period while the GVA dropped by some 4%.

[31] House of Commons/ODPM, 2003b; Gripaios & Paul Bishop, "Objective One Funding in the UK: A Critical Assessment", *Regional Studies*, November 2006.

[32] CLG, Technical note accompanying the Public Service Agreement, 2002.

[33] Reasons given for using GVA rather than, say, GDP per capita combined with other measures, are, amongst other factors, that the former is internationally comparable and may also be less susceptible to political manipulation. Since it is a single measure, it cannot be manipulated through shifting the weights of the various measures.

commuters tend to live. Some estimates put the Greater London's upwards bias in the GVA calculation in the area of 15%.[34]

5.4 This is precisely the case with the infamous example of Lüneburg outside Hamburg, Germany. The district serves as residential area for Hamburg's professionals, and is considered one of the wealthiest commuting areas in Germany, growing by 2,000 residents each year. However, since GVA focuses on workplace, the high income of Lüneburg's residents counts towards Hamburg wealth statistics.[35] Consequently, Eurostat has identified Lüneburg as an Objective One region, marginally poorer than Merseyside. Lüneburg was granted a staggering €900 million from the SCF for the 2000–06 period—only slightly less than what was given to Merseyside for the same time period. This, of course, adds to the criticism of the insufficient targeting of the SCF.

5.5 In addition, GVA does not adequately account for demographic trends, productivity factors and population structure. Neither does it reflect lifestyle choices. For instance, an area that has a large number of pensioners, students or part-time workers will have low GVA per head since that type of income is omitted in the GVA measure. This, without the area necessarily experiencing a shortage of economic opportunities.[36] Many have pointed to Cornwall and Cumbria as being on opposite ends of this problem.

5.6. The ONS' recommendation for measuring regional prosperity and hence for deciding how to allocate the SCF, strike us as fairer, more appropriate and more relevant:

(a) regional GVA per full-time employee, which they argue is the best way to measure regional differences in productivity as it is not affected by the number of non-working residents; and

(b) regional gross household disposable income, which indicates the prosperity of residents.[37]

5.7 But even beyond the measure *per se*, the appropriateness of the EU's distinctly region-based funding system is questionable. Due to the set-up, the SCF often fail to target smaller pockets of poverty that can exist within a region. The flip side is that more affluent areas can end up with substantial amounts of money for no apparent reason.

5.8 This is a major shortcoming in a country such as the UK, where local pockets of poverty often exist within affluent larger areas. In urban areas, for example, discrepancies can come down to as small units as a block of council estates. The SCF are way too inflexible to address such gaps. This problem is also exacerbated by what many observers consider the artificial nature of the UK's regions.

5.9 The South East is a good case study. In 2004, the South East was the 13th wealthiest region in the EU[38] with a household disposable income 12% above the national average. The region was unsurprisingly given Objective Three status—which reflected its wealth levels—and was granted close to £300 million for the 2000–06 financial perspective.[39]

5.10 However, within the South East there are smaller economically deprived areas such as Hastings, where 27% of all children come from families living on out of work benefits.[40] This and other indicators make it one of the poorest areas in England. But Hastings is situated within the NUTS 3 region of East Sussex, which has a GDHI above the national average. NUTS 3 is the smallest unit in the EU's classification system. Consequently Hastings is completely omitted. For the 2000–06 financial period, it has only been given ESF grants worth £1.1 million. This translates into 0.4% of the total ESF amount given to the South East.[41]

5.11 Likewise, some parts of Thanet belong to the 1% of the most deprived areas in the UK.[42] Its NUTS 3 region, however, is Kent, whose GDHI is above the national average. Thanet received some £1.8 million from the ESF over a six year period. Although both towns get substantially more money from the ERDF, it still seems rather odd that they would end up with so little money from the ESF.

5.12 In comparison, Canterbury—a wealthy area by all measures—has been given some £2.6 million from the ESF.

5.13 Examples like these seem to suggest that a substantial share of the SCF ends up with projects and individuals that, comparatively speaking, are not in need of the money, and that the reverse is true.

[34] Roberts 2004.
[35] *Daily Telegraph*, "600m EU aid for Germany's thriving 'fat belt' commuters", 21 June 2007.
[36] Gripaios & Paul Bishop, "Objective One Funding in the UK: A Critical Assessment", *Regional Studies*, November 2006.
[37] House of Commons/ODPM, 2003.
[38] According to the GVA measure.
[39] DTI/BERR, UK Structural Funds Allocations 2000–06.
[40] *End Child Poverty*, 2007. Available at http://www.ecpc.org.uk/south-east.html.
[41] *South East Government Office* 2007, List of all projects by post code and ESF value.
[42] DWP, Indices of Multiple Deprivation 2007. Available at http://www.communities.gov.uk/communities/neighbourhoodrenewal/deprivation/deprivation07/

5.14 We used the ACORN system for UK postcodes—which categorises the UK population according to income, lifestyle choices and a whole range of demographic statistics—to get an idea of where the SCF actually end up. In the South East, we found that postcode areas whose populations are classified as "wealthy achievers" received 5.5% of the funds. The upper half of the population, from the "wealthy achievers" to "secure families" in the "comfortably off" category got almost 30% of the money granted. Only 10% of the funds had gone to the bottom one fifth of households that fall under the category "hard pressed". For the upper categories, we excluded grants that have been given to councils under general headlines, as opposed to specific projects. It is fair to assume that lump sums given to councils could be redistributed elsewhere.

5.15 As said, one of the major problems with evaluating the SCF is the poor quality of the available data. The South East is the only region that provides detailed information on where its SCF money has gone in terms of smaller units. In virtually every other region, data is only available for the NUTS 2 level—at best. As discussed, this is not very useful if we want to investigate whether the funds in reality are targeted at areas where they can do most good.

5.16 If we assume that the South East is indicative for the UK as a whole and using the SCF allocated to the UK for the 2000–06 financial period, which is around £10 billion, more than £3 billion has gone to the "top" 50% of the population in terms of wealth. The wealthiest 20% have received about £550 million from the SCF. Meanwhile, as little as £1 billion has gone to the bottom 20% of the UK's population. Even assuming that all the grants that have been given to Councils in the wealthiest areas have been redistributed to the bottom 20% (something that seem very unlikely), the bottom one fifth has still only been granted £3 billion out of the allocated £10 billion.

5.17 This is a very rough estimate, but it does give an idea of how off target and unfair the SCF can be. Furthermore, it provides a strong argument as to why the EU's criteria and region-based spending structure should not stay in place after 2013.

5.18 As the flaws are so fundamental and cut to the very heart of the distribution/impact of the SCF, it seems highly appropriate to consider them simultaneously with the wider discussions on spending allocation.

6. *What would be the effect of linking the availability of the Structural Funds with compliance to Broad Economic Policy Guidelines?*

6.1 It would not be appropriate for member states which are not members of the euro to face financial penalties (in the form of lost structural funding) for non compliance with the Broad Economic Policy Guidelines.

6.2 The euro member states, where macroeconomic policy is arguably a matter of greater mutual concern, already have in place rules on fiscal policy in the form of the stability and growth pact. Creating a parallel process to enforce the BEPG would be likely to create confusion.

9 January 2008

Examination of Witnesses

Witnesses: Mr Neil O'Brian and Mr Mats Persson, Open Europe, examined.

Q36 ***Chairman:*** Welcome to our sub-committee and thank you very much for coming. This is a public session. You have had the list of topics for discussion. Would you like to make a general statement first or would you rather we started with questions?

Mr O'Brian: We would rather start with the questions.

Q37 ***Chairman:*** My first question is the obvious one to get us started. You make the case for the abolition of structural funds and the complete renationalisation of regional policy. Could you give me a quick summary for the record?

Mr O'Brian: The quick way of expressing that, turning the question round, would be to say that if you take the idea of subsidiarity seriously, why should we run regional policy at European level? It is not intuitively clear why we should do that, particularly given that there are fairly clear problems in doing that in the present system at the moment. The main problems that we identify are, firstly, quite poor targeting of funds—almost all regions get something; and from the limited amount of data that we have been able to find, when you get down to a regional level, we still find that a greater proportion of the money is not being spent in the poorest areas. Secondly, you have quite high bureaucratic costs; you have various levels of administration and very high costs in doing that. Thirdly, you have problems with the kinds of projects that are being funded at the moment. A lot of these things are not really creating as much employment as they could or as much growth as they possibly could. Fourthly, you have quite bad connection with national policies. Certainly that is a problem which the Prime Minister has identified. Gordon Brown said that "there are many things that we want to do to encourage local skills in research and development and local businesses that we are not able to do because of the existing rules". Fifthly and finally, there are problems with vulnerability to fraud in the current system. It is a very complex system. The Court of Auditors has not, as you know, cleared the overall budget for 13 years in a row and the structural funds seem to be one of the main areas of problems. In the ECA's last survey, only about 31 per cent of all of the funds they surveyed were completely free from error. You have five pretty serious problems. The Government I think has made a very good case for renationalising the funds, certainly in the richer Member States. I think we would agree with their case.

Q38 ***Lord Kerr of Kinlochard:*** So we can assume, as I did from your written evidence, that you are more or less against the status quo?
Mr O'Brian: Yes.

Q39 ***Lord Kerr of Kinlochard:*** You make a number of proposals for changes. One is that Member States should be permitted to opt out from the EU structural funds system as a whole. Could I ask you what you mean by that, because you also argue as the British Government has done, that access to the structural funds should be concentrated heavily on the poorest. I think you support that. If the system were to continue, you think that is correct—a poverty focus. But how do you reconcile an opt-out system with a poverty focus? Presumably those who would not be receiving funds via the structural funds would opt out; the structural funds would then be a means of recycling money among the poorest.
Mr O'Brian: I think what we would propose and, as I understand it, what the Government would propose, is to disentangle two different issues. One is the overall net transfer of funds from rich Member States to the poorer Member States and the second is the specific system of structural and cohesion funds that we have at the moment. For example, we would propose, and again, I think the Government proposed, that countries like the UK with a GDP per capita of more than 90 per cent of the EU average would neither receive funds from the SCF nor pay in that amount of money. Overall, the impact would be fiscally neutral on the EU Budget. For example, if you were either to allow Member States to opt out or you were to have the EU-15 no longer receiving funds from the SCF—

Q40 ***Lord Kerr of Kinlochard:*** The opt-out would be an opt-out from receipts not an opt-out from contributions?
Mr O'Brian: Quite so, and that is a good way of expressing it. Not from your net contribution, if you see what I mean; you would opt out of both receiving and paying for SCF but your overall net contribution to the EU Budget would remain the same. Does that explain what I am trying to say?

Q41 ***Lord Kerr of Kinlochard:*** Yes, I see what you mean, but there would be a major difference if, as you recommend at length in your evidence, there was a massive simplification and repatriation of the system for administring the fund. Member States that had opted out from receipts would be making a contribution into a system which had very light central controls. The present system is criticised by you because the central controls are fairly heavy, but you would maintain your recommendation for a lightening of central control even if Member States like the United Kingdom, if they followed your advice, would have opted out of all receipts but not opted out from a major contribution, which would be basically a budgetary transfer to the poorer Member States, because you would have greatly reduced the administration of the programme from the centre?
Mr O'Brian: There are two quite distinct questions there. One is about whether the richer Member States in particular, the net contributors as it were, should be able to opt out of receipt of SCF. Then there is the question about for those Member States that continue to receive it, how should that be run? I think we would advocate even for those Member States a lighter and simpler way of administering the funds, and also possibly the types of projects that they could spend on might be widened as well. It is like the debate we have in international aid about direct budgetary support versus specific funding for projects. The advantage of giving money and allowing Member States to spend it on what they would like to spend it on is of course that they know where the funds are best spent and they can spend it on the kinds of things that they need. The disadvantage is that all these funds are fungible and if you allowed them to spend EU funds on one thing, that means that they can spend less on themselves and you are less able to direct from the centre. There are two quite distinct questions. One is about our involvement and the second is about what kind of regulatory regime we should have the funds from Member States that remain in the system.

Q42 ***Lord Kerr of Kinlochard:*** These questions are linked to the extent that you make both.
Mr O'Brian: Yes. I would agree with both.

Q43 ***Lord Kerr of Kinlochard:*** You believe that the UK taxpayer would be perfectly happy to see a major reduction in the control over the expenditure, in the poorer eastern European states, of his money; he

would go on contributing at present levels but would see no benefit in the United Kingdom, and much reduced control of expenditure. Do you think that is consistent with your point about fraud?
Mr O'Brian: In answer to your first point, the UK taxpayer is not going to be paying any more than he or she currently is at the moment, and so in one sense there is no reason for them to be obsessed about this. As to your second point, I think in truth we can distinguish between problems with fraud and problems about what kind of projects the money can be spent on. For example, one issue is of course about council housing. If we allowed Member States or the poorer Member States to spend SCF on those kinds of projects, that would be an extra dimension of freedom which they would certainly appreciate. I do not see why that should make this system as a whole more vulnerable to fraud. You definitely can distinguish those two problems.

Q44 ***Lord Watson of Richmond:*** Frankly, I am still very puzzled by this problem. Are you saying in effect that a Member State that decides to become a non-receiver—in other words, it totally takes itself out of the system—should continue to remain a donor so that there would be two differences for that particular state: one, it would be receiving less; and, secondly, it would have less control over what is spent? It seems a very curious proposition.
Mr O'Brian: But it would be receiving less and paying in proportionately less, if you see what I mean, so that the net effect is neutral.

Q45 ***Chairman:*** No, I am sorry, I do not see that. This may be at the core of our confusion. If you are paying something in and you are not getting anything back, that is fine. It may even be Government policy. Nobody may mind doing that but there is a difference for the UK taxpayer: they are not receiving anything for the money they put in.
Mr O'Brian: I have obviously explained what I am saying very badly. For example, if the UK, say, is receiving £4 billion worth of structural funds every year, the UK would pay in within its contributions £4 billion less and not receive back £4 billion. The net contribution would remain exactly the same.

Q46 ***Lord Watson of Richmond:*** The net contribution could still be very considerable.
Mr O'Brian: It would be unchanged.

Q47 ***Lord Haskins:*** Effectively that would mean that the structural funds would be Bulgaria lending money to Romania?
Mr O'Brian: No, it would be still us making a net transfer into the Budget and them receiving.

Q48 ***Lord Woolmer of Leeds:*** How would you propose that that adjustment be made in the contribution from the UK? If the effect on the UK is contributing, let us say for the sake of argument, £20 billion a year but receiving £4 billion a year, in your eyes they do not get the £4 billion and only pay out £16 billion.
Mr O'Brian: Exactly.

Q49 ***Lord Woolmer of Leeds:*** How would you secure that adjustment because the gross cost presumably is out of the general UK contribution to the EU?
Mr O'Brian: That links to the wider question about reform of both contributions and receipts. In terms of this proposal and this discussion, we are talking really about the spending side of the EU Budget. You can fix the contribution side of the EU Budget really how you would like. There are people, particularly in Brussels and here who would like to simplify the current system. As you know, we have a mixture of own resources which are a diminishing share of the Budget. We have the VAT based resource; and you have the GNI based resource. You can balance these things how you would like. The really important thing is the overall net contribution.

Q50 ***Lord Woolmer of Leeds:*** To some extent in countries like the UK, there is an argument—I do not mean an economic argument but a purely political argument—that if we are contributing so much to the EU, we might as well get something back and hence an argument for at least getting something back under the regional policy. If you did net it out, as you suggest, it would mean going back to the drawing board and finding convincing ways in which you can adjust the UK, German and French contributions to the EU Budget. That would all have to be renegotiated in some way.
Mr O'Brian: Interestingly, as I understand it, from talking to people at BERR, we did have quite good support for our proposal from France and Germany and some of the other net contributors.

Q51 ***Lord Kerr of Kinlochard:*** I can see why it is more attractive to them than to us because they do not have a rebate system. We have a system whereby two-thirds of the difference between what we pay in and what we get back is refunded to us a couple of years in arrears. You left that out when you described to the Chairman how the net of that would be exactly the same.
Mr O'Brian: Yes, I think that is an extremely good and important point that you are making. All Member States are roughly having to co-fund all these projects and to say, "We are providing half the funds from the national level", and then for the UK, you also have—

Q52 ***Lord Kerr of Kinlochard:*** I am sorry, that is a different point. We are talking about the UK rebate, which of course France and Germany are very keen to see eliminated.
Mr O'Brian: I was just trying to add to your point, which is that not only is the UK Government having to fund half of the new project itself, but on top of that it is losing two-thirds of the money that it gains from every successful submission for SCF because of the way that the rebate works. Really for a given project, the EU is only ever providing one-sixth of the money in the UK, and so it is a less attractive system, I suspect, for the Treasury and that is probably why the proposal came from the Treasury.

Q53 ***Lord Kerr of Kinlochard:*** It is very ingenious, but the fact is that if your proposal is, as you explained to the Chairman this morning, that rich Member States opt out of receipts but are required to remain in for contributions, the Member State which would lose enormously disproportionately compared to the others would be the United Kingdom because of the working of the UK rebate?
Mr O'Brian: I have may have misunderstood. Why would the UK particularly lose?

Q54 ***Lord Kerr of Kinlochard:*** Because the UK obtains a rebate of two-thirds of the difference between what it puts in and what it gets back, in broad terms. If we were opted out of the system, we could not possibly expect that the UK would continue to get back two-thirds of the moneys that had been spent in eastern Europe. Indeed, we have already, as I understand it, signalled that we do not expect the rebate to apply to expenditure in eastern Europe.
Mr O'Brian: That pass has already been sold.
Lord Kerr of Kinlochard: What we do get back is two-thirds of our contribution to Structural Funds expenditure in western Europe, and we would no longer obtain that, because there would be no expenditure in Western Europe.
Chairman: Lord Kerr, you may have to explain this to me quietly afterwards. For the moment, I would like to ask Lord Trimble to ask his question.

Q55 ***Lord Trimble:*** If we all were to be dependent on an expanded United Kingdom regional policy replacing the existing EU programmes, could we be sure that the United Kingdom Government would continue to make extra funds available? What if the Government was in financial difficulties in a way that the present Government may be in terms of public spending over the next year or two? Might it not then be tempted to cut back on its UK-funded regional policy and would we not also lose the benefit of the existing EU multi-annual programme as well so that the regions might find themselves worse off if they were dealing simply with the UK Government rather than dealing, as they are to some extent, with Brussels at the moment?
Mr O'Brian: Mats Persson may well turn to this. By way of preface to that, I would say that you could apply that argument to every single item of UK Government spending. Of course, the reality is that the amount that the EU spends is not really any more predictable in the UK Government system.
Mr Persson: One of the fundamentals flaws of the structural funds is that they are negotiated at the EU level in a bargaining type of manner. I think that makes them quite unpredictable as well. Striking deals at the EU level when leaders and ministers get together and negotiate the Budget make the funds less about development as about securing as much funds as possible to assure voters at home that they are getting something back. One of our criticisms is that the funds are not necessarily development driven; they are more driven by bargains at the EU level, and so where is the development strategy in the first place here? I think that makes it all unpredictable as well.
Mr O'Brian: May I add a rather striking example of that? Instead of having a rationally driven Budget, it is one driven by deals. In the last two days of the negotiations in December 2005 over the financial perspective, the budget for administration was increased by €1 billion and when we asked the Parliamentary question in the other House about this, we received the very blunt answer from the Government that said it was "necessary to secure political agreement". They are spending €1 billion, they are almost admitting, as a political sweetener. That gives you a flavour of the kind of negotiations.

Q56 ***Lord Trimble:*** My experience of negotiations at EU level is limited but I was involved in the discussions way back in 1999 or 2000 with regard to structural funds for Northern Ireland. The key discussion took place during the German presidency with the German European Minister in Bonn. It was a discussion that involved him, me and Paul Murphy, who was the Northern Ireland Office Minister responsible. There was not any question of which I was aware of any deals or trade-offs being done on a UK-EU basis. It was simply a matter of discussion of the changes in the criteria which had to be negotiated as a result of Northern Ireland getting over 75 per cent of the EU GDP limit, which meant that we were going to lose our status. I do not see this point that you are putting so much weight on. I did not see it in that case. It may be the case elsewhere but I do not know that it is always the case.
Mr O'Brian: One way to look at this would be to say that it is a concern. I think the concern underlying your question is that, given the overall Budget, it should be spent in the areas where it is needed most;

it should be rationally allocated. Is the best way to do that to do it on a UK basis where you are closer to the decisions and you do not have rules, for example about going over the 65 per cent of the EU average GDP and you do not have these various constraints and you can just make a straight forward decision on a UK basis.
Lord Trimble: You may also be having to weigh up which administration has a more positive attitude to regional policy: the Treasury in London or the Commission in Brussels?

Q57 ***Chairman:*** That could be interesting.
Mr O'Brian: It is a question of whether you believe you can win the argument better in Westminster or do you believe you can win the argument better in Brussels. Where do you feel that Northern Ireland has more clout? It is an interesting question.

Q58 ***Lord Trimble:*** At least in Brussels they listen to you. I do not know that the Treasury does!
Mr Persson: In terms of predictability, consistency and continuity, there seems to be a certain absence of that in having the EU running regional policy as well. As you know, six English regions had their funds cut off just this past spring. It was not clear from talking to the people on the ground why that happened. They felt that they had complied with the regulations and yet the funds were cut off, which of course meant a lot more work and added uncertainty to the whole situation.
Mr O'Brian: Certainly some of them felt it was a political move as well.
Mr Persson: It is not necessarily that keeping the structural funds as they are right now at the EU level brings this type of certainty and continuity that we seem to be discussing.

Q59 ***Lord Woolmer of Leeds:*** If I can turn to a little bit of theory and see what your thoughts are on it, one view about regional policy is that it interferes with the market. You should actually allow for movement of labour and movement of capital and regional policy slows that down. Another view is that there is a trade-off between efficiency and equity. If you do introduce regional policy, you need to accept that it is going to slow down growth. The third and final view of regional policy is that lagging regions have under-used resources and regional policy is actually good for growth in the economy. Really, there are quite different views. Where do you come from on that theoretical side of things?
Mr Persson: In the report we argue for targeted tax cuts as a possible better solution, or a passive solution rather than active intervention. We would probably therefore subscribe more towards the framework that it can actually be, if not detrimental, at least irrelevant to growth and for job creation. Obviously there is at least a risk that it can divert resources and talent and inhibit labour flexibly by mis-targeting interventions. Looking at the targeting of the structural funds, that risk is not insignificant. You also have this problem of a possible dependency culture. For example, if you look at the poorest regions in the EU, they have increased their dependency on grants for disposable income. These are not good signs. There is also the so-called Mezzogiorno problem where funds are going one way and the people are going the other. If you look at migration trends, that is also something that should be of concern. Obviously a lot will depend on the way regional policy is pursued and implemented, but in terms of what theoretical framework falls closest to our report, that would probably be the one.

Q60 ***Lord Woolmer of Leeds:*** You could apply exactly the same arguments of course to regional policy within that, could you not? Do you believe in regional policy at all anywhere?
Mr O'Brian: This is a good question. The fundamental question is: what regions we are talking about and how big a unit are we interested in?

Q61 ***Lord Woolmer of Leeds:*** Say the United Kingdom?
Mr O'Brian: The same question I was asking still applies. Are we trying to target very small pockets of poverty, say the size of a town, or are we trying to bring the average productivity to quite a large region of five million people, say, for the NUTS regions in the UK? Are we trying to make those converge and, if so, why? I would certainly personally be more inclined to the approach which is about targeting pockets of poverty rather than very large regions. One of the problems with the SCF is that we are effectively spraying a lot of money around. When we did a bit of analysis of the small amount of data we were able to get hold of—and there really is very little data in the public domain about all this—we found that only about 10 per cent of the money in one region that we studied was being spent in the poorest one-fifth of areas defined by postcode. That is not really getting to the stubborn pockets of poverty in which we are interested. When we talk about regional policy, what exactly do we mean?

Q62 ***Lord Woolmer of Leeds:*** Finally, on that and taking Mr Persson's point that on balance you acknowledge that policies if anything interfere with work in the marketplace and slow things down rather than helping, you say that if there is anything done, it should be targeted very much more narrowly than the broad concept of the region and should be by way of tax incentives rather than grants. Would that mean in summary as far as European policy is that rich countries like the UK should devolve within the UK

and regional policy *per se* is itself harmful rather than helpful and a re-think is needed entirely? In that case, why should the UK even support any regional assistance within Europe, even on the net basis you are advocating? That is with the UK vigorously opposing any form of regional policy in Europe, whether gross or net contributors.
Mr O'Brian: I think you could have an interesting debate about what kind of regional policy you would like to see within the UK.

Q63 ***Lord Woolmer of Leeds:*** Within Europe?
Mr O'Brian: Within Europe as well.

Q64 ***Lord Woolmer of Leeds:*** You do not believe in a net contribution really, do you?
Mr O'Brian: No, I think you are trying to put words in my mouth here.

Q65 ***Lord Woolmer of Leeds:*** I am not being aggressive because I think your paper is interesting and challenging. This is really pushing to understand where you come from.
Mr O'Brian: I certainly think the economics are not clear cut at all about regional policy. There are areas where you could argue that it has succeeded but then you have areas where they pretty clearly have not. Look at the divergent of performance of, say, Ireland, Greece and Portugal, all of the large recipients. I do not think it is at all clear which of the kind of effects that you initially identified, the adjustment-stopping effects versus the effects of liberating unrealised resources in backwards regions, dominates the economics. I just do not think that is clear at all. My instinct is that we should have some kind of regional policy and it should be much more targeted on poverty. One thing which I would identify as being unambiguously true is that these things would be better run at a national level without the kinds of constraints that you have from the EU's set rules. Certainly you would then have the freedom to experiment and try these other means of doing things.
Chairman: I would like now to start asking you about some of the figures in your report.

Q66 ***Lord Kerr of Kinlochard:*** In the press release and your report there is a very striking number of £670 million a year given as the cost to the UK of administring the structural fund. You build this on four elements. Could I take you through these four elements in turn? First, the largest element is £500 million a year, which you say is the cost of the regional tier of the administration of the structural funds. You base that on a table which shows the cost of Regional Development Agencies, and apparently assumes that all these costs arise from the structural funds and without the structural funds would not exist. Second, your table counts overseas spending by regional development agencies; that is export promotion, inward investment attraction, that sort of thing, nothing to do with structural funds. Thirdly, it counts the administrative costs of government policies for the regions, which you assume would not exist but for the structural funds. I do not think that is a widely supported view. Last, grants to Regional Assemblies, which you also insist would not exist but for the structural funds. You top that up to a staggering number and claim that the cost of the regional tier of the administration in the UK of the EU structural funds is £500 million. I do not understand this. I may be misreading your table. I do not support the view that we would not have regional offices and regional assemblies but for the structural funds. You believe that, and you therefore believe that it is fair to charge as a cost to the structural funds in your calculation anything that a regional assembly or regional development agency does. Is that really fair?
Mr O'Brian: As has been pointed out in the report, and we make this very clear, clearly not all of those costs are to do with the structural funds. We do point out in the report that the problem is that we cannot find any data to disaggregate the cost of running the structural funds from the rest of those costs. On your second point, how this should be charged to them, the point I would make is that you cannot get rid of any of these structures if you continue to be in receipt of structural cohesion funds because you need this tier of regional government and it was indeed originally set up to administer the SCF.

Q67 ***Lord Kerr of Kinlochard:*** In order to come to your estimate of the costs of the structural funds, you need to assume that the British Government and the regions want rid of these things. It would then be perfectly fair to charge their costs as a charge to the structural funds, but there is no evidence that I know of that this British Government or any of these regional assemblies wish to commit suicide.
Mr O'Brian: Whether they wish to commit suicide is one point. The point is that you cannot get rid of that entire regional tier of government—

Q68 ***Lord Kerr of Kinlochard:*** You say that in your paper and you have repeated that. I am trying to establish whether it is fair to charge all the costs of the regional tier of government in the United Kingdom to the structural funds simply because the regional tier is used as a mechanism for administering the structural funds.
Mr O'Brian: We make it clear in the paper that you cannot do that. You cannot say that all that money is driven by SCF spending.

Q69 ***Chairman:*** This is a point of particular interest to the committee, the actual costs of administering the funds that come from the EU. I think you have just said that you could not manage to disaggregate them except in particular cases the Scottish Parliament. You have suggested that the structural funds in Scotland cost them £30.9 million.
Mr O'Brian: There are two pieces of data that it would be wonderful if this committee could find, which we were not able to find in the course of our investigation. The first is the disaggregated administrative costs for the regional agencies in terms of how much they spend running SCF versus other things. The second is of course an important cost which is not included in our figure and would be a very important part of the costs of running the structural funds and we have no data on at all. That is the cost to the recipients, because that is one of the largest costs, in complying with the EU's financial rules: for example holding records for 12 years, even if they are very small projects, and the costs of applying for the money. That is the most striking omission really from our report. When we spoke to participants in SCF spending, they were all very clear that they were spending a lot of their time and a lot of money trying to draw down these funds. We have no data on that amount of money.

Q70 ***Lord Kerr of Kinlochard:*** I noted you were not able to do that. I agree with you that there is a cost and it is not clear, but I am sorry, I think we need to be clear about your evidence. You appear to be saying now that you have used the costs of regional government as a proxy for the costs of the structural funds because you were unable to obtain data for the costs in the regions of administering the structural funds. Is that correct?
Mr O'Brian: Yes, that is what we say in the report.

Q71 ***Lord Kerr of Kinlochard:*** Can I also ask about the first level, the EU level costs, where you say correctly that there is a line in the EU Budget for administration of everything: the institutions, including the Commission with all its Directorates and so on, and it costs about 5 per cent of the EU Budget. It is a separate line. You then go up the budget until you come to the structural funds and you say let us assume that 5 per cent of structural fund expenditure is spent on the EU administration of the structural funds. Forgive me, that seems to me to be a big jump because there are only a couple of Directorates in the Commission which handle the structural funds; they are by no means the largest. There are a huge number of EU organisations which are funded from the administration line of the Budget. It seems to me that 5 per cent of the overall Budget going on administration does not mean that the costs of the very small number of people in Brussels who have the job of administering the structural funds must amount to 5 per cent of the size of the structural funds. I do not think it is the case: I think the extrapolation is a rather wild one.
Mr O'Brian: I am sure you are right and I absolutely agree with you that all the data could definitely be improved upon, and I hope that you will be bale to get better numbers than we had available. You say it is a wild one. You may well be correct that it is not right because, as we have made clear in the report, it is a ballpark calculation. We just had to assume that its percentage administrative costs are roughly the same as the rest of the EU spending. You may well be right that that is not correct.

Q72 ***Lord Kerr of Kinlochard:*** You cannot assume it. The structural fund is a tap through which a huge amount of money moves. If you take something like the Competition Directorate of the Commission, its only cost is administration. That is the only thing it does; it administers the competition laws. You are saying that because 5 per cent of the EU Budget as a whole is spent on administration, it is reasonable to assume that of the structural funds money, 5 per cent goes in administration. It is not true. Take the Common Agricultural Policy: huge amounts of money go through but a rather small number of people in Brussels administer it. This is in the same category; a rather small amount of people handle the structural funds. I think the extrapolation does not quite work. Could I also touch on the last layer you mention, which is the cost to central government. You say €100 million a year or just over is your central estimate, which you base on the fact that one department spends €10 million a year, it says according to you, on the European Social Fund administration. I would say, from my Whitehall experience, that you are overestimating it by at least by 100 per cent the costs for central government. The structural funds are not a major concern for central government precisely because the decision-taking has largely been devolved to regional governments and to Scotland and to Northern Ireland. These are the three elements that tot up to your £670 million a year. The first you admit is a proxy. The second is an extrapolation, which you are not really defending. The third I strongly suspect is an exaggeration. Do you really think it is wise to put round numbers as hard as £670 million a year as the UK cost of administering the Structural Funds when they are built on such an inadequate foundation?
Mr O'Brian: In answer to your first point about the costs of central government, we did ask parliamentary questions to all these departments and unfortunately several of them refused to answer. There is not much we can do about that if they will not provide the data. I hope that you will force them to answer in this committee because I am as keen as

you are to find the right number. You say it might be £50 million rather than £100 million. There is only one way of finding out and that is for this committee to get the numbers out of the departments, which we were unable to obtain. On the overall figure, as we make very clear in the report, all we are able to do is give you ballpark estimates, rough magnitudes. As I said before, you are right that there are good arguments for the various points you make, but then again there is a very large, if not the most significant cost, which is the fourth thing, the cost to recipients, which we do not have in there at all. The data is as good as one can get by not being in central government and not being able to get government departments to answer parliamentary questions. I hope that you will be able to improve on that.

Q73 ***Lord Watson of Richmond:*** Mr O'Brian, you have been on the receiving end of the so-called analytical dissection for which Lord Kerr is known and feared throughout the Civil Service.
Mr O'Brian: I always enjoy it.

Q74 ***Lord Watson of Richmond:*** It has been fascinating. I just want to report that I started to be puzzled by these figures, but I am now really startled that you provide this type of evidence. I really just wondered what your actual motive is. It is quite clear that you are saying that you cannot get disaggregated data. Nevertheless, you offer this enormous eye-catching sum and, as we have just seen, it clearly does not stand up. What is the purpose of this? If you are simply trying to provoke this committee to try and get its own answers, well, I am sure we will do our best, but it is a very strange way of approaching this.
Mr O'Brian: If our evidence provokes this committee to find its own number, I would be delighted and I think that would be a wonderful and satisfactory outcome to the process.

Q75 ***Lord Steinberg:*** I am afraid I am going to go on to the attack and the detailed figures and percentage points in them. I am referring to paragraph 1.11 in the written evidence which points out that in Northern Ireland £57.1 million or 11 per cent was allocated for the programme and yet Scotland, which has a population three times that of Northern Ireland, has got an allocation of £30.9 million. Those are the sums presumably that are allocated. My first question is: how much of that allocation has actually been spent? Secondly: do you trail it down, bearing in mind that there is now an Assembly again in Northern Ireland, yet the costs for the regional operation of the Northern Ireland Office have increased enormously and within the last year there have been 46 extra premises taken by the Northern Ireland Office? I know this is not directly related to some of the points we are talking about but it concerns me very much. You have accurate figures here. How far does the trail go and where do you stop?
Mr Persson: In all fairness, we have not looked into the devolved administrations that much in terms of—

Q76 ***Lord Steinberg:*** And yet you have exact figures here for allocations?
Mr O'Brian: We cite figures from a report that was released in Northern Ireland, so the figures are, I am sure, accurate.
Mr Persson: The Scottish figures are from the Scottish Parliament.

Q77 ***Lord Steinberg:*** Did you trail them any further than just taking figures from the report?
Mr Persson: We have not trailed them any further. Basically, we were still trying to get numbers from the English regions, which obviously was quite hard to do.

Q78 ***Lord Kerr of Kinlochard:*** Your source for the number of £57.1 million, from reading the footnote, is "PA, September 10, 2007". What is PA?
Mr Persson: Press Association.

Q79 ***Lord Kerr of Kinlochard:*** A report of what? The Press Association does not make up a number. They report somebody giving a number.
Mr Persson: The report came from one of the people involved in the Peace 2 programme.
Lord Kerr of Kinlochard: I am sorry but it will not do to tell us that this is a Press Association—

Q80 ***Chairman:*** Can we perhaps ask you to write about that as to where it came from?
Mr Persson: I can forward you the name and the title and the status of the person that reported that number. That is no problem at all.

Q81 ***Lord Steinberg:*** As you are dispensing this, can you tell us how much of the allocation has been spent?
Mr Persson: In Northern Ireland and Scotland?

Q82 ***Lord Steinberg:*** Yes?
Mr Persson: I am not sure. I know the overall number for the UK for 2000-2006 period is something like 83 per cent.
Chairman: We would be very grateful for a bit of writing on that too. I would now like to move on and ask Lord Haskins.

Q83 ***Lord Haskins:*** You give, as always happens in these cases, a number of examples of some exotic investments, up Vesuvius and such like, implying that this is the responsibility of the Commission in the EU for this waste of money. If there is waste of money there, and obviously there is to an extent, is that not more a reflection of national Member States and their attitude towards it? If you pursued the mood of subsidiarity, then you must, by the nature of things, give people at local level discretion over how that money is spent and to what might look to be—and obviously from a point of view in Vesuvius—quite meaningful to the people who live around Vesuvius. It is a problem for Member States rather than for the Commission.

Mr O'Brian: I expect Mats probably wants to answer that.

Mr Persson: First of all, the one does not necessarily have to exclude the other; that the projects are poorly targeted or that there is poor project selection can mean a number of things. As we have pointed out in the report, there are some fundamental flaws in the system that facilitate poor project selection. One would be that the funds are allocated at a level that is very far away from the recipients who are actually affected by the funds. A second point is the N + 2 rule, which means that there is enormous pressure on spending fast rather than spending wisely; you have to get the money out of the door. That could negatively impact the kind of projects that are being funded. Thirdly, we argue that there are complex EU regulations involved here that are specific to the EU level, which could deter particularly smaller projects; those projects that are in most need of the funds, that are struggling, that do not have the resources to absorb the cost involved in applying, these are the projects that could be neglected in the process. There are also regulations that limit the capacity of national, regional and local actors to apply for the funds. There are a number of issues here not specific to the EU level that, we argue, lead, in the extension, to poor project selection.

Mr O'Brian: One way of expressing that is to say that it manages to combine the worst effects of the top-down and bottom-up system because effectively you have large sums of money that have been allocated to a region burning a hole in the pocket of the people in charge of getting the money out of the door, so there is pressure to spend, which is a problem with top-down systems, and yet at the same time it is not a command and control system, so you need to find local people who will bid for the money. You have the kinds of problems you sometimes have with bottom-up systems.

Q84 ***Lord Haskins:*** That happens in national government here too.

Mr O'Brian: Absolutely, I agree with you that it is quite possible for national governments and local governments to make mistakes too. The question I pose is: is it more likely to make mistakes with the system we have at the moment which does clearly create pressure to spend the money? I think it is more likely that you will make mistakes and select bad projects, given that you have these problems with N + 2 and so on.

Mr Persson: This is not particularly an odd point to say that there is pressure to spend money fast. That has been pointed out in several different Member States. The Court of Auditors made that point very strongly, that this is a major flaw in the structure.

Q85 ***Lord Haskins:*** They may deplore all public expenditure right across the Commission; that happens in every Member State as far as I know?

Mr O'Brian: I think there is a particular problem here that you recognise.

Q86 ***Chairman:*** Can I ask you to comment on this? There is a recent report to the DTI from ODPM which found that over 80 per cent of the sample of stakeholders found structural fund programmes offered additional benefits compared to domestic ones, which rather goes against your point. Over half also thought they brought additional costs, which also follows your point, but that on balance the positive views seem to outweigh negative ones. They thought the structural funds did different things depending on your own national region.

Mr O'Brian: I think I would want to have a look at that report. What you are saying about there being additional costs and additional benefits sounded rather confusing. We do cite some polling data of recipients in our report as well, which found that by a margin of I think something like 60 per cent to 5 per cent people found the structural funds more difficult to deal with and more burdensome administratively than national policies. I think that kind of fair question is probably more reflective of the opinions of the recipients.

Q87 ***Chairman:*** Could we turn smartly to the future? To what extent do you consider the simplification in the 2007-2013 programme of the administrative processes together with the principle of proportionality would make some difference to the problems you identify?

Mr Persson: It would be interesting to know exactly what reforms you had in mind there. You mention the proportionality principle. What other reforms?

Mr O'Brian: There was a slew of different things that the UK and other Member States were trying to achieve in 2003. There were many different attempts to change the system slightly. I do not know if there is anything that you want us to focus on particularly.

Q88 ***Chairman:*** It is the self-certification on small projects and the minor but no doubt useful administrative reforms that we are after.

Mr Persson: On self-certification of projects, it is quite puzzling to try to find out exactly what type of reforms and what kind of practical difference they will make. If you talk to the people involved in the process, particularly the civil servants, they are not quite confident in talking about exactly what kind of practical difference this will make on the ground. In terms of simplification of the whole programme, I understand that the number of programme steps have been reduced. What that simply means is that, according to our understanding, the Government Office used to have to produce this report called a programme complement, and that has now been taken away. That document was intended, ahead of the last financial period, as a simplification, because in the mind of the Commission this would give the Government Offices, the regional actors, more ownership of the process. Obviously, as is the case with most of these types of EU reforms, it only led to more paperwork and additional administrative burdens. So they took that away. That is failed simplification. If you want to call it simplification, that is fair enough but it is not really going to do anything because it was just a failed reform to start with.
Mr O'Brian: I might also put it into the context that we do present rather a long table in our report of all the different steps involved in administering the SCF and it is a fiendishly complicated process. Whether the overall level of complexity has been significantly impacted by the reforms between the last period and this one, I do not really know. There were certainly some clear and good ideas. I think the UK Government did attempt to get a relaxation for small projects of the rules about holding accounting records for 12 years but I do not think they succeeded in getting that agreed or certainly if it was agreed, it was then reversed. There are things we can do to make the system slightly better but I am not sure whether this tinkering with reforms is really fundamentally going to change the problems with the administrative complexity and costs that we are identifying.
Mr Persson: In terms of the proportionality principle, I am not sure it applies. I think what you have in mind here is Article 74 of the Structural Funds Regulations.

Q89 ***Chairman:*** The administrative costs should be brought into line with the value of the project?
Mr Persson: Yes. Does that apply to the ESF for example? Does it apply to ERDF in England or the UK? I am not sure. I have been in touch with DWP, CLG and BERR and no-one has said that is going to have any effect in the UK in terms of programmes being able to opt out. This is not about projects; this is about the programmes. Our suggestion is that the opt-outs should be project-based and that there should be more focus on projects; they should be able to opt out if they are small enough. But the reforms have to do with programmes. They do not make any difference and they do not apply to the ESF. To my knowledge, they do not apply to the European Regional Development Fund either. Again, no-one knows, so we are not sure, but I am not confident that this will make any difference.
Chairman: I do not think we can take that any further. We are running out of time. I will ask Lord Watson to ask his question.

Q90 ***Lord Watson of Richmond:*** My question follows from Lord Haskins's question quite closely. You have highlighted the concerns of the European Court of Auditors over the substantial errors in reimbursement of structural fund projects, but as the day-to-day controls over these are actually the responsibility of the Member States and not of the Commission, could this failing really point far more directly into the procedures of the Member States than those of the Commission? Does it follow therefore, if that is the case, that repatriation of regional policy will not necessarily reduce the problem at all because the problems are at the Member State level rather than at the EU level? I think that is a relevant question.
Mr O'Brian: I thought the operative word in what you said, and basically I agree with what you are saying, is "necessarily". It is certainly true that if you were to continue to run the funds in exactly the same way by having to renationalise them, you would have many of the same problems. One of the interesting things is that if you are going to return overall regional policy to the UK or Member State level, you have the opportunity to do things in a fundamentally different way. For example, if you have, say, a targeted tax cut for a particularly deprived region, you do not have any of these problems with spending money; you do not have levels of administrative complexity. You sweep away all the problems.

Q91 ***Lord Watson of Richmond:*** I think, Mr O'Brian, what has become clear during your evidence is that really the main thrust of your attack is against regional policy *per se*.
Mr O'Brian: I would not agree with you on that.

Q92 ***Lord Watson of Richmond:*** Let me finish. Really the only regional policy in which you would be interested is regional policy which uses as its main mechanism tax relief and has as its main target relatively isolated bits of poverty. That is a totally legitimate position.
Mr O'Brian: Again, I think you are putting words in my mouth.

Q93 ***Lord Watson of Richmond:*** It seems a bit odd in terms of the criticism of what exists now.
Mr O'Brian: I do not agree with the way you are characterising my position. I think politically we will inevitably continue to spend money anyway with some kind of spending programmes, even if we did renationalise it. I think there may well even be a case for doing that. You will continue to spend money on project-based regeneration. I am not completely against that. I am saying that perhaps the balance between these things should change. I do not believe in no regional spending. Let us be fairly clear about that. I think the attraction of returning control of these things to Member States is that it allows you to explore these other options and, even if we do continue to have essentially project-based regional spending, I believe we could run it in a better way if we got rid of some of the problems that we have inherent in the SCF system.

Q94 ***Lord Watson of Richmond:*** Do you accept, because it is quite important to your argument, that repatriation is not in itself going to solve the major problems that you are concerned with?
Mr O'Brian: It gives you the opportunity to solve those problems. It does not necessarily solve them.

Q95 ***Lord Moser:*** So much of what we have been talking about ultimately depends on how you measure regional prosperity. I was rather struck and slightly surprised by how severely critical you are of the current measures which, as I understand it, is basically GDP per head. Your criticism seemed to be that GDP depends largely on GVA plus taxes and subsidies, et cetera. Supposing those are the poor measures. The measures that ONS, which I used to run, recommend as substitutes do not seem all that fundamentally different to me. You end up almost saying that the data are so poor that there is really no way of doing this thing properly on the ground, which is rather negative.
Mr Persson: Yes, it is rather negative but when you have a situation with a region, Lüneburg, outside Hamburg getting €900 million, although it is one of the wealthiest regions in Germany, then something is fundamentally flawed. If you mess a little bit with the measures and the last two regions end up in very different positions in terms of prosperity, then something is wrong and something needs to happen. It seems to us, without necessarily having the expertise in the area of statistics at that detailed level, that it would be more appropriate to have something that would measure, for example, the prosperity of the residents, so that wealth statistics would count towards the people who actually live there, rather than the workplace. That is a fundamental point. You do not have to be particularly involved in order to figure out that there is something flawed with these measures.
Mr O'Brian: I do not think it is one of the most negative things in the report really. Broadly speaking, looking at the academic literature, I think there is a fairly broad consensus that the measure could be improved on in a relatively simple way that would give you better targeting. Even if we did very little else in the way of reform, that is one area that we could pick off as relatively straightforward.

Q96 ***Lord Moser:*** I am all in favour of trying to improve the basis, but the way it reads, it almost ends up as if the thing is so unmeasurable, and you cannot end up like that unless you say "drop regional policy". What at the moment is your best recommendation for how to judge on the ground what should be used?
Mr O'Brian: I thought that the ONS proposal seems like the reasonable one. I think they make a good case.

Q97 ***Lord Moser:*** That still depends on GVA.
Mr O'Brian: But also you are bringing together a number of different measures rather than simply having one club, if you see what I mean.
Mr Persson: You have regional GVA per full-time employee, for example. That makes a difference. You can also bring in regional gross household disposable income, which is appropriate because, as you say and as has been pointed out, obviously one of the main things about the structural funds is that they are supposed to add value to public policies, and to us disposable income seems most appropriate for measuring if they in fact do. There is a main concern with measures because they have to be internationally comparatively and also internationally meaningful. As I understand it, household disposable income on the regional level is only available in nine Member States. So it would be very hard to change this while the structural funds are at the EU level. In extension, this would obviously be an argument for repatriation of the structural funds. I do not know if you have noticed, that is our main point.

Q98 ***Chairman:*** We need to stop, having exhausted both witnesses and ourselves. If I have managed not to let one of my colleagues ask a burning question, please do feel free. If we have not let you say anything which you are absolutely burning to say, please say it.
Mr Persson: I just want to make a general point, and we have pointed to this many times. And it is about the availability of data in terms of the structural funds, which is not the way it is supposed to be. I come from a culture of political transparency and this lack of availability is something that needs to be addressed immediately. In terms of value for

taxpayers' money and in terms of transparency, this is not acceptable. You have to be able to know where the funds are going. That is a fundamental criticism. You cannot spend half the year trying to figure out basic issues such as how much money goes to this particular area. One region in the UK holds detailed data on where the money is going in terms of postcodes. That is the South East Region and they have been the most accommodating. Even the central government is very unwilling to provide the information. This is something that I would challenge you to really pick up on and do something about.

Q99 ***Lord Kerr of Kinlochard:*** I think that is a very interesting admission of defeat. There are a number of statements in the evidence and in the press releases about the evidence which are, I think we have established, guesstimates; they are speculative. The list of horror stories is sourced to newspapers. I think one needs to be told facts rather than reports like I very much fear one will read perhaps in *The Mail on Sunday*, that £670 million must be the UK cost of running the structural funds because it is in "evidence" given to a House of Lords committee. I think this is very dangerous.

Mr O'Brian: Would you like a final statement from me? It will be very brief. I do not think for a second this is an admission of defeat. It is a challenge to you to go and find better data on all these different issues. I think the case we are making is a strong one, which is also the case which the UK Government makes and accepts. These issues will return, I am sure, when the next financial framework is negotiated. I think a good report from this Committee finding more data and challenging these points would be very welcome.

Chairman: Thank you very much.

TUESDAY 29 JANUARY 2008

Present	Cohen of Pimlico, B (Chairman)	Trimble, L
	Moser, L	Woolmer of Leeds, L

Examination of Witness

Witness: **Professor John Bachtler**, University of Strathclyde, examined.

Q100 ***Chairman:*** Professor Bachtler, it is good of you to come. May I say by way of introduction that the discussion is on the record. We are being recorded for webcast. You will receive a transcript of whatever is said during the session and you will have an opportunity to correct it. Thank you very much for coming. Would you prefer that we just started asking questions or is there a general opening statement you would like to make?
Professor Bachtler: I am happy for you to start asking questions.

Q101 ***Chairman:*** With the Chairman's prerogative, I will have the first warm-up question. What do you see as the major differences between the 2006–2013 and the earlier Structural Funds programmes in the areas of the allocation and disbursement of funds and the aims and objectives of Cohesion policy?
Professor Bachtler: In short, the geographical distribution of funding has shifted eastwards, and the thematic orientation of funding is apparently focusing much more on areas of research and development and entrepreneurship. Perhaps I could explain each of those in turn. Firstly, in terms of the spatial distribution of funding, clearly with the accession of much poorer Member States, the focus of the funds has moved very significantly to central and eastern European countries, although more than half of the funding is still being allocated to the old Member States, the EU-15. What has essentially happened is that the funding in the old Member States has gone down on average by about one-third. The degree of change varies from country to country. Ireland and Spain took very significant cut-backs, but overall the EU-15 change is just over one-third of a reduction. In the new Member States obviously the reverse has happened. There are very significant increases, a doubling of funding allocations overall, but again it has varied from country to country. Poland is of course the key country where over €60 billion is being spent; something like one-fifth of the whole Cohesion policy budget is going to Poland. A lot depends on what happens there. The way in which funding was allocated used the same formula as was used in 1999; it is called the Berlin formula, which essentially gives more money to the poorer countries, so there is an inverse relationship between allocation levels and GDP per head. However, that formula only applied in practice in the old Member States. If the Berlin formula had applied in the new Member States, then the Cohesion policy budget would not have been sufficient in order to provide the scale of allocations that the formula would have given those countries. What effectively happened was that a limit of just under 4 per cent of GNI [Gross National Income], as a measure of absorption capacity, as it was called, was used to limit the allocations to the new Member States. The reasoning there, apart from the cost, was that it would be difficult—

Q102 ***Lord Moser:*** That is 4 per cent of what?
Professor Bachtler: The figure of 4 per cent of national GNI, basically of national income, was the ceiling. The amount of money that was allocated in terms of Structural Cohesion funds to the new Member States in each country could not exceed just under 4 per cent of GNI because that was felt to be the maximum that these countries could absorb in terms of their institutional capacity and systems. As a result there were somewhat perverse outcomes in the sense that the richer countries like the Czech Republic received more per head in terms of funding and countries like Latvia received less. That was the main change in terms of the spatial allocation of funding. As in 1999 for the 2000–06 period, most of the funding was allocated to the poorest regions, those with a GDP per head of less than 75 per cent of the EU average. Whereas in the 2000-06 period, only selected regions outside the poorest parts of the EU were eligible for funding—those with higher unemployment rates for example—in the 2007–13 period the whole of the EU is eligible for funding, so not just the poorest regions but also areas outside the poorer parts of the EU. Outside the poorest regions, it is for national governments to decide where they want to focus the money in geographical terms. The second aspect of the changes in the allocation of funding relates to the thematic focus. The EU has tried to ensure that more funding is being allocated to what is called the Lisbon Agenda (basically the growth and jobs or competitiveness agenda of the EU). The way this has been done is to use rather a crude instrument or mechanism whereby a specified percentage of expenditure under the various Structural Fund programmes has to go to certain categories of spending, particularly areas such as research and development, the information society, entrepreneurship, these sorts of so-called

competitive-oriented areas of funding. It is difficult at this stage to be precise as to what the implications of this so-called "earmarking" mechanism are. According to European Commission figures, what is happening in the 2007–13 period is that the amount of money being spent on these so-called "Lisbon categories" is trebling; in other words, there is a three-fold increase in spending in areas like entrepreneurship, R&D and the information society, on the basis that these should be the priorities for the EU. In other words, to reinvigorate the EU economy, it is believed there is a need to focus on these areas. However, this statement carries a health warning because the European Commission is basing their estimate of spending allocations on what the Member States are saying in their programmes. The figures are effectively forecasts of where the Member States and regions are going to commit or spend the money. We cannot be certain of that spending until after the programme period is over. To a certain extent, there has been a bit of, shall we say, presentational classification of expenditure so that if Member States wanted to do what they were doing before, maybe focusing on certain areas of infrastructure or certain generic categories of business aid, they perhaps presented it as being more competitiveness-oriented. So there is a health warning there. Those are the main changes in terms of where the money is going.

Q103 ***Lord Woolmer of Leeds:*** Could you tell us how you think the Cohesion policy in the Union has worked to date? Has it been successful with regard to the Member States? It has now been going for quite a few years, about 20 years. What is your view about that?

Professor Bachtler: One of the problems with Cohesion policy is that it is so difficult to be definitive about what the successes or failures have been, at least in quantitative terms. If one looks at the evidence from evaluation and other research, one can see very mixed results. When the Commission presents its periodic reports on the effectiveness of the funding, it relies quite heavily on macro-economic models which have been used to project the impact of funding over the time. The Commission also uses *ex post* evaluations undertaken after the programme period is complete. Essentially, the Commission argues that if one looks back over the last 15 to 20 years one can see that there has been a narrowing of disparities between the poorest countries and the rest of the EU, and between the poorest regions and the rest of the EU. On the other hand, it is very difficult to be definitive as to what the contribution of Cohesion policy has been to that narrowing because there is a whole series of other factors, such as increased openness to trade and so on, that could play a part. If one goes down to the level of individual projects, if one goes out into the regions and one does evaluations on individual projects, reports show that there is a high degree of what is called additionality; in other words, that the EU funding has led to genuinely new things happening—additional employment being created and projects going ahead in a faster timescale or at a larger scale. The problem is aggregating up from the experience of individual programmes to the Member State level or to the EU level. If one tries to generalise across the research that has been undertaken, some of the assessments of the totality of research have concluded that Structural Funds have perhaps contributed an additional 0.5 per cent of GDP growth per year in the poorest parts of the EU and maybe between one and two million jobs during the 1990s. There is a big difference between one million and two million jobs, and again these are generalisations. There has also been a fair amount of criticism in the research that has been conducted. Indeed, some studies have found it very difficult to find clear evidence of impact. There are three factors which come through from all the research that has been undertaken as to the problems that there have been and the difficulty in being definitive. The first problem is that there has been an excessive focus on infrastructure, particularly during the 1990s, with insufficient attention being given to things like education and human capital; in other words, a focus on building the infrastructure but not necessarily giving enough attention to the demand side or those parts of the economy which would benefit from using infrastructure that is put in place. Secondly, a lot of emphasis has been put on attracting inward investment or attracting economic activity into the poorer regions and it has not always been the right sort of inward investment. Thirdly, and perhaps the most important factor, there has been insufficient attention given to what is called institutional capacity; in other words, having the administrative organisations and systems in place to be able to make best use of the money: to plan, to draw up good strategies, to ensure that the money is being spent in the right way, and also to ensure that the Structural Fund's spending is accompanied by other measures such as labour market reform or aspects of deregulation. Unfortunately, therefore it is very difficult to give a definitive answer to your question. One other difficulty is that a lot of the research relates to experience of Cohesion policy in the 1990s and it is only now that the European Commission is undertaking a major evaluation of the last period, 2000 to 2006. The experience of the most recent period may well change this somewhat mixed assessment that we are talking about. I have also been talking solely about the quantitative impacts. I can say a bit more about the added value, if necessary.

Q104 ***Chairman:*** It was occurring to me as you spoke whether you would support the use of funds to improve administrative capacity; ie to fund improvements in the public sector?

Professor Bachtler: Yes, I think that is absolutely critical. That is one of the key lessons that have been learnt from the last programme periods. Much more attention is being given to administrative capacity in the new Member States in this new period. One of the reasons it is so important is because a potential area of added value of the policy is improving governance. We can see that very clearly happening in countries like Poland right now, that the requirements of Cohesion policy in terms of audit, financial management, control, monitoring, public procurement, state aids, as well as environmental sustainability, gender quality and everything else, are actually forcing changes to domestic systems of policy, its design and governance; ie changes are going beyond Structural Funds to more general aspects of reform of public management and the way institutions operate.

Q105 ***Lord Moser:*** It is quite difficult. Structural Funds have so many purposes. It would be good to hear from you what you regard as the central focus objectives of the funds. It is a basic question and linked to that how things can be improved so that they can help Member States and regions to do even better. Then there is a question that you were beginning to touch on, I think: the way they are delivered, where they can be perhaps more performance-related, more friendly, et cetera. It is a basic question of what they are for and how they work. It is really back to basics.

Professor Bachtler: Historically, the central objective of Cohesion policy in the European jargon has been economic and social cohesion, by which is meant the reduction of economic and social disparities between regions. That has been pursued partly on the grounds of equity and on the grounds of solidarity, in particular because it has been recognised that the process of European integration has an unequal distribution of benefits and costs. Cohesion policy is partly trying to compensate for the costs of measures being taken for example to implement the single market programme to provide for the free movement of labour, capital and so on, or to compensate for the effect of competition policy restrictions on state aid. In the UK for, instance, we are much more constrained these days in terms of what we can provide in regard to our own domestic regional aid to firms in the poorer parts of the country. Cohesion policy has partly been seen as compensating for that, but its core purpose has been the reduction of socio-economic disparities. Looking at the way things are changing now and the way things are possibly going to change in the future, this reduction of disparities will continue to remain an important objective, particularly because of the big development gap between the EU-15, (the old Member States) and many of the new Member States, in particular countries like Latvia. One can see signs that the objectives of Cohesion policy are becoming more varied. In the Lisbon Treaty, alongside economic and social cohesion, there is now reference to territorial cohesion. This is a term which is much less clear and the term "territorial cohesion" is used in very different ways by different people, by different governments and different interest groups. Essentially what the European Commission and some Member States have argued is that the challenge of convergence, the challenge of economic development, is not restricted to economic and social issues. There is a whole variety of policy challenges in terms of spatial differences in educational opportunities, environment, transport, R&D and so on. Those challenges do not always lend themselves to policy action at the regional scale. Sometimes you need to work intra-regionally; sometimes you need to work locally. This is where the term territorial comes from because it is less specific to regions than the former objectives have been. What that broadening of the remit or objective may mean in practice is that the role of Cohesion policy becomes much more diffuse. The policy may become involved in a variety of policy areas, such as the ones that I outlined. One can see that already happening now whereby the current Cohesion policy is linked very much to the Lisbon Agenda which is very much about promoting growth and competitiveness across the whole of the EU. In its recent consultation exercise, the Commission has also proposed that Cohesion policy should have a role in addressing future challenges such as climate change or demographic issues, such as ageing or migration, energy security, these kinds of issues.

Q106 ***Lord Moser:*** The broad objective sounds a little bit like the way our politicians talk and I wrote down some of the words—the broad vision, solidarity, lessening disparity. That is all great, is it not, but you then you went on really to explain that now almost anything fits.

Professor Bachtler: Of course in political terms part of the rationale for this shift is to try to safeguard the future of Cohesion policy by making it more relevant to the core ambitions of the European Union, the core policy areas, those which are seen as important and to prevent it Cohesion policy only being seen as something for the poor. The aim is to ensure that Cohesion policy is not just of interest to central and eastern Europe, a sort of welfare policy, but that it is a policy that is relevant also for countries like the UK, the Netherlands, Sweden, Finland and so on and the other parts of the EU. This is part of the thinking, but there is also a policy logic behind it, because increasingly economic development challenges are very complex. If you are trying to address issues like innovation or productivity or sustainable development, you have to try to bring together a whole variety of policy areas to work together. The European Commission and some Member States see Cohesion policy as having a role here to try to make these different policy areas work together for the benefit of regions.

Q107 ***Lord Moser:*** Looked at from the point of view of the Member States and the regions, if you were the dictator in charge of it all, how could you make it more effective from the bottom up rather than from Brussels?

Professor Bachtler: Maybe I could answer that in two parts, firstly by saying what I think is wrong or what needs to change in terms of delivery system and then how it might be improved. Firstly, in terms of what needs to change one aspect is that there needs to be a far greater recognition of the diversity of economic development situations across the EU. The kinds of issues that are being addressed in countries like Poland and other new Member States are different from those in southern Europe, which are different in turn from those development challenges that we are addressing. Also, the way in which we go about regional development in countries like the UK is now quite different from when Structural Funds were first introduced and that needs to be recognised if one wants to find ways for the EU to create added value. Secondly, the system needs to have more flexibility. The seven-year planning periods for Cohesion policy provide predictability in terms of funding for regions of the Member States but they do also lock in regions and countries to plans that were designed at the start of the period. An example of that is the following. The 2000–2006 programmes were designed in 1998–99. In the early 2000s, there was an economic downturn. Many of the programmes had quite ambitious targets for promoting business investment, R&D and so on and they found it a real struggle to adapt their programmes to a new situation because the economic environment had changed. There needs to be more flexibility within the seven-year programme period to adapt. Thirdly, there needs to be less prescription. On the one hand, the top-down specification of EU objectives and themes helps to set an agenda—it provides focus, it can encourage changes in thinking among those new Member States and regions—but the way in which challenges like climate change in the future, demographic ageing, migration and so on are going to affect regions is very varied and unpredictable. There needs to be more scope for flexibility here. Lastly, in terms of what needs to change, I think much more emphasis needs to be placed on what one might call policy additionality or innovation; in other words, the EU funding being used to do something different or do something extra. Often it seems to me that in countries like the UK, Finland, the Netherlands, Sweden and so on—outside the poorest regions—the money is being recycled to a certain extent. Effectively EU money is being used to do much the same thing as national funding, providing bigger budgets or safeguarding budgets from being cut back. Essentially it is doing rather similar things. I think we need to find incentives for innovation, not just innovation in terms of R&D but innovation in doing something different in policy terms so that Cohesion policy can really bring added value. In terms of how one might go about that, one could say we need a smarter Cohesion policy, a smarter way of managing the policy; not just thinking about where the money goes and controlling where the money goes but providing almost a toolkit of policy support. This means having much clearer strategies at EU and Member State levels. To a certain extent, that is now happening with the national strategic reference frameworks. Of course financial resources are important but, as you said, Chairman, more emphasis needs to be placed on institutional development and the development of human capacity; in other words, support for systems and for people, help with designing better strategies, designing better programmes, managing expenditure and evaluating interventions. We also need to place much greater emphasis on knowledge transfer; in other words, the European Commission having a role to encourage an exchange of experience and learning about the kinds of policies and interventions that work and those that do not work. Particularly, as we try to deal with these challenges of encouraging innovation, productivity, responding to climate change and so on, there could be a far stronger role for the European Commission to improve the flows of knowledge across borders. Lastly, there is a need for Cohesion policy to promote co-ordination. At the moment we have different funds: we have the European Regional Development Fund and the European Social Fund as the main Structural Funds. We then have a Rural Development Fund, but that is under the heading of the Common Agricultural Policy. There are then other policy areas that also have spatially-oriented or regionally-oriented programmes, such as under R&D policy. There is a real need to co-ordinate these instruments and policy areas much more. In improving policy management we need more strategic vision; of course we need financial resources but we need institution building, human capacity development, knowledge transfer and co-ordination. Those are the areas for improving effectiveness in my view.

Chairman: That is just for a start! I would now like to switch track and ask Lord Trimble to ask you about subsidiarity.

Q108 ***Lord Trimble:*** That comes up when thinking about what you were saying on territorial cohesion, taking the funds in a different direction. Do the funds, particularly with regard to that, meet the principle of subsidiarity?

Professor Bachtler: That is a good question. The starting point is whether you believe or not that the European Union has a valid role in the field of regional policy. If that is accepted, then I would say that in many respects Cohesion policy is one of the most decentralised policies that the European Union has. The European Union uses the term "shared management", meaning that Cohesion policy is a shared responsibility between the European level, Member State level and sub-national level. There is a range of partnership approaches. The degree to which certain functions ought to be exercised at European level or Member State level is really at the heart of your question. The problem is that the European Commission has responsibilities that it needs to discharge to the Council the European Parliament and the Court of Auditors in terms of accounting for how Cohesion policy money is spent, whereas a lot of the decisions about how the money is spent and used are taken at Member State level. If one looks back at the last 15 to 20 years, there has been a constant struggle between the European and Member State level with Member States saying that far too many decisions are being taken in Brussels, that there are far too many constraints and we need more subsidiarity; on the other hand, the Commission says that it has to have some mechanism to ensure that the decisions taken at European level, and the objectives set for the policy, are met. The trend over the recent period has been in the direction of more subsidiarity; in fact, the Commission probably has less influence now than it has had since the reform of the Structural Funds in 1988. Now, the Commission role is focused on laying down strategic guidelines. Member States have drawn up national strategic reference frameworks as to how those guidelines are going to be translated, and then the operational programmes are being implemented. That framework may be appropriate for a country like the UK with very well developed regional policies and other institutional systems of policy management and implementation. I would question whether subsidiarity has gone too far in the case of a country like Poland because there, if you talk to European and Commission officials who are responsible for overseeing the way in which €60 billion (£40 billion) is being spent, they have really quite limited information to be able to determine whether that money is being spent effectively or not because the accountability requirements in terms of the strategic decisions are much less in this period. The main mechanism by which the European Commission can hold Member States to account is through the monitoring system, through the financial control and audit system, which is not particularly satisfactory because a lot of the controls are effectively after the event. The degree to which there is too much or too little subsidiary varies depending which Member State one is talking about.

Q109 ***Lord Trimble:*** If over the last number of years the emphasis has shifted more from the Commission level to Member State level that then raises a question which some people have put to us by saying that what should really happen is that these funds should be repatriated to the Member States or the distribution of these funds should be repatriated to Member States. What are your views on that?

Professor Bachtler: Repatriation is a term I have some difficulty with. It sounds fine in principle but if one assumes that there is a rationale for a Cohesion policy at the European level and one wants those Cohesion policy objectives followed through, not just in countries like Poland but in countries like the UK and Finland, and one then gives the funding or one allocates the funding to the Member State level to spend, the question is: what guarantees does one have that that funding is going to be spent on EU objectives rather than national objectives, or even on national regional policy objectives as opposed to any other national objectives? There is a question of how one ensures that if one does repatriate, if you like, the funding, then EU objectives which have been agreed by Member States are met. Having said that, I think one could imagine quite a different system from one at the moment whereby instead of the European Union effectively determining funding for regions, essentially the system were to be simplified. You could allocate the funding to Member States based on some formula, say based on GDP per head, and then it would be the responsibility of the Member State to implement programmes or funding through its own strategies. If one were to go down that route the key issue would be to build in some sort of mechanism whereby there was accountability to the European Union; for example, some sort of contract between the Member State and the European Union defining certain outcomes that the Member State would aim to meet in terms of aspects of innovation or employment.

Q110 ***Lord Trimble:*** In view of what you were saying in reply to earlier questions about the way in which there are different problems in different areas and problems about governance in eastern Europe and a different set of problems in southern Europe, would it not then make sense to move in the way that you have suggested? What you then have is not just an allocation of money to that Member State but also, as it were, a negotiation between the Member State and the Union generally as to what should be the priorities for that Member State in terms of the things it is going to tackle, whether it is questions of governance or human capital or economic competitiveness or whatever, rather than to operate in the present regime? That is the direction your mind is going in, I take it.

Professor Bachtler: I would say that is certainly a valid argument because, as you say, there are these big differences. What would be possibly a more effective route would be to say that the task of the Cohesion policy is to strengthen support to national regional policies; in other words, to assist the national regional policies to work better. If you go back to that toolkit that I was talking about earlier, in different countries you have different combinations of money, institution building, human capital development, co-ordination, knowledge transfer and so on. Therefore, you could adapt the mix of support mechanisms from the European level to suit each country's particular needs. One important benefit of that is that it would almost "liberate" the European Commission from one of its current problems, which is that the Directorate-General for Regional Policy is horrendously overloaded and under-staffed in order to deal with the task of supervising and monitoring this enormous number of programmes and is essentially focusing very heavily on the monitoring of expenditure—in other words, how the money is being spent—rather than how well is the money being spent. Having a different system focusing on the Member State level would allow it also to deploy the available resources to make a more substantive policy input to regional policies.

Q111 ***Lord Trimble:*** One other thing comes to my mind on subsidiarity. We have been talking about subsidiarity as between Commission level and national government level. There is then the question of regions within Member States. Is there not a problem in that, particularly with some of the new Member States, they are so small that they are effectively just regions themselves, like Latvia which you have mentioned, whereas Poland will presumably have regions within it and then the larger existing Member States will have regions within them? Is this a problem? What do you think about that?

Professor Bachtler: It is not a huge problem but it varies from Member State to Member State. As you say, Poland in fact is the only central and eastern European country that actually has regions in terms of having an elected regional level of government. The other Member States, the larger ones like the Czech Republic, Hungary and Slovak Republic, have regions but essentially, a bit like in England, they have regional development agencies which are accountable to central government or regional councils made up of local authority representatives and so on. The regions over which Structural Funds operate in, say, the Czech Republic, do not accord with the natural regional sub-divisions of the country, so there is an element of artificiality in terms of the way in which regional policy is being allocated. You are quite right that in countries like Latvia or Slovenia the country is a region, if you like, on the "map of Europe". I think it is a valid objective of Cohesion policy now and in the future to promote the involvement of sub-national partners in the Cohesion policy process but in a way that suits each particular country. In the UK (and not just in the UK because I think the same would apply to countries like Finland, Sweden, France to a certain extent, the Netherlands and Italy) Cohesion policy has played an important role in encouraging the development of a local or regional level of competence and in encouraging the development of regional institutions that are able to take a strategic approach to regional needs. One can see that the way in which regionalisation has developed in the United Kingdom, particularly in England, is partly a consequence of the role of the Cohesion policy.

Q112 ***Lord Woolmer of Leeds:*** Before I turn to the question of the proportion of the Budget allocated to Structural Funds, in his evidence to us the Minister for Competitiveness in the Department of Business Enterprise and Regulatory Reform said a couple of things. One of them is in paragraph 10, which you will not have but I will tell you what he said. "The Integrated Guidelines for Jobs and growth and National Reform Programmes", agreed at EU level, "set out the key challenges that the EU, Member States and regions . . . There is no need for a separate set of challenges to be identified for Cohesion policy. Instead, the task is to identify how Cohesion policy can support Member States' polices . . . . Where money is needed to achieve Cohesion policy objectives it should mainly come from national, regional and local sources. EU funding support for Cohesion policy needs to be better focussed on the poorer Member States . . . " Is that not effectively saying that at EU level policy needs to stick to doing something about real inequalities between Member States and that the other issues are really things that all the Member States should be getting on with and the agreed policies and so on across the EU really are not the purpose or substance of Cohesion policies. Effectively, in terms of additionality and added value and so on, it is saying that there is a danger that the EU may be getting into things that they should not be getting into.

Professor Bachtler: As you say, I have not seen the letter. It seems to me that what is happening in the current period is, to a certain extent, what the Minister is advocating because the current Cohesion policy objectives—in the way that they are set out in the Commission's Integrated Guidelines and thus in national strategic reference frameworks—flow pretty much directly from the integrated strategy on growth and jobs the so-called Lisbon Agenda, or at least that is the way it has been designed, and not just in the area of Cohesion Policy; the Guidelines for rural development and fisheries and other areas as well also flow from there. Secondly, I agree very much that the focus should be on regional inequalities. Something like 80 per cent of Cohesion policy funding is going to the poorest countries and the poorest regions. Of course the problem with the UK line from the EU perspective—and this is something that the new Member States are very aware of and alive to—is that if you say that Cohesion policy is essentially a policy for the poor, it becomes a sort of welfare policy. What happens is that the richer countries are not going to have an interest in that policy area, apart from cutting down the size of the bill; in other words, the share of the EU budgetary cake allocated to Cohesion policy. What the European Commission, supported by quite a number of Member States, has sought to do is to ensure that Cohesion policy is not just for the poor; although 80 per cent of the funding is going to the poor, the rest is going to other Member States and other regions in order to ensure that they continue to have an interest in the policy and thus safeguard it in the longer term. The European Commission of course—in its arguments or its initial thinking about the future of the policy—is trying to continue to link what Cohesion policy does in future to the coming major challenges that the EU is going to have to address, such as (currently) growth and jobs, but in the future possibly climate change, demographic issues and other challenges. I can understand where the UK is coming from on this.

Q113 ***Lord Woolmer of Leeds:*** Before I move on to the question of the proportion of the Budget, I must say that that is the first time I have heard argued that policy should not simply concentrate on reducing the inequalities between Member States because the rich Member States would regard that as just helping the poor and then they might not want to do it, if I summarise what you have said. I have never heard that argued. Therefore, even rich Member States have got to have some because then they will take an interest. That is effectively, again paraphrasing what you think, what some people would argue. I have to say that I have not heard that argument but other members of the committee might have done. Can I turn finally to the question of the criteria to guide decisions on the proportion of the Budget to be allocated to Structural Funds, and again this is a quote by the Minister in his letter to us. He said: "The priority is to ensure that the review of the EU Budget provides the basis for a more effective and efficient Budget, including a significant increase in the percentage of Structural and Cohesion funds spent on poorer Member States." The Minister told us that was an issue, and I do not argue about the proportion which is all right but it is not just an issue about proportion; it is the fact that money should really go where it is most needed. What do you think about the guidelines on the proportion of the Budget? Is that not related to what the money is being used for? We could hardly argue for a bigger proportion if it is going to go to rich countries.

Professor Bachtler: No. The argument that I put forward or the way I outlined the European Commission's thinking is essentially a political argument. A few months ago *The Economist* had a very nice way of putting the point that you made in quite blunt terms. However, although it is a political argument the approach to Cohesion policy is not unique. The way that the German national regional policy system works is not dissimilar; it is basically to try and keep all parts of the country in the regional policy system. Ultimately, the development of the policy, the amount of money that is spent in the EU Budget and the sub-division within the Budget among different policy areas is a political decision. At the moment Cohesion policy has an important role to play in the equation because it is the mechanism by which countries are able to determine how much money they are going to get back out of the EU Budget. Of course for the UK that is not unimportant and similarly that is true for other countries. It is of course entirely valid for the UK to push a line which will ensure that its interests are maximised. It is very difficult to say how things are going to develop in the future. The European Commission's budget review is quite clear, at least in its ambitions. It wants to ensure that there is a real added value in the policies and the spending that it has in the future, and its review of policy areas has been undertaken with that in mind. With increasing priority being given to competitiveness issues at European and national levels, there must be a strong likelihood of a strengthening so-called competitiveness policies: spending on R&D, trans-European networks, life and learning, these sorts of things, will increase as a share of the Budget in the future. There will be strong pressures for agricultural spending to go down, partly because of pressures from the WTO in terms of the coming negotiations there. There will be huge resistance, and not just from France which is generally portrayed as the defender of the Common Agricultural Policy, but it is very likely that agricultural spending will fall and that Cohesion policy will continue to be the "adjustment variable", in the future budgetary debate—unless it is possible somehow to disconnect the debate on the Budget from the debate on policy, which is quite difficult to perceive at the moment. As I have said a couple of times, Cohesion policy is trying to reinvent itself in the way that it operates in order to try to command the support of the richer Member States.

Q114 *Chairman:* As a supplementary to that, and you have mentioned climate change a couple of times, I suppose I have really given up thinking that Cohesion policy had really anything to do with climate change because it cannot; it is too big. Can I press you a little on that or do you think this is all part of making Cohesion policy more acceptable to put an emphasis on climate change?

Professor Bachtler: That is quite a difficult one. As a starting point, one would ask what regional policy has to do with climate change. There are other policies which one would imagine are more relevant. However, if one thinks what the consequences of climate change are likely to be, they are going to be territorially quite different across the European Union. The effect of rising temperatures is going to bring real problems for agriculture in southern Europe, and for other parts of the EU there may be more turbulent weather conditions: concentrated rainfall and storms. We have already seen over the last year the problems that flooding has brought to parts of the UK. There is a whole new challenge of risk management associated with rising sea levels and weather patterns. One could see different ways in which the EU might respond under the heading of Cohesion policy. The classic response would be to have a climate change programme for countries and regions and to design strategies and so on to respond to that. However, if one thinks about it in a different way, one could say that climate change will have territorially quite different impacts, but climate change is just one of a whole series of challenges which is going to affect regions over the coming years. So maybe what Cohesion policy should be doing is trying to strengthen the capacity of regions to deal with economic development challenges of a whole variety of types in areas like building up and helping institutional capacity, providing targeted funding perhaps where it is needed—essentially taking a bottom-up approach. It is interesting that a number of English regions have started to develop regional climate change strategies. Essentially they are asking what the consequences are going to be for, say, the East Midlands or for East Anglia as a result of climate change, such as a rise in temperatures or variability of climatic events, and what it is that they need to be doing. It is when you get down to that very specific level of what the impact is going to be on one or other region and what it is that is needed in terms of policy support, then one can think about what it is that the European Union could usefully do, if anything, to support national efforts in this area. In my view, that is the line of argument that one should be taking.

Q115 *Lord Trimble:* I ask your view of the current tests for the eligibility of regions to receive support under Structural Funds and do you think they should remain in place the way they are?

Professor Bachtler: The main eligibility test is of course gross domestic product per head, GDP per capita. It is a relatively crude instrument and its measurement has a whole variety of problems. A bit like democracy, it is the least worst option. There has been a lot of discussion about using other criteria, but GDP does encapsulate a lot of what one is trying to do through regional policy and through Cohesion policy. In practical terms, the issue is two-fold. Looking to the future at the European level, one can continue to say that we should have this cut-off point or threshold, for defining poor regions; as now, where a region has less than 75 per cent of the EU average of GDP per head then it is defined as a poor region and it should receive support. However when the current eligibility map for 2000-06 was drawn up, it was on the basis of an EU 25, excluding Bulgaria and Romania. If one factors in Bulgaria and Romania now and one thinks about what a map of an EU 27 would look like, straight away it starts to shift the relative eligibility position of individual regions. Similarly if one factors in relative growth rates and looks at the regional trajectories in terms of GDP in the future. If the eligibility decision on the next period is being made in 2010 or 2011 (enlargement is probably not going to be an issue apart from Croatia but let us take that as a scenario), one would find that virtually all the eligible regions would be in central and eastern Europe, some in Portugal and a few in other parts of the EU-15, (the old Member States). Cohesion policy would become pretty much *de facto* something that is of interest to the new Member States and not to the old Member States and that straight away changes the political configuration of countries that would have an interest or not in the policy.

Q116 *Lord Trimble:* The present criteria, as you say, are essentially economic. A lot of discussion earlier on added value was looking at things which were not directly economic in terms of governance and human capacity. Are there any criteria that can reflect those or other things which would be regarded as significant added value or would bringing in a weighting for that just accelerate the tendency to focus on central and eastern Europe?

Professor Bachtler: What happens at the moment is that there are two levels of calculation for allocating funding. The first stage is to decide the regions that are eligible through the 75 per cent GDP per head criterion. The second stage is then to decide how much money should go to each of those eligible regions. At the moment that is principally based on GDP per head but it also factors in criteria like national unemployment rates and then, as part of the political bargaining, a whole series of other little adjustments are made in order that the countries get the level of support they want. The problem, if one goes beyond GDP at an EU level, is that one does not have comparable data that are reliable enough at a sub-national level in order to be able to factor it in to the eligibility calculations. You have regional unemployment rates or regional employment trends which one could factor in, and they are taken into account to a certain extent. Unless somebody does come up with something imaginative, one probably will continue to use a criterion which has now lasted for 20 years—it is probably one of the only things that all Member States have actually agreed on. If one then finds that the regions that one wants to designate for the provision of aid do not fall into the category of eligibility, one would need to make adjustments, for example by building in some transitional support for regions between 75 and 85 per cent or 75 and 100 per cent (of average EU GDP per head). Having defined those regions (or if one allocated funding at a national level, defined the aid that is going to the Member State), then within the country or region, one would look at where it is that we should be spending our money and to what extent we should be putting it into institutional capacity development as well as into areas like infrastructure, business aid and so on.

Chairman: Thank you very much, Mr Bachtler. We have kept you rather longer than I meant to but we have found your evidence most illuminating. Thank you very much indeed for coming.

Memorandum by Professor John Bachtler

Following the evidence session, the Committee asked:

What would you introduce if the Funds did not exist and you were designing the Funds from scratch today?

If the Funds were being designed from scratch, the emphasis would have to be on rationalising and simplifying the current approach, in two main ways.

First, a more coordinated and coherent approach would be required, avoiding the split between two different Funds under Cohesion policy and a third (rural development) under the CAP, each with separate regulations and administrative requirements. One Fund per objective could be a starting point.

Second, much of the complexity of Structural Funds arises from the separate implementation requirements for Cohesion policy, especially in the fields of financial management and control and audit, due to the Commission's obligation to be accountable for EU spending. This leads, for example, to multiple levels of audit for individual programmes. Despite this, the Commission has to take criticism for spending irregularities which are primarily caused at Member State level. There is a need to re-examine the accountability for Cohesion policy spending and reliance on the use of Member State administrative systems wherever possible, where these can be shown to be sufficiently reliable to meet EU requirements.

25 February 2008

TUESDAY 19 FEBRUARY 2008

Present	Cohen of Pimlico, B (Chairman)	Renton of Mount Harry, L
	Maclennan of Rogart, L	Woolmer of Leeds, L

Memorandum by Keith Boyfield, Keith Boyfield Associates

It came as a surprise to me when writing *Eutopia: What EU would be best and how do we achieve it?*[1] which I co-authored with Tim Ambler of the London Business School, to discover just how large a proportion of the overall EU budget was accounted for by regional funding of one sort or another. Along with the CAP, structural funding represents by far the largest slice of EU expenditure over the seven year time period 2007–13. Following enlargement of the EU to 27 member states, competition for these funds will become even more intense.

1. *What should be the objective of the EU's Structural Funds? How can the Funds become more effective in supporting public policies in Member States and regions? What mechanisms of delivery could make the policy more performance-based and more user-friendly?*

This question assumes at the outset that EU Structural Funds are a good idea. In our *Eutopia* study (see above) Tim Ambler and I questioned the whole purpose of structural funding. Essentially, this policy goal is open to the criticism that it is bribing citizens of the EU with their own money. As we observed, a great deal of waste and fraud with regard to the EU budget could be saved if funds were not being sent to Brussels and back again. We argue that it makes more sense for individual member states to apply their own funds to agreed EU programmes. Only surpluses or shortfalls should move into and out of Brussels. Furthermore, it makes far more sense for wealthier member states to address economic development in their own economically troubled regions.

However, there may be a good case for the EU supporting economic development in certain accession states. But it would be wiser to do so on a specific, targeted basis and not one that involves supporting economic development in relatively wealthy member states.

2. *Do structural funds meet the principle of subsidiarity? Could the same cohesion objectives be met through repatriation of the distribution of these funds?*

Subsidiarity can be defined as the right of any member state to legislate in any area not specifically reserved for the EU. Structural funds essentially act as an additional source of funding to support regional development in various parts of the EU. As such, they serve as "bolt-on extras" to the funding already available from national governments and the private sector. In terms of subsidiarity, EU structural funding represents an alternative source of funding, which can raise tensions with member state governments. What is more, there is every incentive for regional governments of one form and another to apply for these EU structural funds, particularly where their goals may be at odds with their own central governments. When one visits Brussels these days, one is struck by the profusion of representative offices housing the representatives of various EU regions: Scotland, Wales, Greater London Authority, Bavaria, Liguria, Catalonia, etc. Economists might refer to this as "rent-seeking behaviour". In practice, European regions are lobbying for as much of the available European Structural Funds as possible. This lobbying activity can be expensive and wasteful; it can also trigger tensions with other regions and member state governments.

As argued in my response to the first question, I believe it makes more sense for member states to address their own regional development issues. Accordingly, I would support moves to repatriate the distribution of regional funding, albeit such a move might well provoke resistance from regions within the EU that have poor relations with their own member state government. This is a crucial political point that appears to have been overlooked by many in the past.

[1] Published by the Adam Smith Institute in 2006.

3. *What impact has enlargement had on Structural Funds, and are any changes necessary to meet the challenges of further enlargement?*

Enlargement has made competition for structural funds considerably tougher. The fact that many accession states have lower GDP per capita figures than the EU 15 also adds to the demand for greater structural funding.

Moves to further enlarge the EU will only add to these demands for larger expenditure on regional development. When deciding on whether to enlarge the EU, existing member states and their citizens will need to recognise these pressures. Those who believe the purpose of the EU is to act as a catalyst for greater economic prosperity across Europe will be relatively relaxed about these implications, but suffice to say that the EU has not always been perceived as an engine that drives economic prosperity. Those who question the purpose of the EU and its role in creating greater wealth will inevitably be suspicious about moves to expand the EU and spend higher amounts of taxpayers' money on regional development schemes in the remoter parts of Europe.

4. *How will the EU's commitments on combating climate change manifest themselves in the distribution of Structural Funds for the post-2013 period? How will the response to other challenges facing the EU economy (eg migration, growth of the service sector) shape future policies?*

As yet I have not undertaken any study of the EU's commitments to combat climate change and their influence on expenditure in the post 2013 period, so it is better that I make no response to this question at the moment. As for other challenges facing the EU economy in the post 2013 period, one could write several books and still not adequately answer the issues involved. One point is worth highlighting however: the primary aim of the EU is to establish a single market in goods and services. Fifty years after the EU was first established, it remains the case that the goal of a common market remains some way off, particularly in the area of services.

5. *What criteria should guide decisions on the proportion of the EU budget to be allocated to Structural Funds?*

As set out in my answer to the first and second questions, I remain sceptical as to whether regional funding by the EU is a good thing in the first place, particularly where it involves financial support in relatively wealthy member states. I believe EU regional funding should be fundamentally overhauled and reduced, targeting schemes that may have merit in the poorer accession states.

The EU budget process is excessively lengthy and complex. It invariably ends up being resolved in one last minute summit where decisions on matters of huge importance are often taken in the early hours of the night and as part of some complicated, Byzantine horse-trading session.

It must also be pointed out that the EU budget making process involves setting ceilings in terms of individual member states' GDPs. Since the ceilings are set way ahead of actual expenditure, and since it remains uncertain what rate of economic growth individual member states will enjoy, the whole process is seriously flawed. What is more, the Commission fails to spend the annual amount it is given (In 2001 it was left with a surplus of €15 billion, €7.4 billion in 2002, €5.5 billion in 2003 and €2.7 billion in 2004).[2]

6. *Are the relative eligibility tests for regions to receive support under the EU's Structural Funds relevant, fair and appropriate? Should they remain in place after 2013? Is it appropriate that they are discussed simultaneously with wider agreements on allocating EU budget spending?*

As yet I have not undertaken any detailed study of these eligibility tests so I would prefer to miss out a response to this question. I suspect that these tests are discussed simultaneously with wider agreements on allocating EU budget spending as part of the horse-trading that characterises spending by the EU throughout Europe. Those member states that receive relatively little by way of funding will inevitably complain; those that do relatively well will support the process.

[2] *Eutopia: What EU would be best and how do we achieve it?* Adam Smith Institute, 2006, page 36.

7. *What would be the effect of linking the availability of Structural Funds with compliance to Broad Economic Policy Guidelines?*

In a word, salutary.

9 January 2008

Examination of Witnesses

Witnesses: Mr Keith Boyfield and Ms Florenica Ahumada Segura, Keith Boyfield Associates; and Dr Robert Leonardi, London School of Economics, examined.

Q117 *Chairman:* Good morning. First let me say that we are broadcasting. You will get a transcript of everything you have said to have a look at and comment on, but it is all being recorded. What I would like to ask—and there are three of you—is if anybody would like to make an opening statement we would be glad; or if you would rather just sit and we will start on questions that would also work. We would hope to let you go by about 11.40. Who, if anyone, would like to start?

Mr Boyfield: I would like to make a general statement about why I first became interested in this subject. I go to Brussels quite a lot and I have to declare an interest. I do work for the European Commission—an excellent organisation—for their Competition Directorate and Transport Directorate. I also write for the *Wall Street Journal*, whose main offices are in Brussels. When I go on my visits to Brussels I have been very struck by the number of representational offices of EU regions and I think to myself why is this? Then a couple of years ago when I wrote *Eutopia*, published by the Adam Smith Institute—and I wrote that with Tim Ambler of the London Business School—I was surprised, I have to say, to discover that 35 per cent of the EU's budget is channelled into regional development aid—I was quite surprised at that. I was also interested in this whole general trend towards the emergence of city states; the world is becoming more and more like Renaissance Italy, dominated by cities like Florence, Venice, Genoa. I think that London and New York have far more in common with each other; and the people who work there tend to work for the same sorts of firms, go to the same sorts of restaurants, shop at the same sorts of shops, and often criss-cross the Atlantic and spend much more time with each other than they do, for example, with people in the north-west of England, which is my home region. Similarly, people in New York feel more at home in London than in Wichita, Kansas. It also makes me think that there is an analogy with soccer—and I will be brief about this. Increasingly, people seem to support major soccer teams and it is a global market place, so people are supporting Manchester United, Inter Milan, Real Madrid—they get their talent from all over the world. The people who support England or Wales, I am told, tend to be the people who support Brentford or Millwall because those teams tend not to win so much. So you will see increasingly a dominance of city states. Then it also made me think—and this is probably the last thing I should say—about the EU's budget and how it is being spent on regional aid for many laudable reasons. It is often said that Brussels is a centralising influence, but I think there is an interesting argument to suggest that this regional development funding is acting as an encouragement, if not a catalyst, for the increased fracturing of Europe, by-passing the nation state. In areas like Catalonia and the Basque country it will be interesting to see how the money is spent there. That is why Florenica, my colleague, who speaks fluent Spanish and Italian, is helping me on this. We are also interested to see how the regional development funding is working in places like Scotland, which of course is keen on taking a much more independent line; and a whole host of other places like Belgium where the Flemish, as I understand it, are increasingly seeking to plough their own furrow. The last thing I would say is that we are not the Delphic Oracle; we have not come with a battery of statistics and we are really just earnest seekers after truth. So that is my general statement.

Q118 *Chairman:* Thank you. Dr Leonardi.

Dr Leonardi: Could I add to that? I teach at the London School of Economics and this term I am teaching a course on the social and economic cohesion policy of the European Union, so therefore I follow very closely what is happening throughout the EU. One thing that needs to be established here is that the Cohesion Policy or the Regional Development Fund and the European Social Fund, which are the primary funding bodies, concentrate this funding in the less developed areas. At the present time 81 per cent of the cohesion budget is concentrated in the convergence areas—that is, Central and Eastern Europe, bits of Greece, bits of Italy, bits of Spain and bits of Portugal. Therefore, we do not have an equal distribution of the funding. In the non-convergence or the ex-Objective 1 regions there is very little money that is provided, but the cohesion policy has had a very important impact in leveraging private funding; therefore this is one of the main elements why the non-convergence regions would like to continue with the cohesion policy because it is a very strong stimulus for the mobilisation of private investment. So usually the relationship is one to five, one to six in terms of EU funding and building on that, because there is this idea that if the funds come from the EU they are first predictable—you know that they are there, they are not going to disappear from one budgetary year to another; secondly, they are going to have strong controls, therefore it is difficult to misuse the money; thirdly, it is money that is seen as oriented to economic restructuring and therefore it has a positive impact; fourthly, it allows a certain amount of multi-level governance, that is with the participation of the private sector, regions, national funding and European funding, so therefore this creates a much greater European feel. This is something that is not just locally oriented but it has a European focus to it.

Q119 ***Chairman:*** Thank you very much. This has strayed promptly into the territory of question one, which is about how successful the cohesion policy from 1988 to date has been with regard to all the Member States. Let me remind myself, the convergence funds go to people whose income is less than 75 per cent of the average of EU GDP per head?
Dr Leonardi: Right.

Q120 ***Chairman:*** Your point is really that as well as the 81 per cent of people whose GDP is less than 75 per cent of the EU national average, that even people in the regions with GDP above that level regard these funds as very important?
Dr Leonardi: Yes.

Q121 ***Chairman:*** Because they are secure, cannot be taken away and are generally European.
Dr Leonardi: Yes.
Mr Boyfield: Could I just add something there?

Q122 ***Chairman:*** Of course.
Mr Boyfield: I suppose they would hardly refuse this largesse from Brussels. I entirely take into account what Robert has been saying about how you can leverage this funding with private sector funding, and this might well be a very good thing, but it strikes me that the picture is mixed. If I might just quote a couple of sentences from the OECD Economic Survey of the EU—and you might well have seen this already—it came out in September 2007, they say of the regional development cohesion policy: "Its record so far has been patchy: regional disparities are not falling . . . "—I would be interested to hear what Robert has to say about that—" . . . "or at best are declining very slowly. The budget is too small to make a real dent in income gaps, so the challenge is to get the maximum benefit from the available funds by making sure Member States focus on activities that will spark sustainable growth, such as education, research and important infrastructure projects." In many ways that entirely concurs with my view. Go ahead, Robert, because I would be most interested to hear what you say.
Dr Leonardi: I have just come back from a trip to the United States where I went to the World Bank on Thursday and the Inter-American Development Bank and Harvard University and this issue came up and that is completely wrong; it is false. That is, in the EU regional disparities have fallen at a much faster rate than we have ever seen historically in any single Member State. If you take the United States, if you take Germany, if you take Japan, large Member States that have a lot of national funding, the disparities between developed and under-developed areas have fallen at a much slower rate than has taken place in the EU during the last 20 years. Remember that Ireland was an Objective 1 region in 1988; it had an average GDP of 66 per cent of the EU average. Now it has 147 per cent. Athens in 2005 had an average GDP of 131 per cent of the EU average—Athens, Greece. Greece as a country by 2008 is going to surpass Italy in terms of average GDP, and so on. Spain has already surpassed 105 per cent, so we have this massive change in regional disparities, and what we are seeing in Central and Eastern Europe is higher than average growth rates in all Central and Eastern Europe states. Therefore, if you look at the GDP data, you see certain turning points or certain points of acceleration, and the Central and Eastern European countries have experienced a fast acceleration in 2004 when they came in and they will probably now have another acceleration in 2007/2008 because of the amount of money being made available. Latvia, Estonia and Lithuania are now growing like Ireland used to grow in the 1990s—they have double digit growth rates.

Q123 ***Chairman:*** Could one, however, put all this down to the benign influence of structural funds? Surely not? It has to do with trade—
Dr Leonardi: Absolutely not. But that is why we have the important element of two things: the single market coming into that, which changes completely entrepreneurial strategies because you can go to Estonia and set up a plant there and serve 450 million people and not just the Estonian population. That completely changes the strategies of entrepreneurs.
Chairman: Can I bring in Lord Maclennan?

Q124 ***Lord Maclennan of Rogart:*** We have heard two very fascinating and contrasting views; indeed, I might even venture to say conflicting views. You will understand, Mr Boyfield, that you did say that you were not going to trouble us with statistics, but I think when making such bold statements as you have about lack of impact I would be greatly assisted by any statistics—

Mr Boyfield: I am glad I did my preparation in that case and I hate to fall out at such an early stage with my friend from the LSE, as it is my old Alma Mater.

Q125 ***Lord Maclennan of Rogart:*** Just before you do, may I complete my question? Speaking as someone who represented the Highlands of Scotland or a large part of it in the House of Commons for 35 years, I certainly have witnessed statistical change in the relationship of that economy to the rest of Scotland. At the beginning of that period of a structural assistance we saw that that area came within Objective 1 of the European Union structural funding and at the end of it it no longer qualified. So in the words of the then Secretary of State for Scotland in the middle 1960s, "The Highlander had been the man on Scotland's conscience," but by the end of that period it was no longer true, and the points that have been made seriously by Dr Leonardi about leverage and about convergence within one country seem to me to be entirely borne out by that little microcosmic example. Where am I wrong in that discussion?

Mr Boyfield: Let me make these points to you. I am not saying that they have no impact; I am just trying to take it in context. First of all, *The Economist* magazine suggests that EU development aid raised annual GDP growth in Ireland in the 1990s by perhaps half a point, and they based that estimate on what they describe as authoritative studies when I looked at the magazine. Other factors such as favourable demographics, the opening up of EU markets after the 1992 reforms, and fiscal policy, were more important drivers of growth. Also, we looked at a speech given by Commissioner Hubner in Brasilia on 29 November 2007, looking at the impact of cohesion policy, and she argues that Greece has closed the previous gap with the EU average in terms of GDP. Allowing for the new accession countries it appears to have climbed from 74 per cent of average GDP in 1995, when the EU was of course 15 Member States, to reach 88 per cent. That is in 2005. What I was confused about was whether those statistics were based on the 25 Member States of the EU or the EU15. She talks about Spain climbing from 91 per cent to 102 per cent over the same time period. Interestingly, Ireland, which had already got to 102 per cent of average GDP, has risen to 145 per cent. I was wondering how far that was attributable to Ireland's success in receiving CAP grants and adopting a more entrepreneurial, friendly fiscal policy? The last point I would make is that Open Europe—and I gather you have already taken evidence from them and had a candid exchange of views—point out that in 1989, when Objective 1 status came in, of the 44 regions that were designated, as I understand it, as Objective 1, 43 were still eligible for such funding in 2003, which basically suggests that the poor regions are still poor. The last point I would make, refers to an excellent paper by Tim Leunig, which I have been reading over the last few days. I heard him at the Institute of Economic Affairs a couple of weeks ago—he is an academic at the London School of Economics—and he came out last year with a paper called *Cities Limited*—

Q126 ***Lord Renton of Mount Harry:*** Chairman, is it possible to get back to our questions; we are just having speeches, which, personally, I find rather irritating.

Mr Boyfield: That basically says that regional development policy is not working.

Lord Renton of Mount Harry: We have a lot of questions to ask.

Chairman: If I may, I will now try to get through our list of questions. Lord Woolmer.

Q127 ***Lord Woolmer of Leeds:*** The lead-in question is what should be the objectives of the EU Structural Funds? I would like, before we finish, to come back to some of that conversation, but if I can start on that question that would be very helpful.

Dr Leonardi: In terms of the Treaty, the single European market, which has been repeated in other Treaties in the preamble, is the reduction of regional disparities. Therefore, the reduction of regional disparity means to reduce the gap between developed areas or core areas and peripheral or undeveloped areas. That has remained as the primary objective.

Q128 ***Lord Woolmer of Leeds:*** Mr Boyfield may want to comment as well, but given that it seems very straightforward clearly individual Member States are also concerned about regional disparities.

Dr Leonardi: Absolutely.

Q129 ***Lord Woolmer of Leeds:*** One of the important questions is, first of all, which is the most effective way to address regional disparities—is it through policies within Member States? Is there actually a role at an EU level? Is that because Member State policies fail in some way and there is a failure of the policy of Member States? So given the objective is to reduce the disparities why do that at an EU-wide level? Is that not what Member State government polices are concerned about?

Dr Leonardi: What happened in the 1980s was that most Member States went away or closed down the regional policy—in the UK it was closed down in 1979, in other countries it was closed down in the 1980s—because national regional policies had not produced any impact whatsoever and therefore what national regional policies did was to create a culture of dependence on the government handouts because they tended to be without significant controls and therefore they created a culture of trying to capture these funds, keeping the funds and then repeating them over time. Therefore, there was no evaluation, there was no exit from the policy and the areas remained under-developed and that is why they were closed down. Secondly, and one of the reasons why the policy then was closed down in Spain and in Greece, which happened, is that they had difficulty in just meeting the requirements of co-financing. That is, the EU funds do not cover 100 per cent of the programmes; they cover either 50 per cent in the UK, Italy, France, Germany cases, or 75 per cent of the cost in the case of the cohesion countries, Greece, Portugal, Spain and Ireland. Even though the national governments had to come up with *only* 25 per cent they had difficulty in doing that. Therefore, that is why national regional policy was closed down because they just did not have any extra funds to do it. The other element that is important is that national regional policy looked at the national market—the focus point was the national market. So when you moved to the European market then your entrepreneurial choices, strategic choices differed significantly. What we have seen in Europe is that with the creation of the single market and the coming into fruition of the cohesion policy countries and regions were able to restructure within a European context, within a wider market context, and this is the important element. We have to remember that we have moved in many cases from very small national markets to a huge European market.

Mr Boyfield: Can I make a short point? It strikes me that there might be an argument for the European Commission having a role in regional development policies, particularly amongst the accession countries and the smaller countries such as Cyprus, Malta and so on, if it can be shown that they add value and they are a repository of expertise and experience. That is one of the things we are seeking to look at in our study. I think that there is an argument that for the richer countries—and this is something that I gather Britain was spearheading in 2005 –regional policy might be "nationalised", I think that is the phrase that is used, and go back to those Member countries. And there seems to be support from other countries, including Germany, France and Sweden for that view.

Q130 ***Lord Woolmer of Leeds:*** So the answer to the question that I will pose, which is if regional funds are used to help reduce the disparities, Dr Leonardi's answer to that is that historically Member countries did not do a very good job at regional policy and EU policy is a lot better. So it is not a question of the regional funds and cohesion funds being more effective in supporting public policy Member States, in Dr Leonardi's view but actually substituted for ineffective policy in Member States, if I understand that, which is an extremely bold statement and certainly one to which we can devote an awful lot of time. Does that remain the current position? Is it the case that Member States, despite the desire of some Member States to repatriate or bring back to home base regional policies, is it your view, both of you, that that is quite wrong? That at the EU level things can be done to reduce regional disparities that Member States would not do? I find that a bold statement but that is certainly the burden of Dr Leonardi's evidence. Would you both have that view?

Mr Boyfield: No, I am rather sceptical about that. I have yet to be convinced that they are doing things which could not be done, particularly in the wealthier Member States. But then I am pretty negative and sceptical, particularly having read this Policy Exchange study, on the impact that regional policy has in this country.

Chairman: We seem to be now clearly in the area of subsidiarity and I would like to hand over to Lord Maclennan.

Q131 ***Lord Maclennan of Rogart:*** I am grateful, Mr Boyfield, for your evidence. You mention in your written evidence that there could be a problem in the present situation of regional funding by the EU, flowing from differences and tensions, as you put it, between regions and Member State governments. Is that a hypothetical concern or an actual historical fact because I am not aware of the skewing of the problem sufficiently to make it something of which we need to take much account?

Mr Boyfield: That is my hunch, it is my candid view.

Q132 ***Lord Maclennan of Rogart:*** A hunch but is there any evidence?

Mr Boyfield: We all start off with hunches but—

Q133 ***Lord Maclennan of Rogart:*** You cannot have a hunch without having some basis of evidence—

Mr Boyfield: Material I have read, including the report from Open Europe, points out that the priorities set by Brussels may well differ not only from national governments' priorities for regional development but also for regions' priorities for local development. You might take the view that Brussels' priorities are better than the others but there is obvious tension there, it strikes me, and that is something we are going to be looking at.

Q134 ***Lord Maclennan of Rogart:*** What you seem to be saying is that some national governments may not satisfy their regions, but that does not necessarily

mean that the regions are not on the right track and have a higher aspiration for regional policy than the national government which—
Mr Boyfield: I entirely endorse that; I concur with that.

Q135 ***Lord Maclennan of Rogart:*** What is wrong, in that case, with the regions looking to Brussels to give them something of a leg up?
Mr Boyfield: Nothing at all.

Q136 ***Lord Maclennan of Rogart:*** Good.
Mr Boyfield: And that is the interesting thing, from my point of view. As I heard Lord Trimble say when you took evidence from Open Europe, Ulster got a much more sympathetic ear in Brussels than they did from HM Treasury.

Q137 ***Lord Maclennan of Rogart:*** So we do not need to be too concerned in that case about differences and tensions, as you put it, between national and regions. In fact, it seems to me that you are now turning your written argument on its head and that if what we are interested in is regional development that we should be ready to look to the Union—
Mr Boyfield: No, the question, which I am still looking at as we have only just begun this study, is how far are the priorities set by Brussels, Member State governments and regions identical? And I would have thought, inevitably, that they are going to differ across 27 Member States.

Q138 ***Chairman:*** Can I pose a question arising? The thing we are rather struggling with is the whole question of repatriation of structural funds, whereby the rich countries would fundamentally turn themselves into a position where they were contributors rather than recipients. I think perhaps the way to focus this question is to ask you both whether you would actually support a position whereby the richer States made only a net contribution to the budget and spent what money they would have received in their own countries as they were going to. Dr Leonardi?
Dr Leonardi: Just to pick up the last point. When you look at the formulation of the policy, because the policy then is formulated in terms of a community support framework or a national strategic reference framework, then it is divided into national operational programmes and regional operational programmes. So therefore at the EU level they establish parameters of the policy; they do not dictate what the money should be spent on. They say that money should not be spent in only one sector; therefore, they say infrastructure, vocational education, capital investments, etcetera. But then the weight is determined by the national government and national operational programmes and the regions in regional operational programmes. So therefore Brussels is not dictating. The regional and the national governments are able to emphasise their priority if they want to put more on infrastructure, more on vocational education or whatever; so therefore that is up to the various national governments. To your point about the repatriation, I would be very much against this because on the one hand we have to look at the reasons why regional policy was closed down in the first place at the national level; secondly, we have to look at the important elements that have come out of the EU cohesion policy, and that is the semester reporting, the unification, the standardisation of the reporting, the creation of evaluation, which was not present in the national regional policy; and then the creation of the three management units, so the management authority responsible for day to day, and therefore there is a person, staff, building, telephone, email, whatever. There is a payment authority that has the responsibility of paying the invoices. And then a certification authority, so that the invoices are checked with the physical progress of the projects. Therefore, all these three elements have significantly reduced the space for misuse, corruption or whatever. Therefore, these things were not present in national regional policy. In Germany they are still not present in national regional policy. Therefore, I would be very, very reluctant because at the national level we do not have the safeguards in place.

Q139 ***Chairman:*** Thank you very much, Dr Leonardi. Mr Boyfield, we are trying to decide whether we are in favour of repatriation of funds or not.
Mr Boyfield: I think I am in favour of repatriation of funds to the richer countries. I think there might well be an argument, as Robert was saying, that you should concentrate funding on the accession countries, the poorer countries; and it is also quite noticeable that Brussels seems to be tightening up its monitoring and reviews. I think there is an important question about how far the Court of Auditors' recommendations are really being picked up by the European Parliament. There has been a weakness there, but they do seem to be tightening up, as was evidenced in the *Financial Times* article last week about the Dutch refusing to sign off the accounts.

Q140 ***Lord Maclennan of Rogart:*** May I follow up this point about the rich and poor, or relatively rich and relatively poor? Your written statement again speaks about it making more sense for Member States to address their own regional development issues. That could allow the relatively rich simply not to have a regional development policy. That is an

option, but is it conformable with the overall objectives of the Union of trying to spread the benefits of the market from the city state that you are talking about throughout the whole population of countries? And is it not also the case that the contraction of the proportion of the budget devoted to structural aid in the richer countries, which Dr Leonardi mentioned, has reflected the lessening of the need of the greater countries and not simply the growth in the need of the convergence countries? Would that be reasonably true?
Dr Leonardi: If you look at the distribution of CAP funds they are going towards the richest countries.

Q141 ***Lord Renton of Mount Harry:*** Which funds?
Dr Leonardi: The CAP, the market mechanism. There it is going to France, it is going to Germany, it is going to Italy and going to the UK. So the CAP funds go to the opposite people, vis-à-vis the cohesion, and that is why we had the budgetary battle in 2005, 2006—you might remember that—because there was the feeling that the attempt to lower cohesion funding was exactly detrimental to the interests of the new accession countries, and instead the guarantee of CAP funding up until 2013. There was a guarantee to the bigger countries and the richer countries that they would get theirs because the other thing is that CAP has had no impact in reducing regional disparity because of this mismatch—the richer you are the more money you get.
Chairman: I think it is reasonably clear to all of us that something has to happen to the CAP Fund, but I strive to keep my mind firmly on the structural funds.

Q142 ***Lord Maclennan of Rogart:*** Dr Leonardi, is it your view that it would be acceptable European Union policy to effectively say that regional disparities in the rich countries are not something that the Union ought to be involved in; it is marginal to the interests and they should consequently be repatriated?
Dr Leonardi: No because it varies in terms of some countries are interested in this and others are not interested in this. Therefore, to leave whole swathes of regions that may be suffering I think needs to become a concern of the overall European Union. I think that the European Union provides a check to make sure that there is a more equal distribution, but in many countries there is not this orientation. We see this again in Ireland, in Portugal and in Greece. There the use of the funds have been very good, have promoted convergence but disparities have increased within the countries.
Mr Boyfield: If I could add very quickly, I do not think it is any business of Brussels really, the way in which these things are done by the Member States, in other words the richer states if they are repatriated; it is up to the electorate when they vote in elections, and if the Scots want to do their own thing and go independent, then let them.
Chairman: I think that possibly follows from repatriation. If I may, I would like to move on to consider what is to be done with structural funds in the future, not what has been done in the past. Lord Renton.

Q143 ***Lord Renton of Mount Harry:*** I think, Chairman, that that is the point on which we should now concentrate rather than the past. Personally, I do not think there is going to be very much change. I think that the cohesion fund will continue to exist; I think that the richer countries would never actually allow themselves not to get anything from it at all because it would be impossible to sell that politically. If we look at the 2008 EC budget which has just been approved, there is actually no change in the figure for the cohesion fund. It started at €46.8 billion and it remains at €46.8 billion. I think realistically that is likely to continue. Therefore, looking slightly more at the minutiae, accepting that there are new countries coming in that are very much poorer, or there is migration, the service sector is growing, there is all the worry about climate change, what changes to the funds do you think may be necessary to deal with these new problems, which were not there ten years ago, etcetera?
Dr Leonardi: One thing is that migration has become a European-wide problem. In terms of now, we live it as a Northern European or Southern European or Western European phenomena but all predictions are that in Central and Eastern Europe we are going to have in five years a mopping up of the unemployment levels.

Q144 ***Lord Renton of Mount Harry:*** A mopping up?
Dr Leonardi: A drastic reduction in unemployment levels, and therefore the need to either repatriate their nationals who have emigrated from Romania, Poland, etcetera, or to import labour from the Ukraine, Belarus, Russia. Therefore, migration is a very, very important thing and it has not been dealt with adequately. You see it clearly in the cities because in the cities we have a growing phenomena of migrant communities not being well integrated or not integrating into the general society and therefore creating points of conflict with the resident populations; and leading to a decline in the physical infrastructure, the abandonment of education and increased crime and terrorist-type activities. Therefore, it is something that has not been adequately addressed because that was not on the remit at the beginning, and I think that needs to be introduced into the remit much more. Secondly, I think that we have to be much more sensitive to the

environment. In many of these Central and Eastern European countries—but we saw it also in Portugal and Spain and Greece—development is considered to be good no matter what the costs, and therefore in the middle to long-term we see the negative impacts of these types of developments, especially coastal developmental, river development and so forth. Therefore, we have to be much more sensitive to the environmental impact of projects. So even though Environmental Impact Statements are required for large infrastructure projects I think that they need to be also introduced for medium sized projects and an overall consideration for the development programmes.

Q145 ***Lord Woolmer of Leeds:*** Within that context particularly do you see the EU over the next three or four years specifically putting structural fund money substantially into climate change projects?
Dr Leonardi: It could. This really requires a consensus among the Member States to say, "Okay, we want to change the objectives," and that is part of the legislative process at the European level, and Member countries do have a role in initiating these types of policies. I would not discount it at all; I think if the UK were to raise this banner and carry it forward then many other countries, Sweden and other countries in Western Europe, would readily support that.

Q146 ***Chairman:*** We posed a question in terms of potential further enlargement and indeed I guess you are answering it in terms of enlargement because enlargement will lead to more migration.
Dr Leonardi: We get migration without enlargement. Once the States come in there is an ability to stabilise migration. That is what I am arguing for Central and Eastern Europe. The flows that we have seen from Poland I think will stop and will reverse in the coming years, but we have on the eastern side of the European Union borders with the Ukraine, Belarus, Russia, and I think these areas do have employment problems and therefore are readily capable of providing extra labour, to say nothing of the southern Mediterranean area because they have the ability to go into all European countries—not just the southern European countries, but we find significant Moroccan and Tunisian groups in Holland, in Denmark, in Sweden and in other places.
Mr Boyfield: Can I just say one thing? Is the migration not already happening? If you go around London there are a heck of a lot of Ukrainians, Turks and other immigrants. They might be illegal or whatever but the catering industry would not operate without a lot of these people.
Chairman: What we are trying to nail down is whether structural funds will be any contribution to dealing with these problems.

Q147 ***Lord Renton of Mount Harry:*** This is a difficult one, I know. Do you think it is possible to add more specific criteria to guide decisions on the proportion of the EU budget to be allocated to structural funds? It follows on in a sense from what you are saying.
Dr Leonardi: It is perfectly possible. I think that for the management of migration, if you think of the European Social Fund it was created in 1958 in order to exactly respond to that issue of migration of southern Italians to France and to Germany, and therefore it was seen as a fund to educate them, to integrate them and then to protect them in terms of their job rights. So I think that the social fund could be brought back to its original purpose and more focused on the management of migration problems. But in this new round of cohesion policy, 2007 to 2013, there is a possibility of proposing projects within city centres, so about two per cent of the funds are earmarked for metropolitan types of initiatives in the various Member States. But there is a certain amount of denial on the part of Central and Eastern European countries; they state flatly that they do not have a migration problem—now. I think that they will have a migration problem within five years.
Chairman: If I could just have a pick on this because it is quite important. It seemed to us when we tried to prepare what we were thinking about structural funds that with any luck they would increase, Lord Renton, perhaps only as the proportion of CAP goes down. There is some scope in terms of the European budget.
Lord Renton of Mount Harry: Of course it is a very relevant point because with climate change, does it come out of the CAP budget, or whatever?

Q148 ***Chairman:*** The other point that the European Commission keeps making is that indeed it is policy to link the priorities for some funds with the Lisbon Agenda, something to do with competitiveness. Do either of you in fact support that?
Dr Leonardi: Yes.
Mr Boyfield: It is a bit like saying are you in favour of not beating your wife; the Lisbon Agenda is just a long wish list which seems to have so far appeared elusive in terms of achieving those targets. Can I also be a bit of a cynic again about the regional development funds? Although they are there for laudable reasons—and I am not saying that in places like Caithness and Ross they might not have had an impact—there is this perception amongst a lot of people in Europe that they are a kind of slush fund, and that the Member States come together at these summits and they work out basically how much they

are prepared to pay to two big items in the EU budget, which comes to something like 90 per cent of the overall budget at the moment—that is the CAP and these regional development funds. They look on the development funds, it strikes me, as a bit of a sweetener—one keeps reading these press reports that at three o'clock in the morning at the Brussels summit in December 2005 when the British and the Germans were trying to persuade the Poles to agree to some particular item they said, "We will give you another 100 million Euros for your subway development—

Q149 ***Lord Renton of Mount Harry:*** But it was ever thus.
Mr Boyfield: It was ever thus and actually, as you were saying, I am also of the opinion that we are not likely to see any radical changes; we can come up with various criteria to do with particular fashions the moment like climate change, and some of these might well be laudable, but you can ask yourself, I guess, how far is the European Commission really a repository of expertise and experience in climate change? My experience of working with the European Commission is that they are often very good at acting as a switchboard of advice, and they will put people in touch with the experts in Europe and all that is very positive, but I am not really entirely sure what added value they provide for the money that is spent on them.

Q150 ***Lord Renton of Mount Harry:*** Climate change has to be an EU problem because it is not a single national problem.
Mr Boyfield: I absolutely agree with that.

Q151 ***Lord Renton of Mount Harry:*** It just has to be a continental and global problem.
Mr Boyfield: But you could also have voluntary cooperation amongst the Member States. Switzerland presumably is concerned about climate change and presumably voluntarily goes along with a lot of the very fine initiatives from the EU.
Dr Leonardi: Can I respond to that? In terms of the Lisbon Agenda, the difficulty with the Lisbon Agenda is that we have the open method of coordination as a way of achieving these, and the open method of coordination has still to be proven as effective, as an effective way of managing these policies and achieving the goals because at the end there is no compliance mechanism; there is just blaming and shaming and that is it—you cannot take money away or you cannot give money. So where the Lisbon Agenda has been effective is where it has been integrated into the cohesion policy. Therefore, for the convergence countries it has become a very important objective as part of the overall objective of reducing disparities, so the Lisbon Agenda has been given teeth by the cohesion policy. Secondly, the allocation of money in the cohesion policy is not based on everybody putting in a bid and being able to use their political weight to get it because the allocation of funding is done on the basis of a formula that is proposed by the Commission and agreed by the Council of Ministers. Therefore, once the formula is in place the budget can increase, decrease or whatever in terms of the allocation that is determined by that formula; and these types of things. Secondly, all of this has to pass by the European Parliament, and therefore the Member States in December 2005 agreed on 1.0 per cent of GDP and the Parliament did not accept it; then the compromise of 1.07 per cent. Therefore, we should not at all believe that Member States can do whatever they want in terms of these financial arrangements because there are strict rules.

Q152 ***Lord Maclennan of Rogart:*** On the formula and on the initiative for change you did earlier say, Dr Leonardi, that if there were a consensus the objectives could be enlarged.
Dr Leonardi: Yes.

Q153 ***Lord Maclennan of Rogart:*** But I wonder if that is actually consistent with or allowed for within the formulae? The formulae are macroeconomic in a way but the problems sometimes appear to be micro problems. For example, the shoe industry in Italy has been so threatened by China that a whole area is really at risk. But could the formulae allow a sensitive response to that kind of national or regional problem?
Dr Leonardi: Yes, it can because here we are talking about an area that is not going to be a major beneficiary of the cohesion budget, it is not part of the convergence objective; but it is part of that leveraging structure where the shoe industry, say in Tuscany, can be a focus of it and therefore the Tuscany government can say, "I want to put the money that I receive from the EU on this as a way of then leveraging the private equity that is necessary." And that is the only way they are going to do it because in many of these situations had the private sector been in a position to take care of the problem it would have taken care of it already. But we still have these lingering problems and so they need a certain amount of focus from the public authorities to make sure that everyone is on board in terms of the regional officials, the local officials, the banks, the entrepreneurs and the representative associations of the entrepreneurs.
Mr Boyfield: Can I quickly add something? I was talking to a very prominent private equity guy last week, who was telling me that he has invested quite a lot in Wales in recent years, and there is now quite a

thriving consultancy business out there in directing private equity firms and other investors in terms of what is leveraged from the European Community. Next week I am going to Munich to the Super Return Private Equity conference and I notice that there are some sessions there on what you might be able to do with the European Commission in terms of investing in particular regions of Europe. That is a very interesting thing to follow.

Chairman: This is of course evidence of leverage.

Q154 ***Lord Woolmer of Leeds:*** Could you remind me what the current eligibility tests are for regions to receive funds under the EU's structural funds. Do you regard them as fair, relevant and appropriate and should they remain in place after 2013?

Dr Leonardi: There is one criteria and that is 75 per cent or less of the EU average.

Q155 ***Lord Woolmer of Leeds:*** Just that one?

Dr Leonardi: Just that one; 75 per cent or less of the EU average. Now we have 27, but when the calculations were made for 2007–13 we had an EU of 25 and therefore we did not take into account the weight of Romania and Bulgaria, which have lowered the average in terms of the absolute number for the EU average. So that is the only measure. But in the allocation of funds, once you qualify, then you have population, unemployment levels, activity rates in terms of what percentage of your population is in employment; and also introduced in 2003 was the ultra peripheral position to take into account the Azores, the Canary Islands, in terms of these others that did not have big populations and therefore required more funding. But those were the criteria in terms of the allocation. One last point, the absolute level of development of the country as a whole is taken into consideration. So under-developed regions in a wealthy country such as Italy, the UK or France receive less than a poor region in a poor country.

Mr Boyfield: Sweden, I think.

Dr Leonardi: There it is a special situation for Sweden and Finland because in those areas the qualification is that they have to have less than one person per square kilometre.

Mr Boyfield: The Tundra Belt.

Q156 ***Chairman:*** Do you feel that these are about the right criteria or would you make a change?

Dr Leonardi: This is the only criterion that is uniform throughout the EU and therefore it is EU-defined, it is not nationally-defined, and the problem that we get with nationally-defined parameters is that each country—and one example is unemployment—defines it differently; therefore, in one place part-time work is employment and in other places part-time work is unemployment. So unless we have a uniform, a homogenous definition throughout the EU then it is difficult to accept anything else.

Q157 ***Lord Woolmer of Leeds:*** So your answer is that there are tests for allocation, but in applying those tests actually the data and the definitions that individual countries apply differ?

Dr Leonardi: Yes.

Mr Boyfield: I would go along with that.

Q158 ***Lord Woolmer of Leeds:*** So what if anything do you think should change?

Dr Leonardi: If we could guarantee the definition of unemployment is the same throughout the EU, if we could guarantee that there is not under or over reporting because that also is another matter, and if we were to have those guarantees across the EU 27 then I would also add unemployment and activity rates, then they could be used for the allocation of funds once eligibility is established. But unless we have homogenous definitions of criteria, it is very difficult to change the present system.

Mr Boyfield: I really endorse that but ultimately the 75 per cent figure is an arbitrary figure. I was looking at *The Times* yesterday about the GDPs of some of these candidate countries in the former Yugoslavia and some of them have very, very low GDPs and very high unemployment rates. Inevitably I think we are going to see more funding going to these candidate states, and that is not necessarily a bad thing.

Q159 ***Chairman:*** I think that must be right. I am conscious that we have not asked one of our witnesses anything. Ms Segura, would you like to say anything about any of this? What is your research subject about which you would like to speak?

Ms Segura: My knowledge about this particular topic is not very deep but what I have seen so far is that the cohesion funds have had a very good intention coming from the European Union in order to leverage these regions that are in different circumstances. I think if the management of the funds by the Member States were more rigorous they could actually have a better impact in this area. I think a lot of money, as far as I can see, is spent in administration and the management of these funds when allocated. This is my point of view at the moment.

Q160 ***Chairman:*** If I have picked up Dr Leonardi's argument correctly, yes, there may be some money spent on administration but it is worth it.

Dr Leonardi: Very, very little—very, very little.

Q161 ***Chairman:*** We have manuscript figures for England and some for the Commission.

19 February 2008 Mr Keith Boyfield, Ms Florenica Ahumada Segura and Dr Robert Leonardi

Dr Leonardi: The technical assistance, there is a line in the budget as technical assistance that pays for in-house activities as well as bringing people in, and that technical assistance is one per cent, 0.7 per cent—we are talking about very small figures. But it also pays for all of the evaluation, all of the oversight and all of the semester meetings that take place.

Q162 ***Chairman:*** If there was anything that any of you had to attribute on administrative expense—we received Open Europe's figures with some scepticism but there is a difficulty about getting figures and it is something I would like to cover so that if there is any evidence around I would be glad to have it.
Mr Boyfield: We would gladly like to write back to you on that if we discover any.

Q163 ***Lord Maclennan of Rogart:*** As a follow-up to something that was said a little earlier about sources of extravagance or waste. It was rather broadly stated by Mr Boyfield in his written evidence that lobbying was wasteful, but how can a political system work to redress imbalance when you say that the Union is now increasingly dominated by the city states if the peripheral regions do not actually lobby and come together and find common ground. It seems to me that that is such a broad generalisation.
Mr Boyfield: Speaking as a lobbyist, because I have been a lobbyist for the last 25 years of my life, even I see when I go to Brussels, (which is now the second capital after Washington for lobbyists), I think, yes, I am all in favour of lobbying because it can provide more accurate information and you can advocate your best case, but there are excesses, and I think that one can install a ceiling to this type of activity. Speaking as a lobbyist, I think when I go to Brussels that there is an awful lot of lobbying going on and there is an awful lot of excess there.

Q164 ***Lord Maclennan of Rogart:*** But the lobbying is not a function of the European Union, surely it is a matter for the Council themselves.
Mr Boyfield: No, it is rent-seeking activity because quite rationally these representative offices are pursuing funds and if 35 per cent of the EU budget goes on the regions it is quite rational that you will see a lot of rent-seeking activity.
Chairman: It is a very tempting digression but I am going to haul us back out of it because Lord Woolmer has a final question.

Q165 ***Lord Woolmer of Leeds:*** Going back right back to basics, to the start as it were, to get a sense of perspective. There are three ways in broad terms, three underlying causes why regional disparities might change, let us say reduce. One is countries entering into a single market in which capital flows is increasingly moved around freely, and where certainly trade seems not to make any difference and trade in services less so but increasing, and mobility of labour. So there is that single market issue. There is the operation of regional policies within Member States and then there are EU-wide regional funds. To get a sense of perspective what work has been done to demonstrate, to try to calculate the effect of each of those elements in reducing regional disparity? Because we have been talking, as inevitably we do in inquiries, as if our central interest is the one that is making all the difference. To me, on the face of it, it must be—but I may be wrong—that this entry into a single market for trade, capital and so on must have made overwhelmingly the biggest difference, and some Member States have had regional policies. So what work has been done to try to disentangle those because otherwise we could be arguing a great deal about something that actually does not really make a lot of difference? It is important but—
Dr Leonardi: Is Lord Woolmer an academic?

Q166 ***Chairman:*** The Irish case is, I would suggest, particularly difficult to disentangle some sensible fiscal policies and the ability to trade from what, if anything, structural funds did for them.
Dr Leonardi: We had a special issue of Regional Studies last year addressing the point and it is difficult because we do not have a clear and precise accounting for the funds that are spent at the regional level because in this policy we have national operational programmes which are multi regional, for example for the large, infrastructure projects, that cover more then one region. Therefore in the regional operational programmes we know how much is being spent in the particular region and we can figure out from the accounting when it was spent. But with the multi regional projects we do not have a regional breakdown of the multi regional expenditure. For example, in Spain two-thirds of the money is being spent in the national, multi regional programmes because they have built a lot of infrastructure and so as a result we have regional convergence taking place but we cannot pin it to what is being invested because we do not have this regional breakdown of investment. So we do not know where it is being spent and when it is being spent; therefore, we are stuck with a minimum amount or a minority of the information that we would need in order to sort out these two. Also, given that they take place simultaneously, they overlap.

Q167 ***Lord Woolmer of Leeds:*** That is the public spending element whether it is national Member State or the EU; but what about the trading case, movements of capital and labour and so on as opposed to public spending. In very simple terms, is

it overwhelmingly—as my instinct is that it must be overwhelmingly the biggest impact? That must be the biggest impact in Ireland, for example?
Mr Boyfield: I was just going to say that that seems to be the theme of what comes out of these *Economist* articles about Ireland and why it proved to be that this Celtic Tiger, has proved successful partly demographics, a lot to do with fiscal policy, but also the opening up of the EU. Its something we want to look at. I will gladly write to you about it but I cannot quote you chapter and verse on the academic literature because I am not as learned as Robert Leonardi on this; I defer to his excellent knowledge.

Q168 ***Lord Woolmer of Leeds:*** Dr Leonardi was shaking his head at that. It is an important issue and we can all spend a lot of time worrying about this issue here in front of us but actually it might be very marginal in its actual impact.
Dr Leonardi: One of the interesting aspects of the cohesion policy is that large infrastructure projects arguably need to justified and from the EU point of view a large infrastructure project should be financed if it has a European-wide impact, not just a local impact but a more national impact. One of the things that one sees in national infrastructure is that you have a tendency of creating a star system with the national capital in the middle and all the roads leading out from the national capital to the periphery, and instead in the EU it has to link up to an EU infrastructure grid and so therefore that significantly changes the nature. Once you have the infrastructure in place then it helps to reduce the cost of production in particular peripheral areas. The important thing in Ireland is that they restructured the ports in Ireland.

Q169 ***Chairman:*** They restructured the connecting links.
Dr Leonardi: Exactly, and then they created the infrastructure connecting the ports because the ports were the crucial elements—and also the airports were another element.
Mr Boyfield: Can I just say that I do quite a lot of work on Sub-Sahara and Africa and it is very noticeable that the money which China is putting into places like the Democratic Republic of Congo is going into the development of the harbour and the railway system and so on, so that they can get their cobalt and copper out more easily. I think it is very interesting what is happening with regard to investment in places like Angola and The Congo; it is really focused on the infrastructure, roads, rail and harbours.

Q170 ***Chairman:*** I think I have probably exhausted everybody, including my witnesses. It remains for me to say thank you very much for what has been a very interesting session and to plead for any evidence that you have which you can conveniently lay your hands on on administration costs.
Dr Leonardi: I shall leave a copy of my book on this subject with you.

Q171 ***Chairman:*** Thank you. It is always argued that the costs are always too high and outweigh the benefits and if I can get a decent handle on the costs and they are as small as you suggest, then that is another bit of the puzzle.
Mr Boyfield: We will gladly keep you informed of our progress.
Chairman: Thank you very much.

TUESDAY 26 FEBRUARY 2008

Present	Haskins, L	Renton of Mount Harry, L
	Kerr of Kinlochard, L	Steinberg, L
	Maclennan of Rogart, L	Trimble, L
	Moser, L	Woolmer of Leeds, L (Chairman)

Memorandum by Stephen Timms MP, Minister of State for Competitiveness, Department for Business, Enterprise and Regulatory Reform

Further to your Committee's Call for Evidence from the Department for Business, Enterprise and Regulatory Reform on the Future of European Structural Funds, please find enclosed the Department's response.

THE FUTURE OF EUROPEAN STRUCTURAL FUNDS—CALL FOR EVIDENCE RESPONSE

What should be the objectives of the EU's Structural Funds? How can the Funds become more effective in supporting public policies in Member States and regions? What mechanisms of delivery could make the policy more performance-based and more user-friendly?

1. The European Structural and Cohesion Funds are instruments to help achieve the objectives of the Union's Cohesion Policy. Article 158 of the Treaty establishing the European Community is the basis for this Policy:

2. "In order to promote its overall harmonious development, the Community shall develop and pursue its actions leading to the strengthening of its economic and social cohesion.

3. In particular, the Community shall aim at reducing disparities between the levels of development of the various regions and the backwardness of the least favoured regions or islands, including rural areas".

4. This, in turn, is based on Article 2 of the Treaty which sets outs the Union's overall economic and social objectives, including a high level of employment, balanced and sustainable development and the strengthening of economic and social cohesion.[1]

5. These articles give the Union considerable scope to determine the priority given to the different objectives, what should be achieved within each objective, how it should be achieved (by spending, regulation or coordination), over what time scale (short or long term) and by whom (the Commission, Member States or sub-national authorities).

6. The Regulations negotiated for the 2007–13 period formalise Cohesion Policy objectives as being:

- Convergence—to help the least-developed Member States and regions catch up more quickly with the EU average by improving conditions for growth and employment.[2]
- Regional Competitiveness and Employment (RCE)—to strengthen the competitiveness, employment and attractiveness of regions other than those which are the most disadvantaged.
- European Territorial Cooperation—to strengthen cross-border, transnational and inter-regional co-operation.

7. Under existing arrangements all Regions of the Union will receive funding under either the Convergence or RCE Objectives and in addition all Regions are eligible to receive funding under the Co-operation Objective.

8. We believe the principle method of addressing the aim of EU Cohesion Policy, that all European regions should fulfil their economic potential, is by focussing on the drivers of growth as set out in the Lisbon

[1] The Reform Treaty, when ratified, will introduce the additional concept of Territorial Cohesion.

[2] The convergence objective covers all NUTS-2 regions across the EU with a GDP per head below 75% of the EU25 average. In the UK, Cornwall and West Wales and the Valleys are covered. Convergence also covers regions that are being phased out of the convergence objective due to the statistical effect of enlargement. In the UK this applies to the Highlands and Islands.

Integrated Guidelines. We need to consider the best means for achieving this goal. A principled approach, as set out in our recent publication "*Global Europe: Meeting Economic and Security Challenges*"[3] should guide this:

- The EU should act only where there are clear additional benefits from collective efforts, or "EU value added", compared with action solely by individual Member States.
- Where EU-level action is appropriate, it should be proportionate and flexible. Expenditure is just one of a number of policy levers, alongside coordination, sharing best practice, and legislation or regulation.
- Where spending is appropriate: sound financial management alongside continuing budget discipline

9. Given the above, the introduction of the new strategic approach to cohesion policy in 2007–13, including the Community Strategic Guidelines on Cohesion is welcome. In particular, during the negotiations we were strong supporters of the links made to the Integrated Guidelines for Jobs and Growth and National Reform Programmes.

10. For the future we believe this strategic approach should be further simplified. The Integrated Guidelines for Jobs and Growth and National Reform Programmes set out the key challenges that the EU, Member States and regions face in relation to their economic development. There is no need for a separate set of challenges to be identified for cohesion policy. Instead, the task is to identify how cohesion policy can support Member States' policies (at national and regional level) to address the guidelines and recommendations agreed by the European Council. The guidelines and National Reform Programmes should therefore drive cohesion policy and its programmes.

11. The objectives of Cohesion policy are supported in large measure by actions and funding at national, regional, local and neighbourhood levels. Where money is needed to achieve Cohesion Policy objectives it should mainly come from national, regional and local sources. EU funding support for Cohesion Policy needs to be better focussed on the poorer Member States, to help them make the investments needed to support their economic growth; this in turn will help to develop the wider EU economy. As already stated the best way to achieve the aim of Cohesion Policy is through the Lisbon Growth and Jobs Agenda, however, the main focus of this funding should be on activities that help build the Member States institutional structures and financial strength providing them with the ability to pursue their own regional policies in the future and limited by an absorption cap. The full range of financing options should be considered, for example a loan from the European Investment Bank may in some instances be a more appropriate form of financing than a grant from the EU budget.

12. Cohesion policy should continue to place emphasis on the performance of Structural Fund programmes in terms of the shared goals in the Lisbon strategy. The targets and indicators of programmes should set out their contribution to the relevant national strategies outlined in National Reform Programmes. These targets and indicators should be the primary means of monitoring the performance of programmes. This monitoring should be done by national or regional authorities (depending on Member States' arrangements) in partnership with the European Commission. The European Commission could have a role to play in commissioning independent research to assess the evidence available of the impact of Structural and Cohesion Funds spending on regional and national economic growth, and where possible identify the relative impacts of SCF spending and actions by Member States/regions.

13. Cooperation activity is an area in which structural funds could potentially add value. Funding could help to promote partnership across borders and encourage more balanced economic development. Cooperative working between Regions across the Union should be encouraged to identify and spread effective practice, for instance to identify the interventions that have the greatest effect on growth and productivity and provide greatest value for money. This process would exchange and disseminate best practice across Member States, and provide analysis and evidence to inform the design of future programmes.

14. It is important that the highest standards of financial control are applied to EU funds. The recent simplification of the financial management, control and audit systems is welcome but the systems remain complex and there are still opportunities for further improvements. Current systems should be subject to further review with the aim of identifying further simplification that maintains a high standard of financial control while minimising the administrative burden. The Commission should ensure that there is a uniform approach to quality assuring Member State's audit arrangements.

[3] Global Europe: Meeting the Economic and Security Challenges (October 2007), p 23 http://www.fco.gov.uk/Files/kfile/FCO_BEU_DOC_GlobalEurope71022.pdf

Do Structural Funds meet the principle of subsidiarity? Could the same cohesion objectives be met through repatriation of the distribution of these funds?

15. In the Treaty the principle of Subsidiarity states[4], "... the Community shall take action, in accordance with the principle of subsidiarity, only if and in so far as the objectives of the proposed action cannot be sufficiently achieved by the Member States..."

16. In a Modern Regional Policy we argued that "In line with the principle of subsidiarity, those Member States which have the institutions and financial strength to fully develop and pursue their own devolved and decentralised regional policies in support of these objectives should be encouraged and enabled to do so. Other Member States which have not yet reached this position will continue, for some time, to benefit from assistance—in particular, financial and administrative—to promote regional development with the goal that these Member States would ultimately no longer need such support".

17. As outlined above, it is our view that there needs to be a significant increase in the percentage of Structural and Cohesion Funds spent on poorer Member States. By separating the means of Cohesion Policy from the aims any repatriated funds would continue to contribute to these aims.

18. One of the main criticisms of the existing arrangements is that the administration of the funds is complex and burdensome. However, supporters of the existing arrangements would argue that the Structural Funds provide a wider added value than just the redistribution of money. For example:

- The multi annual planning process encourages a more strategic approach to regional development.
- Partnership in the SCF has brought enhanced transparency, cooperation and coordination to the design and delivery of regional development policy.
- Monitoring and evaluation obligations have improved the efficiency of programme implementation and led to more transparency and better policymaking.

19. A Cohesion Policy that separates means from aims can still achieve these benefits. Through a strategic framework linked to the Integrated Guidelines and Member States National Reform Programmes all Member States could receive these benefits whilst allowing for a significantly increased percentage of the funds being spent in the poorer Member States.

What impact has enlargement had on Structural Funds, and are any changes necessary to meet the challenges of further enlargement?

20. The UK Government strongly supported enlargement which has strengthened EU Member States economies, offering businesses and citizens the full benefit of a competitive market of 450 million people.

21. Enlargement has seen a significant change in the nature of disparities across the Union. The EU now has large disparities at national level in terms of GNP per head, but the main eligibility for Structural and Cohesion Funds continue to be at the regional level. Each of the ten new Member States that joined the EU in 2004 had a GNP per head below the average of the then EU. The same is true for Romania and Bulgaria who joined on 1 January 2007.[5]

22. In current prices, the SCF budget is now equal to €347 billion in 2007–13. This includes allocations to the new Member States, Bulgaria and Romania. The UK has long stressed that the EU SCF budget needs to be sustainable. This means that it has to take account of future planned enlargements as well as respecting budget discipline.

23. Over the period 2007–13, richer Member States (ie the original EU15 Members excluding Greece and Portugal) are set to receive a significant proportion of Structural and Cohesion Funds, with only 64% of budget commitments being allocated to the poorer Member States.[6] The pattern of allocations shifts over the period, with the funding moving progressively to the poorer countries so that in 2013, the budget commitments allocated to poorer countries should reach 67%. We would like to see this percentage increase significantly.

[4] Consolidated Version of the Treaty Establishing the European Community, Article 5.

[5] As the Commission Fourth Cohesion Report notes, "This enlargement added 8.6% to the Union's landmass and 6.3% to its population—a similar addition to when Austria, Finland and Sweden joined in the mid-1990s—but only 1% to its GDP measured in purchasing power standard terms, less than any previous enlargement. GDP per head is, therefore, only 35% of the EU average in Bulgaria and 38% in Romania. Accordingly, the accession of the two countries will lower the EU average level of GDP per head by just over 4%".

[6] In practice, the proportion of actual payments to the poorer Member States could be less than 64%, according to absorption levels and phasing.

24. As stated above the best way to achieve Cohesion Policy aims are through a strategic approach linked to the Lisbon Agenda, however, the main focus of funding in the poorer Member States should be on activities that help build their institutional structures and financial strength providing them with the ability to pursue their own regional policies in the future and limited by an absorption cap.

25. The EU is committed to the accession of Turkey, Croatia and other countries of the Western Balkans, a commitment which the UK Government strongly supports.

How will the EU's commitments on combating climate change manifest themselves in the distribution of Structural Funds for the post-2013 period? How will the response to other challenges facing the EU economy (eg migration, growth of the service sector) shape future policies?

26. Current Cohesion Policy already has a strong focus on climate change issues. Programmes are required to be assessed for their environmental sustainability and various activities which support the environment are already supported.

27. The full impacts of climate change on the economy and workers are not yet fully understood. There are major challenges, but also opportunities. For example, the transition to a low carbon economy will also be a significant employment opportunity.[7]

28. It is not possible at this stage to predict the outcome of negotiations for the next Financial Perspective and Structural and Cohesion Funds Regulations. The challenges facing European regions, for example, globalisation, climate and demographic change, are not new and are already being considered and addressed at a European, national, regional and local level. Cohesion Policy should remain focussed on achieving sustainable growth and jobs. If the scope of Cohesion Policy were widened then this could result in a shift in resources away from addressing disparities in economic development, the primary aim of Cohesion Policy.

29. Cooperative working between Regions could also be used to identify and spread effective practice in addressing these and other challenges. This process would exchange and disseminate best practice across Member States, and provide analysis and evidence to inform the design of future programme activities and also promote closer cooperation between Regions.

30. Wider consideration of the role that the EC Budget could play in supporting these challenges should take place as part of the EC Budget Review.

What criteria should guide decisions on the proportion of the EU budget to be allocated to Structural Funds?

31. It will be important to consider Structural and Cohesion Funds in the context of the EU Budget as a whole. The UK Government is considering its approach to the European Commission's ongoing Budget Review, guided by the three principles outlined in the answer to Question 1.

32. We have set out in our recent publication "*Global Europe: Meeting Economic and Security Challenges*" that a priority for the UK will be reform of the budget so that the EU is better equipped to meet the challenges of the 21st Century. The priority is to ensure that the review of the EU Budget provides the basis for a more effective and efficient Budget, including, a significant increase in the percentage of Structural and Cohesion funds spent on poorer Member States. We acknowledge that consequences of significant changes to funding patterns arising from future reforms will need to be considered, for example, whether it would be appropriate for transitional arrangements to be made, but this can only be done in the context of the availability of EC budget resources, and the priorities that are agreed.

Are the current eligibility tests for regions to receive support under the EU's Structural Funds relevant, fair and appropriate? Should they remain in place after 2013? Is it appropriate that they are discussed simultaneously with wider agreements on allocating EU budget spending?

33. The main aim of Cohesion Policy is to focus on disparities in development. Therefore it is right that the focus of eligibility be based on economic indicators. It would not be appropriate to speculate at this point in the current financial perspective what would be the best approach to distributing the Structural Fund budget for 2014–20. We can, however, look at the impact of existing arrangements on future spending and some of the issues that arise.

[7] The environmental industries in the UK are already worth more than £25 billion and employ some 400,000 people.

34. As already stated in question 3, over the period 2007–13, richer Member States (ie the original EU15 Members excluding Greece and Portugal) are set to receive a significant proportion of Structural and Cohesion Funds, with only 64% of budget commitments being allocated to the poorer Member States. The pattern of allocations shifts over the period, with the funding moving progressively to the poorer countries so that in 2013, the budget commitments allocated to poorer countries should reach 67%. We would like to see this percentage increase significantly.

35. Under the existing system of allocation there are currently 19 additional provisions to deal with Member States individual issues. This indicates that the current system fails to address many issues Member States would want it to. Any revision to existing arrangements should focus on simplification. One possible approach could be the allocation of funding at a Member State level rather than to regions specifically.

What would be the effect of linking the availability of Structural Funds with compliance to Broad Economic Policy Guidelines?

36. If Conditionality were to be extended to the other Funds and its scope widened there would be potential risks. Any move to extend conditionality would require a system that was both clear and transparent and with a consistent decision making processes. By making the compliance with the Broad Economic Policy Guidelines a prerequisite of funding this may lead to pressure to use the Structural Funds to specifically meet these guidelines in too restrictive a fashion. The Broad Economic Policy Guidelines of course cover areas of policy that are broader than the aims of the Structural Funds, for example, reinforcement of social security systems and wage-bargaining.

9 January 2008

Examination of Witnesses

Witnesses: Mr Pat McFadden, a Member of the House of Commons, Minister of State for Employment Relations and Postal Affairs, Mr Andrew Steele, Director of National and European Policy, Regions, and Mr Neil Bond, Head of the Structural Funds Team, Regions, Department for Business, Enterprise and Regulatory Reform, examined.

Q172 ***Chairman:*** Minister, thank you for sparing us your time this morning. You have an hour, which will be very helpful. Is there anything that you would like to say by way of introduction before we go to the questions?
Mr McFadden: No, I do not think so. My predecessor in this role, Stephen Timms, sent you a written submission a couple of months ago, which you can take as the basis of the position and I am quite happy to go straight into questions. Perhaps before we do that, I should allow my colleagues to introduce themselves and tell you what they do.
Mr Steele: I am Andrew Steele. I am Director of National and European Policy in BERR's Regions Directorate.
Mr Bond: I am Neil Bond. I am Head of the Structural Funds Team within BERR Regions Directorate.
Chairman: We have reordered the questions but will cover them all eventually.

Q173 ***Lord Renton of Mount Harry:*** Minister, I have read your letter to Lord Grenfell of 31 January and also the enclosed Government answer on the question of Cohesion Funds, but I wonder if we could start at the beginning and you could tell us, in your judgment, what should be the basic objectives of the Structural and Cohesion Funds and how can the Funds become more effective in supporting public policies in the EU States and regions?
Mr McFadden: The basic objectives of the Funds are economic; they are about jobs and growth and about closing the gap between the poorest regions and the rest of the EU. The Government is quite keen to maintain that economic focus of the Funds. We set that out quite clearly in the Global Europe pamphlet, which was published about four or five months ago. Keeping that focus on jobs and growth is the key thing for us; it is how we try to use them in the UK and that is how we want them to be used across the European Union.

Q174 ***Lord Renton of Mount Harry:*** Are you satisfied with the Funds as they are at the moment, and what mechanisms of delivery could make the policies simply more performance-based, more user-friendly and perhaps less complicated?
Mr McFadden: There is a good argument for simplification, you are right about that. The best way to make them more user-friendly, or more performance-based, is to align them more closely to the Lisbon Agenda on growth and jobs. If you take this in a wider context, the European Union is hopefully emerging from a lengthy period of an internal focus—the Treaty is being debated day-by-day in Parliament—and, as the Global Europe pamphlet said, our aim would be to move on from

having that approved to getting on with what was decided in Lisbon. The truth is the European Union has probably spent too long with an internal focus and not long enough with an external globalisation focus on how to compete and how to succeed in a much more open and competitive world than was the case in the past. The best way to make these Funds more effective, more user-friendly, is to align them with those goals—the Lisbon Agenda.

Q175 ***Lord Renton of Mount Harry:*** I still think the Commission might disagree with you about those words "internal focus"; after all they have just taken on board six or seven new members.
Mr McFadden: They might, but we have spent some time debating the internal rules.

Q176 ***Chairman:*** Many proponents of significant European level Structural and Cohesion Fund policies argue that there is more to it than economic issues. Article 158 of the Treaty emphasises strengthening economic and social cohesion. You have not mentioned social cohesion at all in your response, is that because you think it is less important than economic issues?
Mr McFadden: No, you are right; there are other things to be taken into consideration. There is also the question of institutional capability, which these Funds are supposed to promote. I am not denying these other things for a moment, but if you want my clear answer on what the main focus should be here, it should be on growth and jobs and improving the economic performance of the poorer regions of the EU.

Q177 ***Chairman:*** So, in paragraph 10 of your written submission to us, where you say that Integrated Guidelines for Jobs and Growth at European level and National Reform Programmes set out the key challenges, there is no need for a separate set of challenges to be identified for cohesion policy; the task is to identify how cohesion policy can support Member States' policies at national and regional level. So, is it fair to summarise Her Majesty's Government's view about that to be that if Member States apply national reform programmes in the framework of integrated guidelines for jobs and growth—pursue the Lisbon Agenda—there is no different agenda for Structural and Cohesion Funds and their underlying policies: get on and do something about growth and jobs and that would do the job, essentially, of European social cohesion.
Mr McFadden: We would take the view that it would be wrong to have two different agendas. There is an overarching Lisbon Agenda around growth and jobs that is supposed to drive the European Union in a whole number of different ways in the next few years, and that you should somehow have an entirely separate agenda is odd. I am not denying the social dimension, I am not denying the institutional capability, these are important, but if you are asking in simple terms what I think these Funds are for, I would say, jobs, growth and pursuing the Lisbon Agenda.

Q178 ***Chairman:*** Do you find that our European partners share that view of where social cohesion fits in? Do you get any different views from that of the UK?
Mr McFadden: In a club of 27 Member States you will always hear different views.

Q179 ***Chairman:*** Which particular views would you be listening to, taking account of and responding to?
Mr McFadden: My brief experience of ministerial involvement in dossiers and so on, leads me to believe that you will always have a moving set of alliances in the EU. What we have tried to do, as a Member State, particularly in recent years, is to try to focus the EU more on the external challenges that I mentioned at the beginning; on globalisation and on competing in a more open world. The current Commission for the most part are supportive of that agenda, and are allies of that agenda; certainly President Barroso is supportive of that. On that broad front, we have many allies in Europe but, of course, with 27 different countries with their own histories and their own views, there will be different emphases in different Member States.

Q180 ***Lord Kerr of Kinlochard:*** When John Hutton wrote to the Commission about the present review of Cohesion Policy, he stressed the need to respect the principle that the EU should only act where there was clear additional benefit from a collective effort—or EU added value—that EU action should also be proportionate and flexible and that sound financial management should be applied. I am sure this Committee agrees with that. The first principle, which he put at the top of the list, was the requirement for EU added value, which is another way of saying that it is necessary to satisfy the subsidiarity test. The Lisbon Treaty spells out the subsidiarity test clearly: the Union shall act only if and in so far as the objectives of the proposed action cannot be sufficiently achieved by the Member States, either at central level or at regional or local level, but can rather by reason of the scale or effect of the proposed action be better achieved at Union level. Was Mr Hutton saying, and do you say, that the present Structural Funds respect that principle, or was Mr Hutton calling for a reform of the Structural Funds better to reflect that principle? Is there an added value test? Is it sufficiently applied? If not, could not the same Cohesion objectives be achieved by Member State management of the distribution of the money?

Mr McFadden: That is a very good question. What the Government means by the statement that you read out, which is also repeated in the Global Europe pamphlet, is probably more towards the latter of the two positions that you offered, that this issue of EU added value probably becomes more true in the poorer Member States, where there is the most catching up to do, and probably less true in the richer Member States, which is why we have argued that a greater proportion of these Funds should be allocated to the poorer Member States. It is easier to see the EU added value in those circumstances and that is the trend that we supported with the current round of expenditure from 2007–2013. I would expect that is also the trend that we would support in future consideration of the Funds.

Lord Kerr of Kinlochard: That is a very interesting answer. But I will defer to Lord Haskins on the natural follow-up to what you have just said.

Q181 ***Lord Haskins:*** I understand that two or three years ago the merit of rich countries putting money into the budget in order to take the same amount of money back was questioned. The Commission's response was that this was an excellent PR exercise for the Commission –that people in rich countries would feel that the EU was doing something good for them. Not a tremendously convincing argument to me. On the other hand, I am a board member of Yorkshire Forward Regional Development Agency, and there are people there who would say that if this money was not being redirected by the European Union, maybe Her Majesty's Treasury would be less generous about these Funds than the European Union is. Would you like to comment on either of those points?

Mr McFadden: There would be people in Yorkshire who say that and, indeed, in other parts of the country. How these Funds are viewed is perhaps affected by where in the country you live. For example, if I lived in West Wales and the Valleys, or in Cornwall, where there is proportionately a lot of help from these Funds, I would probably see them as very valuable and important. But I think there is a question of scale in this; in the current round of expenditure, the UK will receive something like 9.5 billion euros over seven years. That is worth having; it is nice to have but compared to public expenditure as a whole, compared even to the Yorkshire Forward's budget over seven years, it is not a vast amount. That does not mean it is not worth having or that I do not value the projects on which this money is spent—I am sure we will go on to talk about some of those—but for a country like the UK, I think it is worth keeping a sense of proportion about the added impact of these Funds over a seven-year period. I agree with you that if you are a beneficiary in the Yorkshire area, you would say that this is a good thing, but I would not want to overstate the impact of this expenditure compared to the annual expenditure of Central Government, RDA expenditure or, for example, the expenditure of the devolved administrations which would be vastly greater.

Q182 ***Lord Haskins:*** It is difficult for me to understand why Cornwall or South Yorkshire benefit from the scale or the added value that the European Union gives, which a British Government should not be able to supply itself.

Mr McFadden: In theory, it could; I am not saying that would be impossible, but we were allocated the Funds for this current round of expenditure; those programmes are being implemented and they will add value. What I am saying is that there is a question of scale here compared to say, what Poland is getting from these Funds over this current round of expenditure, where they are responsible for a fifth of the total; we are a few per cent of the total. So there is an important question of scale when you consider the added value. It goes back to Lord Kerr's question about whether these funds match the principle of subsidiarity and how we see that added value. I think scale matters here and the impact and the difference that these Funds can make compared to where you are starting from also has an impact on that. There is not a uniform answer to that question of where you see the added value throughout the European Union.

Q183 ***Lord Kerr of Kinlochard:*** I would like to come back on that. You are quite close to suggesting that the EU added value is in respect of expenditure in the poorer Member States only. I do see the added value in that the standards and rules which are laid down by the Funds will be helpful to those stumping up the money in ensuring that the money is, for the most part, properly spent on the right kind of things in the poorer countries. You are not saying, Minister, that these rules and standards, which perhaps cover translators, paperwork, hassle and bureaucracy, if you look at it the other way round, are unnecessary and inappropriate to this country. You are not saying that there is no EU added value in having projects in West Wales.

Mr McFadden: No, I am not saying that there is no EU added value, I am very careful not to say that. As I said, if I lived in West Wales, I would see the benefit from these Funds. In the debate on 6 February, when the new treaty was being debated, several Welsh Members spoke and said that these Funds have had a significant impact; my colleague Nia Griffith, the Member for Llanelli, talked about the projects in her constituency. So, I see the value. What I am saying is that there is a question of scale on both counts, both the jobs and growth economic impacts, which will obviously be greater in somewhere like Poland, which is receiving about one-fifth of the total allocation for this current round of expenditure. And on the question of institutional capability, you mentioned both ends of this lens, is it good stewardship or is it paperwork and bureaucracy. Good stewardship is important—this is public money in one sense or another—it is important that we have sound financial management, that is also one of the things that we set out in Global Europe. Again, where you have—probably less true over time—relatively new democracies there probably is added EU value in terms of stewardship, of Funds, of project management, of partnership working, which are going to have a greater impact than, hopefully, in the richer Member States where some of these systems have been developed and have been in place for some time. So, I am not saying there is no added value in the UK, but I am saying on a scale both on the economic side and on the institutional side it is probably less than in the newer and poorer Member States.

Q184 ***Chairman:*** May I press you on this basic question of whether richer Member States should receive any funding at all, in principle. In paragraph 16 of the written evidence to the Committee, the Minister argues that "In line with . . . subsidiarity, Member States which have the institutions and financial strength to fully develop and pursue their own devolved and decentralised regional policies . . . should be encouraged and enabled to do so. Other Member States which have not yet reached this position will continue, for some time, to benefit from assistance". Is that not very close to saying that richer countries do not need these kind of Funds—they have got the financial strength; they have got the capability to get on with their own policies. Is that not what the written evidence to us says?

Mr McFadden: It is certainly a question of scale and I hope the Committee does not think that I am being repetitive in coming back to the same point a few times, but it does apply here. Let us be honest about how this would be viewed in the next round of negotiations on these things at EU level, there will be richer Member States that want to hang on to some of these Funds for particular regions within their countries, and I understand that. That is what happened the last time, in the run-up to the current round of expenditure. What we are saying in that paragraph is that there is less of a need in richer Member States—to go back to the discussions we have just had with Lord Kerr and Lord Haskins—for reasons of economic development having developed at a greater pace over the years, and for the institutional capability. Now, does that mean that richer Member States should not get a penny? No, I am not saying that, but what I am saying is that proportionately we want to see a situation where most of these Funds, and a greater proportion of these Funds, is spent on the Member States and the regions that really need it, and those are the poorer Member States.

Chairman: That leads us on to Lord Moser. Thirty-six per cent of the Funds currently do not go to the poorer countries. That is not negligible; that is a very substantial proportion.

Q185 ***Lord Moser:*** You said in your evidence that you favour an increase in that figure—not the 36 per cent, but the 64 per cent—to 67 per cent. That seems a rather modest forecast. Looking at the other side of it, is there a worry in the Government's mind, or your mind, that the poorer countries cannot cope with more anyhow, that they cannot absorb more than that? Is that one argument for not going either the whole hog for the poorer countries, or rather more than a 3 per cent increase?

Mr McFadden: There are two points there and I will bring Mr Steele in in a second. On the 64 per cent and 67 per cent, I should clarify that. The 67 per cent is where we think we can get to within the current round of expenditure between 2007-2013; that does not refer to a long-term target after that for the next round of expenditure, that is a prediction of where we can get to.

Q186 ***Lord Moser:*** If I can interrupt you. Why is that the limit, why is that all you can get to?

Mr McFadden: That relates to the second part of your question. There is an absorption cap which is around the proportion of GDP, it varies between 3 per cent and 4 per cent of GDP in individual Member States. Part of that is about additionality because, of course, these Funds have to be matched by expenditure from within the Member State that receives them. It is also partly based on experience about how Member States can absorb and use these Funds. I am happy to bring Mr Steele in on this.

Mr Steele: To be clear about the 64 per cent and the 67 per cent: the 64 per cent is an average over the period 2007-2013. It starts lower, at something like 57 per cent, but finishes higher in 2013 at 67 per cent. The 64 per cent is an average over that seven-year period. That is largely caused by the phasing out in existing richer Member States of some of the regions that were Objective 1 in the previous period that are no longer Objective 1, but which are getting tapered funds at the moment, but tapering down, so that by 2013 they will be at the regional competitive and employment levels. That I hope explains what the Minister said about a rising trend in favour of the poorer Member States over the current period; but our ambition goes beyond that for the future period.

Q187 ***Lord Moser:*** Beyond 67 per cent?
Mr Steele: Yes.

Q188 ***Lord Moser:*** How many countries are we talking about when we talk about the poorer, as opposed to the richer countries?
Mr McFadden: We tend to focus on the newer Member States who have joined in the last few years, although there may be regions within other Member States. If you wanted to refer to "old Europe"—to use Donald Rumsfeld's phrase—Greece and Portugal were the two States that tended to be regarded as poorer Member States. Many of the newer Member States have significantly below average GDP per head, and the European Union uses the definition itself of Member States where GDP per head is less than 90 per cent of the EU average, and most of the new Member States, if not all of them, come into that bracket.

Q189 ***Lord Haskins:*** Concerning the absorption point, having spent my life in the private sector and spent the last five years in the public sector, this obsession with absorbing public money at the end of the financial year has always intrigued me—the "hockey stick" effect—it is not only a problem for Bulgaria, it is a problem for Yorkshire also. Is this a serious issue that places like Bulgaria simply are not in the position to spend the money that is available for them because they do not have the structures and disciplines and they cannot pass the tests that are needed? Is that a real problem and how are we going to get around that?
Mr McFadden: That is one issue. But there is also the issue of them perhaps having to borrow to meet the matched funding. We do not want to have a perverse effect, where the Funds that are meant to help poorer countries, end up getting them into huge debt because of borrowing in order to make up the matched funding. My colleagues will correct me if I am wrong but one of the reasons the absorption caps have been set is also with an eye on the level of financial commitment that is needed from the receiving Member States, as well as the institutional capability.

Q190 ***Chairman:*** Does that lead to the thought that co-financing should be changed, or moderated, if one of the problems is that a poor country might have to borrow to co-finance, to relax the co-financing? If there really is poverty and there are difficulties, why is not the funding on a more generous basis?
Mr McFadden: By co-financing, you mean the requirement to match Funds?

Q191 ***Chairman:*** Yes.
Mr McFadden: We have taken the view that this is probably the right principle that the receiving Member State should have a stake in this too. We have not always thought that you could just have a basic grant system, where there is no requirement required on behalf of the receiving Member State.

Q192 ***Lord Steinberg:*** Concerning the comment that you made about Bulgaria, which you said was one of the weaker countries, on which we all agree. You are saying that they have not got the structure or the ability to spend the money that was being allocated to them. Is it not slightly immoral that we offer them a carrot which they are unable to take? Should we not be working rather to try and improve their structure, rather than purely offering them money which we know they cannot take.
Mr McFadden: I do not think it is as stark as that. If you look at the table of the beneficiaries for example, of the expenditure in 2007-2013, there is -as we were talking about percentages a few moments ago—most of this is going to the poorer Member States. I agree with you that part of the ethos of being in the European Union is that we should try to work to improve the performance, improve the quality of life and improve the economic development of those countries that have joined which, for one reason or another, are not in the same position as the majority of countries in the EU. These Funds are supposed to be an important weapon in that. So I agree with the general premise and, as we said in the paper which we sent to you, we also want to see a greater proportion of these Funds going to the poorer Member States. We have also said that this should be done in a way that means sound financial management and is properly run and managed. When you are dealing with the stewardship of public funds, that is always a principle that should be borne in mind. I agree with the general premise of what you are saying, but I am not sure it is as stark as us offering money and saying that there are so many strings on this that it is not really a benefit to you. It is a matter of getting the right management and stewardship in place.

Q193 ***Lord Maclennan of Rogart:*** I am a little puzzled, Minister, why the Union should take the view that the totality of the Funds should go in a higher proportion to the Member States that are catching up, but that the conditions and terms on which the money is made available should not be variable across the Member States regardless of their needs. Prudent financial management does not mean that the contribution should be necessarily required to be the same.
Mr McFadden: They are variable to some extent. There has always been a requirement of these Funds that there is also a commitment shown on behalf of the receiving Member State. It does not operate quite as uniformly throughout the European Union but perhaps Mr Steele can say a bit more about that.

Mr Steele: There are different co-financing rates in the regulations depending on where you are in the league table of relative wealth, so the poorer Member States have a lower co-financing rate, broadly speaking, than the richer ones do so they have to provide less matched funding in absolute terms.

Q194 ***Lord Maclennan of Rogart:*** Could you give us any indication as to what the significances are and where these differences operate?
Mr Steele: I will send you a note on that, if I may. Broadly speaking, from memory, the co-financing rate is about 25 per cent.

Q195 ***Chairman:*** It would be very helpful if you could do a note on this.
Mr Steele: Yes, certainly.
Lord Kerr of Kinlochard: I would like to bring in a note of mild dissent if—not you, Minister—but if we were arguing about a co-financing rate of zero. The free good is not valued and is very dangerous. I have never believed in the absorbtive capacity arguments; Spain disproves them totally. We debated at great length in the 1980s how much Structural Funds money Spain could absorb. In the end, Spain acquired much more than we, in London, thought was absorbable in Spain. The huge take-off of the Spanish economy in the 1990s had very little to do with the Structural Funds; the country was absorbing an enormous amount of investment and shooting up the per capita GNP league tables, with the kick-start of the Structural Funds helping a bit; of course, the co-financing rate was quite high.

Q196 ***Lord Trimble:*** I turn to the question of the eligibility tests for the Structural Funds. What view do you take of the eligibility tests; do you think they are fair, reasonable, or what?
Mr McFadden: This goes back to my first answer. The eligibility tests are essentially economic and we think that is right and that should continue.

Q197 ***Lord Trimble:*** This is the percentage of GDP that is still at 75 per cent for Objective 1?
Mr McFadden: Yes, there is also a definition of a poor Member State, which is that the whole Member State is beneath 90 per cent. There is a regional impact of being 75 per cent or less.

Q198 ***Lord Trimble:*** I am curious about the interrelationship between this uniform criterion, which you define throughout and the way in which you are dividing them between the EU 13 and the rest; one-third going to the EU 13 and two-thirds to the others. How does that work out? Does it not result in a situation that within the EU 13—the originals, minus Greece and Portugal—that there is expenditure that would not be justified on the criteria that apply to the poorer States?
Mr McFadden: They certainly would not say that. There are two or three things in play here; there are regions, which will have, for example, in West Wales and the Valleys in the UK, where you have a GDP per head of less than 75 per cent of the average. That would be true in whole Member States in the eastern side of the European Union. There are also those whole Member States which have less than 90 per cent of GDP—that applies to the Cohesion Fund, not to the other two—and all these factors come into play.

Q199 ***Lord Trimble:*** What do you think should happen after 2013?
Mr McFadden: As you know, the Commission have launched a consultation on the EU budget. This will be part of that. We, as a Government, will make a submission on our views on that later this year. These Funds will still be part of the future but—I am not trying to duck the question—until we have a broader discussion of the EU budget for that period, it is difficult to predict with any accuracy how much they will be, or what proportion of the budget. It has been a longstanding position of the UK Government that less of the European Union budget should be spent on agriculture and more on other things; that will continue to be part of the position. Again, if you look at the Global Europe pamphlet, beyond the Structural Funds we set out a number of issues around competitiveness and other areas which we thought were priorities for the European Union in the future. All these things will be reflected in our submission to that consultation on the EU budget. Structural Funds will be a part of that and I would not want to start predicting numbers.

Q200 ***Lord Trimble:*** This obviously comes on to something that was suggested to us in other evidence that we have heard; it has been suggested that it is undesirable to have discussion of Structural and Cohesion Funds taking place within the same context as discussion on wider issues and that quite often the Structural and Cohesion Funds are adjusted in order to buy support of wider issues, or to affect them.
Mr McFadden: I am not sure that I quite understand the question. I am not sure that it is undesirable to have discussion on it; it is a perfectly reasonable issue to discuss. Certainly, the UK Government's view of the future of these Funds would be taken in a broader view of what the priorities of the European Union should be. We referred earlier to areas that we are phasing out that had support in the past, their performance has hopefully improved and I completely take the point that Lord Kerr made that this may be only one factor of many factors in a particular region or country's economic performance

improving. The picture will change over time and if these Funds are effective, maybe not in 2013 but in the future, some of the countries currently benefiting from them may not need them in the future.

Q201 ***Lord Moser:*** You referred several times, understandably, to GDP figures. Are these national figures or do you use regional data also?
Mr Steele: In terms of the qualification for payments from the Cohesion Fund, which is one of the three European Structural and Cohesion Funds, it is on a national GNI basis, which is very similar to GDP. In terms of the regional selection for the convergence regions, it is on a regional GDP basis.

Q202 ***Lord Moser:*** Why the difference?
Mr Steele: The aims of the Cohesion Fund are aimed specifically at those countries that fall below 90 per cent of average, whereas the European Regional Development Fund, as its name suggests, is more focused on the regional level rather than the national level.

Q203 ***Lord Moser:*** Getting back to the absorption point which was raised earlier, some poorer countries have rich regions and so to judge them as poorer countries because they have low GDP per head is rather misleading.
Mr Steele: I can really only explain how the current system is, rather than what we think it should be, but that is how the Cohesion Fund is set up and operates.

Q204 ***Chairman:*** That brings us very nicely to the question of what the Government thinks the system should be. What would be your guiding principles if you are looking at the whole question of Structural and Cohesion Funds from scratch?
Mr McFadden: We have set them out in the Global Europe pamphlet and indeed in the written evidence that we presented. I think there would be three things: the EU added value point; that EU action should be proportionate and flexible; and the third point would be sound financial management and stewardship of the Funds. If we were starting this from scratch, those would be the three things that we should think about in setting up such a system. Even if we cannot start from scratch, those are the three things that should hopefully inform it in the future.

Q205 ***Chairman:*** If you applied those principles, what changes would we see in the system?
Mr McFadden: This goes back to some of the discussions we have had. You would probably be spending more of this in the poorer EU Member States, which reflects the discussion that Lord Kerr and I had about EU added value. You would always be asking yourself about the long-term necessity of the Funds; we know it may be a feature of bureaucracy in general, not just these Funds, that once something gets set up it tends to live forever. Regarding the question of stewardship, there are issues of simplicity and there will always be a balance between—this is a generic regulatory question, I suppose—of asking people to account properly for the money that is spent, which is an important principle, and also managing it so tightly that you do not get the benefit of local knowledge. That is why in this current round of spending there has been an attempt to get the stewardship into three levels of the European Union, the strategic approach of the European Union, the national reference framework at the national level, and then the implementation at the more regional level.

Q206 ***Chairman:*** In paragraph 8 of your written evidence, on the second of those principles, the Minister told us that expenditure is just one of a number of policy levers, alongside co-ordination, shared best practice, legislation or regulation. Which are the most important of the non-expenditure policy levers and do you think that balance is right at the moment, or needs to change? You made the point that spending is not the only thing.
Mr McFadden: Yes, I understand the question. It is a good question about regional policy—what else is important? Governance is important; accessibility and transport are important; I believe local and environmental factors are important in regional policy and effectiveness, in other words, creating a good physical environment and a good business investment environment; and we would also stress, and have done as a Government, capability and skills to compete. There are a number of things which are not purely investment and expenditure but which are certainly helpful to you if you want to succeed as a region.

Q207 ***Lord Maclennan of Rogart:*** I have a particular question about the compatibility of the guidelines and these principles that you have been outlining, with the objectives set out in the regulations for the current period, the third objective in the current period is to promote European territorial co-operation, to strengthen cross-border transnational interregional co-operation. Are you able to say which of those integrated guidelines deals with that issue? It seems to me that if you leave these matters simply to national reform programmes, you will not necessarily get that integrated territorial co-operation across borders.
Mr McFadden: For example, in the second point, there is a reference to legislation and regulation. That can be a critical friend or foe in terms of encouraging greater cross-border territorial co-operation. There are many unseen barriers that we know about. The battle for a single market is not quite fully won, and

if we want to see more cross-border trade and cross-border co-operation, there is a substantial regulatory agenda, which may not be quite our main subject today, but it is substantial.

Q208 ***Lord Maclennan of Rogart:*** You would not see Cohesion Funding as being part of the weaponry to deal with this?
Mr McFadden: Cohesion Funding can be, but following on from the Chairman's question about non-financial instruments, getting the regulatory balance right is critical to economic growth and jobs, it can help you or it can hinder you. Hopefully, this Government can be a good influence in encouraging the EU to pay close attention to the regulatory environment.

Q209 ***Lord Steinberg:*** I am sure you would agree with me, Minister, that the whole format and shape of the European Union has changed a lot over recent years and will continue to change in the future, and that we will have more so-called "weak countries" entering the EU in time. Bearing that in mind, and bearing in mind that the strong must always help the weak, is the Government satisfied that the current budget that they have in relation to this, are they happy with this, bearing in mind also that budgets are usually best-guess estimates and can go wrong quite easily. Is our Government happy about the current size of the budget?
Mr McFadden: There are two points there. We have been strong supporters of enlargement; we think it has been good for Europe, economically, politically, culturally.

Q210 ***Lord Steinberg:*** Pardon me, but I think this Committee agrees with that position.
Mr McFadden: Yes, I am sure. I got that from your question. Under both the last Government and this Government we are supporters of enlargement. Your question is that enlargement brings with it a number of countries which have been poorer in the past, so is the budget up to the job, which I suppose goes back to the question that Lord Trimble asked me a few minutes ago. There will always be a discussion about the EU budget and I suspect it would be unwise of me to comment too closely—I can feel my Treasury colleagues watching over my shoulder even though they are not in the room—if I commented too freely on what I thought the size of EU budget should be in the future. That will be the subject of much negotiation.

Q211 ***Lord Steinberg:*** Pardon me for interrupting you your flow, but I am just asking about the current EU budget.
Mr McFadden: Is the current budget up to the job? I am sure people will always argue that they want more. Our view, as you know, was that we would have liked to have seen less of the current EU budget spent on agriculture and more on other priorities. In terms of the Structural Funds, maybe that would come into that, but we have the budget we have; we will have to do the best job that we can with it and as for the next round, that is for another day.

Q212 ***Lord Maclennan of Rogart:*** Minister, is it your judgment and that of the Government that the Structural and Cohesion Funds are being sensibly and effectively applied and what kind of criteria of success do you have in judging what is going on across the Union?
Mr McFadden: The criteria of success are economic and we will have to judge the success by the performance in the future of those regions that are receiving help from these Funds. We want to see the raising up of the regions that are poorer; an increase in their capability and that contributing to an overall better performance for the EU in the future. Remember, the Lisbon goal was for Europe to become the most successful and competitive transnational economy by 2010. That is a very ambitious goal and this expenditure is supposed to help in some way towards it. So, that is how we will have to judge it.

Q213 ***Lord Maclennan of Rogart:*** With respect, that is a sort of "rolled-up" application of the criteria to many different factors. What I was trying to get at, you have mentioned in another context, regulation and the single market, and all those things might contribute to the economic turnaround, but are there criteria that you can apply to the application of the Structural and Cohesion Funds, in particular, within the areas where they are being deployed?
Mr McFadden: The Funds have different aims. For example, in the European Social Fund, one of the aims is around skills and the capability of individuals, so you would judge that as to whether that expenditure has had an impact for them and an impact in the regions in which it is applied. In this country, it works through Job Centre Plus and others. It depends on the Fund and the aims of the Fund. I am not trying to duck your question but these Funds have some quite specific aims.

Q214 ***Lord Maclennan of Rogart:*** Are you satisfied that the Commission can do the necessary appraisal of whether these micro aims are being achieved, or do we ourselves look at them?
Mr McFadden: If you are looking at how effective, take that example we have just been talking about, the European Social Fund expenditure will have been in say, the East Midlands region. I am not sure the

Commission is always going to have that detailed level of knowledge; that is going to have to be done closer to the ground.

Q215 ***Lord Maclennan of Rogart:*** By whom?
Mr McFadden: In that case, I would say by the regional body administering the Fund.

Q216 ***Lord Maclennan of Rogart:*** But that is a self-serving body and they, as you pointed out in the context of Yorkshire, would always be making the strongest case. Is there any external critique?
Mr McFadden: There is stewardship of RDA expenditure.
Mr Steele: There is an increased emphasis in the current, relatively new, round of Funds on evaluation of the impact, focusing not only on the direct outputs which have tended to be in terms of jobs or start-up of new businesses, but also looking at the real economic impact of the Funds and trying to adjust for the other factors which are clearly important also in terms of regional economic growth.

Q217 ***Lord Steinberg:*** This goes back to an earlier point. We were told at a previous meeting that some countries find it very difficult to measure, and to evaluate what happens in the regions within the country because of poor statistics. Is that a worry for you? It has been mentioned and I understand it.
Mr McFadden: It is a worry, but it is probably a fact that capability certainly differs from country to country. We talked earlier about the value of these Funds beyond the—I should not say pounds, shillings and pence, as I will be wrong on two counts—actual sums of money and improving institutional capability and project management and a number of other things is part of all this. Of course, there will be different statistical and data collection capabilities, but that would be true even in the EU 15, not just in the new Member States.

Q218 ***Chairman:*** Before we turn to the last question, is it not the case that most Objective 1 regions that were Objective 1 regions even in the 1980s, are still Objective 1 regions and if that is the case, does that not appear to show that it has not been the kind of success that one would have hoped for?
Mr Bond: I am aware that this is something that Open Europe referred to in their evidence, but the comparison they make was not entirely accurate. Of the regions that were nominated in 1989, which was approximately 44, half of them now still have coverage by successors to Objective 1, ie, the Convergence objective, and half of them have not. They were referring to regions in a particular year and they picked the middle year of the last financing round that was still receiving support from the funding, but that also meant that you counted those regions that were getting transitional support because they had moved over three-quarters of the EU average, and that included, in the UK, Northern Ireland; it included southern Ireland including Dublin, so there were some areas of substantial population. If you would like them, we can provide the actual figures on that.
Chairman: That would be extremely helpful to us, rather than take time today.

Q219 ***Lord Kerr of Kinlochard:*** May I take you back, Minister, to added value. Supposing the Structural and Cohesion Funds did not exist. Would UK regional policy be very different? What would we be doing differently; and are there things we would not be doing at all?
Mr McFadden: I do not think, in policy terms, we would be doing a huge amount differently. In geographical terms, you might not see the benefit which those regions of the country that have the largest share of the expenditure may be getting at the moment if these Funds had never existed. I do not think that they have changed our policy, but they will have had some beneficial impact on the geographical distribution of money to the regions that have benefited from them.

Q220 ***Lord Kerr of Kinlochard:*** How much does this added value—if it exists—cost, how much do we pay for it, what is the added cost? We had remarkable estimates from Europe and have had a lot of very interesting evidence. I was looking last night at evidence from the East Midlands Development Agency, which says that the RDA administration costs for England as a whole amount to about £11 million, of which the largest component is £3 million from the South West Regional Development Agency; the South West being the only English region with both full "convergence" and "competitive" allocations, and therefore some £400 million; administering that costs them just under £3 million. Is that order of magnitude about right; about 1 per cent of the amounts of money we are talking about; the Structural Fund money that comes to a region? That is the Regional Development Agency cost; is that out of line with the average, or is that about it?
Mr McFadden: This might be one to add to the list of two or three things on which we will have to come back to you on paper; it is perhaps best done in that way. One point I would make is that there is recognition in the Funds that there will be administrative costs in using the money and it is built into the Funds and recognised in the way that they are structured.

Q221 ***Lord Renton of Mount Harry:*** Minister, I declare an interest because, as the Chairman of a conservation board in Sussex and Hampshire, we have received quite, for us, substantial sums of money from the European Regional Development Fund, particularly under what is known as the Interreg Programme, in which a number of countries go forward with the same idea about covering the environment, having more volunteers, etc., and I cannot avoid stressing that, at a moment when money is very short from DEFRA and others for environmental agricultural purposes, we are looking—some of us in the conservation boards and national parks—very much to help from Europe. This is the European Regional Development Fund, in our case we use SEEDA quite frequently, but much of the work we have to do ourselves. It has proven a very important element in helping the agri-environment issues that are not subsidies to farmers, at a time, and it is going to be even more so, because money is going to be short. DEFRA, of course, is the ministry with which we deal.

Mr McFadden: Is that new? Have not people, quite understandably, always tried to get help from funding sources that are available. I appreciate what you are saying, but I am not sure it is entirely new and I quite understand why you are doing it.

Lord Renton of Mount Harry: I am saying this in praise of what happens. It has been very helpful and we hope it will go on being helpful.

Chairman: On that positive note, Minister, could I thank you and your two officials for your direct and helpful answers to our questions. We are most grateful to you all. Thank you.

Supplementary memorandum by Pat McFadden MP, Minister of State for Employment Relations & Postal Services, Department for Business, Enterprise & Regulatory Reform

At my Evidence session on the 26 February, I agreed to provide further information on three issues.

The first issue was the levels of funding required from Member States to "match" those provided by the Funds. These are set out in the Regulation laying down general provisions on the European Regional Development Fund, the European Social Fund and the Cohesion Fund—Council Regulation (EC) No 1083/2006. Article 53 and Annex III set out the contribution from the Funds at the level of operational programmes. The maximum levels vary from 50% through to 85% dependent on the Objective, the Fund and the relative prosperity of the recipient Member State. The relevant text from the Regulations is attached at Annex A. The difference between these levels and 100% is the contribution required from other sources. Thus, for example, if a Fund is providing a maximum of 75% under the Regulations, the match funding to be provided from other sources will be a minimum of 25%.

The second issue concerned the cost of administering the Funds in the UK. The running costs of administering the Funds in the UK for 2007–08, above those co-financed by the Funds through Technical Assistance, is estimated to be £15.45 million[8]. This figure includes work on the 2007–13 programmes as well as on the 2000–06 programmes which are still running.

In addition, there is some capital expenditure; for example, £3.02 million is being allocated by Communities and Local Government in 2007–08 to develop their IT system for the 2007–13 period.

Article 46 of the Structural Funds General Regulation, cited above, allows for a proportion of the Member States Allocation to provide "Technical Assistance" for the running of the Operational Programmes. This can be used to finance the preparation, management, monitoring, evaluation, information and control activities of Operational Programmes together with activities to reinforce the administrative capacity for implementing the Funds. The maximum limits for Technical Assistance are 4% of the total amount allocated under the Convergence and Regional Competitiveness and Employment Objectives and 6% of the total amount allocated under the European Territorial Cooperation Objective.

Any funding provided by the Commission under Technical Assistance needs to be match funded by the recipient. For example, the domestic costs of the RDAs, as the body designated by the Member State to administer the 2007–13 ERDF Operational Programmes in the English regions, are match funded by Technical Assistance.

The third issue was the current status of Objective 1 regions designated in 1989. Our analysis shows that of the 44 Regions designated across the EU as Objective 1 regions in 1989, 21 remain as Convergence Objective (the successor of Objective 1) regions for the 2007–13 period. Details of this analysis can be found at Annex B.

12 March 2008

[8] This covers the budgets of Business, Enterprise and Regulatory Reform, the Department of Work and Pensions, Communities and Local Government, the Welsh Assembly Government, Scottish Executive and Northern Ireland Executive

Annex A

RELEVANT TEXT OF COUNCIL REGULATION (EC) NO 1083/2006 IN RELATION TO MATCH FUNDING LEVELS

ARTICLE 53

Contribution from the Funds

3. For operational programmes under the European territorial cooperation objective in which at least one participant belongs to a Member State whose average GDP per capita for the period 2001 to 2003 was below 85% of the EU-25 average during the same period, the contribution from the ERDF shall not be higher than 85% of the eligible expenditure. For all other operational programmes, the contribution from the ERDF shall not be higher than 75% of the eligible expenditure co-financed by the ERDF.

ANNEX III

Ceilings applicable to co-financing rates (referred to in Article 53)

Criteria	*Member States*	*ERDF and ESF Percentage of eligible expenditure*	*Cohesion Fund Percentage of eligible expenditure*
(1) Member States whose average GDP per capita for the period 2001–03 was below 85% of the EU-25 average during the same period.	Czech Republic, Estonia, Greece, Cyprus, Latvia, Lithuania, Hungary, Malta, Poland, Portugal, Slovenia, Slovakia	85% for the Convergence and Regional competitiveness and employment objectives	85%
(2) Member States other than those under (1) eligible for the transitional regime of the Cohesion Fund on 1 January 2007.	Spain	80% for the Convergence and phasing-in regions under the Regional competitiveness and employment objective 50% for the Regional competitiveness and employment objective outside phasing-in regions	85%
(3) Member States other than those referred to under (1) and (2).	Belgium, Denmark, Federal Republic of Germany, France, Ireland, Italy, Luxembourg, the Netherlands, Austria, Finland, Sweden and United Kingdom.	75% for the Convergence objective	—
(4) Member States other than those referred to under (1) and (2).	Belgium, Denmark, Federal Republic of Germany, France, Ireland, Italy, Luxembourg, the Netherlands, Austria, Finland, Sweden and United Kingdom.	50% for the Regional competitiveness and employment objective	—
(5) Outermost regions referred to in Article 299(2) of the Treaty benefiting from the additional allocation for these regions provided for in paragraph 20 of Annex II	Spain, France and Portugal	50%	—

Criteria	*Member States*	*ERDF and ESF Percentage of eligible expenditure*	*Cohesion Fund Percentage of eligible expenditure*
(6) Outermost regions referred to in Article 299(2) of the Treaty	Spain, France and Portugal	85 % under the Convergence and Regional competitiveness and employment objectives	—

Annex B

ANALYSIS ON THE CURRENT STATUS OF OBJECTIVE 1 REGIONS DESIGNATED IN 1989

Progress of the Regions Eligible for Objective 1 (Obj 1) in 1989

Programming periods	*1989–93*	*1994–99*	*2000–06*	*2007–13*
No. of Obj 1/convergence objective regions	44	44	38	21
No. of regions receiving funding from Obj1/ convergence objective	44	44	43	30

Explanatory Notes

In 1988, 44 regions were designated to receive EU Objective 1 funding for the period 1989–93. All of those regions were still eligible for Objective 1 in the following funding period 1994–99, with the exception of Abruzzi in Italy, which only received support until 1996.

For the 2000–06 period, five regions had GDP above 75% of the EU average. They received transitional funding from Objective 1 for the period. So, although 43 regions were receiving Objective 1 funds, only 38 of them were still Objective 1 regions.

As part of the reforms of the Structural Funds for 2007–13, Objective 1 was replaced by the convergence objective, with the same qualifying criterion. The regions eligible for the convergence objective were designated in 2005 on the following basis: regions with a GDP below 75% of the EU-25 average were designated as convergence objective regions. Regions with a GDP above 75% of the EU-25 average but below 75% of the old EU-15 average were given convergence objective funding on a transitional basis (and designated as Phasing-Out regions). Regions which had received Objective 1 in 2000–06 but now had a GDP above 75% of both the EU-25 and EU-15 average were given transitional support from the competitiveness and employment objective (and designated as Phasing-In regions).

Of the original 44 regions eligible for Objective 1, 21 were eligible for its successor, the convergence objective. An additional nine regions were designated as Phasing-Out regions.

Additional Points

- These tables only cover the progress of the original 44 regions designated as Objective 1 in 1988. They do not cover any regions that became eligible after 1988.
- In 1988 the EU consisted of 12 Member States (including pre-unification West Germany).
- Ireland was a single NUTS-2 region between 1989–99. To enable consistent comparison, it has been counted as two regions throughout the tables.
- The Spanish NUTS-2 region Ceuta-Melilla was split into two for 2007–13. To enable consistent comparison it has been counted as two regions throughout the tables.

Details

MS	*Region*	*Status* *1989–93*	*1994–99*	*2000–06*	*2007–13*
Spain	Andalusia	Obj 1	Obj 1	Obj 1	Convergence
	Asturias	Obj 1	Obj 1	Obj 1	Phasing-Out
	Castilla y Leon	Obj 1	Obj 1	Obj 1	Phasing-In
	Castilla-La Mancha	Obj 1	Obj 1	Obj 1	Convergence
	Ceuta	Obj 1	Obj 1	Obj 1	Phasing-Out
	Melilla	Obj 1	Obj 1	Obj 1	Phasing-Out
	Comunidad Valenciana	Obj 1	Obj 1	Obj 1	Phasing-In
	Exrtemadura	Obj 1	Obj 1	Obj 1	Convergence
	Galicia	Obj 1	Obj 1	Obj 1	Convergence
	Canary Islands	Obj 1	Obj 1	Obj 1	Phasing-In
	Murcia	Obj 1	Obj 1	Obj 1	Phasing-Out
France	French Overseas Depts	Obj 1	Obj 1	Obj 1	Convergence
	Corsica	Obj 1	Obj 1	Transition	
Greece	Anatoliki Makedonia, Thraki	Obj 1	Obj 1	Obj 1	Convergence
	Kentriki Makedonia	Obj 1	Obj 1	Obj 1	Phasing-Out
	Dytiki Makedonia	Obj 1	Obj 1	Obj 1	Phasing-Out
	Thessalia	Obj 1	Obj 1	Obj 1	Convergence
	Ipeiros	Obj 1	Obj 1	Obj 1	Convergence
	Ionia Nisia	Obj 1	Obj 1	Obj 1	Convergence
	Dytiki Ellada	Obj 1	Obj 1	Obj 1	Convergence
	Sterea Ellada	Obj 1	Obj 1	Obj 1	Phasing-In
	Peloponnisos	Obj 1	Obj 1	Obj 1	Convergence
	Attiki	Obj 1	Obj 1	Obj 1	Phasing-Out
	Voreio Aigaio	Obj 1	Obj 1	Obj 1	Convergence
	Notio Aigaio	Obj 1	Obj 1	Obj 1	Phasing-In
	Kriti	Obj 1	Obj 1	Obj 1	Convergence
Ireland	Border Midlands & Western	Obj 1	Obj 1	Obj 1	Phasing-In
	Southern and Eastern	Obj 1	Obj 1	Transition	
Italy	Abruzzi	Obj 1	Obj 1/ Transition*		
	Basilicata	Obj 1	Obj 1	Obj 1	Phasing-Out
	Calabria	Obj 1	Obj 1	Obj 1	Convergence
	Campania	Obj 1	Obj 1	Obj 1	Convergence
	Molise	Obj 1	Obj 1	Transition	
	Apulia (Puglia)	Obj 1	Obj 1	Obj 1	Convergence
	Sardinia	Obj 1	Obj 1	Obj 1	Phasing-In
	Sicily	Obj 1	Obj 1	Obj 1	Convergence
Portugal	Notre	Obj 1	Obj 1	Obj 1	Convergence
	Centro	Obj 1	Obj 1	Obj 1	Convergence
	Alentejo	Obj 1	Obj 1	Obj 1	Convergence
	Algarve	Obj 1	Obj 1	Obj 1	Phasing-Out
	Acores	Obj 1	Obj 1	Obj 1	Convergence
	Madeira	Obj 1	Obj 1	Obj 1	Phasing-In
	Lisboa	Obj 1	Obj 1	Transition	
UK	Northern Ireland	Obj 1	Obj 1	Transition	

Notes
* = Abruzzi was Objective 1 for 1994–1996 only

TUESDAY 4 MARCH 2008

Present	Cohen of Pimlico, B (Chairman)	Steinberg, L
	Kerr of Kinlochard, L	Trimble, L
	Moser, L	Woolmer of Leeds, L
	Renton of Mount Harry, L	

Memorandum by Graham Meadows, former Director General of DG Regional Policy, European Commission, and Honorary Professor in the School of City and Regional Planning, University of Cardiff

1. The European Union's structural funds are financial instruments in support of, respectively, European regional and cohesion policy (using the European Regional Development Fund, the Cohesion Fund and the European Social Fund) and European policy for rural development (the European Fund for Agriculture Rural Development). Taken together, these instruments account for 40% of the EU budget but just 0.4% of EU GDP. As such, the instruments are of less significance to the Inquiry than the policies and political objectives of the Union which underlie their deployment and my answers to the Committee's questions will therefore address the latter.

2. These answers are supplied to the Committee in a personal capacity. While their focus of attention is on EU regional and cohesion policy (hereafter EU regional policy), many of the arguments apply by analogy to rural development policy which follows many of the same operational principles.

QUESTION 1

(a) *The objectives the European Union's regional policy*

3. The objectives of European regional policy remain valid and should not change if the Union is to maintain its high level of integration reflected in the single market and, for 15 Member States, the single currency. The policy concerns itself with the economic growth of regions and the Union's single market for labour, and thus contributes to the Union objective to improve the well-being of citizens through "balanced economic growth" and the achievement of a "highly competitive social market economy aiming at full employment and social progress".[1] The benefits, and costs, of market-driven growth do not fall equally on Member States and regions. Regional policy is the Union's response to the concerns raised by the uneven distribution of the costs and benefits of the single market.

4. European regional policy is one of a trinity of economic policies through which the Union seeks its objective of balanced growth.[2] The three are:

- market-opening, both internally (the Single Market) and globally;
- the single currency, the Euro, with its common rules for the macro-management of the economy (the Growth and Stability Pact) and its common guidelines for managing the supply side of the economy (the Lisbon and Gothenburg agenda); and
- regional policy, which encompasses financial support for the Union's Single Labour Market.

5. European regional policy plays a double function within the trinity:

- it seeks to help the weakest regions to close the gap between their income and the Union average thus seeking greater balance to growth; and
- it contributes directly to a faster overall rate of growth, both for Member States and for the Union as a whole, by raising the growth rate of the slowest growing regions, where resources are underused.

[1] Both quotations are from the recently-signed Lisbon Treaty.

[2] This emphasises the rôle of Union policies in economic growth, whereas most national governments would argue that their growth record—especially if it is good—is due to their own economic management. In part this is true, national macro-economic policy is obviously crucial to growth. But at the same time, national macro-economic policy is made within a Union context. All Member States benefit from the growth inducing effect of the Single Market and from the Union's trade agreements with third countries.
Member States who are also members of the Euro zone must heed Stability Pact rules. Even those outside the Euro-zone manage their currencies so as to keep within a particular relationship with the € and with an eye on Stability Pact rules. And all Member States accept the Lisbon and Gothenburg agenda.
Just as all Member States benefit from the positive effects of growth induced by the Single Market and Single Currency, so they may suffer, perhaps disproportionately, from the imbalances caused by the more rapid growth.

6. The policy also supports the operation of the Single Labour Market through the European Social Fund, which is equal to 10% of the Union budget.

7. The policy's delivery mechanism provides the additional benefit of inciting regions to pursue strategic investments (see Question 2 below).

(b) *The effectiveness of European regional policy*

8. Modifications to the operation of the European regional policy over time have made it more effective in supporting other public policies in Member States and regions. Its structure has proved to be adaptable to changing circumstances. Introduced, in its present form in 1989, alongside the push towards the Single Market and the Single Currency, the policy has coped with successive enlargements which have more than doubled the number of Member States, increased the number of regions and widened regional income disparities. At the same time, it has proved itself capable of adapting to the different public policies of individual Member States.

9. The core principles of its delivery system have proved effective. The policy's *co-financing* rule produces a leveraging effect which will transform the €350 billion of Union resources for 2007–13 into an investment fund of €525 billion by attracting matching finance from national public and private sources; the effectiveness of these financial resources will be further increased by the *concentration* of investment co-finance in space, time and by development priority; the tasks of strategy-making and *programming* are devolved to partnerships of economic actors in the regions themselves (see Question 2, "European regional policy and subsidiarity").

10. Yet, devolved management takes place within a frame of *investment guidelines* and priorities approved by the Council of Ministers which ensures a European added value for investments. Thus, in the current period, the policy's total €525 billion budget will secure the double benefit of working to balance growth and inciting investments which are deemed by the Council to have a strategic importance for the Union. Thus, the policy's delivery system produces important advantages in maximising the value of Union expenditure.

11. Changes introduced for 2007–13 programmes have again demonstrated the policy's adaptability and will further increase its effectiveness in the pursuit of sustainable growth. They strengthen the policy's link to the Union's agenda for economic modernisation, expressed in the Lisbon and Gothenburg agenda, and have led regions to increase their use of EU co-finance for investments to increase their competitiveness. The better-off, or "Competitiveness", regions will use 80% of their EU co-finance in this way; the "Convergence" regions—where investments in basic infrastructure continue to be essential to make up for inadequacies in provision—will use 60%.

12. Thus European regional policy seeks to achieve many of the benefits of the fiscal equalisation systems used by other, older political entities such as the United States, at only a fraction of the cost to the taxpayer measured as a percentage of GDP.

(c) *Room for improvement: making European regional policy more effective and user friendly*

13. European regional policy has become less user-friendly over the past few years due to the increased complexity of aspects of financial management, including its specific auditing requirements. It is urgent that this should be corrected. If audit requirements could be brought into better balance, and more in line with national practices, the way would be open for programme management to focus more on performance and the improvement of value for money.

(i) Financial management and control

14. The growing burden of administration and financial management being passed to project sponsors earns the policy a bad reputation, even among direct beneficiaries.

15. The background is the tension between the different actors in regional policy's shared management—the EU, the Member States, the regions. They frequently address questions of financial management in a conflictual way, and this saps mutual confidence and the possibility of dialogue. The result is that financial management systems become more burdensome and costly as requirements multiply and are simply passed down the bureaucratic line from the European Court of Auditors to the Commission, from Commission to Member States, from Member States to the regions, from regions to the citizens. It has been said that few categories in the UK national budget would meet the auditing standards currently imposed by the European Court of Auditors.

16. The Lisbon Treaty has redefined financial responsibilities for the Union budget in a way which might be especially useful for a policy which is the subject of shared management, like European regional policy. Revised policy regulations go in the same direction. But it will be several years before the benefit of these changes becomes apparent. Also, present practice in interpreting financial regulations is such that, unless there is a co-operative and consensual approach between the European Court of Auditors, the Commission and Member States, there can be no guarantee that the new rules will lead to a substantial reduction in the requirements faced by end-users.

17. Therefore, in view of the mounting criticism it would be desirable for the Commission and the European Court of Auditors, as two European institutions created by the Treaty and bound by its objectives, to lead a Union-wide response. They might, for example, establish a forum where they and the Member States and regions could analyse together the burdens they are imposing on citizens, and their costs, and look for ways to lighten the administrative workload, while still ensuring sound and efficient management of the Union budget. The "reform" which might be looked for in this area is not, therefore, changed regulations—at least not in the first instance—but a new approach. Such an initiative is becoming a political imperative.

(ii) A better assessment of performance

18. Target-setting by means of performance indicators and regular evaluation are integral parts of operational programmes co-financed by European regional policy. Programmes are evaluated in the preparatory phase, during implementation and again at their conclusion. The results of evaluations are widely disseminated.

19. A number of recently-introduced elements in the policy aim to help regions improve their performance, both in terms of investment and administration.

- The Jaspers initiative, operated by the European Commission and the European Investment Bank, provides technical support to EU-12 Member States to help prepare and implement large projects, especially in the fields of environment and transport.
- Two initiatives, Jeremie and Jessica, aim to help regions increase their use of recyclable loan funds alongside the more usual grant mechanism.
- Another recently-launched initiative will encourage and enable regions to use European regional and cohesion policy funding in the establishment of micro-credit schemes.
- The European Investment Bank group is a partner to the European Commission in each of these schemes.

In addition, the policy's budget includes considerable funds for technical assistance and Interreg, the initiative for inter-regional co-operation, which is operated in a fully-devolved way, encourages regions to form regional networks to share good practice and learn from one another's experience.

20. The steadily-mounting requirements for financial management make it difficult for programme managers to devote sufficient attention to performance assessment. The same applies to the auditors themselves who lack the resources to add performance audits to those they carry out for financial management. This is a part of European regional policy which requires further development. It may be that a Union-wide system of performance assessment would be a promising route to the introduction of conditionality (see Question 7).

QUESTION 2

21. I will argue that, as a result of its unique system of multi-level governance, the principle of subsidiarity is more fully-incorporated into European regional policy (and rural development policy) than any other European policy area. Also, I will argue that the repatriation, or re-nationalisation, of European regional policy would risk the loss of important advantages, among them the curtailment, to some extent, of subsidiarity.

(a) *European regional policy and subsidiarity*

22. European regional policy's way of working—its delivery system—is distinctive. It is as important to its results as its funding. The delivery system aims at a great degree of decentralisation to Member States, regions and cities and is integral to the policy. It represents the Union's political choice for a particular form of economic governance and embodies, and gives full expression to, the principle of subsidiarity.

23. An examination of the policy's decentralised implementation system provides a vision of subsidiarity in action.

— The policy is founded on the principle that regions will chart their own distinct pathways to economic growth. Taking account of Union, national and regional priorities, each region writes its own development strategy and operational programme, building on its strengths and addressing its weaknesses. No region is obliged to adopt a "one-size-fits-all" solution. Regions choose the projects they wish to support with EU co-finance. Thus, planning and project decisions are taken where understanding, either of the opportunities they wish to exploit or the problems they seek to confront, is greatest.

— European regional policy provide a precise focus on economic growth to help guide regions in the preparation of their strategies and development programmes.

— The Union's investment guidelines (and, in the United Kingdom, those of the UK government) ensure for the region (and the UK) a higher added value for the total investment spend—the double benefit of stimulating growth and of enabling and prompting strategic investment.

— Regional policy encourages an innovative approach to economic development and the incorporation of positive results into development programmes.

— The contact which the policy establishes between the region and the Union enhances the contact between the region and other Union policies, like research and enterprise.

24. The answer to Question 6 below shows how, through the practical operation of the principle of subsidiarity, it is regions and Member States which determine the allocations of the European regional policy budget to the European Social Fund and the European Regional Development Fund.

(b) *Repatriating or re-nationalising regional policy*

25. In the present budgetary climate, it is possible to identify two schools of thought about the role and future relevance of European regional policy. They have a number of important differences. Because both schools exist in the United Kingdom, it may be worth describing them.

26. First some similarities. Both schools:

— recognise that the precise focus for regional policy is to achieve an improved performance in regional economic growth in order to diminish income disparities;

— see the task of safeguarding and developing competitiveness as a constant necessity in successful economies; and

— accept the need for Union co-finance in certain conditions and seek to concentrate it in the worst-off regions and Member States.

27. But alongside these important similarities there is a major difference, which is chiefly motivated by European regional policy's impact on the Union budget.

28. The school which favours the present structure and delivery system for European regional policy—though it may press energetically for changes in the way the policy works—recognises that the benefits and costs of the Single Market are not distributed equally. One result is the creation, or widening, of income disparities. Another is the loss of competitiveness, which affects regions, or parts of regions, in, even, the better-off Member States. This school takes the view that actions to reduce disparities and improve competitiveness are, therefore, in some measure, a European Union responsibility and should be supported from the Union budget. The Union's present European regional policy reflects this school's thinking.

29. The other school argues for a narrowing of the Union's budget responsibility by reducing the scope of regional policy. It would concentrate the budget on the short-term task of kick-starting the poorest regional and national economies. Once this was achieved, and a national economy attained a pre-set income threshold—perhaps 90% of the Union's average GDP—regional policy would become the financial responsibility of the Member State and cease to be financed from the Union budget. Each Member State would be free to choose its own level of financing and its own implementation system. It characterises this reform as ending a "one size fits all" policy. Its followers press for the expansion and deepening of the Single Market, as a *permanent* means to growth, and argue for a *temporary* financial responsibility for the imbalances which market-driven growth creates. Adoption of this school's reforms would "repatriate" or re-nationalise regional policy—in some Member States immediately, for example EU-15, and for all others later.

30. It is worth asking, "What would be lost by the policy's repatriation or renationalisation?"

— European regional policy supports the Union's Growth and Stability Pact since finance from the Cohesion Fund is conditional in relation to the rules for the sound management of public finances.

— It is characterised by micro-economic conditionality in key fields, since it requires full respect for rules on state aid, public procurement, the environment and equality of opportunities. Thus it helps the single market to become a race to the top rather than a race to the bottom where social, environmental and other standards are sacrificed.

— Its seven-year programmes offer Member States, regions, and cities medium-term stability, with financial resources guaranteed, within which to organise and implement their economic growth policies.

— Management of programmes by local partnerships brings the benefit of local ownership, which increases the region's motivation and helps build local knowledge of development techniques. This contributes towards sustainability. An alternative management model frequently selects as leader a "big hitter" which leaves little management capacity behind when it eventually moves on.

— European regional and cohesion policy has encouraged regions to adopt a more sophisticated approach to risk. Fraud or misuse of funding is not tolerated but, in the selection and management of projects, regions are encouraged to manage, rather than avoid, risk. This approach brings development benefits in regions where growth is urgently needed. Examples of projects in the United Kingdom which have managed risk in this way would be the Merseyside Special Investment Fund, which opened the way to EU financial participation in recyclable funds; the Key Fund in South Yorkshire which made it possible to overcome problems of matching finance; the Combined Universities of Cornwall which enabled higher education facilities in the county to combine their specialities to offer a range of university courses and research.

— The development of cross-cutting themes has enabled regions to further increase the added value of European funding. Regions have frequently assessed their entire development effort against themes they considered of major importance—for example, the equality of employment between men and women or social inclusion. Environmental concerns have been a major beneficiary of this approach (see Question 4).

— The policy is built around a Union benchmark—evolution of the Union's average income per head—which has a greater relevance for the balancing of growth than national averages.

— European regional policy contributes to the realisation of the Union's single labour market. The European Social Fund is an important complement to legislative action and policy co-ordination under the renewed Lisbon agenda. It is delivered through regional policy.

— The policy's delivery system transforms a system of financial redistribution into a policy for balanced and strategic economic development. The objective method of determining policy expenditure and its distribution between Member States, as well as the method of its delivery into actual projects, offers assurance to European policy-makers that expenditure will be used to create Union-wide growth and thus be more than financial transfers. Resources earmarked as necessary for growth are thus proofed against other, short-term budget considerations.

— The policy's delivery system provides a framework for Member States, regions and cities which enables them to improve the strategic element in their own policy. In addition, its discipline encourages them to improve their practices of administration and financial management to the best international standards.

— European regional policy provides a framework and resources which allows cities, regions and Member States to work together to promote exchanges of experience and best practice.

31. Member States could do many of these things for themselves if they wanted to—though macro-economic conditionality would be difficult and the national electoral cycle would tend to render the seven-year implementation period difficult to achieve. *But it is clear that it is, mostly, only within the operation of the Union's regional policy that they actually do them.*

32. European regional policy makes the Union visible to citizens and brings it closer by supporting them through severe economic change. Its programmes, managed by local economic actors in regions and cities, have deployed the European Regional Development Fund, the Cohesion Fund and the European Social Fund to co-finance, perhaps, more than half a million projects throughout the Union, to assist the training of 4 million people a year, to help 1.2 million women a year to return to work and another 200,000 from disadvantaged groups. In addition, the Solidarity Fund has helped citizens affected by natural and man-made

catastrophes and the Globalisation Adjustment Fund is helping those who need to change jobs because of business restructuring. If the policy were not there, many citizens would be poorer.

33. But the policy has a poor record in claiming credit for its achievements. Efforts to improve the effectiveness of the policy should make this a major concern and establish a consensus with Member States and regions which will ensure proper recognition of the European Union role in regional economic development and in improvements in the functioning of the labour market. Some United Kingdom regions make this a priority, seeking to go further than the minimum which is required in the policy's current regulations. The United Kingdom would be well-placed to play a leading part in raising citizens' awareness of the benefits the policy brings.

QUESTION 3

34. Most notably, the previous two enlargements of the Union impacted on European regional policy in two ways:

- Accession of additional population with an income considerably below the Union average created a large new budget demand. In the climate of budget austerity this could not be wholly met through increased funding and entailed a switch in support from less-well-off regions in EU-15 to regions in the acceding Members.
- The low incomes of the acceding Member States reduced the Union's average income by 15 percentage points. The immediate result was that a number of regions, still in the process of restructuring their economies, lost their priority status for regional policy support because the Union threshold fell below their own average income. The longer-term result is that high-intensity support from European regional policy is lost to regions earlier in their restructuring process—or, put another way, at a lower level of income—thus leaving them in a less strong position to continue their development.

35. Any discussion of how European regional policy might be adapted to prepare for future enlargements of the Union should be grounded in an understanding of its key features. Notably, the policy should continue to:

- apply to all regions with variations in aid intensity according to national and regional levels of prosperity;
- provide a link between European regional policy and the Union's macro-economic policy and the Growth and Stability Pact (see Question 8);
- operate within its seven-year programming period, thus providing a stable medium-to-long-term framework in which regions can formulate and carry out their strategies to accelerate growth and converge on the Union average;
- set a European target for growth, the Union's average level of income per head, as a realistic benchmark against which to judge performance;
- operate in a decentralised way, fully reflecting the principle of subsidiarity, thus safeguarding against any tendency to force regions into "one-size-fits-all" policies and strengthening their involvement in their own economic development;
- insist on co-financing which, through financial leverage, increases the financial resources available for regional development;
- focus on competitiveness, which is of key importance to all regions, whatever their level of income; and
- link and, as far as possible integrate, investments in business and infrastructure with those in the development of the labour market.

36. In further considering what changes may be necessary to meet the challenges of further enlargement, the following factors will be relevant: a) the size of the acceding countries; b) their degree of economic development; and c) their physical proximity to poles of development. Experience shows that the Union could profit from building further on the policy's strengths.

- Regional policy should continue as an *economic* policy of the Union. But there may be room to develop the use of other European indicators besides GDP per head (for example, for the labour market, environment, research and innovation performance) to give additional guidance to regions as to how they should shape their regional growth strategies. This would further tie the regions into the goal of economic modernisation and sustainable development and provide a basis for pursuing targets like those for carbon emissions.

— Financial leverage and the value for the Union budget is a major preoccupation. It is important that the Union achieves a better mix of loans and grants, with regions allocating more of their funding to recyclable loan funds. The latest reform of European regional policy recognised the importance of capital provision for regional development and introduced a number of pilot schemes. The policy should now go further. Perhaps the Union can establish, through negotiation with each Member State and region, target shares of their regional policy funding to be used in co-financing recyclable loan funds.

QUESTION 4

37. It will be useful to keep in mind that, in effect, European regional policy is implemented in two stages. In the first, the Policy's budget is allocated (distributed) to regions and Member States according to their economic performance and need. This is decided by the Commission and Member States at the beginning of the programme period and reflects the Policy's objective of seeking sustainable improvements in regional economic performance. The second stage begins once the financial allocation has been made when regions and Member States decide for themselves on their development strategy and programme. It is at this second stage that regions would take account of climate change or social inclusion.

38. Ever since the policy's reformulation in 1989, the Union has persuaded regions and Member States that they should give priority to investments in environmental protection and social inclusion, since these both influence the sustainability of growth. The funding devoted to such investments will total around €72 billions in 2007–13 programmes—€62 billions for the environment, €10 billions for social inclusion. The question of migration has risen rapidly in the policy agenda of many regions, including regions and cities in the United Kingdom, revealing itself as a volatile, Union-wide phenomenon, spanning issues like globalisation, enlargement and the Single Market. It is reflected in an increased effort by many regions to put in place improved arrangements for the integration of migrant and ethnic minority communities. It is a question which lends itself to a response at the Union level.

39. The impact of investments for climate change, social inclusion and for actions related to migration will be further magnified by the retention of these three areas of interest as cross-cutting themes in many programmes. This has become standard practice for a number of themes for development. The regional partnership for East Scotland played a leading part in a trans-European network on sustainable development, pioneering and disseminating in the Union an environmentally-aware process for project selection.

QUESTION 5

40. The Union recently succeeded for the fourth time in establishing a multi-year budget framework running until 2013. The existence of this multi-year framework, which does not replace the succession of annual budgets, makes possible the multi-year framework for regional policy. This benefit is transmitted directly to regions making it possible for them to plan for the medium to long-term in full confidence that the agreed amounts of Union resources and the matching finance will be available to them.

41. The proposed EU budget for regional policy is built on two calculations.

— The larger part, that for the poorer Convergence regions, is built by first identifying the regions which have, during the three-year reference period, achieved an income equal to or less than 75% of the average Union GDP per head. Next, harmonised economic data for each region, covering regional GDP and unemployment rates, are fed through a formula, first accepted by the Union at Berlin in 1999, in order to arrive at a financial allocation by region. These regional allocations, capped at 4% of national GDP, are then summed to obtain the total budget required, from which can be determined the Member State shares. This system of construction accounts for 80% of the 2007–13 Union budget for European Cohesion Policy.

— It is the remaining part of the regional policy budget which experienced the most significant reduction for 2007–13 in order to ensure funding at sufficient levels of intensity for the EU-12 member states. Calculating this part of the budget takes account of previous Union decisions and allocates funding between Member States, based on an examination of regional economic data referring to regional GDP per head, unemployment, employment, educational and training attainment, population and population density. These data give an allocation by Member State and are used to derive "recommended" allocations of funding by region. Funding is also allocated to the Interreg instrument for cross-border co-operation, and to technical assistance.

- Once the *total budget is decided* by the Union, the same method is followed in reverse to establish the allocations by region.
- For the Cohesion Fund, an overall allocation is distributed among the eligible Member States according to a formula which takes account of the size of the country, in terms of surface and population. The resulting national allocation is then adjusted to reflect the relative wealth of each country. Eligible countries are those which have, during the three-year reference period, achieved an income equal to or less than 90% of the average Union GNI per head.

42. The present criteria conform with the policy's identity as an economic instrument, which seeks to promote the growth of poorer regions and the competitiveness of better-off regions in order to help them reduce the disparities between their average income and that of the Union. And the *order* in which decisions are taken is fully in line with the principle of subsidiarity. The allocations are arrived at by an objective method, on the basis of harmonised data, and the method is applied across the Union. Small adjustments are made in the political process of the final decision-making, but I have calculated that these amount to less than 1% of the regional and cohesion policy budget. The order of decision hands responsibility to the regions and Member States once the overall European regional policy budget is allocated to regions. It is the regions, through their respective operational programmes decided in line with their own economic conditions, which decide the size of the policy's constituent funds. As long as European regional policy remains an economic instrument, embodying subsidiarity, these criteria will be appropriate.

43. Given that regional policy is an economic instrument of the Union, the Union's GDP per head should continue to provide its essential benchmark. But there is room to develop the use of other European indicators to give additional guidance to regions as to how they should shape their regional growth policies (see Question 3 above).

44. At this stage it will be useful to anticipate the last part of Question 6 on whether it is appropriate that regional eligibility criteria should be discussed at the same time as the wider discussion on the Union budget. Since the size of the European regional policy budget is directly geared—in the way described above—to economic conditions in regions, it is in the interest of budget transparency that regional eligibility criteria should be known (i.e. decided) at the time the budget is set.

Question 6

45. At present, the policy essentially divides the Union's regions into two groups. The Convergence regions have an income (GDP) per head of 75% of the Community average, or below, and receive the bulk of the policy's funding (80% of funding for 35% of population). Competitiveness regions are those above 75% of average income and qualify for a much lower intensity of funding (12% funding, 60% population). A small number of Competitiveness regions—those which were Objective 1 (now called Convergence) regions in 2000–06 and a group which would have been Convergence regions but for the fall in EU average income because of Enlargement—receive extra funding on a temporary and degressive basis in order to palliate their change in status.

46. This creates a situation in which regions in the no-man's land between 75 and 100% of the Union's average income receive little support for their efforts towards economic modernisation, with the consequence that their growth performance is impaired. This might be seen to be important to those regions whose income is not far above 75% of the Union average. In addition, it should be borne in mind that the Union's average income was reduced by 15 percentage points as a result of the last two Union enlargements. This drop in the average, in effect, raised a number of regions above the 75% threshold despite the fact that their economic modernisation was, perhaps, still at a sensitive stage.

47. This makes it appropriate to consider the creation of a third category of regions between Convergence and Competitiveness (perhaps to be called Regions in Transition). This third category could be defined as being between 75% and, say, 100% of the Community average income. The intensity of the financial allocation to these regions should lie mid-way between those for the Convergence and Competitiveness regions. Introduction of such a category would make it necessary to revisit the method of deciding on budget allocations to regions and to categories of regions. Proportional concentration on the very poorest would be reduced, though not necessarily by the same percentage as the absolute level of funding.

48. The gains to the Union would be two-fold: a more determined action to reduce the regional income disparities caused by the process of economic growth; an additional stimulus to growth itself.

Question 7

49. The European Cohesion Fund has, since 2000 been conditional on a Member State's compliance with the terms of the Stability and Growth Pact. The present Cohesion Fund regulation allows for the suspension of all or part of a Member State's commitments from the beginning of the year *after* the decision to suspend. The decision to specify commitments and the time-lag before the suspension enters into force reflect a wish by the Union not to push a Member State further into deficit. This may easily happen if payments from the Union budget are suspended since Member States will be legally obliged to continue co-finance to projects once it has committed to them.

50. This is, therefore, a delicate issue, since a sanction of this nature could make it even more difficult for beneficiaries of the Cohesion Fund to meet the terms of the Growth and Stability Pact, for example, in covering their public expenditure deficits.

51. Any extension of conditionality to take on board the Broad Economic Policy Guidelines would need to take such considerations into account—as well as their non-constraining nature as guidelines—while recognising that the impact of regional programmes is predominantly at the micro-economic level. Rather, it would seem preferable to develop the conditionality of regional policy from within and, in response to Question 1 above, the suggestion is made that financial support from the Union should become more conditioned by the meeting of performance targets.

8 January 2008

Examination of Witness

Witness: Mr Graham Meadows, former Director General of Regional Policy, European Commission, examined.

Q222 *Chairman:* Good morning, Mr Meadows, thank you very much for coming. May I say by way of a preliminary remark that the whole session is recorded and you will get a transcript which you can take a view on. You have of course already provided written answers to many of our questions but we are probably still going to ask them just the same and pick away at the answers. Would you like us just to start or would you prefer to make an opening statement?

Mr Meadows: Thank you, My Lord Chairman; I would prefer you to start.

Q223 *Chairman:* Then we will do that. You get me first putting the formal question, what should be the objectives of the EU's Structural Funds and how can the Funds become more effective in supporting public policy in Member States and regions? What mechanisms of delivery could make the policy more user-friendly? That is the formal general question which you have already provided some answers on, but perhaps you could just start there.

Mr Meadows: The first point to underline is that the EU Structural Funds are instruments of regional and cohesion policy, or agricultural development policy, or policy for restructuring the fisheries sector. The Funds are governed by the objectives of the policies. The objectives of regional and cohesion policy are best seen in relation to the economic objectives set out most recently in the Lisbon Treaty: the pursuit of balanced growth and of social market economy which is providing jobs for Union citizens. These are the overall objectives of the Treaty, of EU regional policy and, therefore, of the funds. Are the Funds effective or is the policy effective? In my answers I tried to show that, although the structure of the policy is quite complex, it brings a number of benefits to the policymaker in the sense of levering in financial resources from other sources into development areas, of on strategic investments, of supporting the creation of the European Union's single market for labour, and so on. The main problem with the Funds at the moment, which makes them less user-friendly than they otherwise would be is the steady accretion of financial management responsibilities. Whereas we would all wish to see public policy managed in such a way that taxpayers' money is used for the purposes for which it is intended by the policymakers, European regional and cohesion policy is reaching a state where you have the impression that financial controls are now into the belt and braces zone: the processes are being over-controlled and there is a need to find a new way of approaching this question of financial control which would make it easier for people and for companies to have access to Structural Funds through regional development programmes.

Chairman: I am going to postpone, if I may, discussion of how might we change the finances to later when Lord Woolmer will ask you about it, but I want to get us into the heart of it. One of the issues that this Committee is having to think about for the report is whether we in any way support a policy of repatriation or we do not; in that context I want to focus very much on that particular question because it is one of the issues for us. Lord Trimble.

Q224 ***Lord Trimble:*** On the question of repatriation of Funds I notice in paragraph 30 of your evidence you have a long list—it runs over the page—of things that would be lost by the policies of repatriation and re-nationalisation, so you see a lot of disadvantages, do you, in the repatriation of regional policy. Do you see any advantages?
Mr Meadows: The first point I would like to make, for my benefit rather than for the Committee's –so that you choose the word "repatriation" to describe the process which makes it sound as if you are bringing home wounded warriors who have been fighting for the realm abroad. Re-nationalisation is a slightly better word in the sense that a process which brought the implementation and direction of regional policy more closely towards central government would actually remove, or would be in danger of removing powers or measures of discretion from the regions themselves. Repatriation focuses only on that part of the process which is bringing something back from abroad, to here in the heart of government as it were. Re-nationalisation makes us aware that there are two sides to the process. It may be that the price of bringing something back from abroad is that we also take something away from either the devolved parts of the United Kingdom or from the regions themselves.

Q225 ***Lord Kerr of Kinlochard:*** You could run a regional policy on a regional basis, it does not have to be centrally run.
Mr Meadows: Perhaps I can come to the question about what you could do in a second part of this answer because you could do many things. It is rather a question of how you assess what you would do if you could. If that sounds Rumsfeldian, I apologise. Let me come back to Lord Trimble's question about advantages. Quite clearly, to the extent that administration may be more difficult because any European Union policy has to apply in 27 Member States and has to try to reflect the conditions in 27 Member States, in theory at least it ought to be possible to have a simpler administrative system if you are only dealing with one particular Member State. Coming back to Lord Kerr's question about could and would, there is no doubt that many of the disadvantages of re-nationalisation could be avoided if that is what the re-nationalising government wished to do. There are one or two things which it would be difficult to avoid, which in my view would represent a loss of quality inside a country like the United Kingdom: one would be the time horizon which European policy gives at the moment—it would be difficult to replicate a seven year or a nine year time horizon: another would be the difficulty of replicating the linkage in terms of economic management between the Cohesion Fund, which is part of the Structural Fund package, and the Union's Growth and Stability pact, or, in other words, management of deficits. To end on the advantage, the advantage ought to be a simpler administrative system, it ought to be perhaps a system which is more responsive to the Member States' needs. The problem is that we have to try to judge—this is why I get into this difficulty between would and could—what a Member State would do if it was re-creating a national regional policy. Here it seems to be fair to consider as important the track record of particular Member States. If you look into the Union there are some Member States who are extremely committed to regional policy and you can see that, perhaps, the transfer back to them of regional policy would have little impact and perhaps bring extra advantages. The Federal Republic of Germany, for example, is one which has a long history of very active regional policy. Then you have other Member States which have a more embryonic or ad hoc regional policy and you have the feeling that if regional policy went back to those Member States, perhaps within a fairly short time some of the benefits which have been established in the past would be eroded.

Q226 ***Lord Trimble:*** I have to say that from that perspective one regards European regional policy as only an aspect of regional policy, there are other aspects of regional policy that currently operate on a national basis, and indeed regional policy existed before we went into the European Union, so I do not regard European regional policy as being regional policy full stop. Can I put to you an interesting experience that I had about ten years ago when we were starting to prepare for devolution in Northern Ireland and I found myself in conversation with a very senior official of the Northern Ireland Department of Finance. We were discussing European funding and he said that European regional funding was quite often more trouble than it is worth, and the reason why he said that was that the Northern Ireland Department was under constant pressure from the Treasury to design its capital spending programme so as to attract as much European funding as possible and that this distorted the public expenditure priorities and sometimes made them adopt projects that would not be high priorities simply in order to ensure a drawdown on European funding. Obviously, this is that particular official's viewpoint and it is a different viewpoint from that of people who are running the regional authorities and already know that they are going to get X amount of money branded as European anyway, but I would just like to share that with you.
Mr Meadows: Lord Trimble, you are right to say that European regional policy is only a part of the regional policy armoury which has been deployed in the United Kingdom. You may have been more aware of regional policy in Northern Ireland than

someone would have been in perhaps the South West of England before European regional policy began. The views of civil servants—I speak as a former civil servant—are sometimes imperfect. I remember that when the politicians in Cornwall and South-West England were lobbying for Objective 1 status which would have meant considerably more resources coming to the county from Brussels that one of the civil servants in the county said to me confidentially at the time "I only hope we do not succeed because we just will not know what to do with the money". Now it is clear that the rate of economic growth in Cornwall is much greater as a result of Objective 1 status and funding being granted to the country. If you went to the county you would find that there is a fairly widespread agreement that European regional policy has helped the county to reverse its fortunes.

Q227 ***Lord Trimble:*** I notice that in the succeeding paragraphs to the one listing all the things that would be lost by re-nationalisation of regional policy, you say that regional policy makes the Union visible to citizens but then criticise it by saying that it has a "poor record" of claiming credit for its achievements. I am again not really sure that I see this because one is accustomed to seeing regularly projects with large signs saying that this project is being funded by blah-blah-blah—one sees that travelling around the regions regularly. The two points in any event seem to me to be somewhat inconsistent with each other.
Mr Meadows: You do see signs, you are right, but the number of signs that you see often bears quite a low relationship to the number of projects which are being financed in any region. At times, from Brussels, the European Commission has launched the idea that there should be, for example, one day a year on which people draw attention to the projects or the training actions which have been co-financed from the European Union, not as a way of trying to detract from an appreciation of what the Member States have done for their citizens, but as a way of saying that here Europe has also been trying to assist you. These sorts of ideas are never really very welcome in Member States' capitals.
Lord Renton of Mount Harry: Can I add something to that last point, simply to say that I am very interested and very glad to hear you say that because I, as very much a supporter of the EU generally, and regional funding, have always thought that it is a very great shame that it is not compulsory that if you are going to get EU regional money as we are talking about, you should advertise the fact that some value is coming from the development of the EU. It happens in Scotland, very much so, but it is totally different and noticeable in my part of the country, south-east England, you never get any credit for the EU but in Scotland it is always very much on the billboards.

Q228 ***Lord Trimble:*** I thought it was compulsory that you did.
Mr Meadows: It is compulsory.
Lord Renton of Mount Harry: It is compulsory, is it, and just ignored, is that so?
Lord Trimble: It may be that there is not much expenditure of regional funds in your area.
Lord Renton of Mount Harry: It is where one knows that there has been expenditure and there is no advertising.

Q229 ***Chairman:*** Mr Meadows, perhaps you can answer the question whether it is or is not compulsory.
Mr Meadows: I was quite happy to hear their Lordships' dispute. It is compulsory but it is, as it were, still something which is honoured or fulfilled in a rather strange way and is often not fulfilled at all, so much so that the European Union has the power to withdraw a percentage of funding if it finds that afterwards proper publicity has not been accorded to the project. In my own time we withdrew money from one quite large project because there was no sign inside the airport to say that this was part funded by the European Union. In the north-east of England once Commissioner Wulf-Mathies was taken to the Theatre Royal in Newcastle, which had been refurbished partly with European Union money, but it was difficult to find the plaque. It was there and the law was fulfilled but people going to the theatre would not have been aware of it.
Lord Renton of Mount Harry: I must say have been to that theatre with Lord and Lady Eccles and I was totally unaware that it had been in any way revamped by EU money.
Chairman: I would like to pull us back to where we were. Lord Kerr, you had a question on the last point.

Q230 ***Lord Kerr of Kinlochard:*** I was thinking about Lord Trimble's point about Northern Ireland and that going for regional fund money is more trouble than it is worth; and about Mr Meadows' point about the South West. The South West was a very impressive story, but post hoc does not necessarily mean propter hoc, and one of the reasons it seems to me why there has not always been the wildest enthusiasm for bidding for Structural Fund money in the United Kingdom is the Treasury rules on non-additionality; in order to maintain the planned total of public expenditure, if you win money from Brussels this is netted off against your money from London. This rule does not create enormous enthusiasm for a huge bidding exercise or perhaps plaques in theatres when you win. Would you like to comment on that?

Mr Meadows: In the past was a tough debate between the European Union and the United Kingdom about this very question, about whether funding was, or should be, additional or not, I think Lord Kerr, who was then Sir John Kerr, was the British Permanent Representative in Brussels at the time. The issue was only partly solved and has been further diluted since. It is true that among officials you may encounter reluctance to campaign for funding, but politicians from Brussels, politicians or political leaders in regions or in the devolved parts of the Union realise that there is at least publicity value in it and there may be a marginal or even considerable value in getting additional funds by going to Brussels. My experience was that there was no shortage of people coming and arguing for funding. One of the problems that the policy faces, and I do not think this is only in the United Kingdom it is in other places also, is that if the amount of funding being granted to a Member States is low, then it is very tempting for the Member States to merely mix it in with its own resources. If you were at the moment running the Polish government it would be very difficult not to make the expenditure additional because there is so much, something like 60 billions euros over nine years. That gives a clue as to how to view things. If one looks at a detailed level in the United Kingdom, the amount of funding being targeted into a particular local authority area by the European Union may be a considerable percentage of the authority's investment resources. I have in mind West Cumbria, which was a very clear case. The Union targeted more money into West Cumbria than the British Government would have otherwise paid to the region, so there was a considerable net benefit. Also, you sometimes find that in terms of the net investment effort in a region, the investment effort will be considerably increased by the fact that European Union funding is chiefly for investment. Looked at it in more detail, therefore, and at the level of smaller units, you do see an additional benefit and you see also the benefit of a different quality of expenditure. You do get additional benefits on the ground therefore.

Q231 ***Lord Kerr of Kinlochard:*** Following that up, one takes your point with regard to Poland because EU funding going into Poland is something like 20 per cent, the rate of increase is 20 per cent above the funds that the Polish Government has, so obviously with regard to Poland regional funding has got considerable added value. With regard to larger, richer states, regional funding has comparatively limited added value, so apart from some ideological point, would it not be actually better to take the richer and larger states out of regional funding so as to concentrate the funding where it is going to make a significant difference?

Mr Meadows: The richer Member States conceal or contain very wide variations in regional incomes or in regional well-being and, as I have just mentioned, we have had experience in the United Kingdom whereby European Union resources coming into the country meant that the Government transferred more of its own resources to less well-off areas. At the end of the exercise it was clear that the regions which had been listed as being eligible for EU funding came out with more funding than they would have otherwise had. One can allocate resources to richer regions and concentrate it on the poorer parts of those regions. Also, it is quite conceivable that without a regional policy which operates in all of the Member States adherence to the single market or adherence to the single currency would be weakened in some Member States.

Q232 ***Lord Renton of Mount Harry:*** Could I just mention, Mr Meadows, that area of northern England that you mentioned? Could this be due to them having a very active MEP and therefore making a lot of noise, and that some of this has therefore been picked up by the local MPs in order to get the EU money and with that more Government money? It seems to me just the sort of suitable target for an MEP.

Mr Meadows: I would like to hand the credit to them, but West Cumbria was two local authority areas and because of the configuration of the areas—it is the coastal plain between the Lake District and the sea—these local authority areas are rather long and they cover the whole area. This was a very particular case, that is why I remember it, and it bore on the additionality argument that Lord Kerr was referring to. The problem for London was the realisation that London had agreed to the transfer to this area of a fairly large amount of European Union resources and then had realised that its own funding to the area was insufficient to provide matching funding. I am quite happy to give the credit to the boisterous nature of Members of the European Parliament or Members of the House of Commons or Members of the House of Lords.

Q233 ***Chairman:*** Can I pick up out of the general question about re-nationalisation of funds or not, in your experience where are the States of the European Union going with it? Is there any general level of support for re-nationalisation? I have no feeling for who thinks what about it.

Mr Meadows: The last time that Member States had to decide whether they wanted to go for some kind of re-nationalisation was, of course, the budget settlement which was reached in December 2005. That is the last time that the question was put. The fact that the policy is going on in a similar to that which existed before, though with some changes, indicates that there was not a consensus among Member States to re-nationalise European regional policy. Under normal circumstances, after an agreement of that kind, it would be some years before the same question was put again. But in the agreement of December 2005, there was a provision to look again in the mid-term at the evolution of the budget, so, strangely, the arguments which were used in that negotiation are still circulating because the Union is now going through its mid-term review of the present budget settlement. The last time that the Member States were called upon to decide this particular question, then, they decided not to re-nationalise. The Member States themselves have a wide range of needs which can be met through the existence of something like European regional policy, even though it is true as Lord Trimble says, that each of the Member States themselves has its own regional policy.

Q234 ***Lord Kerr of Kinlochard:*** As a strictly economic policy—this is between the lines of your admirable paper—skewing towards the poor makes sense. There was a bit more skewing introduced in 2005 and maybe a little bit more in this mid-term review, but in terms of strict economics, that must be right. You have a number of political arguments for maintaining the Structural Funds EU-wide; you say it is supportive of the single labour market; you say it is supportive of the disciplines of the Stability and Growth Pacts and you say it is also good for the image of the Union EU-wide. Probably you would also concede that it is politically tricky in some Member States to agree that they would not be eligible for any money from the Structural Funds, or only for a little bit. But basically the economics of the operation only make sense if it is a way of transferring resources from the richer Member States to the poorer Member States; do you agree with that?

Mr Meadows: By and large, yes, but I would also say that in my view the skewing to the poorer Member States has probably gone too far. One has to have in mind that when the policy began there was a certain balance and the balance was struck around the threshold of 75 per cent of community income. Those regions with a per head income less than 75 per cent of the Community average received something like 80 per cent of the funding and the others 20 per cent. The enlargements of the Union which have taken place have lowered the Community average income by about 15 percentage points. So the balancing point which was thought to be suitable for the policy between 1989 and 2006 has suddenly gone down, although the practice of concentrating funding on the regions below 75 per cent has been retained. You have, therefore, a considerable exaggeration in the skewing effect and you see the effect of this in the United Kingdom. In the United Kingdom, regions which would have continued to receive a fairly large injection of European resources had the enlargements not taken place, in other words had the average income not fallen, no longer receive the same intensity of support. In effect, economically speaking, they are removed from the category of regions receiving the highest intensity of assistance, perhaps before they are in a position where they could continue to sustain the further growth of their own prosperity. This is because the threshold income which triggers the highest intensity of support is now 15 percentage points lower. I find that there is a danger of—if I say it in these terms I do not mean it in an emotional way—abandoning a region before it has reached the position where it can sustain its own development. If one is not careful one will discover that regions—we have seen this in the case of one or two regions—leave eligibility and then bounce back into it, like planes which do not take off. Their economies are in the process of restructuring but when the Union withdraws the funding they cannot sustain the effort and bounce back onto the runway again. I would see that as an economic argument that the balance of the policy has been changed by this lowering of the Community's average income.

Lord Renton of Mount Harry: Perhaps we could just take that point a bit further because it is precisely the question that I was going to ask.

Chairman: We will go back, but do take that point now.

Q235 ***Lord Renton of Mount Harry:*** Indeed, that is precisely the point that you make in paragraphs 46 and 47 of your note to us, this drop of 15 percentage points, and when I read that last night I must say I was taken by considerable surprise. Does this actually show the real difficulty for you or the Commission in getting this right and actually satisfying both the needs and the requests? You then, Mr Meadows, go on to suggest the creation of a third category of regions between convergence and competitiveness, perhaps to be called regions in transition, to cover those who might otherwise be over 75 per cent but really should not be. Would you like to just explain that a little bit more because it seems to be part of the difficulty in always having as it were to create new classes in order to keep up with the mob?

Mr Meadows: The third category exists at the moment but in an ad hoc way. Basically what happens is the Commission proposes some kind of short term transitional arrangement for regions which are no longer to receive high intensity support. The policy offers degressive to help the transition to a lower intensity of aid. This degressive support is time-limited, however. If one looks at the development of some regions, one finds that they become stuck in the, as it were, netherworld. To continue their development, they need an intensity of support which is higher than that given to the generality of regions, although it need not be as high as in the very worst-off. As a result they find it difficult to close the gap between their average income and the Union average. At the moment, the policy is in a certain sense unfair because it removes necessary support from some regions before they are able to sustain their continued development. In economic terms it is not good management to reduce the intensity of support below the level which would be justified by the economic fundamentals. I think it could be done better and have suggested, as you say Lord Renton, a third intermediate regional classification.

Lord Trimble: It might just be worthwhile trying to sort out the factual basis of this because you are assuming that if a region ceases for example to be Objective 1 and then there is a reduction in the amount of European regional fund money that comes to the pot, that then results in a lowering of regional funding for the region. I do not think that actually is the case as far as the United Kingdom is concerned. Just from our own experience when we ceased to be Objective 1 we had of course transitional arrangements regionally after that, but there was no reduction in total funding for the region, it continued to increase in the way that other parts of the United Kingdom expenditure was increasing. The strain did not come in the region; if there was any strain it came on the Exchequer generally and there was no reduction of expenditure in the region. That might not be true of other countries or other regions, but it might be worthwhile just inquiring into that.

Lord Kerr of Kinlochard: Poverty is relative. If you admit a large number of poor Member States what happens to the average is pretty obvious and 75 per cent of that is 75 per cent of something else. I have noted down the years how Member States grappled with that situation, changing the frontiers of their regions, and playing games of that kind. I did it with the frontiers of the Highlands and Islands myself, to get Aberdeen out of the Highlands in order to maintain the great poverty of the Highlands.

Lord Renton of Mount Harry: We now know who was to blame.

Q236 ***Lord Kerr of Kinlochard:*** This is a political game which is nothing to do with the economics. The economics is that you will do most good by sending the money to where the need is greatest and when Spain joined the pressure on the UK was considerable and we fought gallantly to hang on to as much as we possibly could, but the balance tilted to Spain, quite rightly. Now that the East Europeans have joined the balance has tilted from Spain to East Europe, and this is correct, that is where the money is needed.

Mr Meadows: I will come to Lord Trimble but, first of all, yes, poverty is relative. I find it, however, difficult to say to a region which is no better off absolutely on Tuesday than it was on Monday, "You are relatively much better off than you were yesterday because a lot of less well-off Member States have joined the European Union." It is true that poverty is relative, but there is an absolute element to be taken into account. The second thing is you will be pleased to know, Lord Kerr, that as a result of your stalwart efforts with the Highlands a regulation was adopted by the European Union which prevents the gerrymandering of regional borders in the course of a negotiation over a budget settlement. Lord Kerr was quite shameful in the sense that he actually did it when he knew he would derive a financial benefit from it—or he knew that the region would.

Q237 ***Lord Woolmer of Leeds:*** Is that shameless or shameful?

Mr Meadows: Could I answer Lord Trimble? The first thing to remember—and I have only ever seen this through a glass darkly, as it were, is that the United Kingdom has a very firm arrangement, the Barnet formula, for distributing public sector resources between its constituent nations. It may well be possible, as Lord Kerr said, that the removal of European Union finance would in some way be compensated in the application of that formula. If you look into the Irish Republic, I would imagine that support for regions has changed as a result of the fact that intensity of support under regional policy is now much less than it was, let us say five years ago, and if you look into other Member States you do see a difference in the amount of resources being injected into a region if their status inside European regional policy changes. In other words, you can see by the loss of a resource the fact that the resource was bringing an additional benefit.

Q238 ***Lord Trimble:*** This is the point that I put to you earlier, that there are some states where, because of their smaller size and position financially, regional policy has significant added value for those states and there are other states where it does not. That is basically the argument that you are putting to me now.

Mr Meadows: Yes, but I do not want you to interpret me as saying that it is only in a particular group of Member States that the benefit can be derived from regional policy—and here I would probably have to part company with you and Lord Kerr. I believe that even in a quite well-off Member State there are always quite large pockets of low income which would benefit from the application of a regional approach.

Lord Trimble: That is undoubtedly the case but I do not think it is right to assume that the comparatively well-off Member State would not itself have a policy for dealing with the problems of deprivation.
Chairman: I am going to call time on this one and move us on. Lord Steinberg, you were going to ask about the impact that enlargement has had on Structural Funds but much of this it seems to me has already been answered. Have you anything that you would like to ask on that?

Q239 ***Lord Steinberg:*** First of all I would like to congratulate you, Mr Meadows, on preparing a good list of answers to our questions. Whilst we may not agree with all of them, it is certainly a very comprehensive answer, so thank you for that. What I want to ask is we have been talking quite a bit about percentages of effect and whilst I have never been a mathematician I have worked in the question of financial matters for some time. I am concerned as to how you arrive at the 15 percentage points. Where have you taken that figure from? How many new entrants were there; have you taken that then with the full 27 in and what was your previous starting figure because 15 percentage points is an awful lot, and I am really very much concerned that you might not have taken it from the right starting point and you may have gathered this figure from some statistic. I found it very, very strange when you have large numbers of countries already with rather large Structural Fund positions; 15 percentage points seems enormous to me, could you explain that, please?
Mr Meadows: Thank you, Lord Steinberg. Remember that we are working with harmonised income data which is collected from the Member States so one may have a range of questions about the data, but these are harmonised and to the best of everyone's efforts we can have confidence in the data with which we are working. That is the first point. The second point is that the enlargement of the Union to take in the ten new Member States—that is the 12 minus Romania and Bulgaria—because the national income per head of those Member States is so much lower than the Union average, and in some parts of Poland it is only a little more than a third of the Union average, the effect of taking in ten rather poor Member States meant that the average income fell by about 12 percentage points at the first stage, and it was on the basis of that reduced income that the present period was decided, and that produced, as Lord Kerr said, a shift of resources towards the new Member States. In the United Kingdom a number of regions like Merseyside and South Yorkshire, for example—which had been below 75 per cent—as a result of this change came above 75 per cent and moved into this transitional group that I mentioned earlier. What is significant is that even with that percentage drop in income, there are still parts of the United Kingdom which are below 75 per cent of the average, which is really a significant finding. Since that political agreement was reached in December 2005, of course, Romania and Bulgaria have also joined the Union and they are also poorer than the new average, so they have pulled the average down by another two percentage points although the lower income of 15 percentage points has not yet been applied for the policy. In other words we have never had the selection of regions on the basis of this full 15 percentage point drop. Quite clearly, however, a region like Cornwall or West Wales and the Valleys would no longer qualify for the high levels of support they are getting on the basis of the present level of income in the European Union, they would both now be above 75 per cent of the new Community average.
Lord Steinberg: I can understand all of that and I know of course that there has been a shift, but you still did not tell me where you started off from, how the 15 per cent was arrived at, because 15 per cent is a colossal figure and Romania, Bulgaria and Poland would not change it by that amount. I entirely agree with my colleagues that there is a shift and that the poorer countries are not only entitled but are receiving much more in terms of aid. Here I have to declare an interest: I have just bought a sizeable business in Poland a week and a half ago, so I am obviously confident about the future of Poland. If you are telling me that that 15 percentage points has come from when we were 15 then I can understand it better, but if you are telling me that it has happened with Romania and Bulgaria coming in, going from 25 to 27—if I am right you said that effect was about two or three percentage points.

Q240 ***Chairman:*** I can see that this is an important question, I was wondering if we could ask Mr Meadows to write to us about it because I am dying to get on and ask about financial matters, but it is sufficiently technical that we could perhaps ask Mr Meadows to write—you have understood the basis of the question?
Mr Meadows: Yes. I could probably answer it in two sentences.

Q241 ***Chairman:*** Okay, go.
Mr Meadows: The enlargement from 15 Member States to 25 Member States lowered the average income per head by 12 percentage points; that is Poland plus the other nine. The further enlargement from 25 to 27 lowered that average income by a further two percentage points to give you a total of around 15 percentage points in the reduction. The 2005 deal was struck on the basis of 25 Member States—in other words on the basis of the average income for the EU-15 member states minus the 12 percentage point drop which resulted from the

accession of ten new Member States in 2004. But I will write and explain it.

Lord Steinberg: Yes, thank you for that answer but I am not happy about that.

Chairman: We need to move on. Lord Moser.

Q242 ***Lord Moser:*** Mr Meadows, we have talked at some length about how to split the total, poorer versus richer countries et cetera et cetera; I am interested in the size of the total cake and your paper is very helpful in explaining how this is determined and also the order of decision-making—first the total, then the regions and then the Member States. It reads like quite a sophisticated process, but in fact it is not very sophisticated because as you say in your paper everything ultimately rests on GDP per head. I know enough about that to know that that is the most important single measurement, but it is by no means the only one, and I was rather cheered by an aside in your paper that maybe other criteria should be brought into play. Could you say something first of all about your view upon the total size of the cake, which is 0.4 per cent of regional wealth so to speak, whether you think that is appropriate or whether you think it could be more or less—the total, never mind the composition—and then, secondly, whether you are really happy about so much resting on basically a single macroeconomic figure?

Mr Meadows: In terms of the size of the cake, when we were negotiating the continuation of the policy the total figure for the Competitiveness regions started off as a somewhat political figure . In the negotiations we felt that the figure was eroded, or reduced to be close to a level at which the basic policy would have to perhaps be changed. What is my idea about the size of the cake? In the present structure of the policy, bearing in mind the effects of this fall of 15 percentage points in income, there is probably an argument for making the cake slightly larger. How much larger is something which would need to be determined by Member States, but 0.4 per cent of Community GDP at the moment is probably 50 or 60 billion euros short of where one really ought to be to have a sufficient impact. In terms of other indicators, the last 20 years have seen the emergence of aspects of the policy which are of considerable concern which are not captured necessarily by GDP. I am thinking of some sort of environmental indicators and things of this sort in addition to the labour market indicators. Labour market indicators are taken into account in the calculation, but in terms of the way in which resources are used, either within Member States or within regions, it appears that there is an enhanced role which could be given to indicators which reflect degrees of economic modernisation or reflect environmental concerns, reflect some social concerns. The difficulty that the Union would have is that these data do not exist on a regional basis, which is harmonised. One would be reluctant to use them as a way of actually allocating resources from the Union to the Member States. Within Member States it would possible to use them.

Q243 ***Lord Moser:*** If I could just have one follow-up, what you have just said was certainly correct in the old days and when I was in charge of statistics here I of course spent much time in Luxembourg, at the statistical office, but in those days figures were fairly crude and one could understand this kind of thing being based on average—which I do not like—GDP per head but hiding many, many variations. I do not like policies being based on percentages, policies should be based on actual figures, numbers. Nowadays, as we all know, statistical systems have become enormously sophisticated and I have a feeling that somebody in Brussels or Luxembourg is being rather lazy to go on basing it basically on GDP per head. Using GDP regional figures does not take advantage of those systems—I am not talking about Romania and Bulgaria which have less sophisticated systems, although they will come up—and I would have thought the time was ripe for the decision-makers to say that these allocations should be done on a much more sophisticated basis and that countries that do not yet have the figures to make that possible should bloody well get them. I find it all a little bit out of date.

Mr Meadows: Right. As I say, the problem is that the Union requires regional data for all of the Member States which is harmonised. Only that kind of data is suitable for allocating finance between Member States and between regions, otherwise people pay the price for statistical defects. The way in which I would see other indicators coming into the process in the short tem would be as a way of trying to give greater insight into the allocation of EU resources within regions for particular purposes. As these other databases develop then obviously, as you say, they could become more and more key in allocating resources in the policy.

Lord Kerr of Kinlochard: I confess I find Lord Moser's purism is admirable but it does not fit in the Council of Ministers. The more sophisticated your indicators—Mr Meadows cites environment, research, innovation and reforms of the labour market—the more room you are creating for political argument and fudge. I would not go as far as Mr Meadows goes actually, there is plenty of fudge already even with the GDP per head criteria which is reasonably unfudgable.

Chairman: This has been a riveting discussion but we are rapidly running out of time and I really would like to arrive at your views upon the increasing burden of financial management and I would like to ask Lord Woolmer to ask about this.

Q244 ***Lord Woolmer of Leeds:*** Thank you. Mr Meadows, in your original written submission and your later one you are fairly frank about the costs imposed by the administrative and financial management arrangements, from the top down to the bottom as it were, from the staff at the Commission through to the final project and in your words has earned the policy a bad name, even amongst those who are benefiting. Can I ask you two questions about that? First of all, how does the Commission quantify the cost of administering further funds from the applicant on the ground, through the management, through the different layers of regional, national and then Brussels levels? Has this been assessed and what at the Commission level have they made of these costs that are being imposed?

Mr Meadows: Has there been an attempt to actually measure the cost of administering the Funds? I think no, but viscerally you can see that the cost is rising because of events in the European Union and the state of public opinion. It is not possible to have a frank discussion about the way in which financial control and financial management is evolving. I can give you a very recent example. In December of last year the European Parliament's Budget Control Committee refused at that stage to grant the discharge on Structural Fund expenditure for 2006, because the Court of Auditors reported that there was an error rate in this expenditure of something like 12 per cent. This came back a couple of weeks ago to the same Committee and, in the meantime, to try to show that it was dealing with this problem the Commission produced a rather large programme of work that it was going to undertake to actually give confidence to the Budget Control Committee of the Parliament. This programme of work now risks to add further controls. I suggest, therefore, that it would be useful if it were possible for the Member States, the Commission and the Court of Auditors to discuss ways of arriving at the level of financial management which is required in a more cost-effective way. At the moment, events push the institutions forward in so that no one can actually stand back and ask "Can we achieve these ends differently?" We have reached the position where, when auditors reveal that something is not up to European standards, it is difficult to say whether something is really wrong or the standards too high. It would only be right, I think, to allow ourselves a doubt as to whether in fact controls are being piled on controls to such an extent that we are demanding too high a level of accuracy in financial management. The level being imposed by the Union on the United Kingdom is probably higher than the level that the United Kingdom imposes on itself. I do not see any virtue in that. I think it is a question of management and what I plead for in the notes is that some way is found outside the formal processes to look at this particular question. At the moment the regulations are being changed and people are hopeful that the new regulations will ease matters; the Treaty is being changed and people are also hoping that will make financial control easier. My own view, however, is that as long as the present attitudes which underlie financial control are not changed, or are not given a chance to reappraise themselves, the new possibilities will be interpreted in exactly the same way as the old possibilities and we will not actually escape from the present circumstance. It is a very thorny question because, of course, one can easily be accused of looking for lax financial management and allowing people to make off to Bermuda with large packages of taxpayers' money and so on, which is of course no one's intention. At the moment one has the impression that some extra thought is needed, that the institutions need, under a flag of truce, to be able to talk about these issues and ask themselves "Are we really going about this in the right way?"

Chairman: Thank you very much, Mr Meadows. I am going to allow an extra couple of minutes for Lord Kerr.

Q245 ***Lord Kerr of Kinlochard:*** I was interested in what Mr Meadows said in his paper about a better mix of loans and grants, that the Union should allocate more of its funding to recyclable loan funds. This is news to me; could you explain, Mr Meadows, what you have in mind; how much more, and how this would fit with the role of the European Investment Bank?

Mr Meadows: As regions approach the point in their development when they can sustain their own economic effort, their needs for investments in basic infrastructure diminish and they use more of their EU resources to support business in different ways, for what we used to call "softer" investment purposes. In these circumstances, it seems suitable for the regions themselves to decide to use—so it is not something which would necessarily be enforced from outside—the European Union resources in recyclable loan funds instead of grants to achieve some of the objectives that they want to achieve. The advantage would be that after the period of programming these funds would come back as the loans were repaid and the regions could carry on using the funding to pursue the same objectives. Years ago, when I was responsible in a detailed way for European regional policy in the Federal Republic of Germany where, Lord Trimble is right, there is a very large national or regional policy, I discovered—this was around 1989—that Marshall aid was still being recycled. These were investable resources which were delivered into the German economy and used for recyclable loans. You get some impression from this of the staying power of that kind of instrument as opposed to grants, which, of course, are necessary for certain purposes but could be diminished for others. The suggestion I make is that the Union should negotiate with each of the regions a percentage of the support coming from the European Union that the region would feel comfortable in using in recyclable loan funds, the advantage to the region being that when European Union funding diminished they would still have the benefit of what they had in the past. The United Kingdom has done this. The United Kingdom a few years ago put quite a large amount of funding into recyclable funds, and this money is still going around. It is a rather good way of softening for the region some of the funding changes which take place as regional income rises and they change categories within EU regional policy. It gives the regions more control over managing their own economic performance and is therefore a good thing.

Q246 ***Chairman:*** Thank you very much, Mr Meadows. We have kept you much longer than we should have, but we do thank you very much for coming and have found this most helpful.

Mr Meadows: You are very kind; it has been my great pleasure.

THURSDAY 6 MARCH 2008

Present Cohen of Pimlico, B (Chairman) Woolmer of Leeds, L
Trimble, L

Examination of Witnesses

Witnesses: MR DIRK AHNER, Director General DG Regional Policy, MR NICOLA DE MICHELIS, Head of Unit—Additionality, Economic and Quantitative Analysis, DG Regional Policy, MR ERIC DUFEIL, Head of Unit, Spain, DG Regional Policy and MR PASCAL BOIJMANS, Deputy Head of Unit, Poland, DG Regional Policy, examined.

Q247 ***Chairman:*** Good morning. We are reasonably short-handed this morning because some of our colleagues are attending the tripartite meeting between the European Parliament, Lords and Commons.
Mr Ahner: A real stressful day for you.

Q248 ***Chairman:*** It is very good of you to receive us. We have taken quite a lot of evidence on this inquiry and we are boiling up to arrive at a provisional set of conclusions. You have had a copy of the topics we would like to discuss.
Mr Ahner: Yes.

Q249 ***Chairman:*** If I introduce my colleagues: I have here Lord Woolmer, a member of my Committee, and Lord Trimble, who has enormous regional experience from Northern Ireland. Would you like to introduce your colleagues?
Mr Ahner: My colleague, Pascal Boijmans, who is working in the unit which is responsible for regional development in Poland. Nicola De Michelis is the Head of our Economic Analysis Unit. We have reorganised our Directorate-General and we have one directorate which is policy planning, policy evaluation and economic analysis. Nicola heads the Economic Analysis Unit team.

Q250 ***Chairman:*** You have had the various questions we want to ask. We can either chunk our way down them with refinements or is there an opening statement you would like to make?
Mr Ahner: If I may suggest, I will go very rapidly through the questions and leave the details for my colleagues. In the meantime, Mr Dufeil has joined us, who is responsible for Spain. In addition, Eric has worked on Germany for many years so he can compare two quite different countries as far as their development patterns are concerned. Let me start with two or three sentences about where we are to get into the subject. Last year we had a very, very intense year of programme approval for the new programming period, 2007-13. Practically all programmes were approved last year; there are very, very few still missing. This year the implementation has started. Some countries started the implementation last year, but this year the bulk of the countries and regions will start the implementation process. To say something about the new period, I think it will make sense in terms of evaluation in two or three years' time. At the end of this year and early next year we expect a whole set of evaluation reports and evaluation studies of the 2000-06 period and it is our intention in the first half of next year to come with an overview and synthesis report of the outcomes of these evaluation studies. This year, and this is why I am so grateful that we have the possibility of this exchange today, we are starting our work on the future Cohesion Policy. This is work where we look a year ahead, so it is a window of opportunity to discuss, exchange and analyse the situation. This work is ongoing, it started just a few weeks ago. Looking at the past and coming back to your questions, let me first of all underline that I am a complete—I do not know how you say it in English—greenhorn. This has been a good year to work in regional policy. I worked in rural development policy before, which is familiar but is a different field, much more agricultural and sectorially oriented. I will give you my first reactions to your questions and then we will attend to the detail. The first question was has the policy been successful so far. It is extremely difficult to have a benchmark for success: when do you speak about success and when do you not speak about success. If we look at the period for which we have comparable statistics available we can see that convergence has taken place but Regional Development Policy, Cohesion Policy, in our view at least, is not only about the question of convergence. First of all, yes it is about convergence because it is a question of solidarity and this is why a lot of the money is concentrated on the poorer regions, or on regions which have particular problems of structural adjustment, but at the same time it is a policy which helps us to sustain a model of development which we think is the model we have in Europe, which is one of a relatively spatially balanced economic development with a polycentric orientation. In our view, this makes sense in economic terms for the very simple reason we believe if we accept there is a strong

concentration of economic activity on very few areas we would very rapidly have a double problem, first of all negative externalities in the big agglomerations, and this is something with which we are already living today in some cases, and the other point is we would probably lose a lot of potential which exists and which would remain unused if we did not have this approach to more balanced development in spatial terms. If you look at the EU-15, where we can observe 10 years from 1995–2005 where we have comparable statistics, convergence took place. It is extremely difficult to say that was exclusively because of Cohesion Policy. I would say it was also because of Cohesion Policy and the evaluation studies which exist for this period, if I understand them correctly, confirm this. When we say we have cohesion, we have development in those regions which were lagging behind, but very often what one should not forget is this has feedback effects on the economies of the other countries. We have made a static calculation for the year 2004 where we saw about a quarter of the money which was spent in the poorer regions of the Community went back in the form of demand for equipment and other things to the richer regions of the EU. There is an ongoing effect which takes place. That is my answer to the first question. If you want figures and details, let me say you have a lot of figures in the Cohesion Report of last year but my colleagues can go into more detail if you want. What lessons can be learned from Spain? Is Spain a model? I must say, we have such a diversity of situations in Europe, even within Spain, that I would be extremely cautious speaking about models. It is true we are testing policy and approaches. One of the specificities of the Cohesion Policy which I think makes sense, and as compared to Rural Development Policy I am delighted to see how it works in the field of Regional Policy, is what is done at the regional and local level is worked out and decided by the regional and local level. It then comes up in the form of programmes to the Commission but the Commission is not really the body which decides on programmes; the Commission has the role of a sparring partner and adviser. We get a programme from the region or from a Member State, we discuss this programme with them and look at whether this programme, since it is EU money being spent, is in line with the priorities which we have commonly set at the EU level and does this programme really address the problems of the regions. Each programme has to carry out an analysis where they show what are the weaknesses and strengths of their regions and what are the opportunities. In our teams we have people who have worked for a number of years with these regions concerned and we discuss it with them. Normally in these discussions, and some call it a negotiation but it is not really a negotiation, what we see is generally we have what I call an improvement of these programmes and at the end we have an outcome where both sides say, "We have brought together something on which we agree which makes sense". I lived through it for the first time last year during the programme approval phase we had, and this is why I am particularly impressed, and we had very hot and heavy meetings. I remember, Eric, you had one prime minister from a German länder one evening in a restaurant in Brussels and you were discussing the questions of this programme up to midnight. Something comes out of this dialogue which in my view generates a real value-added, but we can discuss this further if you want.

Q251 ***Chairman:*** Mr Ahner, I would like to pause at this point but, on the other hand, are you able to be with us all morning?

Mr Ahner: I can stay with you for as long as you want.

Q252 ***Chairman:*** That is very helpful. If we were going to lose you after an hour—

Mr Ahner: You will lose me when you throw me out!

Q253 ***Chairman:*** That is terrific. I wonder, therefore, if I could stop on this question. We shall see Valencia this afternoon and I would very much welcome a comment on the Spanish experience.

Mr Dufeil: Thank you very much, Chairman. If you will allow me, I would like to outline four conclusions I feel I am able to draw from the Spanish experiment. As an introduction, Spain is a very interesting example. It can be looked at as one of the success stories we have recorded in the last 20 years or so. Even if the case study on Ireland might look more impressive, please remember that on the European scale Ireland remains a relatively small country whereas Spain now tends to belong to the biggest countries and to that extent the weight of the Spanish experiment is higher. The first conclusion is convergence in nominal and real terms has taken place over the 20 years at a rate which is quite constant and regular, a little less than one per cent convergence per year on the long-term average, which is very significant. This means that Spain has been able to develop from a level of roughly 90 per cent of the GDP per head indicator at the beginning of the 1990s up to 102 per cent this year. Spain is very proud of the fact that recently they have overtaken Italy. When you travel to Spain you come across that information all the time because for them it is a signal that they have achieved an important step. The second conclusion is if it is true in general terms, in macroeconomic terms at national level, comparing member countries to other countries, within Spain at regional level you see that there is a more differentiated picture. This is not really a surprise when you have growth phenomenon. If you refer to the growth theory of somebody like WW Rostow that explains that as well. It increases the original disparities. It means that in Spain there are winning regions everywhere and every region has developed but to different extents and there are some that have been winners more than others. What is obvious is that the strongest regions, like Catalonia, Madrid, the Basque countries, which are the strong pillars of Spanish growth, have grown more than others, and you still have regions, like Extremadura, which is a remote part in the south, which have development difficulties. However, there are also intermediate stories like the Canary Islands, which was always recorded as part of the Objective 1 region and ultra-peripheral region, that has now become a phasing-in region so they are in the process of joining the competitiveness. That in itself is a very good signal. I have other examples I could quote. This is something we need to observe and differentiate the processes of intervention. The third conclusion is that the growth which took place in Spain over 20 years was primarily based on the construction sector and the development of infrastructure and the result is very visible. If you travel to Spain you can see big panels everywhere with the blue flag and the 12 stars: "Co-financed with ERDF". It is possible to say for the road system, the rail system, some of the port system and other basic infrastructure the network is now up and running and this is one of the requirements of a modern economy. You can record that and check that is physically present and useful, not only to the country itself but to all of Europe, whether for the purpose of tourism or investment. To that extent it is a good move. Of course, this is not sufficient and in Spain they talk about deceleration of the growth, which means they have moved from a rate of four per cent a year to maybe 2.5. That is still more than countries like Germany and France but it is less. They are confronted with a necessity to find a second path of growth which inevitably, if they want to join the club of more developed countries, has to be reoriented towards research and development, technology and innovation. This is where we are now and what we are trying to achieve with the assistance of Structural Fund programmes 2007–13 in Spain. The European Council has decided to attribute a special allocation to Spain as political agreement to compensate for the loss of the Cohesion Fund, but the negotiators have tried to make the most of it and are saying, "Okay, you are attributing money and this is to create a so-called technological fund and with that money in the range of €500 million, please see what you can do with your undertakers, with your universities and laboratories, your public administration", the so-called triple helix model, "and build clusters, foster innovation, especially in the field of small and medium-sized undertakings because this is where it is critical". Just to mention one figure: when the Lisbon Strategy speaks of a target for 2010 which is three per cent of GDP in terms of expenditure in the field of research and development, at the current moment Spain records a level of 1.2 per cent, which is extremely low even compared to other countries like Germany and France, so clearly there is a need. If you do not look only at the publicly financed research but, more important perhaps, the research which is privately financed, which is to say the research which takes place within the companies, then the figures are even smaller. I do not have the details here but we could find that out. That figure is not satisfactory now. We have a success story that we can show and demonstrate more in physical terms. We, together with Spain, are confronted with other challenges of a new type if they want to grow as a modern economy. Those are my four conclusions. There is convergence, there is terrific improvement in the environment, like the sewerage system or cleaning the water, things like that, and also a huge reduction in the indicator of unemployment which culminated at the levels of 18 or 20 per cent and now is in the range of eight or nine per cent, like France or Germany and other Member countries, and like the United Kingdom, but you make us jealous. However, there are still huge environmental problems in Spain relating to water management, among others. Drought is an issue and how not to ensure the transfer of water from one river basin to another and how to mitigate using agriculture, tourism and so on is still an issue that we want to look at because we are going not only for the Lisbon but the Gothenburg Strategy which is environmental sustainability.

Q254 ***Chairman:*** I have two questions before I pass on to my colleagues. Could you remind me what the Spanish allocation under the Regional Development Fund is for 2007-13?

Mr Dufeil: Yes. Altogether, which means ERDF and Cohesion Fund, we are talking of figures in the range of €35 billion, an annual average of €5 billion.

Q255 ***Chairman:*** Obviously, with all respect to the European Commission and the efforts on regional development, this growth was not achieved solely by our efforts. Have you done any work on separating out the effect of growth by becoming a member of the EU and by the trading opportunities from this? It is a question, I do not know that you should have, I am just asking.

Mr Dufeil: We do bear that in question in mind, of course. I am not sure we are able to do that because it is very difficult. I would like to quote another fact which in my opinion is very relevant in the case of Spain, which is a demographic fact. If you look at the population of Spain at the beginning of that period it was very comparable to Poland, in the range of 40 million people, and whereas Poland's population has diminished to 38 million, Spain has grown to 44 million inhabitants, which is a growth of ten per cent, and that is a lot. You could partly explain Spanish growth by the demographic factor, which is due to immigration from Africa, Sub-Saharan countries and Latin America.

Q256 ***Chairman:*** That I did not know.
Mr Dufeil: Very important.
Mr Ahner: In answer to your question, we have done some model analysis where, with the help of economic models, we tried to identify which part of the growth in Spain could be attributable to the Cohesion Fund money. This analysis was carried out in Nicola's unit. Nicola, perhaps you could say a word on this. I think it was around one percentage point a year in growth terms which was directly attributable to the European funds.

Q257 ***Chairman:*** I see the difficulties, that was why I was wondering whether you had done that.
Mr Ahner: This is a model analysis so it must be taken with caution.
Chairman: I think that leads us on very nicely to the second question which, Lord Woolmer, perhaps you would address.

Q258 ***Lord Woolmer of Leeds:*** Mr Ahner, you are going to respond to the question here but can I frame it in a slightly different way. Remind me, how many regions are there in the EU?
Mr Ahner: 268.

Q259 ***Lord Woolmer of Leeds:*** That is the Eurostudy, is it?
Mr Ahner: Yes.

Q260 ***Lord Woolmer of Leeds:*** Can I make a general proposition to you and then ask question two. If there was a single country with a population of 470 million and there were 268 sub-units of government, and you were considering how best to use less than half a per cent of overall income to help development and do other things, I suggest to you that you would be very, very selective across that kind of population and that number of regions, yet the programmes and so on are not very, very selective, every region gets something. I am looking at this strategically. If I was running a business and I had got, heaven forbid, 268 operating units across 470 million people I would think very hard about which business unit needed my intervention from the centre. I put that as a proposition to you. That is looking at a clean sheet as opposed to where we are. With that in mind, if you were designing the system from scratch now, would you really do it the way we are doing it? Is that really the best way to deliver targeted strategic intervention at a pan-European level?
Mr Ahner: Let me answer your thoughts.

Q261 ***Lord Woolmer of Leeds:*** It is quite an important issue.
Mr Ahner: I follow your proposition totally. I would say I have to target my money, I have scarce resources and I want to use them in the best way. The next point is I would ask what do I want to achieve, what are my objectives. In this case I would be confronted with three objectives. The first objective is to try to improve and strengthen the competitiveness of Europe, generate growth and jobs across Europe and take the formulations of the Lisbon Strategy. Then there would be a second objective which would be to say, "Do this, but please do it in a sustainable way". Then there would be a third objective which would tell you, "Whatever you do, you should make sure that there is an overall balanced development in your territory". When I have these three objectives in front of me I would ask myself how can I best put my money in a way to achieve these three objectives. Then I would look at the leverage effects of the money. When I put money there I have a number of objectives. I want to use the little amount of money which I have for this territory as a lever. I want to make sure that it brings development across the whole territory. I would come to a model where you can discuss should it be 80 per cent, 60 per cent or 50 per cent. I would come to a model which I must say is not that far away from the model which we have. Honestly, in economic terms I think this makes a lot of sense. What would be the alternatives? The alternative would be a model where I would say I would let it go, the market would decide totally and fully on this. That is a possible model. In this model I would come to a situation where—

Q262 ***Lord Woolmer of Leeds:*** Mr Ahner, nobody is suggesting that. I was saying if you have got those resources and you have got some objectives, would you be more selective? If you were really prioritising a strategy is not everything. Do not put up an Aunt Sally that no-one is suggesting.
Mr Ahner: With these three objectives in mind I would honestly go for a similar model. If one of these objectives did not exist, if there was not an objective of balanced spatial economic development, I would look for a different model, absolutely. If there was not an objective of long-term environmental sustainability you might look for a different way of spending your money. I must say I would follow this

model which has a very strong concentration of the money on a few regions, which we should not forget, 80 per cent in the current period goes to the poorest regions of the Union.

Q263 ***Lord Woolmer of Leeds:*** How many regions would that be? 80 per cent goes to how many of the 268 regions?
Mr Ahner: Seventy.[1]
Lord Woolmer of Leeds: So 80 per cent goes to 70. Thank you.
Chairman: I am sure you see where we are going. We are picking away at the question of whether you would say of these 270 regions, "I have only got a very limited amount of money to sprinkle about, I am just going to forget about 200 of those regions and I will concentrate my money on the remainder".
Lord Woolmer of Leeds: You would not say forget, you would say leave it for the Member States.

Q264 ***Chairman:*** Yes, just say to Member States, "You can do that".
Mr Ahner: What I want to obtain is a number of common objectives and I see in 200 out of these 270 regions with a relatively small amount of money I can have a leverage effect in the direction of these objectives which is extremely positive.
Mr Dufeil: Mr Ahner, would you like me to outline the negotiation we had with Baden-Wurttemberg?

Q265 ***Chairman:*** That would be most helpful.
Mr Dufeil: Baden-Wurttemberg is one of the most prosperous regions in all of Europe with very successful stories and they get a very limited amount of money from the Structural Funds, €142 million, €20 million a year. According to your line of thought, you could have said, "Why take the trouble" and just forget it. Under Mr Ahner's authority we have negotiated very fiercely and strongly with Baden-Wurttemberg and in the end they have thanked us for that difficult negotiation because we have tried to obtain from them something with a leverage effect which is exemplary in the field of research and innovative development, which they have, but which they could transfer with Structural Funds into pilots and demonstrative projects of high value transferable to other cases. To that extent, we have attributed a much higher value to that €142 million and we gained value from that money.

Q266 ***Lord Trimble:*** Would Baden-Wurttemberg not have done that themselves?
Mr Dufeil: No.

Q267 ***Lord Trimble:*** Why not?
Mr Dufeil: Really, they would not.

Q268 ***Lord Trimble:*** Do you mean to say that they were not into research and development? Of course they were.
Mr Dufeil: No, I am not saying that because they do it, but with 142 million they were only thinking of very classical measures in the field of rural development, which is fine in principle but in their case it was a second-best solution. Looking for that leverage effect we think that we have been able to reach an upper level of efficiency on the Structural Funds.
Mr Ahner: Let me come back to the model for a second. In fact, the policy is extremely simple in its principles. We have a policy there which to a very large extent is an investment policy. It is investment in physical capital, social and human capital and research and development. These are the pillars of this investment. These investments are directed towards objectives which have been defined beforehand which are commonly agreed. Within this framework it is the regional, and in some cases the local level that is most concerned, but in a few cases the national level. After an analysis they elaborate the programmes they see as being the best for themselves. As an additional step they have a discussion on this programme which adds to what is being done at the national level. They have to justify, they ask a number of questions, and at the end comes a programme on which they then have a stability guarantee for over seven years as far as the money that is available is concerned with the possibility that if within the seven years there are changes in the overall objectives and adaptations of the programmes which are needed, for whatever reason, that is possible and can be discussed. In reality, it is an approach, a method where different levels of governance, European, national, regional and sometimes local, are involved in a discussion in order to find solutions to specific problems to achieve a number of objectives which have been commonly defined. This has a leverage effect because what we see is that each euro which is spent through this investment policy brings other euros from the private side into the game. These are the principles of the policy. I call it almost a common policy in the modern sense of the word. It is not a common policy in the sense of the Common Agricultural Policy, it is really a shared policy where all the different levels participate in a process to achieve common objectives. I must say, after one year of discussion and having lived through the very intense period of last year I have been personally astonished at how

[1] *Note by witness:* Seventy is the number of convergence regions. Yet, more regions are covered by 80% of cohesion funding: 116. These include regions covered by the Cohesion Fund and phasing out regions.

well this works, I did not expect that it would work this well.
Chairman: Can we push a little, Mr Ahner. Lord Trimble.

Q269 ***Lord Trimble:*** Just to make sure I have got it right, I gathered from what you said that 80 per cent of the money goes into the poorest regions, the one that used to be Objective 1 but are now called convergence regions.
Mr Ahner: Yes.

Q270 ***Lord Trimble:*** Why 80 per cent? Why not more?
Mr Ahner: It is a little bit more than 80 per cent, but the 80 per cent is the outcome of a political negotiation. The basis of this negotiation is a methodology which we have applied which looks at the gap which exists between the poorest regions in terms of gross domestic product per head and the average. This methodology was the basis for the calculations which was accepted by all Member States. On the last night of the negotiations under the UK Presidency, you will remember there were some final gifts made here and there in order to come to a compromise and the basis was a methodology that had already been agreed in the 1990s.

Q271 ***Lord Trimble:*** If you could, would you want to spend more on the poorer regions?
Mr Ahner: I must say "if you could" has two conditions. The first is if I had more money available and I set this aside. I would say a very cautious no. In particular I see in the poorer regions of today there must be a capacity to use the money which is available for good programmes, and this must not be overlooked. This is one of the big discussions we have with the new Member States, for example. Yes, we have agreed on good programmes and they are programmes which look good to us, but the programme in itself is a framework and within this framework they have to put the money to concrete projects. To come forward and find good projects which fit with these programmes is not easy. That is the first point. The second point is the money which is spent is European taxpayers' money so we ask them to have in place a control capacity, a management capacity, which in some cases they are still building up, if you look at Romania and Bulgaria in particular. Finally, when they want to spend the money they are under rules and supervision which sometimes, let us be honest, are hampering the process. When we insist from Brussels that public procurement rules are respected and if they are not respected they cannot use the money on the projects—

Q272 ***Lord Trimble:*** I understand entirely and we take entirely the points about capacity.
Mr Ahner: I would not see much more capacity in these countries to absorb more money today and in the foreseeable future.

Q273 ***Lord Trimble:*** With regard to the poorest regions, you think they are getting as much as they can cope with?
Mr Ahner: I believe that they cannot cope with what they are getting and I would be reluctant to give more. They may not be at 100 per cent of their capacity, I do not know, but I would be reluctant to give more. First of all, I would like to see the money they have got now they are able to spend on good projects and in three years' time I would like to see the first interim evaluation of what has been done. As far as the more administrative aspects are concerned, we have a yearly monitoring of what is going on in these countries. I would like to see this before I make any decision whatsoever. When the Marshall Plan was decided for Europe after the war I think it was about two per cent of all gross domestic products and we are going up to three or four per cent of GDP sometimes and this is a lot in terms of money which has to be absorbed. At this stage, if I have more money I would not put it in this game, I would let the system grow.

Q274 ***Lord Trimble:*** Just to be slightly provocative, the 17-20 per cent that goes to countries that are not the poorest, is that simply done for political reasons to buy their consent to the existence of this or is there any real objective for it?
Mr Ahner: For me there are certainly political reasons but there is a real objective behind it. In these regions we are very often confronted with quite serious problems of adjustment and restructuring and the fact that statistically the income per head in these regions is higher does not necessarily mean that there is immediately a public capacity available to launch such a process. We have a number of Member States and regions which even today have big problems matching the money which comes from the Community with national money. The little help they get from the EU with its leverage effect can accelerate the adjustment process in these regions considerably sometimes.

Q275 ***Chairman:*** Thank you very much, Mr Ahner. We are juggling to arrive at a recommendation for the future of the Structural Funds and one of the things that bears on the question is, of course, the costs, which Lord Woolmer is going to ask you about shortly. From the point of view of many other European principles, like subsidiarity, it still strikes the ear of a rich country oddly, a rich country with plenty of administrative capacity. In a way, one would see a more rational structure whereby EU assistance was confined to the poorer countries and to fewer of them, to fewer regions, because then you would think you could get more concentration. I think you have probably made the case for intervention in the richer countries which may still have pockets, but is this being done at a very high administrative cost? If you could turn all the administrative talent in the Commission and in other places into the poorer regions, one sort of feels as a businessman you would get a terrific result.

Mr Ahner: I am not 100 per cent sure. If you put all the money into the poorer countries, at this stage of development I think you would get a real problem with digestion. That is the first point. The second point is using the money in the richer regions brings a certain number of advantages which are important. I mentioned some of them and the other advance, which is also important, is this makes the richer regions participate in the overall process. I will come to the cost of the process in a minute. What was quite interesting to see was in the negotiations in general we had to be much more convincing with the richer regions than with the poorer regions in terms of convincing them to do things which were in line with the common objectives. This is strange because very often it was the richer regions who in the past have said absolutely to go for innovation and money has to be put into research. When we saw the programmes and ideas that were developed, we had to have a real discussion about what innovation means, what could and could not be done. This dialogue brings added value to the whole process. That is on the economic side. On the political side, personally I am not 100 per cent convinced that within Europe it would be a good thing to have a situation where you could say, "There are the poor countries, they get the money from the rich countries and that's it". That is not how I would see a European-wide policy of development and improvement of competitiveness. If I may say, everybody is under a "common discipline" and you are not only under a discipline because you are a poorer country, others also have to follow a similar approach under discipline. I agree totally you can discuss all this but last year I was extremely surprised, to be honest, because with my prejudice as an economist I had not expected the costs would go so far.

Q276 ***Lord Woolmer of Leeds:*** Just remind me, of the 70 regions, what proportion of the 470 million Europeans live in those regions? What is the population of those 70 regions?

Mr De Michelis: About a quarter, about 100 million people.[2]

Q277 ***Lord Woolmer of Leeds:*** So it is about the same proportion. It is about a quarter.

Mr De Michelis: Yes.

Q278 ***Lord Woolmer of Leeds:*** There are two issues of cost that I would like to explore with you. One is at Commission level itself, which is relatively easy I suspect, how much it costs the Commission in terms of funds and if that varies between countries. Secondly, the cost of the programmes is felt from particular applicants, particular projects through to administering regional authority or whatever it is, through to Member States and yourselves. There is a series of layers of cost of management, administration, financial systems, controls and so on. That is going to vary between the regions you are dealing with and the Member States you are dealing with. Have you done any serious examination or study of those costs and how they relate to the spend and how that varies?

Mr Ahner: On what happens in the Member States, we are currently carrying out a study and we will have the results next year. We are carrying out a study on what the costs are of control in particular Member States.

Q279 ***Lord Woolmer of Leeds:*** Just the control. If it is not impolite to ask, would it be possible for you to send us a copy of the terms of reference of that study, that would be very helpful, rather than go over it now.

Mr Ahner: Yes. The next point is as far as the Commission is concerned we have made a standardised calculation on the basis of standards which we normally use. If I take the overall concrete management of the funds in DG Regio, so financial management but also the overall management of the programmes, and I take the managers, I set aside the economic analysts and these people, I come to an amount of about €50 million per year for €35 billion which we spent. This is about half a per cent. If I take the whole of the Directorate-General and I say everything has to do with Cohesion Policy I come roughly to a good one per cent because there are all the other services, legal advice, the economic analysis and so on. In total we have 600 officials in DG Regio. We spend €35 billion a year, €350 billion over the seven year period. When you compare it to other Directorate-Generals, the biggest Directorate-General in the Commission is the Research Directorate-General which has about 3,000 people

[2] *Note by witness:* In line with footnote n.1, the 116 regions covered by 80% of the cohesion budget are home to around 200 million people or 40% of the total EU population.

working for €70 billion. In fact, at the Commission level the cost is not exorbitant. Part of the problem is you have to be fair and our colleagues in DG Research are in direct management of research programmes whereas we are in shared management with the Member States and there is a lot of management which takes place at the regional level. Let us be honest, even if no money is spent from the EU, the management at the regional and national level would have to take place. If I take the last enlargement which we had with richer countries—Austria, Finland and Sweden—when you looked at these countries there were quite sophisticated management systems already in place and also for development purposes.

Q280 ***Lord Woolmer of Leeds:*** One last question on this. In relation to the study that you are doing, that you will send us the terms of reference of, it will not look at the overall proportion of cost right through from the project level to the regional authority level to the Member State level. There are certainly one or two regional authorities in the United Kingdom which have commented to us that when you take all of that it is really pretty substantial. That raises this question: in some countries, and this is just a fact of life, it is not an adverse comment on countries that do not meet this criteria, the experience and processes of management, systems and so on are well-established, financial management systems, and in principle, again I think in business terms, one would not run a parallel process of systems, one would say, "If your systems meet our satisfaction we are not going to duplicate those". Is there not room for this in some countries? I am obviously thinking of the UK where our Regional Development Authorities, for example, have to go through all kinds of hoops in relation to grants of finance from the UK Government. Is there not room for this to have a simple way of dealing with things? That is not to say it is not proper and appropriate, and what have you, but are you not able to sign off in some countries saying, "If you do it the way you do it, we agree with your systems", that will simplify things?
Mr Ahner: My colleagues may correct me, but my impression is that is the way it is done. I will repeat what you said. You said, if in a Member State or a region there is a system which corresponds to the requirements of the European system—

Q281 ***Lord Woolmer of Leeds:*** I did not say that. I said which you would accept is as robust and as good as you would want. It is not the same.
Mr Ahner: As long as it fulfils the requirements which we make there is no problem. If you go across Europe, in Germany they have 60 different systems which are working because they were in the regions' existing systems which they have partly adapted and could use as they were. As far as a number of rules that we have with respect to how Community money has to be managed and controlled, which by the way are rules that have been decided unanimously by all Member States, we do not see any problem. I remember in Spain we had a very, very long discussion with the Spanish authorities because of the separation of the management and the control functions. We finally accepted their system after they could show us that their system, although optically it did not correspond to what we expected, fulfilled the same functions that we expected them to do. As far as I see it, where the problem often comes is the requirements at EU level, rightly or wrongly, are so rigorous that what is done at the Member State level does not correspond.

Q282 ***Lord Woolmer of Leeds:*** We took evidence from Graham Meadows, the former Director General, and in his written evidence he said the following: that a black spot of present European regional inclusion policy is the growing administrative and financial burden being passed on to project sponsors. These burdens earn the policy a bad reputation, even amongst direct beneficiaries.
Mr Ahner: Absolutely.

Q283 ***Lord Woolmer of Leeds:*** You would not have thought that from what you have said to us so far.
Mr Ahner: I would agree with Graham, but the question—

Q284 ***Lord Woolmer of Leeds:*** "There is nothing that needs to be done is my impression", you said.
Mr Ahner: I did not say nothing needs to be done. The point is we formulate and define requirements which have to be respected at the EU level. These requirements are decided by our Member States and we have to make sure, that is our work at the Commission, that these requirements are respected. For the final beneficiary that can sometimes create a lot of problems. I would completely agree with Graham that this damages the image of the policy. Part of the problem is if we were allowed to have a looser system we could be much more flexible. The point is when it comes to the point of putting our regulations on the table, what we often see is that in our countries, for whatever reasons, the Court of Auditors want there to be a certain safeguards and control levels within the system. What is true, as far as I understand it, is a number of national systems are less rigorous in their requirements than the EU systems and we have to ask ourselves seriously are the EU systems too rigorous in their requirements. Once we have the rigorous requirements, and there is a national system already in place, although it is not

exactly the construction we would have liked to have seen but it responds to our requirements, then we say, "Please go ahead". I do not see a conflict between the two. The real question remains—I am sorry, I am a little bit exercised on this because I have just come out of a discharge procedure in the budget where we had a lot of discussion with the Court of Auditors and the European Parliament where we were told, "With what is on the paper and the regulation, you, Commission, are not rigorous enough. You must do much more and put much more pressure on Member States". When we see these different echoes, we have to strike a balance. I personally would agree with Graham and say the balance is perhaps too much on the rigorous side. When we prepare the next legal framework I think we will have to have a serious look at what can be simplified. That is a problem for me. Whenever I go to the Member States and the regions and I meet entrepreneurs, the first thing I hear is it is an awful lot of red tape and bureaucratic. I ask them regularly, "Please come with concrete suggestions. Tell us exactly what did not work well and how you think it could work better". I have done it four times and until now I have got no response back, it stays at this level, you go there and speak with them and they say it is awful. I am prepared to go, with the agreement of my Commissioner and the Commission, of course, to the Council and say, "Here in our regulation we have something which is stupidly complicated, let's change the regulation". My real problem at the moment is I need to know exactly where it is too bureaucratic or if it is just a general impression. I am still waiting. Each time I meet these people and I say, "Please come" and they all promise, so perhaps I will get something this year, "Please come and tell me exactly where". I am prepared to change this. This is not the problem.

Q285 ***Chairman:*** The difficulty is the response, the intuitive business response, does tend to favour repatriation of funds, "Don't let's have the EU in this at all, we will do it. We will contribute our bit to the poorer nations". There is very considerable acceptance, there is no problem at all in the United Kingdom about accepting that funds should be going to the new countries in the EU and very considerable difficulty with facing what they see as an extra layer of bureaucratic requirement on top of national bureaucratic requirements. We are kind of used to dealing with national bureaucratic requirements. This fuels the whole idea of a policy of repatriation. I do not think you are ever going to get a terrific amount of sense from asking businessmen what could be simpler, you just have to simplify. The simplification has to be done centrally. No businessman can ever define what is wrong with the system.

Mr Ahner: Yet you must be told. You can discover things where we have said, "This is relatively complicated, why have we done this? What was the reason? Is it really needed?", but you need feedback which goes beyond the simple feeling of "This is all too bureaucratic". Let me make one more point. Sometimes I have the impression, and also in my former work in the field of Agricultural Policy, that only partially you add the Community layer to the national layer and it goes the other way round, there is a Community layer and at the national level layers are added to this because the Community layer is a perfect opportunity to put national layers on it.

Q286 ***Lord Trimble:*** I think we suspect that happens too. I wonder if I could move to something slightly different. We had an interesting discussion earlier about the impact of the funds on Spain and we are also very much interested in the experience in Poland and I wonder if you could take us through that.

Mr Boijmans: In general Poland is in the situation where Spain was 20 or 30 years ago and mirrors the developments that Spain went through. If I could start with factual information. For the new programme period Poland is the largest recipient of Structural Funds and Regional Funds, almost 20 per cent of the budget which is slightly more than €67 billion. It is a lot more than even Spain is receiving during this new programme period. To take you through the negotiations and what we have been negotiating for this new programme period, one of the first things is that Poland is a Member State still with a very high unemployment rate which is decreasing rapidly, partly due to immigration to some of the other Member States. It still has a very large agricultural sector which is under restructuring. The GDP per capita, the income per capita, is still one of the lowest in the European Union. Taking that as a starting point, it means that quite a lot of investments have to take place in basic infrastructure in Poland. Nevertheless, Poland committed itself to the objectives of the Lisbon Strategy to create growth and jobs and to have a more forward looking strategy than purely building only roads and sewerage plants. It has allocated almost 64 per cent of its budget to Lisbon-relevant areas of expenditure, which is quite high taking into account the size of Poland, the size of the budget and the situation Poland is in. As you know, Poland was not obliged as a new Member State to do this but they did this on a voluntary basis. If we look at the three main areas of investment for the new programme period, transport is one. Almost one-third of the budget goes to transport infrastructure but in a wider sense, not only roads but also railways, airports and public transport. We believe that is justified because there is a big backlog in Poland in transport investment even if you take

Poland within the context of the new Member States. For example, Warsaw is one of the very few capitals which cannot be reached by motorway. If you travel by Berlin to Warsaw it is not possible to do that by motorway, only parts are motorway. A large part of the investment goes into trans-European networks and, as I said before, not only motorways but also railways. The second largest area of investment is research and development and innovation and entrepreneurship and that is contributing to the Lisbon Strategy. Poland has the objective that 1.5 per cent of its GDP by the end of the next programme period should go to research and development. At the moment they are still at 0.5 per cent, so there is still a lot of work to be done. There are certainly some areas of excellence within Poland, not only in Warsaw but in other regional capitals, for example Poznan and Wroclaw, which is one of the candidates for the European Institute for Technology. They are trying to promote this image of research and development. This is wider than only research and development, this budget also goes into business support where the strong focus is on small and medium-sized enterprises. Of direct support, 70 per cent should go to SMEs. The budget is also available for foreign direct investment but we have put a clause into the programme that where it is relevant the money will not be used for delocalisation, it will only be used for foreign direct investment for new investments in new plants. The third largest area of investment is the environment where the major part of the budget goes to those investments which help Poland to meet its obligations in the acquis communitaire for the environment. A large part goes to water treatment, not only sewage treatment plants but water supply. More and more areas are being supported by other areas in the environment in the area of solid waste treatment and nature preservation. Those are the three most important areas of investment under this new framework for this new programme period. Looking at the strategy within Poland, the territorial cohesion, you can make a very big divide between east and west Poland. It is a bit crude to divide but that explains the situation best. Next to Warsaw, which is the largest city and where a lot of investments are concentrated, you can see regions in the western part of Poland around Wroclaw, around Poznan, and I understand you will meet a delegation from Wielkopolska this afternoon, which is one of those regions which is catching up very quickly and attracting a lot of foreign direct investment where unemployment is decreasing very rapidly. The other part of Poland, the eastern part, bordering Belorussia and the Ukraine is in a totally different situation where there is still a very strong share of employment in the agricultural sector where people are losing their jobs and it is very difficult to create alternative employment because there is some growth but not as strong as in the western part of the country. That is the reason why there is one special programme for eastern Poland. We have four national programmes in Poland, 16 regional programmes, one for each region, and for the five poorest regions in eastern Poland we have a separate programme on top of that. The idea of this programme is to develop flagship projects, projects which really distinguish themselves whilst supported under the national and regional programmes. To give you one example: there is a project of €300 million which is being prepared to introduce a broadband network in those five eastern regions which would reduce their natural handicap of being on the outside of the European Union. One of those five regions is Lubelskie, the other delegation you will meet this afternoon, so you will have a comparison of two different regions. Next to all these financial investments and concrete investments in infrastructure, one effect of the Structural Funds which should not be forgotten is the indirect effect which it has on the administration. A large part of the money now goes to strengthening the administrative capacity, so Structural Funds can be used for this, but also, for example, because of the Structural Funds Poland has decided to create a new Ministry for Regional Development which will be the central co-ordinator for all investments related to Structural Funds, ERDF, European Social Fund and also the Cohesion Fund. It has helped to strengthen the co-ordination within Poland between these different sector policies where, for example, the people in the transport sector do not communicate with the people in the environment sector. This is not a directly measurable effect but it is certainly an important effect which is a result of the large amounts of money available for Poland. We are trying to do a lot with the Cohesion Fund project but also the major projects in the new programme period to give more support to project planning, that is the final beneficiaries, municipalities or other public bodies, and train them to better plan their projects and develop them quicker so that they can be implemented faster and absorb the money faster, because that is the ultimate target, to absorb the money which is allocated to Poland. I would like to mention these two side-effects of the Structural Funds which have an important impact on the administration of Poland.

Q287 ***Chairman:*** Thank you very much, Mr Boijmans. I am always relieved to see that so many of the capable Poles working in England at the moment have started to go home because the prospects have got better. Mr De Michelis, I appreciate we have not heard much from you. Would you like to add anything on any of this?

Mr De Michelis: Maybe just a word on what Pascal said on the impact of the policy. Since Poland has just received funds for a couple of years it is very difficult to assess what the impact has been. We are running a number of impact assessment models that estimate what the likely impact of this policy will be over the next 15 years. We use different models to avoid being too constrained by one single format. All of these models suggest that particularly for Poland the impact will be between three and five per cent of additional GDP over the period and the creation of about half a million jobs in Poland because of Structural Funds. That is compared to a scenario without Cohesion Policy. Obviously all these estimates have to be taken with caution, like all models, but they at least give an order of magnitude.

Q288 ***Chairman:*** I should have asked before, and I meant to, do you use inward investment as a measure? When I was in regional policy we used to add it up by thinking how much private sector investment we had generated.
Mr De Michelis: Yes. If you are interested, over the next few weeks we will be producing very detailed sheets explaining all the different effects on the basis of these models. This suggests that the private investment mobilised because of Cohesion funding inflows is on average about five per cent, so there is five per cent additional private investment over the 15 year horizon.

Q289 ***Chairman:*** I think we may have exhausted you all, but we are most grateful for your time and the information.
Mr Ahner: It was a pleasure, thank you very much.

Q290 ***Chairman:*** We shall see the Commissioner at the end of the day.
Mr Ahner: She will be delighted.

Q291 ***Chairman:*** So we can ask her a few things. I have met her before and she is a very capable person. Thank you very much, this has been most interesting and we feel much better briefed for our meeting with the Polish and Spanish representatives.
Mr Ahner: Enjoy them. Have a very successful day in Brussels.
Chairman: Thank you so much, Mr Ahner. Thank you all.

THURSDAY 6 MARCH 2008

Present	Cohen of Pimlico, B Kerr of Kinlochard, L	Trimble, L Woolmer of Leeds, L

Examination of Witnesses

Witnesses: Ms Monika Kapturska, Head of Delegation, Ms Anna Wasowicz, Information Officer, Ms Izabela Gorczyca Information Officer, Wielkopolska Regional Representation (Poland), and Ms Marta Lorens, Head of Delegation, Lubelskie Regional Representation, (Poland), examined.

Q292 Chairman: Welcome to UKRep. It is very good of you to come and give evidence to us. We are putting this on the record so that we can use it. Sue is our shorthand writer and you will get to see what you said before it is published. Can I say that the general initial questions, which you have all seen, but I want to read them on for the sake of record, that your presentations will address are: what the role of a Regional Representation in Brussels is; how does your Office represent your region's interest; what is the size of each region's allocation from the EU and how is your allocation utilised, what kinds of projects, what kinds of activities are you doing with it. Since the Wielkopolska region has not yet had its presentation photocopied, could we ask Lubelskie to start.

Ms Lorens: Of course. First of all, I would like to thank you very much for the invitation. It is an honour for me to be in such a distinguished assembly today. Before commencing with the presentation I want to make one point, a caveat. I cannot be called an expert on EU funds in our region, I simply represent my region here in Brussels in my Regional Representation and I co-operate with my friends and colleagues from the Marshal's Office of Lubelskie voivodship which is the managing body of the EU funds. We have prepared a presentation which has been supplied to you. It is a very detailed one full of facts and figures which can be left for evidence afterwards. I would like to make it presentation-friendly and it may have been better to have the projector and equipment to show it, but since we do not have that I will try to make it accessible in a different way. Referring back to the first question about the Regional Office, if I may start with that, our Office of the Lubelskie region is a small one. I am the only person who represents the region in Brussels for now. The activity so far has been focusing on two areas: promotional and representational. The Office is in the process of restructuring and at the end of this year we expect to have the Representation proper with staff and divisions and sections, but due to certain changes on the local authority level it has not been possible to arrange it so far. The promotional area means the participation of our region in different activities here, such as open days. This is an initiative in Brussels organised by the Committee of the Regions and DG Regio. It is a great event and regions from all over Europe present their good practices here, their co-operation, their programmes and projects. We do participate in that. The other part of my activities here in Brussels is simply representing the interests of the voivodship by liaising between the institutions and facilitating communication for the authorities supporting the actions undertaken by the authorities. That is the main thing. Maybe I should have started with a presentation of the region as such because that could be of some use. At the back of this document is a map of Europe and the Lubelskie region is the dark orange. We are at the very border of Europe bordering with Ukraine and Belorussia. Poland is divided into 16 regions and Lubelskie is quite a large one, the third biggest as far as Poland is concerned. It covers 25,000 square kilometres. This is eight per cent of the surface of Poland. The population last year was 2,180,000 inhabitants which ranks it twelfth in Poland as far as density is concerned. It is a sparsely populated region. It is 76 per cent of the European average as far as population density is concerned. It is also one of the regions with the lowest urbanisation indicators in the country, less than 47 per cent. The main city, Lublin, is an academic and economic centre, the biggest town, which is on the right-hand side of this map. Looking at the economy and the challenges for the regions, we are aware of the weaknesses and challenges. There are certain weaknesses typical of such poorly developed regions, such as a low level of economic development which translates to low income among the population, a poorly developed innovation market, a poorly developed SME sector, system of supporting companies and so on. However, these weaknesses are balanced by certain advantages and strengths, namely the potential for the production, for instance, of green food because agriculture is a stronger sector than industry. It is the potential of the region for the production of bioenergy, biomass, biofuels, but also tourism. Such characteristics will be important for the part of the presentation when I tell you about the Regional Operational Programme which has certain priorities that apply to the current situation and the challenges. I will not go through the previous Financial Perspective of the Integrated Regional Operational Programme, 2004-06, the current Financial Perspective is more important for us now.

6 March 2008 Ms Monika Kapturska,Ms Anna Wasowicz, Ms Izabela Gorczyca and Ms Marta Lorens

Q293 Chairman: Yes, please.
Ms Lorens: If we look at the size of the allocation that Lubelskie receives, slide number eight shows quite a good visual representation of the allocation for 2007-13. I will try to describe it briefly. Within the National Cohesion Strategy for 2007-13, over €2 billion of EU funds were allocated for the region for investments. This amount includes allocation for the Regional Operational Programme, which is very important because this is the first ever large-scale programme, this multi-annual programme, financially stable programme, of development measures for the region. The ROP is crucial here. Also, a component of the Operational Programme is the Human Capital and Operational Programme—Development of Eastern Poland. On the graphic we show the share of Community assistance and national contribution which makes it clear that the EU funds constitute the basis of that. If I can focus on the Regional Operational Programme, that will show the principles that guide how we distribute the funds to different projects. We should have in mind one specific goal, that is improving the competitiveness of the Lubelskie region, which triggers faster economic growth and growth of employment complying with the natural and cultural qualities of the region. This is the main goal of the programme and it is divided into three sub-goals concentrating on the competitiveness of the region, on improvement in investment conditions, and also improving the quality of life of the region. Behind the Regional Operational Programme there is the strategy of the voivodship's development and there are certain criteria that allow projects to be co-financed. If we could look at the criteria, they would be the impact on the increase of economic activity, competitiveness, quality of inter-regional relations but also improving the environmental quality and promoting the image of the region, that is also important. What constitutes the core of the programme are the axes. The axes overlap certain levels of co-financing and there are nine such axes. The programme is divided into sections. The first one is entrepreneurship and innovations, then economy infrastructure, third attractiveness of urban areas and investment premises, fourth information society, fifth transport, sixth environment and pure energy, seventh culture and tourism and co-operation between regions, eighth social infrastructure and, finally, technical assistance. From that division we see the highest level of co-financing from the ERDF is attributed to the transport axis, and that is 22 per cent, and entrepreneurship and innovations. They have the highest level of co-financing.

Q294 Chairman: Thank you Ms Lorens, we will read what you are doing afterwards. I would very much like to look at some of your specific projects. We are particularly keen to ask you, when you have told us that, how you find your dealings with the EU and how well it works, how useful it has been. If you could move us to that, because I do want to have time to discuss.
Ms Lorens: Of course. The evidence that I was presented with was the evidence from the previous Financial Perspective 2004-06 and the evaluation of the main beneficiaries and the main activities focusing, for example, on improving the infrastructure, the educational and sport infrastructure as well as roads infrastructure and social ones. For the new Perspective, 2007-13, today I got the information that on 17 March we will start the call for the new applications, so the assessments of these new proceedings will be known in two months. That is the reply that I got, that in two months' time we will be able to give the reply on what are the main problems with utilising the funds and management. I can forward that question and supply you with it in written form as soon as possible, by Monday.

Q295 Chairman: That would be very helpful. We are running an inquiry which says there are these Structural Funds and we know roughly how they are allocated, but we are very keen to find out the views of a recipient of these Structural Funds. Do the conditions strike you as onerous? Is there an awful lot of administrative cost? Has it been helpful? Anything you can tell us.
Ms Lorens: The answer is they have been really helpful indeed. From the data I have with me today I cannot give you precise examples. As I have mentioned, the allocation from the previous Perspective was 80 per cent, so quite a high utilisation of the funding. I have no data on the present Perspective but just for indicative projects, which is at the end of the presentation.

Q296 Chairman: That would be interesting to see.
Ms Lorens: That is an indicative schedule for individual key projects. The key project for the city and region is the regional airport. As I said, the region is quite a big one but it does not have an airport, so that is the first thing. Another thing is the construction of a regional geographical system and culture meetings point and, finally, sports facilities such as a stadium. I understand what you need for your evidence and if I could put down the question and provide you with that, would it be okay if I provide you with that?

Q297 Chairman: That would be most helpful. My Lords, is there anything else that we can ask Ms Lorens? We can always come back to her at the end.

Q298 Lord Trimble: The amount of money the region is receiving is €2 billion per annum, is that right?

Ms Lorens: That is the complete allocation.

Q299 Lord Trimble: For the period from 2007-13 you have a total of €2 billion.
Ms Lorens: €4 billion.
Lord Trimble: That is quite a difference. This may be a silly question to ask you but could you handle more?

Q300 Chairman: Could you use more money?
Ms Lorens: If we look at the previous experience, utilisation of 80 per cent, it was like a period of training for us from 2004-06 and it turned out that we managed.

Q301 Chairman: You managed to spend 80 per cent of what you were given?
Ms Lorens: Yes.

Q302 Lord Trimble: Would you expect to spend more than 80 per cent in this current plan?
Ms Lorens: I would be optimistic.

Q303 Lord Trimble: If you had even more could you spend it?
Ms Lorens: The needs are great. With good management, yes of course.

Q304 Lord Trimble: What I am getting at here is we know from speaking to the Commission that they are operating on the basis that countries, regions, cannot absorb more than the equivalent of four per cent of GDP per annum. Do you share that view? Do you think that is the right sort of figure? Do you think it would be possible to absorb more? I am just looking for a response to that.
Ms Lorens: Thank you for the question and I will give you the answer in written form.

Q305 Chairman: Can we move on to Wielkopolska. We may come back at the end, but it is nice to give somebody else a chance to present because your two regions are very different.
Ms Wasowicz: Have you received our presentations?

Q306 Chairman: No.
Ms Wasowicz: We are still waiting for the photocopies to come.
Ms Kapturska: I just wanted to tell you that we have prepared our Regional Operational Programme and it is in English. This is almost the last version because it is 30 August 2007 and we signed it with the Commission on 6 September. Here you have the presentation from my colleague on Structural Funds.

Q307 Chairman: Perhaps while we are waiting we could ask you how many people you have in the Office here.
Ms Kapturska: Three of us.

Q308 Lord Trimble: So the Office is empty now!
Ms Kapturska: We have a stagiere from the Marshal's Office of the Wielkopolska Region and she is watching the Office.

Q309 Chairman: Answering the telephones.
Ms Kapturska: Yes.

Q310 Chairman: You have heard the sort of things we want to know, and I think we can probably ask you those independent of your presentation. You are a richer region than Lubelskie. How much funds are you in receipt of?
Ms Wasowicz: In the current Financial Perspective we received €1.2 billion in the framework of our Regional Operational Programme for Wielkopolska Voivodship. However, that is not the final sum that we are going to absorb because beneficiaries originating from our voivodship can apply to the funds on a national level also. This is not the final amount of money that will be absorbed in our region, we expect more than that.

Q311 Lord Woolmer of Leeds: More European funds?
Ms Wasowicz: Yes, European funds. That is only the co-financing in the framework of the EU Funds.

Q312 Chairman: Do you find you are able to absorb as many funds as are available to you?
Ms Wasowicz: This is a very difficult question at this stage of the procedure because we could only participate in the first Financial Perspective from 2004-06, so we do not have any evaluation reports carried out yet. We will have to wait for these results. We do not have any official data or indicators at this stage. Let me remind you that this programme is still going on, it is not closed, the projects are running this year. I suggest we should wait for the first outcomes. We are very sorry that you do not have our presentation in front of you but it will give you a progress overview of the Perspective that is being implemented right now.

Q313 Chairman: We would find that useful. I have got a general question that is slightly difficult to answer. You are the first representatives of a country we have talked to that are really new to the whole business of Structural Funds. There is a considerable movement in the old European states to say that more money should be given to the new countries and the Commission, I am sure, would tend to agree that

6 March 2008 Ms Monika Kapturska,Ms Anna Wasowicz, Ms Izabela Gorczyca and Ms Marta Lorens

they are worried about absorption but the Commission seem to feel it is all going very nicely. I would like to know what problems, if any, you have found in your dealings with the Commission. Are there problems of not understanding or not being able to get them to finance projects that you would like financed?

Ms Kapturska: If I could answer because for ten years I worked for local authorities and now in Brussels, so I have got some experience. The local authorities say they can absorb as much money as possible. Usually, for example, the communities built one road every two years but they could build more. Now the Marshals, which are dividing the money and which are the managing authorities of the Structural Funds, are the presidents of the regions. We have got everything in our presentation.

Q314 Chairman: We will catch up.

Ms Kapturska: They tried to divide all the money very carefully but everybody is complaining we do not have enough money. It is the lack of information first and the bureaucracy which is too much and is a barrier as well.

Q315 Chairman: Your bureaucracy or the EU bureaucracy?

Ms Kapturska: Both of them. There are many rules created by our government which do not exist under the rules of the Commission.

Chairman: The Commission said something like that to us. They said that often they felt the rules which stood in the way were those imposed by the states.

Lord Woolmer of Leeds: If the Commission asked your region to produce some concrete evidence of the bureaucracy and the costs and your suggestion how this could be improved, would that be possible to do? The Commission said that everybody complains but nobody produces the evidence. That is not in your region.

Q316 Chairman: Generally.

Ms Kapturska: We have no time to do it because we have a lack of staff dealing with Structural Funds. We have almost as many inhabitants as Ireland, it is over three million people, and in the last period we had just 80 people to deal with Structural Funds in our region at a regional level. We are trying to get more and now we have a maximum of 120. You can imagine this is a problem and that is why it is very difficult for them to prepare reports like that.

Q317 Lord Woolmer of Leeds: They just have not got the time to do it, they are too busy getting on with the job.

Ms Kapturska: Yes.

Q318 Chairman: Are you short of people because you are short of trained people or you just have not had time to hire them? Half of Poland appears to be in London at the moment and I sometimes wonder if we have taken a few of your trained people. Is it a shortage of people who know how to do the work?

Ms Kapturska: Yes. Many of them came in at the beginning of the summer so they had time to read all the documents and so on to do the work but the problem, which is a really important one, is the Marshals' Offices at the regional level which deal with the Structural Funds do not pay enough money. Salaries are very, very low.

Ms Lorens: That is true for my region as well. The private sector offers better working conditions and remuneration for such experts. They do not stay with the local authorities at this level, they go to the private sector. The Marshals' Offices suffer from lack of qualified people.

Ms Kapturska: People who were experienced in the period of 2004-06 went to private companies or became directors. The others are quite new and this is a problem. It does not go against implementing the Structural Funds in Poland because all the communities, provinces and so on are waiting for the money and are ready to absorb the funds, I am perfectly sure about that.

Q319 Chairman: Colleagues, do you want to ask any more questions now or shall we ask Ms Kapturska to do her presentation, now that we all have it? If we could ask you to get through it in about ten minutes and that will leave us time to ask questions.

Ms Kapturska: First of all, I wanted to tell you what a great honour it is for us to present our Regional Office to the House of Lords. I would like to present Anna Wasowicz, who will speak about Structural Funds, and Ms Izabela Gorczyca, our third collaborator. I would like to speak about the Office for four minutes, a maximum of five, and Anna will speak about Structural Funds. I will start with the Office. As you can see, as with all self-respecting regions, we are in the heart of Europe.

Q320 Chairman: Yes, you are, are you not?

Ms Kapturska: In Poland we have just 16 regions but they are quite big. We are the second biggest one and, as I said, we compare with Ireland and we say we are as big as Belgium in the sense of area. Here you have our administration, which I would like to show you. The Marshal, which is the president of the region, implements the Structural Funds with the Regional Board. Wielkopolska has 54 per cent of the EU average GDP.

Q321 Lord Kerr of Kinlochard: What is Poland as a whole?

Ms Kapturska: Fifty. We are third after the Mazowia and Silesia regions. Mazowia has 57 as far as I know. I will tell you about some tasks and activities of the Wielkopolska Office. You know what our regional officers do in Brussels.

Q322 Chairman: You have three of you.
Ms Kapturska: I just wanted to tell you we have got three employees and we stay in the same building with the German Hessen, Italian Emilia-Romagna and French Aquitaine. We have three main areas of activity. They are promotion, funds and co-operation with the other institutions and regions. We participate in conferences, seminars and so on. We inform our region about possible funds and the opportunities. We organise the study visits of the Commission in our region and the visits of our representatives here in Brussels. We co-operate with our Permanent Representative and in the sense of cultural and economic promotion with the embassy in Brussels. We monitor all the funds and inform our local authorities of any possible funds and projects. We promote our economy. We have got a member in the Committee of the Regions, which is the Marshal of the region.

Q323 Chairman: If I may ask a general question as you go through. We notice, as it were, that you are here, not in Poland.
Ms Kapturska: Yes, for five years.

Q324 Chairman: Do you find it very important to be in Brussels and, if so, why?
Ms Kapturska: Yes. As you know, there are 268 regions and 264 of them have their offices in Brussels, which means something.

Q325 Chairman: It must.
Ms Kapturska: All Polish regions, except Swietokrzyskie, have their offices in Brussels. When we compare with the German or Spanish offices, they have something like 15 people in their offices so they can share the competences. It is quite difficult for us, but the important thing is we are here, we can promote our region here and we try to build consortia for projects and try to attract our communities and local authorities to co-operate with the other authorities in Europe to exchange knowledge and best practices, which is very helpful for us.

Q326 Chairman: Thank you.
Ms Kapturska: As my colleague said, we have internships in our Office which is very helpful for the local authorities because people in the region have to know what we are doing and how they can use this knowledge. It is still not enough for us so we try to attract people to Brussels. On one of the last slides you will see our last very interesting project, the Brussels Club of Wielkopolska. We created this a few months ago and our colleagues from other regions have been very surprised that we have had this idea. Because there are just the three of us we wanted to co-operate with all the people from our region who work in the European institutions in Brussels. We have found out there are more than 70 people working in the European institutions from Wielkopolska. We meet and they can help us in our work here. I want to go to my colleague, Anna Wasowicz, who will give you a short speech about the Structural Funds.
Ms Wasowicz: My Lords, given the limited timeframe I will present you with an outline on Structural Funds in the Wielkopolska region. This will be an overview of structural assistance that we have received in past years. I am glad that my colleague presented you with the details on the new Financial Perspective in Poland in her region of Lubelskie Voivodship. Our presentation is a bit different and it should give you the historical approach to structural assistance accessible to Poland. Let me start with Pre-Accession Funds that our region received in the framework of three main programmes starting from 1996. Wielkopolska could participate in the Phare programme, which is Poland and Hungary Assistance for Reconstructing of their Economies. This was a major programme for Central and Eastern Europe, initially established only for Poland and Hungary but later extended to ten candidate countries, as I am sure you know. In 1996 Wielkopolska became eligible to use the cross-border co-operation component within the Phare programme. Since our region is perceived as doing well Wielkopolska cannot participate fully in all editions of these programmes, they were directed mainly to poorer regions and that refers to the economic and social cohesion component. We were also able to participate in the instrument for structural policies for pre-accession that was a Cohesion Fund for implementing the project. We managed to implement four very successful projects. We also participated in a special accession programme for agriculture and rural development. I would now like to give you some main effects of the implementation of the pre-accession funds in Wielkopolska. We need to consider that not all of them have been measured since the last projects terminated as of 2006. We can observe the effect of Phare assistance to the region but within these limited resources we managed to implement the very spectacular project of building a bypass of Poznan, the capital city of Wielkopolska, gaining co-financing of over €160 million within three years. That was a multi-annual project. More effective was ISPA financing, financially important environmental projects and improving access to drinking water to approximately 20 per cent of Wielkopolska's population. Support under the

SAPARD programme was also effective in our voivodship with significant and effective support mainly for food processing and marketing of agri-products. Thanks to the successful utilisation of pre-accession funds Wielkopolska is listed in sixth position in the ranking of pre-accession aid utilisation. Let me present very briefly the architecture of Structural Funds distributed in Poland in 2004-06. The Community Support Framework for Poland amounted to nearly €12 billion in the period 2004-06 and is being implemented through five mono-funded sectoral operational programmes and one multi-funded Integrated Regional Operational Programme where nearly 40 per cent of resources are allocated. We are implementing Cohesion Fund projections and Community initiatives, INTERREG and EQUAL. The Integrated Regional Operational Programme is of main significance for Polish regions. It was prepared by the Ministry of Economy, Labour and Social Policy but in close co-operation with regional self-governments. Goals, priorities and measures cover the whole of the country but most regions differ in their implementation, it depends on the socio-economic structure and situation in the voivodships. This Perspective has been managed nationally by the Ministry of Regional Development since 2005 but most tasks are performed in the regions by regional self-government, Marshal Offices, which are responsible for project identification, and regional state administration, which are Voivodship Offices, which are responsible for audit, monitoring, payment verification and certification.

Q327 Chairman: I am sorry, I need to move you on a little. Could you take us quickly through what you are looking to do in 2007-13?
Ms Wasowicz: As you can see,—

Q328 Chairman: I see, for instance, that you are hoping to spend a lot of money on communications and infrastructure.
Ms Wasowicz: Yes, that is correct. These are priorities set out by the regional government which is now responsible for programming and implementing the Structural Funds.

Q329 Lord Kerr of Kinlochard: Can I ask what "implementing" means there? If I am an entrepreneur and I want to establish a factory, may I apply to the Structural Funds or do I have to be a public sector body wanting to build a road or an airport?
Ms Wasowicz: Private sector entities are also definitely eligible to obtain co-financing with the priority competitiveness of enterprises, yes.

Q330 Lord Kerr of Kinlochard: What proportion of these numbers do you think would be private sector? What would be the public sector/private sector breakdown?
Ms Wasowicz: In the Regional Operational Programme it is also an obligation imposed by the European Commission to design the financial architecture, so I would encourage you to have an in-depth look at the programme which is on the CD. I do not recall at the moment.

Q331 Chairman: Do not worry.
Ms Wasowicz: I am sure the significant amount will be contributed by the private sector here.
Ms Kapturska: There is a joint instrument for the private sector and enterprises, the JEREMIE instrument.
Ms Wasowicz: €60 million will be implemented under the JEREMIE instrument in our voivodship.
Ms Kapturska: Which is exactly for private enterprise, SMEs.

Q332 Lord Kerr of Kinlochard: But, of course, they can also go to a bank or to the European Bank for Reconstruction and Development or to the European Investment Bank or a private sector bank. I used to think when I knew a bit about it that people who had a very good project, private sector people, would not bother about this sort of money because this takes a lot of paperwork, a lot of approvals, they would go to a bank and get a loan if they were confident they were going to make money and pay off the loan quickly. Is that the case, that the private sector complains that the paperwork and delays and complications are a disincentive to going for Structural Funding?
Ms Wasowicz: There are very convenient preconditions to obtain these loans in the framework of the JEREMIE instrument and probably most of these companies would never obtain an equal amount from a regular bank.
Ms Kapturska: As far as we know, they co-operate very well with the Agency of Regional Development which deals with this fund for enterprises.

Q333 Chairman: Thank you. I am afraid we are running out of time.
Ms Wasowicz: I am truly sorry, since we have also prepared a list of key projects.

Q334 Chairman: I was going to say that while we are running out of time I would be very glad to put these into evidence. One can see from the paper what sort of thing it is, what you are doing and how you are using the money. We will also extract material from the CD. Clearly we will come back and talk to you in a year or so and find out how it is all going. We are

very grateful to you for your help. You have provided us with a great deal of evidence which is here and which we can take home and include in the report.
Ms Kapturska: I am sorry for our lack of knowledge. Normally we do not deal with the Structural Funds.

Q335 Chairman: You have given us a great deal of information.
Ms Kapturska: We have great experts in our regions.

Q336 Chairman: You have given us a great deal of information, which no doubt you had to drag out of your regions, and we are most grateful.
Ms Kapturska: We will send some more information if you need it and we can co-operate with our colleagues in the regions.
Lord Trimble: If you send us anything further, what we would particularly appreciate is your view of how easy DG Regio is to work with, whether you think they are too controlling in terms of what you want to do or whether you find you can do the things you want to do within the programme that they have laid out. A consumer's perspective of how the Commission operates.
Chairman: We know how the Commission thinks it operates, we would like to know what the consumers think, and so would they. They would like to know if they are making difficulties for you.

Q337 Lord Trimble: And we will not tell them who complained!
Ms Wasowicz: Being the biggest beneficiary of Structural Funds we cannot really complain.

Q338 Lord Kerr of Kinlochard: Oh yes you can.
Ms Kapturska: We have got our Commissioner.

Q339 Chairman: Yes, of course you have.
Ms Kapturska: Mrs Hübner.

Q340 Chairman: Who we are seeing later.
Ms Kapturska: The fact she is the Commissioner for Regional Policy is wonderful for us. I can say in the name of Wielkopolska that we have wonderful contact with Mr Beschel from DG Regio. He is the head of the unit for Poland. He is in our region very often and supporting us in implementing JEREMIE and JESSICA. Maybe your Committee would be interested to come to Wielkopolska and have such a visit.

Q341 Chairman: What a nice idea.
Ms Kapturska: It could be a great opportunity for us and the people who are dealing with the Structural Funds to present you with much more information and knowledge.
Ms Lorens: The evidence.
Chairman: For the purpose of this report we feel well-served. Thank you all.

Memorandum by Marta Lorens, Lubelskie Regional Representation (Poland)

Poland has become the biggest beneficiary of the cohesion policy in the EU financial perspective for 2007–13. The total amount for execution of structural operations is approximately €85.6 billion from which €67.3 is EU budget share. The expenditures within the cohesion policy will be co-ordinated with other expenditures, among others the Common Agricultural Policy. The total amount of financial means for 2007–13 for development activities will be above €107.9 billion from which €85.4 billion comes from EU funds.

The Lublin region has become a significant beneficiary of allocation within structural funds, the Cohesion Fund and the European Agriculture Fund. At division of the EU funds the attention was paid to invest in the area of so-called "Eastern Poland" to the higher degree than previously. Within the territory of our voivodship, apart from the Regional Operational Programme we will also become a beneficiary of all national programmes prepared by the Polish government, ie Operational Programme—Development of Eastern Poland, Operational Programme—Innovative Economy, Operational Programme—Infrastructure and Environment and additionally of the programme financed from the European Agriculture Fund: the Rural Development Programme. The total amount of the funds available in our region for 2007–13 for development activities is approximately €5 billion of which over €4 billion comes from EU funds.
The basic index describing economic potential of the region is value of Gross Domestic Product (GDP) per capita. In 2004 the value of GDP per capita in Lubelskie voivodship was PLN 16 800 (€7568 using purchasing power parity), which was 69% of the average level for Poland and 33.8% of the European average. The voivodship's share of GDP is nearly 4.0% and has been successively decreasing.

The basis of regional economic development is the value of fixed assets and capacity for their reconstruction and increase. The gross value of fixed assets in the economy of Lubelskie voivodship was estimated in 2004 at the level of PLN 82.4 billion, 4.5% of the national share (and the 8th largest in the country). The unfavourable phenomenon is a slow modernization and exchange pace of gross fixed assets in the region. The renewal index measured by the value of investment outlays in 2000–04 in relation to gross value of fixed assets in 2004 is

23.8% for Lubelskie voivodship compared with 34% averaged across Poland. The value of investment outlays in Lubelskie voivodship in 2005 was slightly above PLN 4.4 billion, representing 3.4% of the investments in the country (the 11th highest). However the voivodship is located in last position in the country when the level of investment outlays is measured per capita: it equates to PLN 1992 (€583)—the average value in Poland is PLN 3434 (€1005). Many factors influence the quality of the voivodship area and the degree of its relations and connections with remaining part of the country and Europe. The most important factors are those resulting out of environmental and cultural conditions, the colonization system including the network of mutual relations between cities and rural areas highly influencing the level of interregional differentiations. Another important factor determining the area quality and region attractiveness is the level of voivodship basic technical infrastructure connected mainly with communication and transport, environmental protection, production and energy distribution.

Badly developed infrastructure impacts significantly upon the low investment levels and tourist attractiveness of the voivodship. Lubelskie voivodship has been assessed for few last years as the least attractive region in Poland in rankings of investment attractiveness (ie the 15th position in the country (data from 2006)). Insufficient regional communication capacity, the poor condition of technical infrastructure, no areas prepared and ready for investment and a badly developed services network lead to Lubelskie voivodship being classified within the lowest E1 class in the assessment of investment attractiveness.

The aforementioned data prove that the amount of €4 billion from EU funds allocated for the period 2007–13 will be insufficient from the point of the region investment needs.

The attempt to even the level of Lublin region development in relation to faster and better developed regions in Poland and simultaneously dynamic economic development in the European space will require additional funds, both national and European, calculated for longer period of time.

21 May 2008

Examination of Witnesses

Witnesses: Mr José Alberto López, in charge of Institutional Relations, Mr Marco Ortiz, responsible for Environment and Health, and Mr Julian Talens, Head of the Legal Department, Valencia Regional Representation (Spain), examined.

Q342 Chairman: Can I welcome you formally and thank you very much for coming. If I may just introduce my colleagues: Lord Kerr, to my left, Lord Trimble, also to my left, and Lord Woolmer to my right. Mr López, would you like to introduce your colleagues.

Mr López: First of all I would like to express what an honour and pleasure it is to be here with you to share our experiences. I am Alberto López. I work in the area of institutional relations in the Delegation of Valencia. We have a representation here in Brussels. I would like to introduce Marco Ortiz, who is head of the environmental issues department, and Mr Talens, head of the legal department in the Valencia Office. I would like to thank you because in our regional priorities we work on these issues, we have meetings and share with other regions our experiences and policies in regional funds and also promoting inter-regional co-operation. We have prepared some documentation for you.

Q343 Chairman: Wonderful.

Mr López: About what we are doing here, our main topics are the promotion and developmental interesting and innovative experiences of our region as well as initiatives to participate in European affairs. To speak briefly about our economic profile, the Valencian region has a lot of product services, both industrial and agricultural. In the industrial sector we are highly specialised in the traditional sectors: leather, furniture, food processing. We are developing more and more the innovative sectors, like ceramics and optics. Thanks to the Structural Funds we have developed some innovative services in support of the economic sectors which are localised near to the production areas. I am speaking of all the efforts made by the regional authorities and all the efforts made by the universities and so on. The region of Valencia is placed in the Mediterranean area, an area of economic growth and development within the European Union. After 20 years of management of the Structural Funds as Objective 1, I have to stress that since 2007 we are in the new "competitiveness and employment objective." After leaving Objective 1 we have the challenge of facing a new situation after two periods of receiving grants, subventions. We have the challenge to look for alternative financial resources. The regional government promoted a foundation called "Comunidad Valencia—Región Europea" which aims to promote participation of the economic and institutional bodies of the region in European initiatives. With this aim, the Foundation, which is composed of economic institutions, private companies and municipalities, all of these members and with the support of the regional government, have been working very actively since 2003 in the participation of European projects. During this period we have experience of participating in some projects, like LIFE INTERREG or Leonardo. Sustainable energy development, renewable energy sources, innovation research, technology transfer, all of these topics have become more and more familiar to us and they will be more and more familiar in our municipalities and economic and social bodies. We are going to distribute some data to you about our participation in these projects. In Brussels in 1997 we had seven people working in the Valencian Regional office; after 2003 when the Foundation was created, the staff grew to 45 people. I have to say that the economic and social bodies are highly interested in these topics and they can send people for six months or one year periods to gain skills, and experience before going back to Valencia. Young professionals are learning here in Brussels, they are sharing with other regions how to participate in projects in order to participate in European projects. That is one of the special interests in attracting and developing skills in our region. I would like to give the floor to Mr Ortiz to develop these topics more.

Q344 Chairman: That is a most useful general introduction.

Mr Ortiz: I will be very brief because Alberto made a good introduction of the region. I would just say that Valencia is the "ten per cent region." We are more or less ten per cent of the Spanish population and we are globally ten per cent of the GDP. Spain's GDP is $1,200 billion and it would be $90 billion in Valencia, so it is a bit less than ten per cent. The region has evolved a lot in the last 20 years in the sense that the traditional industries, some of which Alberto mentioned, have been transformed thanks to the great amount of funds that Brussels has put into Spain. The region was very wise in the way it managed to distribute and use the funds. The fact is that we are out of Objective 1 now. Our GDP has improved in such a way that we are out and it is good news. Those big amounts of funds were used mainly in the construction of infrastructures and also to transform some industries which depended heavily on manpower. One of these industries was the textile industry. They suffered because of seasonality in the sense that for certain months of the year they were not working, people were out of work and there was a high amount of unemployment. The problems were similar in the agricultural sector. The transformation has been to a more effective and intense industry in the sense that people are working in industries that work for the full year. There is a very big automotive cluster around Valencia with Ford motor industry, a big factory, with a great number of industry around, suppliers and other metallic companies or sectors connected to this industry. There is another big cluster in the north of the region connected to the ceramics industry that Alberto was talking about. The ceramics industry in the last 20 years has been one of the leading industries in the world with Italy, (the region of Emilia Romagna, Bologna). Italy and Spain produce 85 per cent of the European production. It is all located in two areas. You have more or less 200 factories with around 25,000 people working. It is very big. These big clusters have been pulling in a lot of manpower and pushing the local administrations to invest a lot of resources in infrastructure. For instance, in the area of the ceramics industry the natural gas network coming from the north of Africa in the last 20 years is now supplying all these industries on a regular basis. Some of those factories—for instance—"Almost earn more money sometimes, by producing electricity than by selling ceramics." They co-generate energy in their factories, in fact they use so much energy that they have to co-generate electricity in order to make the ovens work, and sometimes they produce so much electricity that they can sell the surplus on the grid. The EU funds have completely changed the landscape in the sense that a region that 30 or 40 years ago was more an agricultural society—"oranges for instance; the first oranges were sent to the UK at the beginning of the last century with the first train cooled carriages from Valencia, and now on boats," and agriculture, which was one of the main pillars of the economy—is three per cent, as a sector, and in the global GDP of the region, agriculture, is down to 2.8%, "which is very low," even lower than the rest of Spain. One of the major topics that Alberto stressed was the creation of the Research Institutes. We have an organisation called IMPIVA which is the Institute for Small and Medium Enterprises which was headed by the regional Ministry of Economy. The IMPIVA was developed a network of 14 Technology Institutes which address each of the sectors—for instance—one for wood and furniture; one for plastics; one for ceramics; another one for the metallic industry. These Institutes work in connection with the IMPIVA sometimes with universities but not always. Most of the time the Institutes work with the companies and they try to address the direct problems that the industry faces. In the case of Valencia, one of the main things was to be innovative because with globalisation and the introduction of many products coming from the Far East it has been a big problem for some sectors in the region. The specialists say that thanks to the fact we have those Institutes we will be able to keep the industries profitable and competitive. The Institutes gave the opportunity to the companies to transform their production systems quickly and they are competitive for the time being. We do not know for how long, but at the moment they are. All this thanks to the innovation which has been applied in the manufacturing sector. We are not a region intensive in R&D development, we use more innovation. We innovate by applying new technology in the chains of production.

Q345 Chairman: In all of this, have the EU funds been critical or would you have done it anyway?
Mr Ortiz: They would have done it perhaps, but the funds were critical in the sense they were used to create these networks of Institutes and these EU funds were used to train the workforce and also to develop many programmes to adapt manpower to the new systems because in many cases they had to introduce new machinery with more sophisticated equipment. They had plans and they developed them. They used these funds on many of the programmes to improve the quality of local manpower. As you know, one of the sectors which is very important is tourism, it is more than 15 per cent of our regional GDP, which is very high, and this sector is one of those where a lot of attention has been focused by the regional government. The regional government is very focused on this sector because in certain areas they have managed to avoid the fact that in some months you do not have many visitors so you have to close some hotels. They have tried to avoid that and create all-year round tourism. They are offering the possibility to very different clients in the sense that in winter we have pensioners, in Spain we have a system called inceso, which is a department from the Ministry of Social Affairs, which allows pensioners to travel around the country at very low prices. It is a way to fill hotels that otherwise would be closed. The system keeps hotels open, and people are working, the government promotes this type of activities in the weak seasons.

Q346 Chairman: I must come and join your hotel immediately!
Mr Ortiz: It is very funny, because in winter in some areas you see all of these people doing gym on the beaches. Hotel owners in all of these areas, where some are well-known and some are less, are very happy because these people are very tidy, they do not bother anyone and do not break anything, which is very different from the summer when we have ten million people coming over. It is one of the ways they try to keep the economy and the system running. I would say in some other areas of Spain it is the same but we have some proper focal points there.

Q347 Chairman: You say you are the ten per cent region.
Mr Ortiz: Yes.
Chairman: I have forgotten what Spain's share of the Structural Funds is for 2007-13.

Q348 Lord Woolmer of Leeds: How much does your region get for 2007-13?
Mr Talens: I think it is about ten per cent too.
Chairman: Spain gets about ten per cent and Valencia gets a little less than ten per cent of that.

Q349 Lord Woolmer of Leeds: You do not know what the Valencia figure is for the seven year period, roughly?
Mr López: We have no figures on that yet. We can provide you with that.

Q350 Chairman: That would be kind.
Mr López: We deal with around €3.5 billion in Public Eligible Spending and we are now at around 2,000 billion, in Structural Funds during 2007-2013 period. That is a new situation for us.

Q351 Lord Kerr of Kinlochard: The old Member States, the existing Member States, including Britain and Spain, invented the new doctrine about absorptive capacity and four per cent as a ceiling on what, say, the Poles could spend because they would not have the capacity to absorb more. We did not invent this doctrine when we invented the Cohesion Fund. Spain, as a whole, and I am sure Valencia, was receiving six or seven per cent of GDP at the peak, is that right?
Mr Talens: I think that percentage is too high.

Q352 Lord Kerr of Kinlochard: It was above four, I think. We have invented a new doctrine for good reasons. You are now going down having peaked at five or six.
Mr Talens: I think so, but I am not a specialist in this field, so I should not be talking about that. I am just a member of the Legal Department and I should apologise again for our not precise English.
Mr López: It has been developed by the Ministry of Economy in Valencian Region.

Q353 Chairman: It would be good if we could be provided with those figures. One of the questions we are trying to address is, if you like, a consumer's eye view of Structural Funds. We know what the Commission thinks, we know what they think they are doing, how they are distributing it and how they feel their relationships are with the people who receive these funds and we are therefore after, and we are asking you and Poland, finding out what the recipients think. Are there any barriers or difficulties? Do you find Structural Funds hedged about with bureaucracy? Are there things that could be improved about the administration of Structural Funds? Any comment would be welcome.
Mr López: For Valencia the most important point is security of management, that is less bureaucratic, but it could be very important for us and we are working on that with the Commission. We are working on the ratio of distribution. The Commission in the beginning are going to send around—
Mr Talens: They are going to concentrate the funding at the beginning of the transfer. In a short period of time they are sending the majority of the funds.

Q354 Chairman: They are frontloading.
Mr López: That means we are ending with this period, so the execution of projects will end and at the same time we will be absorbing this big amount of money and that could mean a complicated system.
Mr Talens: Even logistical problems.
Mr López: That is one of our main concerns for this new period.

Q355 Lord Woolmer of Leeds: According to my calculations, in pounds sterling, which will mean nothing to you now, it is slightly under £10 per head of population per annum, and the Polish visitors we had just now receive £33 per head and another £100 a head, so it is quite a difference now from where you were. Can I just ask a question on the costs of administration and management of these programmes and so on. Some witnesses have said that the costs of administering and managing EU programmes from the project level and beneficiaries themselves through the national government level, through the Commission, really adds up to quite a lot of money but also time, effort and so on.
Mr López: That is a very interesting question.

Q356 Lord Woolmer of Leeds: Is that a reasonable point?
Mr López: The management is an important question and for that reason I think it would be better to contact the Regional Ministry or pay a visit to our region and have a meeting with the Minister of Economy and our Ministry composed of around 120 people with 20 years' experience of managing funds and also the administration of public aid according to the European Commission guidelines, which is very important. This is a very technical question and it would be better for them.

Q357 Lord Woolmer of Leeds: In your Office you have businessmen and women come to your Office to talk about relationships with the Commission and how things are handled and you do not find the private sector complain quietly about the bureaucratic processes and so on? That is not an issue that you find raised with you at all?
Mr López: The funds and procedures have been established according to the administrative procedure and—
Mr Talens: Of course, the private sector wants easier access to finance, but we are managing public funds too. I do not know if we have been able to find the right equilibrium point. I have not heard about any complaints from big companies, but I am not a specialist in this matter, as stated before..
Mr López: Also, the Commission have contacted us to share our experience with the new enlarged Member countries on the management of Structural Funds and how to develop them and the development of acquis communitaire and our experience of the municipalities participating in these complex problems.

Q358 Lord Kerr of Kinlochard: I was very interested in what Mr Ortiz said about innovation and encouraging modernising production methods in industry in Valencia. We were there talking about public sector assistance to the private sector and these are private sector companies. Why did they come to you and, through you, to the Structural Fund? Why did they not go to a bank and say, "We have this brilliant idea"? Coming to you, and the Structural Funds, means a bit of delay, a bit of form filling and bureaucracy, whereas the bank, if it likes the idea, gives you the money. Adam Smith said, "Invent a new mousetrap and the world will beat a path to your door". Convince me that it was not going to happen anyway through private sector banking.
Mr Ortiz: In Spain we are a country with a strong administrative tradition. We have had a Public Administration for 500 years. People rely a lot on the Administration, it is something serious. Apart from the private banks, which are very strong, as you know, because they have been lately merging with some British banks.

Q359 Lord Kerr of Kinlochard: Like British banks all the time.
Mr Ortiz: We also have the savings banks which we call Cajas de Ahorros, which are savings banks which have strong ties with the local regional government and in a way are public banks, they are not considered to be private banks. The Administration works regularly with these banks because 20 years ago—"all these things have changed, interest rates were very high, 20 years ago it was 15/16 per cent and now it is four per cent"—it was a problem to give money to someone because of the risk and these savings banks—for instance—Caja de Ahorros del Mediterraneo or any others in the region, were a way of lending money to people and companies at lower rates with quite good conditions and the risk was taken by the Administration. There is strong confidence normally in the administration. The administration is normally respected. I know that in other countries it is not the same and it is more complicated or more complex, but in our case that was why it was easy to adapt to the new system. In the early 1980s when we came into the EU there was a very big transformation in society. Apart from the political transformation, there was a social and economic transformation because the state was very present, a bit like in the eastern countries, the central state, Madrid, was present, petrol industry and distribution was centralised, the motorcar industry was nationalised and there was a very big movement to decentralisation and privatisation and the regions had some word in it.

Mr Talens: I would like to add some ideas to this. It is true that we have a long tradition of bureaucracy but from what I have read about your administrative tradition, continental Europe is more bureaucratic, even in the private financial sector. I could not say that our public administration is much more bureaucratic than most of our private banks, I could not say that.

Q360 Chairman: An interesting thought.
Mr Talens: In the current financial situation, it seems they have not done so badly. There is a big gap in our financial system because SMEs need the funding, but normally the banks will take a long time to analyse the eventual loan. And maybe the right decision to lend the money is to choose other businesses which are more traditional and safer. If the public sector would not offer this money, they would never grow probably.

Q361 Lord Kerr of Kinlochard: That is a complete answer, thank you.
Mr Talens: This is just from my personal experience. This is a big problem we have and this is why our public finances are trying to help the private financial system to be more open to SMEs necessities.

Q362 Chairman: So the EU funds fell not on stony ground but on quite fertile ground, a public system better administered than a private system. Goodness.
Mr Talens: This is just my own personal opinion. It is not a problem of public versus private, but of good versus bad management of money, a problem of efficiency.

Q363 Lord Kerr of Kinlochard: I find that completely convincing. Of course, I also agree with the thought that a whole lot of things were happening in Spain 20 years ago at the same time and it is hard now to work out from your wonderful growth numbers to what extent did the Structural Funds really contribute, to what extent was it pent-up investment from the rest of the world which was waiting to happen, or to what extent it was the transformation of economic policy, which was brilliantly done by both governments, the Gonzalez government and the Aznar government.
Mr Talens: We do not have those data available now.

Q364 Lord Kerr of Kinlochard: I know you do not.
Mr Ortiz: There was strong investment in infrastructure which was vital if we wanted to be competitive. If you have good roads, good trains, good ports/harbours which are competitive, well-connected, it is difficult not to be competitive. There was a very good job done in the last 20 years to improve all the networks of telecommunications and the networks of roads and trains. Most of the region has been benefiting from this. Valencia, which is luckily on the Mediterranean coast between Catalonia, Murcia and Andalucia, is a corridor on the Mediterranean, so there is a flux of goods going from the north to the south and vice versa. The port authority of Valencia and the Regional Administration have developed the port massively in the last ten years, mainly because Madrid was looking for a gateway to the sea and Valencia is on the same latitude as Madrid, so it was a way of driving the massive economy of Madrid to the Mediterranean. The first economic region in the country is Madrid. People generally think about Barcelona or the Basque country but the highest GDP is in Madrid. It was a bureaucratic city which transformed itself into a productive city. Our transformation was from a society based on agriculture, or the transformation of agricultural products, which we still do, into a more industrialised society. Today services represent 63%, of course, but industry is very strong (around 32%).
Mr Talens: Even more the services sector.
Mr López: In this new period businessmen are thinking of new sectors, logistics, visitor platforms, the knowledge society, audiovisual issues. In this sense we are working with the Propeller TV (Yorkshire). We have new sectors in order to improve our economy and working in the EC growth strategy and employment objectives. Valencia developed the "City of Science, and Arts" attracting people not only because of tourism based in sun and sea but also tourism depending on culture and urban development. These are new sectors.

Q365 Chairman: If one had to analyse which bit had contributed most to growth, the Structural Funds probably do take the credit for building infrastructure. That has been most interesting and I do thank you all for coming.
Mr López: As I told you before, on behalf of the regional government I would like to thank you and take the opportunity to invite you to visit our region.

Q366 Chairman: I am coming for the winter as an old person!
Mr López: The Valencian Region has a Parliament as all the Spanish regions based on more decentralised model and identity promotion.
Chairman: Thank you so much, that was most kind and useful.

Examination of Witnesses

Witness: Professor Danuta Hübner, Commissioner for Regional Policy, European Commission, examined.

Q367 Chairman: Commissioner, we are most grateful to you for receiving us. I think the first sensible thing a guest should ask is how much time do you have, when must you be elsewhere?

Professor Hübner: Actually, any time you need I can help. I have a Director's meeting later on.

Q368 Chairman: That is good to know. We have sent you a whole list of questions. As the day has gone on we have come to refine some of them and found others we would like to ask. If you would like to introduce your colleagues, unless you wanted to say something, I could then start.

Professor Hübner: Thank you very much. It is a great pleasure for us to have you here. Thank you for coming to Brussels. I remember from my previous time as Polish Minister that it is a great feeling to go and be at the hearings. I remember Lord Dahrendorf from my hearings on enlargement and it was always a pleasure to have those discussions. Nicola De Michelis is from DG Regio, who is working on the design of the policy and measuring things that are sometimes impossible to measure. Mr Tokarski is from my Cabinet, who is responsible for Regional Policy co-ordination within the Cabinet. Jörgen Gren is from my Cabinet. Angel Catalina Rubianes is relatively new, a year only. I have two people from the Cabinet and two from DG Regio.

Q369 Chairman: Today we had a very interesting session with DG Regio and Mr Ahner, and that was a great success. We have also met compatriots of yours from two regions in Poland who were extremely interesting on how Poland is getting on with the Structural Funds and have given us a great many facts. In writing our report we are struggling with various strands. One of the most potent strands in our country and, I guess, in several other countries in the west is all these funds are being distributed across 268 regions, including regions in part of the richest nations in the EU. Why, the sceptics ask, are we doing this? Should we not be concentrating the money on the regions in greatest need and leaving any region that is embodied within one of the richer nations to the regional policy of that nation on the assumption that they would actually look after their regions? I wonder if I could ask where the Commission comes out on that debate and how you see the reasons for having an EU-wide regional policy.

Professor Hübner: Thank you. As you have probably heard already we went through this type of discussion in 2005 when we had the negotiations for 2007-13. We also had a discussion on where we should go after the last enlargement and the idea was presented that maybe we should limit it only to new Member States and go to the poorest regions. Just for clarification, we have just the two groups of the poorest regions today, the convergence regions and the competitiveness employment objective for the richer regions. Among the poorest regions it is not only new Member States, about 40 per cent of the regions under the convergence objectives are also regions in the EU-15, including the UK, but also Spain, Greece, Germany, Italy and Portugal, and even one in Austria. We have to understand it is not just the poorer parts of Europe or the club of the poorer countries that join the Union that are under this criterion of poorest regions. Across Europe in different places here and there we have those regions that are poorer, so this argument of dividing Europe into two categories and for some regions having a network and framework of European policy with priorities and a general policy framework for only part of Europe when these regions are so dispersed across Europe from the point of view of methodology would be a rather challenging effort. I believe there are also other very serious arguments. For example, if we look at the challenges which require a type of structural policy from Europe today, they are all horizontal: climate change, energy, globalisation, the pressures coming from global markets. It goes across the whole of the European territory in an asymmetric way affecting different regions depending on their capacity and situation. With these horizontal challenges we believe it will be difficult to justify for some territories that we have a common response to our policy and other parts of Europe would not have the same types of response. This argument of global horizontal challenges which require local and regional responses is also working towards the Europe-wide Regional Policy. You hear arguments also, even those which are based on a solidarity argument, that say even in the richer regions we have pockets of very serious social or economic deprivation or insufficiency. We see this policy not so much as in the past when Jacques Delors thought of the Cohesion Policy but today as less of a redistribution mechanism and more of a development policy which is mobilising the endogenous capitals of the regions and doing it by using this common framework which involves co-operation with exchanges of experience through joint work and joint projects. I think this policy brings more European integration than there would be otherwise. If you think of this policy today we have a very strong focus on the poorest because we have more than 80 per cent of resources going to the poorest, both in the EU-15 and EU-12, and five per cent for the weaker regions and 13 per cent going to the richer regions. It is positively biased to the poorer regions but with a small price, which is 12 or 13 per cent of the resources going to the richer regions, we get huge value-added which is keeping all the regions involved and allowing for co-operation and making them all feel they are part of the European economy. The last argument is we sometimes think of Europe as big because if you look at the map of Europe it is a big continent, but if you look at Eurasia or a map of the entire world we are just a tiny peninsula attached to the rest. Today, if you want to compete with countries like China or India, and I do not know what will happen with Africa with the Chinese there strongly and there might be a big change there, we have to think about the entire European territory as a common market, one economy where we have to measure the competitiveness of the regions against the global background, not just comparing ourselves with our neighbours. We are a network of regions that have to think of internationalising themselves and becoming part of global supply networks and chains. I see it as a must that we are altogether in this policy which is where the value-added comes from belonging to one network and one framework of Structural Policy. I would say for a small price we get huge value-added in keeping those regions within it. After visits to the east of England, Yorkshire and the Humber, when you see how much those people do locally, for example in renewable energy or energy efficiencies, because they have a tiny amount, ten per cent of the funds, that they can put into the projects, they do it in a European framework working with other regions and are thinking of having a meeting with us next year on renewable energies that will take place in England. Those parts of England feel they are a part of Europe only because they belong to these policies. The value-added we get is disproportionately high compared to the resources that we invest in those richer regions.

Q370 Lord Woolmer of Leeds: Can I put a proposition to you, Commissioner, and say what I think you have just said and see if I have got it right. There are 268 regions and the Regional and Structural Funds are something in the order of less than half a per cent of the GDP of the Union.
Professor Hübner: Less.

Q371 Lord Woolmer of Leeds: Covering 470 million people. I put the proposition to you that if the Union was one country, and that would send some shivers through parts of the United Kingdom, and there were 470 million people and the country was divided into 268 administrative areas with a lot of strong local traditions and so on, and you had got less than half a per cent of the income of the country to use for certain policies which you call regional and structural, if you were designing a policy from base zero, you would really say "How can we really use that money targeted best" and you would be amazed if you finished up and everybody got something. That would hardly be targeted strategic policy, that would be far beyond strategic policy. If you were running a business covering 470 million you certainly would not divide it up in that kind of way. If you were designing something afresh, not now but looking beyond, it does seem very odd to some people that everybody gets something. If I understood your answer, I think it was this: there is concentration, over 80 per cent of the resources go to 70 regions which is about 25 per cent of the population, 25 per cent of the regions, five per cent goes to encouraging regional activity and so on, and it is only 12 per cent of funds that goes to nearly 300, therefore the amount that those 300 are getting must be very small. In the terms we are talking about here the average citizen thinks they look large but they are actually very small, yet to distribute those funds and have those discussions a lot of activity goes on. I think your explanation was that it does two things. One is it helps bind everybody in to feel they are part of Europe, even though the figures are actually very, very small in relation to public policy. Secondly, I think you said the whole emphasis has begun to shift away from simply being redistribution dealing with the 70 but to wider dimensions like the Lisbon Agenda, competitiveness, and you talked about climate change, energy and so on. What is the answer to why is it that 12 or 15 per cent of the money is going in a very small amount of a lot of regions with all the bureaucracy, all the administration and all the relations that flow on from that? Is it that it is keeping everybody happy and keeping them part of the team or is it that policy is beginning to move gradually over time towards matters other than substantially one of addressing the problem of consolidation and convergence and so on?
Professor Hübner: You have touched upon many extremely important arguments and issues. One thing I would like to raise is the notion that cohesion has evolved over time. In the past you just invested in different things to get cohesion in Europe but today we have regions in Europe where no investor will go unless you build the first decent road. My home country is probably one of the best examples of this but there are many regions like this. We need this traditional investment to make regions grow faster and to catch up. Today, without investment in what makes a regional economy competitive, which is innovation, and there is probably no better way of getting profits and becoming competitive than to invest in innovation, we are moving towards a different type of investment but with the same perspective of having the cohesion, economic and social, and also with the new Treaty territorial cohesion hopefully, more harmonious development with less barriers that will hamper the development in Europe. This is one thing I think we should take into

account because that changes the understanding of how things look today and that is why the policy has had to evolve in the global context and the context of all the challenges and a better understanding of what we need today for cohesion. This is one thing I would like to say. The other thing you mentioned is we need a foreign policy that has a share in the European budget which on the one hand is big and, on the other hand, we know the EU budget is extremely small. This policy will always have to have a strategic approach. Increasingly, we are moving towards the thematic strategy that we need in Europe to address this policy. We have already done it for 2007-13 focusing on Lisbon, on innovation, research, technology transfer and a different type of less direct support for companies and more investment in public goods around the companies that they can use. The third issue I would like to mention in this context is that we should always remember this is a policy which is functioning within the framework of State Aid rules, so we are not just giving subsidies where we think somebody might need them but there are very strict State Aid rules and we have regional maps of State Aid and are navigating within this territory. Today, the notion of a public good in Europe, which was traditionally the transport networks and domination of the railway, where we think we can bring it about is a state of the art environmental policy and if we talk about networks, it is the energy networks. The public good is increasingly education and research. If we think about this policy as delivering European public good which is needed for growth, but which also heads European value-added, we have to move this policy towards these new categories where we want to invest. It goes across the whole of the European Union. The next issue is related to your doubts or comments. We see public investment over the last ten or 15 years in Europe has been moving downwards and we have less public investment at the national level and in some countries a very substantial increase of public investment at regional and local levels. We are still a small proportion of public investment but we treat our money as seed money or as a contribution from the EU budget to public investment with a huge focus on the leverage function of this money. That is why for us, for example, the private investment contribution on the national side to the EU funds is increasingly important and we have moved to the new financial engineering largely inspired, as usual, by a lot of British experiences at local level. We have now got a combination of grants and loans and the leverage function is much, much bigger than it was in the past and I hope it will be bigger in the future. In addition to directly investing in what is essential today for closer cohesion, we are also shifting the pattern of public investment in Europe. I was told by some of the panel that we are also opening minds because people start talking or thinking differently about what kind of investment Europe needs. When I went to Scotland for the first time in 2005 I was at some meetings with journalists where they were saying, "Stop talking about Lisbon, this euro-speak. We don't want to know what Lisbon is", and then I went to a meeting with mayors, there was an organisation of local leaders, and this was after we started negotiations for 2007-13, and before I even opened my mouth they started to talk about Lisbon because they had taken it down to their level and they had ambition and a network of university links was emerging across Scotland.

Q372 Lord Kerr of Kinlochard: Very intelligent people up there!
Professor Hübner: Normally when you have European policy like Lisbon, and we kept it for five years, 2000-05, at a central level, European level, national level, we just talk about it and nothing happens, but the moment we took it down to the regional and local levels it started to live. That is in the heads and minds of those who have an impact on public investment. I lost what I wanted to say about the strategic concentration on Lisbon. With this small amount of money which can trigger waves of bigger money we understood that at the same time we have to strategically focus the priorities and give everybody access to the policy, but only to those who want to implement the priorities that we have for the whole of Europe. I would say that we have succeeded. If you think of the negotiations that we have had, and my colleagues might have shared this with you, we had the negotiations which started with many Member States and regions without sufficient commitment on their side to innovation and ended up with 200 billion devoted to the regional objectives. There was something in the added value of this policy that we needed in Europe in terms of opening minds, not only roads as we did traditionally.

Q373 Lord Trimble: Coming on the back of the reference to the Lisbon Agenda and focusing on things like competitiveness and innovation, surely these are issues that apply across the whole of Europe. What is the regional perspective? Somewhere within the structures here there should be encouragement for competitiveness and innovation generally, should there not? It is not a specifically Regional Policy.
Professor Hübner: I do not think we can have only regions or municipalities and this will be enough to have growth and jobs and competitiveness of the European economy. Certainly it is not enough to have a declaration at national level that we need innovation policy and a lot of innovation, but we must make it happen. If you think where and how innovation happens, you need proximity of partners and if you do not have universities willing to work with businesses,

increasingly very small and medium-sized companies, if you do not have an active mayor of a city who gets the guys from the universities and from business and puts them in one room, you do not have the innovation. If you do not have a financial instrument which is usually present locally that knows all those partners and is able to invest in this risky undertaking, as innovation normally is, then the innovation does not happen. For the innovation to happen we need proximity of partners. This is happening locally or at regional level, so this involvement of the local and regional level in innovation today is a must. Today I think a characteristic of drivers for growth and for change is networking. It also happens not just because governments decide to say, "We should network" but because enterprises or universities decide to network. This local and regional dimension today in generating change, in generating innovation, is essential because it is all based on mutual trust and confidence, partners have to know each other to embark on a common undertaking. That is why we think the growth machinery and how growth happens is increasingly pointing to the importance of the place.

Q374 Lord Trimble: That may very well be true in individual cases where people are innovating, whether they have come spinning off developments from research in universities or whatever, but that does not have any interaction with the Commission, the Commission is not relevant to that process. That is a personal process that depends on the individuals who are there. With regard to innovation and competition, what you want to do is to think in terms of incentives for that and eliminate those things that are making you uncompetitive, like high social costs, inflexibility in labour markets and things like that. Those things do not have a regional dimension. They might have a national dimension, they might have a European dimension, but they are not really relevant to regional policy, are they?
Professor Hübner: No. I can tell you we first saw it on such a scale in France but today it is probably in many other countries in Europe. We have asked every region to do it, which is the Regional Innovation Strategy. In addition to public policies, I agree with you that there is a need to have a framework at national level created by the legal framework and that differs according to the countries. There are many countries that have innovation agencies at national level that play an important role. There are more and more regions that have established the Regional Innovation Strategies across Europe which are based on what makes the innovation so efficient and enables it to take place based on regional and local partnerships between the universities, business and financial institutions. You find this in Spain and in many parts of the UK. Let me also say that there are examples of innovation that are taking place only because there was seed money, like ten per cent coming from the EU budget, and that was why IBM did not go to Oxford or Cambridge, they went to Wales. That was because there was the involvement of European money. If you look into the statistics you can see how differentiated the indicator of research and development share of GDP is, not at national level but also at regional level. There are regions in Germany or Austria that have eight per cent of research and development at the regional level and regions in Bulgaria where it is close to zero. There is a huge differentiation in terms of research and development and innovation capacity, not at national level but at regional level. The same is true in Finland. If you go to countries that have good national statistics or indicators, they are the result of extremely strong activities which are handled regionally and designed and organised and implemented at a regional level because the partners are there. Incentives at national level seem to be insufficient to accelerate and generate the amounts of innovation we need in the European Union. There are also theories that the Americans have started, Michael Porter and many others, who point out that innovation requires the proximity of partners and that is placed-related.

Q375 Lord Kerr of Kinlochard: I want to ask a two-part question which arises from what you said about keeping the Union on the map in the older Member States and about pockets of deprivation even in the rich Member States. Yes, it is true, but I think the terrible problems of East London are probably basically best dealt with by taxing more highly the citizens in West London, and you probably see two or three sitting in front of you now. You know Sussex very well. The problems of the North-East, West Cumbria or the Forth Clyde Valley are probably a call on the resources of the rich South-East of England. I find it hard to follow the argument, unless it is actually a different argument really, an argument about maintaining political support in older and richer Member States for a major resource transfer to newer and poorer Member States, which I am in favour of. If so, we should be honest and distinguish it as a political argument, not an economic argument. That is not saying it is a wrong argument but it is a different kind of argument. After all, you and I were prophets of subsidiarity, we wrote it right at the front of the best version of the Treaty, which was the first version of the Treaty.
Professor Hübner: Absolutely.

Q376 Lord Kerr of Kinlochard: Are you sure that your argument about pockets of deprivation and keeping the EU on the map are consistent with subsidiarity? My second question, and here I would be thrilled if you gave two answers, first as a Commissioner and then as a very distinguished Polish citizen, is do you really believe that four per cent is an objective economically demonstrable ceiling on absorptive capacity? If so, why did we not think of that when we invented the Cohesion Fund in 1991 and 1992, when we were much more generous to Spain? Two answers would be fine!

Professor Hübner: On absorption capacity, this is a very difficult issue and we have had many discussions and a lot of simulation studies and only when it happens can you see whether they cope with this amount of funds. Normally when we talk about absorption we think about administrative capacity and will they have good quality projects, will they have some financial management, enough administration of good quality, not only at national but also at regional and local levels. There are all of those aspects which are of a more technical nature. We have also introduced the broader understanding of absorption capacity and its impact on the macro-economic situation. With the Structural Funds, as you say, it may be just four per cent of the GDP but it can be up to 20 per cent of the public investment in a country and then if it goes to a region, on a regional basis it can be much more than four per cent depending on the redistribution. This broad understanding of absorption capacity is important. That is why we have always believed, and this should be the case for the future, that the additionality principle is one of the important principles here. We should not think of these funds as just coming and replacing the national level but they facilitate and trigger all sorts of changes which otherwise they could probably wait tens of years for. Absorption has to be taken very seriously in the future because of its impact on macro-economic stability and it can have an impact on stresses on individual sectorial markets, the labour market and then it triggers reforms in the labour market because of this. Understanding of absorption capacity is a very complex issue. I would not dare say today what the maximum ceiling of the absorption capacity is because it is so individual depending on the capacity of the economy. Thinking in terms of a ceiling on the money that can come from outside, that is a must, and that is why the State Aid rules are so important. I would challenge your point about whether we pass the subsidiarity test with this policy because if you take subsidiarity as it was in our Treaty, which is the argument that justification for this kind of action exists when the actions of Member States do not suffice to achieve the objectives of cohesion, I would say this is the case and especially so in the context of the new global challenge, all those new challenges, for which I think we need a common framework. A common framework also needs common legal frameworks, but we combine this common framework with stronger centralisation. We had a strategic approach in 2005 when we established the rules and priorities at European level but then we said, "It is up to you, ground zero, to decide what kinds of projects you want to have to make Europe more innovative, to make Europe grow, to create jobs and address social inclusion, climate, the environment or other issues". We combined the strategic role of the Commission with what I think is subsidiarity with those local and regional level decisions on what the priorities are there. I understand the second test for subsidiarity in this context is that what we do generate benefits entire Europe. When we are present in the richer regions we are triggering certain processes there and leading them to co-operate with others and understand that when the money goes to the poorer it very often comes back to the richer because investment and trade flows are generated. I think we do pass the subsidiarity test throughout this policy and the involvement with richer regions as part of these policies within this framework is justified. There is more and more conviction that if you want to be really efficient in responding, hopefully in advance, to the global challenges, although that is not always the case, you have to give more weight to local and regional levels and those local responses to global challenges, in my view, are very often much more efficient than if there was only the national response. Regions come and they like to share best practice and there are special programmes to share best practice. You can see what excellent projects you can have in a city or in a region to address the demographic challenge, for example what they do for the elderly, and others learn from that. This is a value-added that comes with this policy. I think we need all of those local responses today. To make it more efficient we need some co-ordination across Europe and these local responses, which are a must to global challenges, are very softly co-ordinated by us because we offer the same set of rules and the same seven year Financial Perspective so those who know best what to do and how to do it, we help them to function within a common framework which increases the synergies and allows us to have a stronger result at the European level. That is my understanding. When you talk about taxes, it is a different story to talk about taxes in the UK and what is going on on the Continent when we negotiated, for example, the cross-border programme and had a region in the Czech Republic with a corporate tax of probably 15 or 20 per cent and Austria with 40 per cent and had to accommodate those differences. Taxes are probably an instrument which Europe still does not accept the use of as an incentive, not to mention the fact that we at the Commission have no competence on this.

Q377 Lord Kerr of Kinlochard: Would you accept, Commissioner, that for dealing with problems inside richer, older Member States, the balance between loan and grant finance might be rather different, it might be tilted more heavily towards loan finance rather than grant finance compared to newer and poorer Member States. You spoke about financial engineering and we also heard from Graham Meadows the other day on the possible desirability of having more loan finance, particularly in the richer, older Member States, and I found that rather convincing.

Professor Hübner: This is an important change that we introduced when we started the negotiations with the European Investment Bank and EBRD and the Council of Europe on the urban projects to combine these grants coming from the EU budget with the loans. We had two things in mind. One, to increase the amount of finance available to the policy, because no matter how much money you have the needs of modernisation are so enormous across Europe that you need private capital and money coming from loans. The other objective was we knew with the entry of the Bank into the system you could also increase the efficiency and quality of the projects and the culture of richer public sectors, which is not always the best culture, especially on the Continent, so we took this argument into account. Your idea is very interesting. Today we differentiate strongly between the regions of richer countries and poorer countries through very different co-financing criteria. In the poorest countries they get 80/85 per cent from the EU budget for a project and in the richer countries it is the reverse. This is a factor which we can use. The same is true, as you say, with the proportion of the loans and grants. That is a very important argument. In the poorer countries we would like to have the biggest because the culture is changing and we would like them to move towards loan financing. That is helping them to develop their financial sector, which is very shallow. It is a multi-purpose exercise that is combining loans and grants. The response has been very positive and we are surprised how many of the regions have already embarked on this combination of loans and grants and opening the possibility within the programmes.

Chairman: We now come, as it were, to another of the statement of objections about the spreading of Structural Funds through all countries. Lord Woolmer.

Q378 Lord Woolmer of Leeds: We took evidence from a former Director General of DG Regional Policy, Graham Meadows, and in his written evidence to us on the subject of financial management and control he said the following to us: that a black spot of present European Regional Cohesion Policy is the growing administrative and financial burden being passed on to project sponsors. These burdens earn the policy a bad reputation, even among direct beneficiaries. That is a call which you will recognise. Do you think he has a point? Over time is there an issue here that does need to be addressed and how can it be addressed? I am thinking not just of the Commission level but right down through the Commission, Member States, regional authorities, the applicants and so on, the whole process. Has Mr Meadows got a point recognising the competing pressures on you, so not an instant solution? Is there a way forward over time and in what way could evidence and suggestions be helpful to bring about change?

Professor Hübner: There are one or two issues here. We have been working with Graham a lot on simplification because the costs are bigger and costs of control and for many final beneficiaries it is a burden and a cost. This is public money, so this is money that will always be under special scrutiny and control. As you know, in the EU system we have the Court of Auditors, our duties and the judicial procedure every year. There is a shared management system which means that even though the Commission is finally responsible for the budget, the major responsibility for the daily functioning of the policies is with the Member States. We get the payment claims with two signatures, one from managing authorities and the other from the Minister of Finance usually, and still our auditors go and we discover there are irregularities and we undertake procedures leading to financial corrections. The Court of Auditors agrees that certain simplification may make the controls less painful and less costly if we do it. How much we can go with further simplification we will have to see, but we need the support of the Member States. Usually, the Commission proposes something but then to get agreement among 27 Member States and the Parliament, which is usually very strongly divided on those issues, we get less than we want to achieve. It is very difficult. Certainly simplification of the policy is the direction we want to go in. I do not want to enter into details but we did some changes for the Social Fund when there were some flat rates on costs. We have the real cost approach which means checking everything, every light in the room and all these things, which is a nightmare, but that is the approach that comes from our financial system. There is a whole area here still to consider. My view would be that the Commission should be doing more a kind of performance assessment of the policy. We have discussed over the last few years that some financial management is one area where we could increase the role of the Member States with a Contract of Confidence or national declaration and whatever instruments we could envisage for the future. The Commission could probably do more on the performance and contribution of the policy to growth and real change in the economy. We have to work on this area and this is absolutely the direction for the future that is needed. The second thing related to this, which is very painful for me each time I go to a country that has a tiny allocation of one billion and you have a country with an allocation of 60 billion and they have the same procedures, is it is impossible for anybody who is using this support to understand and it is very difficult for us. We would like to change it. That is one of the most difficult issues, how you can have different rules depending on the size, but we have to think of how we can move on this. What we have done already for 2007-13, which was with Graham Meadows, is to introduce changes to the control system and put more responsibility on ex-ante control and the Member States which would free up on some of the policies in the Commission and more could be done on performance. This is an area where much is happening but much still has to be done. I have already mentioned the Contract of Confidence and Wales was the first to sign that with us two years ago. I am sure you all know about the Contract of Confidence where we do a thorough check of the system and the capacity and we give them some responsibility and that means less audits from the Commission.

Chairman: May I trespass on your time just for one final question which I will ask Lord Trimble to put.

Q379 Lord Trimble: This is moving on to something quite different, namely the current consultation on the future of Cohesion Policy. Are there any conclusions emerging from that process at the moment?

Professor Hübner: We started these consultations in September last year. First we presented a Cohesion Report which more or less shows what is going on in Europe. We are also working on a report showing regional Europe in 2020 so we know more or less what kind of situation we might have with regard to challenges towards the end of the next Financial Perspective we should address with the policies, which we will complete by the end of this year. This work has been done through the Fourth Cohesion Report. We opened the consultation and we have received more than 100 contributions of very different natures, some very complex presentations by some Member States and regions but also partners, the business community, academic community, including NGOs and individual citizens. We are now doing the analysis which will be thoroughly presented in a Fifth Interim Report which will be published in June this year. What we see now is—I am sorry, it may not sound modest but one should not be too modest when presenting somebody's views—there is overwhelming support for the Cohesion Policy for the future, for the special focus on the poorest, but no doubt across Europe there is around 60 per cent saying it should be for all the regions across the European Union with a specific place for the poorest regions. We have support for the need of this policy to cope with all the major challenges which are the globalisation pressures, the demography. This opening of the policy to these new challenges is supported. Also we have very clear support for the role of local and regional levels, which is very much in line with the new Treaty where we have subsidiarity extended to local and regional levels for the first time, for the partnership principle, which is consulting with all the partners on the ground, and for simplification, mostly from the Brits who requested that we should work more on the simplification of the administrative procedures. There is also something I have not mentioned so far which is a strong request to keep the commitment of this policy to the integrated approach. One of the values of the Regional Policy is you can have an integrated approach to development so you are not sectorial, which very often does not solve the problems. The approach is that you cannot solve the congestion problem in a city if you do not solve the transport problem or the waste treatment. This integrated approach at a territorial level is supported. There is a concern that we should aim at further full use of synergies between policies and this is what we have been trying to do between research and Regional Policy over the last two years so that these synergies between policies can be used. We also did a Eurobarometer in January for the first time in the history of this policy, the last time it was in 1991, and it was a representative sample of citizens, but basically we got the same results and views. Colleagues tell me that 65 per cent of British citizens are in favour of Regional Policy for all EU regions, and this is the second highest result among Member States.

Q380 Lord Kerr of Kinlochard: Supposing there were not any Structural Funds and you arrived and there was a decision that there should be Structural Funds, there should be Regional, Cohesion and Social Funds, and you had the job of doing it from scratch, like George Thomson 35 years ago, would you construct exactly what there is now or how would you do it differently?

Professor Hübner: I would probably keep some things and I would change some things because the world is changing. As you know, Lord Kerr, the history of Europe is that this is a policy that has been evolving over time. We did not discuss the issue of policy as allowing for internal market development but it is helping the poorer to participate in the benefits of integration that otherwise would be beyond their capacity and there is this additional function of the policy. I must tell you that very often on the ground we are the first group of people coming to check the transposition of European law, especially for procurement. There is a very tough conditionality with this policy which some people say is the only effective conditionality across the world. We are also exporting that to China and Russia. We have signed Memorandums of Understanding with Brazil, China, the West African Union and also Mercosur because they want to follow the European example. We have had a lot of exchanges and working together. I would certainly change the system in relation to bureaucracy. This is something where we have to be really innovative and think how we can protect the budget, which is one function, and the other one is to contribute to growth and how to reduce the cost of this policy. Do not ask me how I would do it and it would not be accepted by anybody if I had my way. I would probably change this. Incidentally, I would keep this policy for all the regions. I travel a lot and have visited 60-something per cent of the regions so far and I see the value of this policy on the ground. Today people do not want to be informed, they want to be involved in things and this policy gives them the chance to be involved. It triggers innovative approaches to many, many things. I probably should not say it here because one should not praise the UK too much in this room, but the inspiration we get from the UK on financial engineering and the approach to many, many projects which you would never expect to find on the Continent because of differences in economic culture is really very inspiring. Learning from others, which I do taking examples from one region to another, is something that this policy is bringing in terms of change to the European economy.

Q381 Chairman: Thank you very much, Commissioner, that was enormously helpful. I am very grateful to you for receiving us. I would ask one favour. Could I have a copy of your survey on the approval ratings of the policy because it is particularly important to know that in the United Kingdom?

Professor Hübner: Yes.

Chairman: Thank you very much.

Written Evidence

Memorandum by Dr John Bradley and Professor Dr Gerhard Untiedt

Question 1: *What should be the objectives of the EU's Structural Funds? How can the Funds become more effective in supporting public policies in Member States and regions? What mechanisms of delivery could make the policy more performance-based and more user-friendly?*

The EU Structural Funds (henceforth, "SFs") have been enhanced over the last two decades to support the lagging Member States and regions in their objective of generating wealth and convergence in income with the more prosperous regions of the EU. The objectives of EU Structural Funds have always been to facilitate the provision of improved levels of physical infrastructure (henceforth, "infrastructure"), higher standards of job-relevant training and vocational-oriented education (henceforth, "human capital"), and policies aimed at giving direct assistance to firms targeted at enhancing output growth and productivity (henceforth, "direct aid"). These three policy instruments are targeted at the supply-side of the supported economy and are accepted by all modern growth theorists as being essential primary or necessary drivers of convergence within developed globalised economies. Modern theories also point to the fact that growth, once it starts up, can become cumulative, under certain conditions (so called "endogenous" growth).

A general problem since 1989, the year in which the proportion of the EU budget devoted to Structural Funds was greatly expanded, is that relatively little formal consideration has been given to two major "conditioning" factors that strongly influence the effectiveness of Structural Funds:

(a) The appropriate balance between the three main SF policy instruments (ie, infrastructure, human capital and direct aid).

(b) The appropriate supporting policies that are desirable to achieve maximum "return on investment" from SF policy instruments.

An illustration of point (a) is the different emphasis placed on physical infrastructure and human capital by the Portuguese and Irish SF programmes. Portuguese SF expenditures were heavily weighted towards infrastructure, even though education and training standards in the labour force were relatively low. Irish SF expenditures, on the other hand, were initially heavily weighted towards human capital and direct aid, and only in the more recent 2000–06 SF programmes (largely funded out of own resources) did the emphasis shift towards investment in infrastructure to address emerging congestion bottlenecks. This points to a potentially serious problem with the design of SF programmes, namely the need for correct diagnosis of development barriers and in the imperfect integration of SF-supported investments into wider national development plans.

An illustration of point (b) is the relatively poor performance of Greek SFs, compared (say) to those of Ireland and Spain and can be attributed largely to macro instability and a poor record of institutional reform in Greece.

These kinds of timing and identification problems are also observable for East Germany or the Italian Mezzogiorno and being repeated in the new member states, where the dynamics of post-Communist recovery can give rise to overheating on the demand side (consumer and property booms), poor restructuring performance on the supply side (the problem of misallocated "legacy" industries), and problems with institutional capacity (weak and disorganised public sectors). Latvia is an illustration of this phenomenon, and raises questions concerning the relatively rigid and sometimes inappropriate timing of SF programmes.

Within the present arrangements in the European Commission it may be difficult to guide SF policy from a top-down perspective towards greater effectiveness. DG-Regional Policy (responsible for design, monitoring and evaluation of SF interventions) has only a restricted remit in the sphere of economic policy-making, confined to structural policies, and operates separately from DG-Economic and Finance, which is (responsible for wider economic and monetary policy concerns). Such a divide within the Commission between public investment policy and overall co-ordination and oversight of all aspects of economic policy is seldom found at the level of individual member states, where the strong influence of the Finance Ministry (or Treasury) comes into play and forces greater accountability within national policy making.

The wider aspects of EU development aid may be too fundamental to be left to a Directorate-General whose remit is, essentially, to administer a system of investment expenditures. The tensions that have arisen between the wider remit of the renewed Lisbon Strategy and the narrower remit of SFs (tensions noted in the *Sapir Report* of 2003) are a manifestation of a deeper malaise at the core of the EC's role in promoting cohesion and growth within the EU. The fundamental issue here is not one of "user friendliness" and "performance-based" interventions, as noted in the question above. Rather, it is one of integrating and linking all relevant strands of EU development policy and cohesion more closely to the budgetary expenditures that are currently aimed more narrowly at the three main SF instruments. The real targets of the SFs concern the long-run transformation of the supported economy. Short-term "performance-based" indicators that are associated with the spending phase of SF aid are likely to be misleading measures of the desired long-term, post-programme impacts.

Question 2: *Do Structural Funds meet the principle of subsidiarity? Could the same cohesion objectives be met through repatriation of the distribution of these funds?*

It is important here to distinguish two areas where the concept of subsidiarity arises with respect to SFs. First, there is the provision of development "aid" in the form of co-financed funds. Second, there is the question of the actual design and implementation of SF-aided public investment programmes in infrastructure, human capital and direct aid.

The spirit of the term "subsidiarity" as applied to the provision of funds suggests that it is fulfilled in situations where the recipient countries would generally find it very difficult, and sometimes impossible, to make up for deficiencies in infrastructure, human capital and direct aid out of their own financial resources. Other problems, of course, are associated with the provision of development aid: moral hazard, deadweight, market distortion, etc. But the wider aspects of the Stability and Growth Pact tend to ensure that such problems are well monitored and minimised as the new member states progress towards membership of the euro zone.

The issue of subsidiarity with respect to SF design and implementation is more complex. The European Commission, through DG-Regional Policy, exercises considerable power over the design of National Development Plans (NDPs) or National Strategic Reference Frameworks (NSRFs). However, member states retain a high degree of authority over SF planning, if they desire, or have the institutional capacity, to use it. The role of the European Commission here is to act as a watch-dog, and discourage poor use of funds through insisting on rigorous ex-ante evaluation and ex-post financial controls. In the early years of expanded SF programmes (eg, 1989–93 and 1994–99) monitoring and evaluation procedures were less well developed. More recently (2000–06 and 2007–13), the monitoring and evaluation processes have begun to operate more effectively and have tended to promote rigorous and open evaluation of public investment at the member state level, often in situations where the post-Communist legacy (but also the administrations in some old Member States) was hostile to such processes. Achieving the correct balance is a difficult and challenging task, but a very important one.

We assume that the term "repatriation of the distribution of these funds" used in the Committee's question refers to the removal of the EC over-sight role in SFs or the switch to a "net fund principle", and not the dismantling of the SF process with a view, perhaps, to reducing member state EU budgetary contributions. Would this be better than the present situation? Our judgement is that the EC oversight role—when exercised effectively—is a crucial element of the value-added of the SF process. Simply to hand out SFs to poorer member states, some with poorly trained and inefficient public administrations, and exercise no oversight on what is done with these funds would be very ineffective. Within the EU SF programmes, the balance between member state "ownership" and EU "oversight" is a delicate one and a source of constant negotiation. The experience accumulated over the past 20 years has largely worked to the benefit of recipient states, and SF aid has largely avoided the serious problems that bedevil aid programmes addressed at the less developed economies of the Third World (as described in William Easterly's highly critical analysis of Third World development aid).

Question 3: *What impact has enlargement had on Structural Funds, and are any changes necessary to meet the challenges of further enlargement?*

The early main recipients of SF aid (Greece, Ireland, Portugal and Spain) were already market economies, albeit rather poor and inefficient ones. In general, SF aid was absorbed relatively easily into their public sector planning systems that could now operate at a higher level of activity without distorting already strained public finances. In addition, public accountability systems were well developed since all four countries had been long-time members of the OECD and the IMF.

Ten of the new member states that acceded between 2004 and 2007 had undergone massive institutional change in the transition from Communist central planning to liberalised, market-based economies (Cyprus and Malta being the two exceptions). The post-Communist transition to a modern role for the public sector has been slow, and is still incomplete (particularly in Bulgaria and Romania). The role of government as "strategic organizer" in a global economy driven by market forces is very different from the previous role of Communist governments as "central planners", and has to be learned. Government as "strategic organizer" carries out its functions in *collaboration* with private sector actors and not as a *substitute* for the market economy. In the case of development planning, the government must target the provision of a range of public goods whose availability and quality are essential inputs to the growth of any modern economy. Within the EU SF process, the planning and implementation of physical infrastructure, of human capital and of industrial strategy are at the centre of the government's developmental role. Experience suggests that some of the new member states are fast learners—Estonia, Poland, Slovenia—and that the SF process is at its most efficient when the recipient state already has a well thought out development strategy and implements it through working in collaboration with the Commission.

Any future enlargement in the Balkans is unlikely to generate new challenges for the SF process, since these are small states that face developmental challenges similar to—say—the Baltic States and Slovenia. In terms of economic development, the accession of Turkey, with its population of around 74 million, would be more challenging, mainly due to its size and to the large regional disparities between the relatively developed west and the very under-developed east and south-east that greatly exceeds regional disparities found in the present member states.

By the time of an eventual Turkish accession, some of the large regional disparities in Turkey are likely to be much attenuated, but the level of income per head is still likely to be low compared to the EU-average. Preliminary calculations suggest that—everything else being equal—the spatial distribution of the SFs will then alter dramatically towards Turkey and this may introduce difficult distributional discussions among the EU Member States.

Question 4: *How will the EU's commitments on combating climate change manifest themselves in the distribution of Structural Funds for the post-2013 period? How will the response to other challenges facing the EU economy (eg, migration, growth of the service sector) shape future policies?*

The SF initiatives are focused on growth and social cohesion within the EU and should largely remain concentrated to these targets. An overload of targets would destroy the possible effectiveness of the Funds by dispersing their focus and marginalising their impacts. Nonetheless, the wider challenges likely to confront the European Union over the next decades range from changes in the sectoral structure of the economies to climate change, ageing societies, migration etc. These have implications for the intervention areas of the SFs, that will have to be considered when future SF programmes are designed.

(a) SFs, the environment and climate change

The research challenge is to examine the complex links between the economy and the environment and to look at the impacts of the Structural Funds on these links. Since the main aim of the SFs is to foster the economic development of the recipient economy in terms of increased income per capita, leading to increased welfare levels, a useful starting point for looking at the connection between growth and the environment is the so-called environmental "Kuznets curve", which states that the relationship between income per capita and certain kinds of pollution and environmental consequences is roughly shaped as an inverted U. Empirical evidence suggests that economic growth is associated with increased air and water pollution at the initial stages of industrialization, but as countries become more wealthy, the association becomes negative in later stages (ie, higher growth is associated with less pollution). The standard rationale for this general finding is that production technology makes some pollution inevitable, but that more advanced technologies are less polluting and the demand for higher environmental quality (by citizens) rises with income.

Of course, this characterisation of the "Kuznets curve", that seems to claim that if countries promote growth, the environment will eventually take care of itself, is incomplete. Pure reliance on growth to solve pollution would result in a sub-optimal outcome, so there must also be effective government regulation. The interesting contrast is obviously the "old" Cohesion States on the one hand and the New Member States and the candidate countries, on the other hand, since it is possible that these groups may lie on different sides of the "Kuznets curve". In other words, the wider global challenge of facilitating growth in very poor countries, even if this leads initially to higher pollution levels, is replicated, to a degree, within the now rather heterogeneous EU.

What are the implications for the SF programmes? Macroeconomic impact analysis suggests that these programmes accelerate cohesion, albeit to different degrees. In some countries, this will be more rapid than in others. As income per capita increases towards EU average levels, the evidence suggests that the energy intensity of GDP will decline. The case of Ireland shows that this decline can be quite rapid, and the Irish example may turn out to be followed by the smaller New Member States like Estonia, the Czech Republic and Slovenia. But the more gradual decline (or static performance) of Greece, Portugal and Spain is likely to be the pattern that will be followed by the larger new member states, such as Poland and Hungary, and the most underdeveloped states (Romania and Bulgaria), and future member states (Turkey).

(b) SFs and migration

An unexpected development after the EU enlargement of 2004 was the large-scale migration from some of the new member states to the UK and Ireland and, to a minor extent, Sweden (three states that opened their labour markets to the accession states). Historical experience suggests that the duration of such migration tends to be mainly temporary, although can last for many years. As development progresses and increased job opportunities appear, reverse migration usually sets in and returning migrants bring back higher skills and wider experience, which are very beneficial to economies in a development phase.

The relationships between migration and SFs are complex. For example, in Poland skill shortages have developed, particularly in the construction sector, as a result of the large out-migration flows after accession in 2004. This makes it difficult for Polish policy makers to plan long-term infrastructural projects, since wage costs escalate and become difficult to predict. In cases of serious labour shortages, SF projects may be delayed and/or prices are driven up and unit costs rise so that the physical outcome of the SF spending is lower than expected.

However, the migration process has self-correcting tendencies, since the demand-side impacts during the SF implementation phases boosts demand for labour, and serves to reduce out migration. The Irish case may be typical of what can be expected for the new member states, with a legacy of large-scale out-migration that was reversed dramatically as the economy grew and converged during the 1990s.

(c) SFs and the service sector

The increase in the share of market services is a characteristic of post-Communist countries, since this sector was repressed during the era of central planning. Increasingly, market service activities have become complementary to manufacturing activities, through out-sourcing and hybrid activities (eg, ICT equipment (manufacturing) combined with software (services)). Model-based analysis of the likely impact of SF programmes has examined spillover benefits for manufacturing and market services, and suggest that these complementarities are very important in modern development. The current tension between the role of SFs in promoting the *Lisbon Strategy* suggests that there are unresolved issues here that will need to be addressed in the negotiations on the review of the EU budget. But this is an argument for integrating SFs and the Lisbon Strategy, and not for a reduction and/or termination of the SF process.

Question 5: *What criteria should guide decisions on the proportion of the EU budget to be allocated to Structural Funds?*

There is no easy way to judge what proportion of the EU budget should be allocated to the SFs. SF spending competes with other spending categories of the EU budget. Some of these categories are defended for political reasons (eg, the CAP), and not on grounds of economic efficiency. Others are often attacked on ideological grounds, even when there is evidence of relatively high efficiency (eg, SFs).

From a theoretical point of view, the EU's limited financial resources should be directed to those tasks that promise the highest marginal return (social and economic) on investment. This could mean that in the context of a politically determined EU budget (say 1% of EU GDP), the SF share might be reduced compared to the Lisbon Strategy forms of interventions (for example non-spatial bounded support for R&D), but might be expanded compared the share absorbed by the CAP. The former trade-off (Lisbon versus SFs) lies at the core of the future design of SF programmes. If SFs are not fully integrated with Lisbon, existing tensions will grow, strategy will become confused, and outcomes will be inefficient.

However, the absorption capacities of the recipient Member States have to be taken into account. The quality of the policy-making establishment in the recipient country is vital. Poor planning, implementation and administration capacities lead to waste of EU resources. Furthermore, the nature of the business cycle in the recipient country is important, so that the additional inflow of SFs does not lead to overheating of the economy. Finally, the EU's decision on whom and/or what to support, defines the expenditure share of its programmes. For example, if a narrower definition of the SF defining property of "lagging-behind" by member states and regions were implemented, but the financial allocation was to be fixed in terms of share of GDP, then the share of SFs in the overall EU budget would obviously drop, and vice versa. The present defining share of 75% of average EU GDP is quite arbitrary. But, there is no obvious way of knowing that a lower level of relative income of 60%, or a higher one of 85% of the EU average would be more effective.

Question 6: *Are the current eligibility tests for regions to receive support under the EU's Structural Funds relevant, fair and appropriate? Should they remain in place after 2013? Is it appropriate that they are discussed simultaneously with wider agreements on allocating EU budget spending?*

At first glance, the eligibility tests for regions or Member States to receive SF aid seem to be transparent and comprehensible. The classification as "convergence" region at the NUTS 2 level rests on the threshold that the income per capita in PPP is less then 75% of EU average. All other NUTS-2-region are classified under the wider "competitiveness and employment" target. Furthermore, member states are classified as eligible for Cohesion Fund resources if there gross national income (GNI) per capita measured at purchasing power parity is less then 90% of the EU average. The available funding rests mainly on population, corrected by some other economic indicators. Beyond these clear analytical rules, several specific exceptions are negotiated.

The main problem with this classification results from the use of administrative NUTS-2 regions, whereas the use of a functional spatial classification would be useful, in the following sense. The main problem introduced by using the NUTS-2 classification is that areas where people have their home and work outside the region (or abroad) are favoured. This is one area where the eligibility tests could be improved. An other area concerns the question of just supporting those Member States that are below a defined threshold, but this would introduce a series of severe problems within the Member States that are above the threshold.

Question 7: *What would be the effect of linking the availability of Structural Funds with compliance to Broad Economic Policy Guidelines?*

The "Broad Economic Policy Guidelines" (BEPG) define a set of macro-economic and micro-economic policy guidelines for all EU Member States. Some of the recommendations are complementary to the SF interventions while others are directly linked with the SFs. As a consequence of the Stability and Growth pact and the renewed Lisbon Agenda, the BEPG can operate as guidelines for all member states.

But due to the different stages of development, as well as quite different societal preferences, it would be very difficult to link the allocation of SFs merely to compliance with the BEPGs. The introduction of rules that are linked to the BPEG would introduce a quite different system for directing EU Structural Fund to the less developed Member States. This would also lead to the need to define very precisely what exactly would be the best implementation of the BEPC for each Member State. This seems to be impossible, since the Member States follow different routes and have different institutional set-ups. Compare, for example, the economically successful countries Ireland and the UK (on the one hand) with the even more successful Nordic countries, Denmark, Sweden and Finland (on the other hand). With respect to labour market regulations, all such states are likely to claim that their economic policies are successful, even though they can be radically different. Ever worse, national governments could not even agree, in the preamble to the BPEG, that the only task of monetary policy would be to pursue price stability.

Obviously there are links between the efficiency of SFs and the BEPGs. As mentioned in our response to Question 1 above, macro and micro stability are "conditioning" factors that can affect the nature of SF impacts. Serious deviations from the BEPGs are often associated with poor economic performance generally, and poor SF impacts specifically. Conditionality of SF aid based on the BEPGs is not in question. Merely the extent to which other factors are also to be taken into account.

9 January 2008

Memorandum by the *emda* on behalf of the Regional Development Agency network

1. RDA Role in Structural Funds

(a) *2000–06 Structural Funds Programmes*

Firstly, it should be noted that the Government Offices were responsible for the management and administration of the 2000–06 Programmes. The RDAs' role focused largely on the provision of a strategic regional steer to European funding programmes in order to ensure that ERDF and ESF funded activity supported regional strategies such as the RES and Regional Skills Strategies. RDAs also acted as a critical friend to the Government Offices in terms of Programme management and governance issues, and played an influential role on the Programme Monitoring Committees. In some regions, RDAs were delivery partners managing significant programmes of activity or indeed individual projects, however, indicative figures for expenditure incurred for this role will vary widely from region to region and are not readily available.

The Government Office network (via the Department for Communities and Local Government) may be in a position to provide figures regarding the programme management and administration costs for the 2000–06 Programmes.

(b) *2007–13 Structural Funds Programmes*

As delegated Managing Authority for 2007–13 ERDF Competitiveness and Convergence[1] Programmes, the RDAs will be administering the Funds on behalf of CLG.

ESF funding continues to be managed in all English regions, with the exception of London, by the Government Offices with RDAs continuing to play a strategic role in the Programme.

2. RDA ERDF Administration Costs

The following table details the expected annual cost for each RDA's management and delivery of ERDF. Each RDA will be able to access Technical Assistance from the individual Programmes to support their effective implementation.

	Expected annual cost £000
East Midlands Development Agency *(emda)*	800
North West Development Agency (NWDA)	1,396
Yorkshire Forward (YF)	1,712
South West Regional Development Agency (SWRDA)—see footnote	2,900
Advantage West Midlands (AWM)	1,066
One Northeast (ONE)	1,500
London Development Agency (LDA)	900
East of England Development Agency (EEDA)	710
South East England Development Agency (SEEDA)	199
	11,183

The cost of administration clearly differs from one agency to another, and this is primarily related to the size of the ERDF Programme and regional structural issues.

3. *Regional Representational Offices in Brussels*

(a) *Role of Regional Representational Offices*

All RDAs play a key role and make a financial contribution to regional Offices based in Brussels. These Offices are run in partnership with other regional stakeholders such as local authorities, and other public and private sector organisations and there are large variations in structure, partnership composition and management arrangements between all of the regions. Indeed, in some regions there are a number of representational Offices which cover different geographical or sectoral aspects of the region.

Therefore, it is crucial to clarify that regional representation in Brussels is not solely related to the Structural and Cohesion Funds and RDA contributions cannot be considered as expenditure related to this. The Brussels Offices provide information, early intelligence and policy advice; a base in Brussels for the region's organisations and businesses; building partnerships with other European regions; as well as promoting the region within Europe.

[1] NB—The South West is the only English region with both full Convergence and Competitiveness allocations. The South West Regional Development Agency is therefore responsible for the management and delivery of both the Convergence (£313 million) and Competitiveness (£85 million) Programmes for the region.

(b) *Contribution by RDAs towards Regional Representational Offices (£k)*

The details given in the table below are based on information provided in response to a recent Parliamentary Question raised by Eric Pickles MP.

Regional Office	*RDA contribution to Office (£k)*	*Additional Information*
West Midlands in Europe Brussels Office	2006–07—£378k	West Midlands in Europe is the regional office representing the interests of a range of organisations across the West Midlands. The West Midlands Local Government Association and Advantage West Midlands are the Joint Managing Partners for the office. The office is also supported by membership subscriptions from a range of other public and private sector organisations. In addition, in recent years the office has begun to attract income from business services and from European projects. Legally, it is an unincorporated association of interests operating as a special interest group of the West Midlands Local Government Association.
East of England European Office	2006–07—£63k	The East of England Brussels Office is managed and staffed by the East of England Regional Assembly on behalf of the East of England European Partnership. This is a region-wide partnership of mainly local authorities, EEDA, and the Government Office for the East of England. All members subscribe to the running costs of the office. The office is a regional representation office, providing information and intelligence on all aspects of European policy and funding.
East Midlands European Office	2006–07—£315k	This is a regional representation office funded by a regional partnership comprising upper tier local authorities, Universities and other public sector partners. The Office is line managed by *emda* on behalf of the regional partnership and focuses on European policy, funding, representation and relationship building in support of regional partners. Please note these figures represent *emda's* actual contribution to the East Midlands European Office (EMEO). Where expenditure by EMEO is less than the contribution to fund the office, the surplus is held over for the next year.
London European Office	2006–07—£50k	London's European Office is a partnership office representing the Mayor of London, GLA, TfL, the LDA, NHS London, London Fire & Emergency Planning Authority, the Metropolitan Police Authority and Metropolitan Police Service which each contribute financially

Regional Office	*RDA contribution to Office (£k)*	*Additional Information*
		to the maintenance of the office. The office monitors EU policy and legislative developments, engages with the EU institutions on behalf of its partners, and raises London's profile in Brussels and promotes its best practice. The work of the office focuses on transport, climate change, energy, environment, economic development, public services, social policy, equalities, public health, counter terrorism, civil protection and security.
North West Brussels Office	2006–07—£58k	This office is jointly staffed and funded by the North West Regional Assembly and Northwest Regional Development Agency. The NWBO provides intelligence to regional partners, a base in Brussels, assist in partnership development, and promotes best practice. The office is located within a shared facility with offices funded by Northwest local authorities.
North East of England Brussels Office	2006–07—£65k	The office is primarily funded by One North East, The Regional Assembly and Local Learning & Skills Council with a number of associate partners making small subscriptions.
South East England Brussels Office	2006–07—£65k	Office costs are shared with the South East England Regional Assembly, all principal local authorities in the South East, and with a range of other partners including several of the region's universities. (The lease for the representative office rented by SEEDA is held by Kent County Council, which has maintained a representative office in Brussels for the last 20 years).
South West UK Brussels Office	2006–07—£178k	This office is a partnership office supported by all first tier Local Authorities in the South West, the South West RDA, the South West Regional Assembly and HERDA (South West Universities).
Yorkshire Europe	2006–07—£340k	Yorkshire Europe is the region's representation in Brussels, providing information and intelligence about Europe for Yorkshire and Humber, a base in Brussels for the region's organisations and businesses as well as promoting the region within Europe. Yorkshire Europe is solely funded by Yorkshire Forward on behalf of the region and is currently managed by the Regional Assembly.

Evidence submitted by *emda* on behalf of the RDA network.

18 February 2008

Memorandum by Jorge Núñez Ferrer, Centre for European Policy Studies

The opinions expressed are solely those of the author and are not necessarily endorsed by the Centre for European Policy Studies

The Future of European Structural Funds

Fundamental principles

1. All EU budget expenditures should follow certain underlying principles which are presented below.[2]

- ***Subsidiarity:*** The EU should only act when it is better suited to do so compared to lower levels of governance.
- ***Proportionality:*** The EU may only act to exactly the extent that is needed to achieve its objectives, and no further.
- ***Additionality:*** EU financial intervention should generate an impact which would not have occurred without EU assistance. EU funding should not substituted national funding.
- ***Value for Money:*** EU actions should be devised to be cost-effective and should be regularly evaluated.

In addition, all policies and specially those aimed at fostering growth should:

- *create a **value added at European level:*** Value added occurs when the return to the investment superior to the one without the investment and superior to the opportunity costs, ie same resources used for the best first alternative.
- *be aimed at **European public goods:*** Resources should be used at European level when the return to the investment for the whole of the EU is superior to the opportunity costs. This is not only for other objectives at EU level but also for the interventions on the same objectives at national level.

2. Presently the policy is not living up to the listed principles due to the highly politicised manner in which funds are allocated and the policy implemented. The policy needs a thorough review. This short paper presents a list of possible reforms to improve the structural policy interventions, and the coherence with the aforementioned principles.

Subsidiarity

3. Interregional support for underdeveloped regions in the EU should be run at EU level, and thus the underlying concept meets the subsidiarity principle. However, the present rationale is flawed and the implementation suboptimal.

Eligibility, Proportionality, Additionality

4. For a policy to attain objectives efficiently, those have to be achievable and clear. However, various economists have pointed out that the theoretical underpinning is based on flawed notions of economic theory.[3] It aims at the convergence of GDP per capita, which is a measure of production, not incomes, thus implying that the value of production per capita should become similar. This is rather utopian given the heterogeneity of endowments of regions. Not surprisingly, GDP per capita divergence between regions within member states has increased rather than decreased. As Martin (2005) clearly points out, growth is still strongly affected on the efficiency gains of economic concentration.[4] High EU wide GDP equalisation while trying to avoid drastic structural change is utopian. Fostering EU growth by avoiding agglomeration and forsaking the impacts of economies of scale is not a plausible strategy either. One can argue that the actual objective is not convergence but that regions reach a minimum of 75% of EU GDP per capita level at PPP (purchase parity prices), an objective that has some considerable flaws, especially after the enlargement. 75% per capita income at GDP PPP gives a very limited vision of the development needs in the regions. The situation in convergence

[2] See Núñez Ferrer, J (2007), "EU budget and policy reforms in order to promote economic growth", ITPS working document R 2007:015; and Núñez Ferrer, J (2007), "The EU Budget, The UK Rebate and the CAP—Phasing them both out?", Task Force Report, CEPS, Brussels.

[3] See Boldrin M and F Canova (2003), "Regional Policies and EU Enlargement", in European Integration, Regional Policy, and Growth, eds Funk, B and Pizzati L, The World bank, Washington DC, and Tarschys, D (2005), "The Enigma of European Value Added", Sieps 2005:4.

[4] Martin P (2005), "The geography of inequalities in Europe", Swedish Economic Policy Review, Vol 12, pp 83–108.

regions in the EU 15 is not worse (and probably better) than in regions in new member states with a higher GDP per capita at PPP, even of those no longer eligible for convergence funds.

5. Even keeping a GDP per capita target, structural policy should aim better at *fostering the endogenous (and sustainable) growth potential of regions*. The word *potential* is critical and does not imply convergence in GDP per capita. Eligibility and the measures allowed should be based on a composite measure, taking into account the level of existing infrastructures, human capital and access to finance private or public, in addition to GDP per capita figures. This is in line with the proportionality principle. This principle requires interventions in the regions to be proportional to the needs to develop the region. This requires that the EU in coordination with the national and regional authorities deploys the means necessary to help regions have the necessary basis to reach their potential growth in the most efficient way.

6. Such an approach would in fact question the need for EU support for regions in wealthier member states. For such regions, growth is determined more by national and regional development strategies and national policies rather than the availability of EU funds. This is also the case for ESF funding with at times seems to "compete" rather than complement national schemes. It is also questionable whether it is pertinent to maintain a grant system from the EU: support for those regions can be devised using other financial instruments such as loans of the EIB or EIF.

7. The principle of additionality as applied today is rather crude and flawed. It just requires that public expenditure is not reduced when EU funds are used. For the poorest countries, the principle of additionality is generally present by default and the rules are sufficient to ensure that EU funding is generating more investment than in the absence of support. The governments have to use all of their resources to co-finance the EU assistance and this generates a considerable improvement in the infrastructures compared with a non-EU intervention scenario.

8. This is not the case for regions in wealthier EU member states. There the EU funds allow governments to invest less in the eligible regions. Suspicions exist that those member states increase less their investments in the regions as their factor in the EU receipts. Formally, additionality is guaranteed, but the facto there is a substitution effect compared to a base scenario without EU support. In addition, regions with higher levels of infrastructure, services and even social support, gain less for each additional investment from the EU, in particular when directed to such popular infrastructures as additional roads. The opportunity costs are higher. Moreover, the more developed regions tend to have better access to other financial operators. There is a certain substitution effect in place that reduces the value of interventions. There is thus certainly some rationality in considering that regions in wealthier member states should not be supported by the EU budget, or at least not using the usual infrastructure investments. The opportunity costs of structural interventions in relatively well endowed convergence regions may be higher for the EU than the resulting impact of the intervention. As a result, there is a need to have more stringent eligibility criteria.

Value for Money, European Public Goods and European Value Added

9. Developing the poorer regions in particular in the poorest countries can potentially generate economic and social benefits for the EU. At low levels of development, investments tend to create strong economic impacts and high returns to investment with relatively low opportunity costs. Investment in the development of those European regions increases the future potential of these regions to generate rapid growth, which in turn increases wealth in the regions and increases the demand for good and services from other regions. Thus fostering the development of poorer regions can be considered targeting a European public good generating a European value added. For regions already relatively well developed in infrastructures and services, regional strategies and national policies are the main factors affecting their development.

Better Objectives, Reinforced Earmarking and Improvements in Implementation

10. Most of the problems of the structural operations of the EU are not related to the measures, but to the quality of implantation. Strategic planning, appropriate monitoring and appropriate implementation are crucial, and the EU's system is suboptimal at all levels.

11. Strategic planning is *the* main element determining the impacts of the structural policies, which includes the need for coherence of national macroeconomic policies, such as fiscal or labour market policies. Incoherent programmes with badly integrated investments can reduce considerably the impact of EU investments.

12. It is necessary that national strategies are evaluated by an independent body, separate from the European Commission, and also drafted nationally by institutes independent from the main state administration. The European Commission, for example, has clashing responsibilities in the area of policy formulation, evaluation and monitoring implementation. For policy formulation, the evaluations for the impacts assessments should

not only be undertaken externally, but also the process of supervising the evaluators should be run by an external agency. It is not possible that evaluations of Community policies are demanded, evaluated and paid by the same organisation that prepares the policy proposals, controls the budget and supervises implementation; it affects the neutrality of the process. The Commission is also influenced by the pressures to have national strategies for the structural funds approved on time and ensuring the absorption of the funds, with quality and the achievement of objectives taking a secondary place.

13. The European Commission can then concentrate on policy-making, budget control and implementation issues alone. The Commission would retain the mandate to prepare regulatory proposals and monitoring the correct implementation of the programmes.

14. For the Planning process at national level, it is highly advised that member states use also an independent national agency to draw the strategy and evaluate the implementation, reducing political interests and the wish of the administration to have a strategy based on fast absorption rather than impact quality.

15. For the implementation, there is a very complex and illogical shared-management structure with the European Commission, in which national authorities are in charge of implementation, but the Commission is held responsible for the financial implementation which it does not control directly. This reduces the member states' responsibility on the quality of implementation. Cipriani (2006 and 2007) explains at length the implications of such a system.[5] In fact, as EU funding is supranational in nature, implementation and financial flows could be better managed and controlled by agencies at national level funded and controlled by the European Commission, or jointly run with the national administration.

16. There is also a need to make sure that the actual objectives are reached by member states, rather than using absorption capacity as the only measure of success. The intensity of EU assistance should also be decided based on the quality of implementation and the achievement of objectives. "Sunset" clauses should be placed on spending programmes. Funding would be discontinued after a certain period unless the usefulness of the investment can be ascertained.[6]

New Priorities

17. The present Financial Perspectives have very much the same priorities and mechanisms as the previous one. Even if the headings of the budget have been altered, the contents is largely the same. Very little discussion on the underlying substance has taken place during the negotiations besides the division of the funds between member states. It is still very much the "relic" which the Sapir report (2003) described.[7]

18. New challenges are clear and pressing. Adapting the budget to promote growth at EU level, rather than supporting agriculture or development only at regional level, has been recognised as one main objective. Work on ensuring that all policies are growth-enhancing or at least not incompatible with a growth approach is necessary.[8] Another challenge is to protect the environment and particularly combating climate change.

19. A political will to liberate the EU budget from considerations on a "fair" share of returns is necessary, in particular for R&D investments. The recent disputes on the allocation of a share of the Galileo programme to each member state are a sign that the potential economies of scale of EU action can be eroded significantly. The EU budget investments have in several areas a theoretically large potential to generate a European value added compared to individual action by member states. In practice, the politicised way in which the funds are allocated can erode much of the benefits. This in turn reduces also the justification for using the EU budget for any actions.

20. Given the rising environmental challenges, action against climate change to reduce CO_2 emissions and adapting to expected changes is an urgent priority. CO_2 emissions are a clear cross-border issue, not only in terms of impacts but also because many cross-border activities generate emissions, from transport to energy supply. As such, combating climate change should in many areas be handled at supranational level. It is clear that there is a role to play by the EU, including for the EU budget.

21. The first action starts by properly integrating climate change concerns into the budget. Presently climate change is squeezed into the programmes ex-post, or by relabeling existing expenditure as climate change investments. There is no clear integrated approach in place yet. Issues such as energy efficiency or investments to reduce emissions in transport should become better integrated into structural funds and imposed on the

[5] Cipriani G (2006), "The Responsibility for Implementing the Community Budget", Working Document 247, CEPS, Brussels; Cipriani, G (2007), "Rethinking the EU Budget: Three Unavoidable Reforms", CEPS, Brussels, pp 150.

[6] Gross, D and Micossi, S (2005), "A Better Budget for the European Union—More Value for Money, More Money for Value", Centre for European Policy Studies (CEPS) Policy Brief No 66 (www.ceps.be)

[7] Sapir, A, P Aghion, G Bertola, M Hellwig, J Pisani-Ferry, D Rosati, J Viñals and H Wallace (2003), *An agenda for a growing Europe: Making the EU economic system deliver*, Report of an independent High-Level Study Group established on the initiative of the President of the European Commission, Brussels, July.

[8] see Núñez Ferrer, J (ibid).

strategic planning of member states for the use of EU funds. Earmarking funds for climate change could be one approach. This should not only affect structural funds (including the rural funds, for example for investments in the food industry and farms).

22. In addition, for important and central climate change investments, a specific budget heading could be introduced, this would ensure that countries invest a clear minimum share of funds in this area. Funds for improving the energy sector efficiency could become a part of this fund, as well as funds to promote transport by rail or waterways. Elements already exist in the Trans-European Networks.

9 January 2008

Memorandum by Patricia Garcia-Duran and Montserrat Millet, International Law and Economy Department, University of Barcelona

What criteria should guide decisions on the proportion of the EU budget to be allocated to structural funds?

1. The Structural Funds proportion of the EU budget should not be decided on the bases of Member States net contributions.

2. Criteria should include the need to support the development of basic infrastructure in the member states, the need to support all regions compliance with the Lisbon Agenda, and the need to develop a polycentric model of territorial development.

3. The most competitive regions in Europe from the Lisbon criteria viewpoint are also the most prepared to benefit from the Research and Development European budget. The less competitive and poor regions of the EU are the ones that receive the most from the Structural Funds. Rural regions are the ones that can benefit the most from the CAP. What is needed is to clarify the position of medium-income non-rural regions.

4. Middle-income non-rural regions should receive EU financial support, as the other regions do from different sources, so as to improve their compliance with the Lisbon Agenda. This support can either come from the Structural Funds or from a reviewed and adapted Research and Development Policy.

Are the current eligibility tests for regions to receive support under the EU's Structural Funds relevant, fair and appropriate? Should they remain in place after 2013? Is it appropriate that they are discussed simultaneously with wider agreements on allocating EU budget spending?

1. The current eligibility tests are appropriate since they take into account the middle-income non-rural regions. Nevertheless, this support can be modified so as to be included within an expanded Research and Development European Policy. This transfer and revision of the present competitiveness regional objective would allow a greater focus on efficiency and, if necessary, the introduction of conditionality.

What would be the effect of linking the availability of Structural Funds with compliance to Broad Economic Policy Guidelines?

1. The effect of linking the availability of Structural Funds with compliance to Broad Economic Policy Guidelines would be that of depriving the European Regional Policy of its "solidarity" value. Structural Funds have always had an implicit solidarity objective that cannot be made conditional. Conditionality must be reserved to policies that only have an "efficiency" objective.

2. Moreover, the effectiveness of Structural Funds can be improved without the need to linking its support to external conditionality as improvements made since 1988 have proved.

8 January 2008

Memorandum by Global Vision

1. *What should be the objectives of the EU's Structural Funds? How can the Funds become more effective in supporting public policies in Member States and regions?*

What mechanisms of delivery could make the policy more performance-based and more user-friendly?

We take a minimalist approach. The EU's Structural Funds should primarily be geared towards helping the poorest Member States catch up in terms of prosperity with the richest. The richest states should be taken out of the funding mechanisms altogether and be left to decide their own strategy for supporting their poorest and most under-performing regions. Funding for the poorest Member States should primarily aim to improve their economic competitiveness and growth prospects by focusing on enterprise and innovation, infrastructure, and skills and employment. Environmental considerations should also be taken into account.

The issue of making the Funds more effective in supporting public policies in the poorest Member States can only really be addressed if detailed knowledge of the relevant national public policies is available. The delivery of the Funds should be individually tailored to projects relating to the particular needs of these most vulnerable countries and be fully coordinated with their national policies.

If the Funds were geared towards the poorest Member States, instead of to all EU27 states, the task of tailoring individual policies would be a much more manageable task. Administrative costs and the alleged losses through fraud would also be reduced. The current approach smacks of a quite inappropriate "one size fits all" approach to Member States—even though they have hugely disparate economies. (This is especially true since the accession of Bulgaria and Romania.) The EU's regional policies would surely be more effective if more resources went into planning carefully individualized projects, the spending on which is thoroughly tracked and audited, rather than maintaining grand, very expensive, EU-wide schemes.

Concerning the Funds' delivery mechanisms to make them more performance-based and user-friendly, they should be dealt with a case-by-case approach with a clear focus on improving growth prospects.

2. *Do Structural Funds meet the principle of subsidiarity? Could the same cohesion objectives be met through repatriation of the distribution of these funds?*

They clearly do not. Gordon Brown has, for example, said that "when the economic and social, as well as democratic, arguments on structural funds now and for the future so clearly favour subsidiarity in action, there is no better place to start than by bringing regional policy back to Britain".[9,10]

Concerning the repatriation of the distribution of the funds rich countries should simply be taken out the EU's Structural Funds system altogether, as already proposed. These countries do not need to be involved in economic cohesion policies. For the poorest countries, there is a strong case for the Commission and the national Governments working together to develop support packages that complement national policies and give the best expected return, in terms of boosting growth prospects, for the EU funding provided.

3. *What impact has enlargement had on Structural Funds, and are any changes necessary to meet the challenges of further enlargement?*

Clearly the two most recent enlargements, with the accession of relatively poor countries, have significantly changed the balance of affluent and less affluent countries within the EU. The EU has become a much more economically disparate group of countries. As already indicated the accession of the very poor countries of Romania and Bulgaria in 2007 was of special significance. The dramatic changes to the make-up of the EU should have been taken as the opportunity to radically rethink the role of the EU's Regional Policy along the lines indicated above (question 1).

Concerning further enlargement it all depends on its extent. Croatia is waiting in the wings for membership. As it is a relatively small country its accession, in itself, would hardly justify a major reappraisal of the EU's approach to regional policy. If Turkey, a large and poor country, were ever to become a full member (which is unlikely) then its accession would surely call for a major reassessment—making a radical change in policy strategy along the lines already suggested all the more necessary.

4. *How will the EU's commitments on combating climate change manifest themselves in the distribution of Structural Funds for the post-2013 period? How will the response to other challenges facing the EU economy (eg migration, growth of the service sector) shape future policies?*

The funding will have to be geared more towards those countries that, other things being equal, have the most to lose (and/or will incur the greatest costs) by restricting their anthropogenic carbon dioxide emissions in the belief that such an activity will combat climate change.

Migration both within the EU and between the EU and non-EU countries has many ramifications—not least of all in the UK. Concerning its implications for future policies for the distribution of Structural Funds, it depends crucially on other policy objectives insofar as they exist and/or are explicitly identified. If, for example, one policy aim were to be to stem intra-EU migration, then it could be argued that the process of

[9] *Times*, 6 March 2003, quoted in Open Europe, Why the EU should not run regional policy, Open Europe, December 2007.
[10] HM Treasury & DTI, *A Modern regional Policy for the UK*, March 2003 was also critical of the inflexibility of EU regional policy.

building up the poorest countries should be accelerated. Funding support would, therefore, be stepped up. Concerning the growth of the growth of the service sector, this should not be regarded as a challenge to be responded to, but rather an almost inevitable development of maturing economies.

5. *What criteria should guide decisions on the proportion of the EU budget to be allocated to Structural Funds?*

The EU's criteria for deciding the budget allocation to the Structural Funds depend crucially on its priorities as a political entity. But just what are the EU's priorities? How does, for example, the EU balance its ambitions to be an international power and an economically dynamic economic region; and its objective of supporting EU agriculture and reducing income inequalities between Member States? The EU has to make these decisions and decide which of these aims (and doubtless countless others) deserve funding. Then, and only then, can the EU decide what proportion of its budget should be allocated to funding its various objectives—including the proportion of the budget allocated to the Structural Funds.

If, for example, the EU decided that it would shrink the funding for CAP asymptotically to zero, admittedly highly unlikely, then the proportion of the budget available for other projects would clearly rise.

6. *Are the current eligibility tests for regions to receive support under the EU's Structural Funds relevant, fair and appropriate? Should they remain in place after 2013? Is it appropriate that they are discussed simultaneously with wider agreements on allocating EU budget spending?*

Given our earlier comments on the Structural Funds, it must be clear that we believe the current system is fundamentally flawed. The whole system, including eligibility tests for the Structural Funds, should be re-constructed. 2013 onwards is the next obvious opportunity to radically change the system.

It is probably appropriate that the eligibility tests are discussed in the context of the overall allocation of EU spending. They doubtless serve to focus the collective mind on just what the EU's priorities should be. And, given the horse-trading that accompanies debates over the Budget, such discussion is probably inevitable.

7. *What would be the effect of linking the availability of Structural Funds with compliance to Broad Economic Policy Guidelines?*

The Broad Economic Policy Guidelines, as revised in 2005 to deliver "integrated guidelines for growth and jobs" and grouped as macroeconomic guidelines, microeconomic guidelines and employment guidelines, are a constructive and systematic way forward. They could, of course, be modified and improved, and they are perhaps too bureaucratic and inflexible. But this is a secondary issue.

If the availability of Structural Funds is to focus on improving competitiveness and growth prospects, then linking the availability of Structural Funds with compliance to the Broad Economic Policy Guidelines should be considered as a sensible starting point. It could be a positive step towards focusing funding on policies explicitly aimed at improving economic performance.

9 January 2008

Memorandum by Professor Daniel Tarschys, Department of Political Science, Stockholm University

THE FUTURE OF EUROPEAN STRUCTURAL FUNDS

1. In considering the record of EU Structural Policy, it is important to note its many **different motives and objectives**. Measured against some of its explicitly stated goals the policy is not convincing at all, but on the other hand there are important achievements in areas that do not figure prominently, if at all, in the official documents. This creates enduring problems for the evaluation industry, but also for politicians trying to make sense of the policy.

A Multi-Purpose Policy

2. European Structural Policy is a prime example of "goal congestion". Some of its objectives serve as criteria for allocation (Objective 1, 2, 3, etc.) but in this context I am concerned only with the more or less formally recognised motives and purposes. These can be grouped into ten different clusters:

1. *Compensatory measures ("side payments") intended to facilitate agreement on other policy decisions.* While the official documents have nothing to say about this motive for the Structural Funds,

historians are agreed that it has been important at several junctures in the recent past when well-designed increments were successfully employed to overcome resistance to further steps in the integration process:

(i) In the *enlargement* process, there were often regional pockets of resistance both in the old Member States and in the candidate countries that were encouraged to overcome their doubts through targeted benefits. In the UK case, the method involved to overcome some early objections to accession was the introduction of regional policy in the European Community (pioneered by Lord Thomson).

(ii) Objections to the *internal market* reforms in the 1980's in some Member States were met by the doubling of the funds for Structural Policy (Delors I).

(iii) A similar strategy was used to overcome concerns about inequities in the foreseen impact of the *monetary union*, again through a doubling of the Structural Policy budget (Delors II). This time the additional allocation was not integrated into the structural funds but kept apart as a so-called cohesion fund, a separation and a label intended to underscore that it was only a temporary measure.

2. *Compensatory measures to offset persistent disadvantages ("juste retour").* Compensation may also be requested by Member States that, rightly or wrongly, perceive themselves to be victims of persistent disadvantages. Structural policy payments is only one way of handling such complaints; budget rebates is another one.

3. *Distributive justice and solidarity.* The wealth and income gaps between different regions of the European Union are considerable, although not quite as considerable as is often claimed.[11] An important motive for Structural Policy is to redistribute resources from wealthier to less wealthy parts of the continent. Well handled, such transfers can give satisfaction to both donors and recipients.

4. *Visibility and legitimacy of the Union.* To many Europeans the EU is but a ceaseless bombardment of incomprehensible rules. A cure frequently prescribed is to offer more visible and down-to-earth evidence of common European investments and initiatives.

5. *Modernisation and institutional development.* The conditionality linked to the various structural programs involves the promotion of financial discipline and the diffusion of modern administrative and managerial standards. Both before and after accession, the funds have been used to enhance the rule of law and the institutional development in many Member States.

6. *Network-building and Europeanisation.* Many activities in the field of structural policy have promoted cross-border contacts and contacts with the European institutions.

7. *Regional growth, employment and development.* Beyond mere redistribution, Structural Policy interventions aim at boosting the long-term capacity for growth and job creation in economically weaker regions. Whether this aim is achieved is very difficult to say. There is ample evidence for the short-term impact of the various programmes and projects but far less is known about the longer-term effects. The quality of most implementation reports and evaluation studies is disappointing.

8. *Aggregate growth and employment.* Some elements in Structural Policy, such as the "missing links" investments in trans-border infrastructural networks, may be beneficial to aggregate growth, but the main pattern of reallocation from more prosperous to less prosperous areas has probably a weakly negative impact on the long-term growth rates of the whole Union. Even the short-term impact is unknown, however, since Structural Policy evaluation reports tend to overlook the opportunity costs involved. Efforts are made to measure "jobs created" and sometimes "jobs maintained", whatever that may mean, but never "jobs destroyed" or "jobs not created".

9. *Convergence.* Inter-state economic gaps have no doubt shrunk somewhat, but the crediting of this highly complex process to Structural Policy interventions should be taken with a grain of salt. Efforts have been made to sort out the contribution of the Structural Funds to convergence, but the differentials highlighted in these studies tend to shrink when more numerous variables and more sophisticated assumptions are integrated into the models.

10. *Cohesion.* If cohesion is taken to mean, as the Commission defines it, "an expression of solidarity between the Member States and regions of the European Union", then any measure should qualify. In the dictionary version, however, cohesion means a "tendency to stick together" (Webster) or a "tendency to remain united" (Oxford). If we understand cohesion to mean a "sense of togetherness",

[11] The official statistics on regional gaps reflect the gross disparities before taxes, social transfers and public consumption. When such domestic political interventions are taken into account, a substantial part of the intra-national gaps tends disappear. Production disparities are much greater than consumption disparities.

then it seems likely that all EU policies make some modest contributions towards this goal, but it is not self-evident that the Structural Funds are more efficient in this respect than other policies. To find measures that give particular value for money in pursuing the sense of European community, one should probably look to such fields as education, culture, mass media, sports and youth mobility.

European Structural Policy: The Record and the Prospects

3. European Structural Policy has scored some successes with respect to at least the first six of the 10 goal clusters. The contribution to goal clusters 7, 9 and 10 is much more modest, and to cluster 8 possibly negative.

4. The record contains some significant achievements. But what are the prospects for the future? Some tasks assigned to Structural Policy have already been completed. Such results should be gracefully acknowledged but do not necessarily justify continued investments or interventions.

5. The basis for the inclusion of any item in the next Financial Perspectives must be well-founded expectations about future impact rather than historical accomplishments. In assessing the prospects, one would have to:

- assign weight to the various objectives;
- consider whether and to what extent they can at all be successfully pursued by national or European policies; and then
- make educated guesses about the possible future contributions by the instruments in the repertoire of European Structural Policy, as compared to other available policy instruments.

6. The compensatory measures made to achieve particular decisions (cluster 1) have already served their purpose and do not merit being continued. In some other areas, one should probably expect declining marginal returns from established programmes. Eg, if the most urgent infrastructural investments have already been supported, the next round is likely to be less useful. The same may hold for investments in administrative modernisation.

7. As to the grand objectives towards the end of the list (clusters 9 and 10), the slow pace and underlying causal complexity of regional equalisation conspire to make *convergence* an unsuitable policy goal for the European Union. If the goal of *cohesion* is understood to mean "the sense of European community", then the present repertoire of instruments in Structural Policy are not so well chosen. If we are serious about this objective, as we should be, then an entirely different set of measures should be considered.

8. When the usefulness of an established European policy declines, whether through task completion or changing priorities, there are two principal options at hand: the available resources could either be redirected to other pressing needs, or the policy in question could be redefined and filled with a new substance. There are several examples in the past of such exercises in "retro-fitting", in the case of CAP through the invention of rural development as a partial exit strategy from agricultural subsidies and in Structural Policy through a bundle of measures presented under the label of "lisbonisation".

9. While intellectual honesty and considerations of rationality speak in favour of an explicitly recognised transfer of resources towards ascending priorities, the high transaction costs involved in shaping agreements and making budgetary decisions in the European Union will often make retro-fitting more expedient. It is not the best strategy to choose, but at least better than leaving things where they are.

10. The budget of the European Union contains both seriously under-funded and seriously over-funded areas. Facilitating a badly needed redeployment of resources requires increased attention to the political and institutional aspects of *policy termination* through the phasing out of expenditures that have already fulfilled their purpose or cannot be expected to offer satisfactory returns in the future.

30 December 2007

Printed in the United Kingdom by The Stationery Office Limited
7/2008 392305 19585

ISBN 978-0-10-401325-0

9 780104 013250